Memories, photographs, recipes
and history of North Sand Lake,
Burnett County, Webster, Wisconsin

Proceeds from the sale of this book will benefit
North Sand Lake

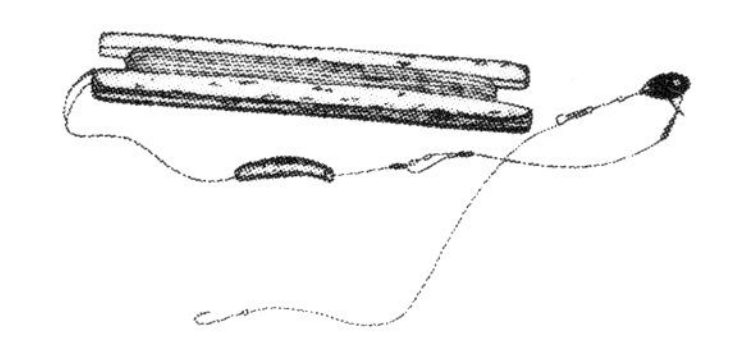

Catherine Tripalin Murray

Up North...remembered
Madison, Wisconsin

Up North: A Father's Summer Legacy
Up North... remembered
1421 Wyldewood Drive
Madison, Wisconsin 53704

Library of Congress Catalog Card Number
ISBN 0-9626346-4-6

First edition.

Editing
Penny DePaola

Design and Layout
Donna Collingwood

Artwork-Logo
Adrian Gay

Some of the recipes in this book have not been tested
and are featured as provided by contributors.

Printed in the United States of America by

omnipress

Published by
Greenbush... remembered
1421 Wyldewood Drive
Madison, Wisconsin 53704

Other books by Catherine Tripalin Murray

a taste of memories from the old "Bush" Volume I, 1988
a taste of memories from the old "Bush" Volume II, 1990
a taste of memories from Columbus Park Volume III, 1992
Recipes of a Lifetime, *Wisconsin State Journal*, 1995
Grandmothers of Greenbush, 1996

Front cover photo: Mike Tripalin and daughter, Catherine, at
Hansen's Resort, North Sand Lake, 1945.
Back cover photo: Mike Tripalin and daughter, Catherine, 1987.

This is a collection of personal reflections from 1945 to the present. Included are remembrances generously shared by others who grew up on North Sand Lake, or in the immediate area, and families, like mine, who drove long distances each year to stay at one of seven resorts along the shoreline. In search of an up north experience, we became spoiled with what the lake and its periphery offered. And, while some stayed lifetimes, others were satisfied with fragments called summer vacations. What you will read are impressions and observations of a time and a place that rapidly developed into an affair. It is an adventure seasoned with history to preserve the past with words and photographs for future generations to taste and enjoy North Sand Lake…just as I have.

They were the best of times ~

[illegible]

Memories are, in many ways, who we are.
Without them, we literally don't know ourselves.

—Joseph Hellique, Professor of Psychology, USC

Dedicated to my father,
Mike Tripalin,
who packed the car with fishing gear,
tucked us in the back seat of the two-tone gray Chevy
and drove up north in 1945
where seeds of love and respect were quickly planted
along the shoreline of North Sand Lake,
then nourished each summer thereafter
to send roots deep into the sand
that sprouted shoots to heavenly heights
with unconditional love
never to be equaled....

...and to my mother,
Mary Tripalin
whose shared compassion for up north
made our family vacations blossom into treasures,
our photo albums swell,
our morning oatmeal nourishing,
our fish fries succulent,
our cocoa and marshmallows soothing,
our pillows warm from the wood stove,
and our summers at the cottage
blessed with fond memories
to last a lifetime.

Table of Contents

Part IV 195

Part V 229

Part VI 299

Part VII 375

1945

Glossary

Barney	Barney Hansen
Florence "Flo"	Barney's wife
Barney's	Hansen's Resort store and snack shop
the store	Hansen's Resort store, snack shop and tavern
Warren	Barney and Flo's son
Paul	Warren and wife Mary's son
Karl	Hansen's Norwegian immigrant handyman
Boy	Karl's dog
dogfish	bowfin
northern	northern pike
popples	local slang for poplar trees
A	County Trunk A, County Road A
H	County Trunk H, County Road H
Mother and Daddy	Mike and Mary Tripalin
Catherine	me
Elaine	my sister
Dick Murray	my husband
Mike, Bill and Bob	our sons, born 1958, 1963, 1965
Gordy	Elaine's husband
Tom	their son, born 1959
Debbie	Mike's wife
Shawn, Jordan and Devin	their sons
Tanya	Bill's wife
Sydnie and Nate	their children
Becky	Shawn's wife
Halle and Kacie	their children
Sugar and Honey	my white toy poodles
Snickers	Bob's cat (America's Funniest Home Video star)
Suzy	my dog
Joe and Mary Tripalin	Daddy's brother and wife
Joey	Daddy's nephew
Joe and Debbie Tripalin	Daddy's (same) nephew
Joe Kovacs	Mother's father
Bill Kovacs	Mother's brother
Billy Kovacs	Mother's nephew

Preface

GROWING UP IN A CITY SURROUNDED BY SPRING-FED LAKES AND EFFIGY mounds, is it coincidental that my summer place on a large, spring-fed lake in Burnett County is comparatively steeped in Native American history?

The isthmus city of Madison, Wisconsin provided lakes in all directions where breezes sifted through trees and windows to cool our home during the warm summer months and beckoned swimming and fishing along shores where Native Americans once lived and buried their loved ones. Our home, located on the northeast side of Madison, is a block from the large spring-fed Lake Mendota, its ancient Indian campsites and a short walk to where an Eagle Mound, with the largest wing-spread of any similar effigy in the Midwest, sprawls a full 624 feet.

My cottage, built on an isthmus separating North Sand Lake from Mallard Lake sends southerly breezes through trees and windows to cool us during the warm summer months and beckons swimming and fishing along shores where Indians once camped and buried their loved ones. A stone's throw from the water's edge carries me a short distance to ancient Indian campsites and mounds studied by the Burnett County State Historical Society. Although the mounds are protected for the privacy of those who today occupy the property, one in particular is marked with a poignant message from a couple who once settled there many years ago.

Doubting that this is nothing more than a coincidence, there must be a connection and underlying reason why I've spent the past twelve years compiling a book interspersed with history and personal reflections. An era ended when Mother and Daddy sold their cottage in 1989, yet the legacy they established nudged me along to make certain their gift of North Sand Lake would be passed on to each new generation.

As you enter this portion of my life at the lake, think of every page being much like an ingredient in a recipe destined to create a Blue Ribbon winner at the State Fair. After the meal, dessert is served and this book, in essence, is the sweetness that preserves history with delectable flavors and heartwarming memories.

Catherine, 15, with Karl's dog "Boy," 1953

Thanks for the Memories

Birch Island Barefoot Annie
Gordy and Elaine Ayen
Tom Ayen
John C. and Sharron Bachman
Bob Barut
Pat and Lucy Basler
Birdie Bowman
Jon Bowman
Mrs. Mildred B. Buggert
Bill Caruso
Father Mike Champlin
Lafayette Connor *
Bill Conroy *
Theman Danielson *
Lefty Darwin
Fred Dhein *
Ray Ellis
Mary Francis
Bob Grindell *
Gary Haas*
Paul Hansen
Betty Hendrickson
Pat Ries Hernandez
Ted and Marge Hildgardner
Mrs. Ray G. Husen
Nancy Jappe
Ed Kellogg
Barbara and Dick * Kenall
Madaleine Lambert
Roger Larson
Emily Leach
Clyde Leedburg
Ainard and June (Chelmo) * Leef
Myrna Leef
Roger Leef
Tom and Bobbie Leopold
Pat McNeal
Virginia Miller
Curt Mommsen
Vi Moser
Rosalie Heuer Mueller
Tom Mulligan
Dick, Mike, Bill and Bob Murray
Gene and Hazel Myers
Betty Pagano
Syliva Kovarik Pardun
Mrs. Frank Preiner
Josephine "Jo Mama" Gehler Robinson
Gary and Helen Rohde
Ray and Eunice Rubin
Tom Rypel *
Valli Preiner Sauer
Bob Scalzo
Dorothy and Ed * Schnaith
Fern Abrahamson Seagren Bowen
Mike Shipanik
Ike Van Sommeren
Jack and Beverly Spittell
Nancee Swenson
Sharon Tarr
Lolita Taylor *
Berniece Thompson
Roger Tollander
Mike* and Mary* Tripalin
Kevin Wear
Austin, Sven, Peter and Paul Wehrwein
Claudia Westlund

* Those known to have passed away before book was published.

Acknowledgements

Great Scott! A History of Northern Wisconsin's Earlier Days, by Beatrice Durand Derrick. *Great Scott* is out of print, but shouldn't be. Printed in 1965, the book is very well written, has been extensively researched by the author and became a treasure to read. It is a must for anyone who appreciates local history and is available to check out at the Spooner library.

Yesteryear: Jackson Township Beginning, by Agnes Mickelson O'Brien. Although unpublished, this is a welcomed effort that describes her experiences in the immediate North Sand Lake area and includes names of early settlers and property owners. The 50-page compilation, edited and printed by the Burnett County Historical Society, is a simple trip to the past and a joy to read.

Although I regret not having met either Durand or O'Brien, their essays were gifts that captured a time and a place well beyond my reach. Growing up here allowed the magic of their minds to record experiences with a priceless passion. First-hand sharing is sweet and pure and without it, fragments of the past often become distorted with time.

I consider myself fortunate to have had the opportunity to meet Lolita Taylor and spend a few hours with her in her home. Retired teacher and author of **The Native American: Ojibwa, the Wild Rice People and Native American**, Taylor's vast knowledge, keen mind and understanding of what this project meant to me was one of the highlights of the undertaking. Her kindness and gracious manner found a place in my heart.

Thank you Burnett County Homemakers Club for documenting **Pioneer Tales of Burnett County**, first published years ago and given to me as a gift from my mother.

Spooner historian Sharon Tarr compiled a wealth of information for her publications, **Spooner, Wisconsin: The 1st 100 Years,** that began with the settlement of Spooner in 1883. At that time, with a population of 800, the community offered a number of blacksmiths, saloons and restaurants, builders, loggers and general stores for its people who were further guided through life's episodes by a drug store, a physician and a lawyer. It took many years following my introduction to Spooner in 1945 to become aware through her research of the large number of Italian immigrants who settled there between 1880 and 1915 because of the regional railroad boom and available land. Each segment of her work is definitely worth reading by contacting her through the Spooner Chamber of Commerce.

A special note of appreciation is extended to Sharon and Eldon Johnson who, in 1989, when Daddy was 85 and Mother was 81, purchased the small seasonal two-bedroom cottage that Gordy built for them in 1966 on the south shoreline isthmus between North Sand and Mallard lakes. The Johnsons, who reside in Hammond, WI, embraced this family treasure—as royal to us as a castle and seat of the Tripalin summer throne that oversaw four lots with three family cottages, and welcomed it into their own lives with the same amount of passion. Understanding the love and respect Mother and Daddy had for the cottage and the lake, the Johnsons preserved their lake roots by hanging a picture taken of the four of them moments after the closing in Siren—a gesture for which I shall be forever grateful.

And to Curt Mommsen, my immediate lake neighbor and St. Croix resident who nurtured my compassion by sharing author Henry Beston's book **The Outermost House** which documented a year spent on the great beach of Cape Cod. Although my experiences as an eight-year-old visiting North Sand Lake are pale compared to Beston's summer of 1924 when he first visited the Atlantic shoreline at the age of 36, a similarity surfaced as he embarked on an opportunity to absorb the area he loved. After purchasing 50 acres of duneland, Beston designed and built a small two-room cottage he named *Fo-castle*. Time spent there wasn't meant to be anything other than a vacation retreat, yet it quickly evolved into a year-long paradise interspersed with unexpected and life-threatening experiences.

Aside from not yet giving a name to my own cottage, yes, there are obvious differences in age, gender, character and location, yet the obsession becomes the common experience in loving the land that surrounded us. For Beston, there were sandy dunes gracing an ocean along the east coast that became his passion. For me, it was a deep spring-fed, crystal-clear lake *up north* in Burnett County in Wisconsin that offered endless adventures.

Many thanks to everyone who entrusted me with treasured photos for more years than I care to admit, and to my good friend Beverly Moffett Otis, for the last-minute finishing touches to complete the book.

Last, to my husband, Dick, whose patience with this 12-year project has been nothing less than admirable (even though it wore thin at times), thank you a million times over. Understanding how important it was for me to compile what began with an innocent idea of writing a 35-page handbook for "newcomers" to know what the lake was like many years ago and then to have the little book grow to a size I never fathomed, had to be a test of his love for me. Now that it is completed, I can return to my old fishing holes in search of the big ones that got away.

The two of us

Visiting Riverview Park, Chicago, 1930.

La Famiglia

Daddy

People gravitated toward him. Five feet, eight or nine inches tall, give or take an inch, with a slight build, olive complexion, dark brown eyes and black hair, plus a personality and smile to warm anyone's heart, Mike Tripalin was a winner. It's no wonder the girls he went to school with remembered him 50 years later as being such a " nice polite person" and "so good looking." Countless times, during conversations, his looks have been compared to a young Al Pacino by those who knew him years ago.

His father, Salvatore Tripolino, whose family had a Coat of Arms and whose father owned a tin factory, arrived in this country from Palermo, Sicily in 1910. Salvatore lived in New York City for about a year before Daddy arrived with his mother, Caterina (DiMaio) Tripolino. After barely existing for a brief period of time there, they moved to Madison, Wisconsin and settled in the Italian immigrant Greenbush neighborhood where they joined Caterina's brothers, Angelo and Dominic.

In 1915, as a 12-year-old boy, Daddy witnessed the murder of his father in the yard of the house where they lived. The tragedy created another burden. With a widowed mother and a two-year-old brother to care for, Daddy quit school and found jobs to support the family. Two years later, he approached his grade school principal and asked to return to classes. Because she denied his request, he visited the Superintendent of Schools and asked to be readmitted with his former classmates. Promising to study hard and bridge the gap created during his absence, permission was granted and Daddy returned to school and graduated from Central High School in 1925.

As an outstanding high school student and athlete who gained instant popularity and recognition to assure him a college education, Daddy set his goals to become a teacher and coach. When I was young, he would tell me how natural it was for him to excel as an athlete and the importance of gaining the respect of his teammates. Immigrant status coupled with derogatory names became a thing of the past and these became the years he described as being some of the best of his life. With a twinkle in his eye and a proud smile, he'd describe how he tucked the football under his arm and ran like hell to keep his small frame from being crushed by much bigger opponents. As a flashy little halfback, he became a sports writer's delight as every football game turned out to be a crowd-dazzling performance which made good reading in the next day's newspaper. One of the writers, "Roundy" Coughlin, compared him to Red Grange and was convinced that Knute Rockne would make a star out of... Mike Tripalin.

During his freshman year at the University of Wisconsin in Madison, the dream to excel in college football never materialized, as the coach thought Daddy was too small for the conference. When the season ended, he accepted a scholarship to play football at Jefferson College, a Jesuit college in Convent, Louisiana near New Orleans. Arriving there on a boxcar as his mode of long distance transportation, he dazzled spectators in Louisiana, as well. Because his coach, Rod Shaughnessy, had coached under Knute Rockne at Notre Dame, Daddy became known in Louisiana as one of the "Four Horsemen of the South."

When his mother's health began to deteriorate, Daddy transferred to La Crosse State Teachers College in La Crosse, Wisconsin to be closer to home. However, the onset of the Great Depression forced him to withdraw from school and return to Madison where he found a job delivering ice for Oscar Mayer & Company. The meat-packing plant was a family-owned operation and those who were hired considered it a privilege to work for the Mayer family. When he was given an opportunity to advance into Beef Sales, he decided to stay with the company and remained there for 42 years until retirement.

Daddy never looked back to wonder what life would have offered him as a teacher and coach. I remember when he was being considered to coach football at one of Madison's high schools. When an existing school coach was selected, it merely prevented any problems to dismantle his job at the plant. He continued to enjoy working with youngsters and retained that throughout his life along with an undying passion for most sports. He also enjoyed the camaraderie and friendships established at Oscar Mayer as well as bonds of respect and friendships with local and regional butchers and meat market owners. Life was good and he was genuinely appreciative of what he had been blessed with along with each accomplishment made in the work force.

On June 26, 1929, Mike Tripalin married Mary Anna Kovacs. My sister, Elaine, was born in 1933, and I arrived in 1937. Eight years later, the four of us headed north on a journey to North Sand Lake for a week that would last a lifetime. Little did we know that we had packed our hearts in our suitcases.

Mother

Mary and Mike Tripalin, June 26, 1929

MARY ANNA KOVACS WAS BORN IN 1908 IN A SMALL VILLAGE near Budapest, Hungary. Her German mother, Margaret Stenger, worked as a cook in a rectory in Germany, and her Hungarian father, Josef Kovacs, whose family had lost their money during a revolutionary upheaval, served in the Cavalry. The family left Hungary and arrived in Chicago where they lived for a short time before returning home. It was during that time that Mother was born. The family sailed again with Mother in tow as an infant. Josef found a job working for the Baltimore Railroad in Chicago, before moving to Madison, Wisconsin where they would buy a new house on Moulton Court on the east side of town.

Life wasn't much easier during that time for German immigrants who were moving into town. Taunted by school age children, Mother remembers removing earrings from her pierced ears one day when she returned home from Holy Redeemer School in Madison's downtown area. It would take 60 years before she wore them again. As an extremely talented teenager whose needlework assignments received recognition in state high school competition, she was offered a job as a seamstress at an upscale women's clothing store on the Capitol Square. She had just completed the 11th grade in high school and planned to graduate the following year. However, when the owner of the store told her the job was hers only if she quit school, she gave in and went to work at Woldenberg's as a teenage seamstress.

At the time of her marriage to Daddy, Mother was employed by the Wisconsin Bell Telephone Company as a telephone operator. When Elaine was born, Mother became a full-time homemaker and remained at home until we both graduated from high school, except for periodic part-time seamstress work at other local stores. Elaine and I took piano and dance lessons and Mother designed and sewed beautiful clothes, costumes and formals for us. After I graduated from high school, she added golf and bowling to her schedule. It wasn't until years later, when I came across some of her English compositions and drawings from high school days that I would understand the extent of her talent.

Mother was also a very private person. She was happy to stay home, keeping it neat and clean and cooking scrumptious and aesthetically pleasing meals. Never making us do anything more than wash and dry dishes, she felt it was more important that we play with our friends. I tested her patience far more than Elaine, and she probably deserved a few medals by the time I was celebrated my 16th birthday. She never raised her voice, but had a subtle way of making me feel bad for disappointing her by stepping beyond the boundary, all of which kept me on the straight and narrow with a simple flash of her eyes. Being the disciplinarian meant that her "precious daughters" never had to worry that their smiling, good-natured, easy-going father would raise his voice to them.

When reflecting on the past, Mother had no regrets other than not having an opportunity to open her own seamstress shop. Otherwise, the formula was perfect. They were satisfied with what they had and never wished for more. We profited as the beneficiaries of a wonderful life together.

Christmas, 1981.

The Family Tree...

Elaine was born in 1933.

She married Gordon Ayen in 1955. They had one son, Tom, born in 1959. Gordy built homes in Madison and our cottages on North Sand Lake.

I was born in 1937.

In 1962 I married Dick Murray. My son, Michael, born in 1958, is from my first marriage. Joining Michael in 1963 was Bill and, in 1965, Bob.

Dick graduated from UW-Madison, flew jet fighters with the Air Force and Wisconsin Air National Guard and was a pilot with TWA. He retired with 25 years of military service in 1978, and as a TWA Captain in 1991 after 25 years with the company.

Michael attended UW-Oshkosh and works for Famous Footwear at Corporate Headquarters. He is married to Deborah Gorman and they have three sons, Shawn, Jordan and Devin.

Bill graduated from UW-Whitewater and works for Promega, a bio-tech firm in Fitchburg, near Madison. He is married to Tanya Huelskamp and they have a daughter, Sydnie, and a son, Nate.

Bob remains single at this writing, married to his music as a drummer with Mirror Black, a Madison-based heavy metal group.

Tom, also single, received two Masters Degrees at UW-Madison and works for Christianson Associates in Madison.

Shawn attended Edgewood College on a scholarship. Following graduation he became a Madison Firefighter. He is married to Becky Sell and they have two daughters, Halle and Kacie.

Everyone lives in Madison.

Happy are those who see beauty
in modest spots
where others see nothing.
Everything is beautiful.
The whole secret lies in knowing
how to interpret it.

Camille Pissarro
1820 - 1903

Introduction

THIS HUMBLE COMPILATION IS NOT TO BE CONFUSED WITH A HISTORY BOOK OF names, places and dates. Welcome it, instead, as a reflection of the past interspersed with an individual's love and respect for a place in Wisconsin valued like a family jewel. However, to offer recollections without portions of its history could be compared to dropping a valuable coin in a pocket with a hole.

Plans to preserve this cherished past for future generations need a foundation. Once built, answers are also necessary for questions that are bound to surface. With this in mind, it is imperative for me to casually skim surfaces of the area's mighty past before attaching personal memories that will stretch the story far beyond and into the 21st century. Only then will my efforts produce an interesting read for everyone to hopefully find a place on coffee tables and books shelves in every cottage, cabin, and year-around home nestled along the shoreline and periphery of North Sand Lake.

As a personal adventure, it all began back in 1945. Although my bare feet left faint impressions in the sand, thoughts of the area's historical significance rarely entered my eight-year-old mind. Instead, I was innocently lost in a fairytale of a vacation composed of water, woods and peace-loving Native Americans. It wasn't until years later that Burnett County became an admitted treasure spreading its branches throughout the expanse of the state's most northwest territory influenced by glacial Lake Grantsburg. Mother Nature's magic wand remodeled the land some 15,000 years before when monstrous sheets of ice, moving from Grantsburg east through Siren and Webster to north of Hertel left behind a magnificent creation of today's 508 lakes, seven major rivers and 30 streams.

The glacial age had been kind to Wisconsin. Prodding, nudging, slicing and chipping away, each massive glacier turned sandstone into sandy soil to deposit a future fortune of 100,000 landscaped acres threaded together by the dominant St. Croix River as a divider between the wilderness of Wisconsin and Minnesota. When the glacier melted, lakes were formed. In the aftermath, the Clam, Namekagon, Tamarack, Totagtic and Yellow rivers made vital connections to complement the final chapter of the Glacial epoch as a natural masterpiece that would one day label Burnett County as the Fishbowl of Wisconsin.

Long before Wisconsin became a territory in 1836 and a state in 1848, population density was confined to a large triangular section of land that stretched from the southwest corner in a northeast direction to the Green Bay area thus filling in everything below to what is now the Illinois border. Above this triangle were three vast stretches of land, the narrowest being St. Croix which hugged the northwest corner of Wisconsin.

The Sauk Indians referred to a small portion of land as *gathering waters.*

Spelled *ouisonsing* by French explorers, the waterway stretched 300 miles from north to south, and 260 miles from east to west. These gathering waters held hundreds of species of fish, and its shorelines, marshlands, and peripheral fields attracted migratory waterfowl and other game birds. Whitetail deer, black bear and many other woodland creates were also in abundance.

When European explorers arrived in North America in 1500, the Chippewa, or Ojibwa as we refer to them today, moved in a westerly direction from the north eastern shores of the Atlantic Ocean to the eastern end of Lake Superior. A century later, they moved again, this time to the southern portion of the Great Lakes thus entering the vast forests of northern Wisconsin. The Ojibwa were identified by the front puckered seam on the moccasins they wore. A religious branch of the tribe, the *Midewiwin*, lived by moral teachings. Their good deeds, they believed, were in view of the Great Spirit who would secure rewards for them after death. As compassionate people, they never passed by the poor without offering food to eat. If a *Midewiwin* tribe member owned a good hunting dog, it was offered to a poor man in need of such an animal. If deer or bear were killed on land passed down from father to son, they were expected to share it with others. With each change of seasons, new horizons awaited with tasks and chores and traditional beliefs.

The arrival of Ojibwa as well as the Sioux laid the groundwork for others to follow, however they often were at war and after the Sioux lost the last of many battles, they left the area. This allowed the Ojibwa to establish their own settlements with entrances and exits of narrow trails destined to become future roads to towns and villages. Knowledge of the land and its seasonal offerings as taught by the wisest men of the tribe served as an unwritten bible to guide each new generation. Alas, the unpredictable was difficult to deal with. An entry in an 1816 diary revealed that temperatures were so low that water froze each month during the year. Also described were two inches of snow that fell during the summer months. The fickleness of the elements spelled disaster for crops. Those who endured these catastrophes became the county's true survivors.

It was during this same time that missionaries, French fur trappers and traders made their appearance. The combination of the Ojibwa, who called themselves *Anishinabe* as "one of the first people," and the French traders and voyageurs, made historical and invaluable impact in Wisconsin during the mid-1650s. For the next two-hundred years, Indian families welcomed the new arrivals and made attempts to teach them long-used methods of survival. In return, the French shared their knowledge of the fur trading business by trading and bartering at fur trading locations. Allow your thoughts to carry you back in time to business of the day when these lonely fur trading log out-posts along waterways momentarily bustled with activity. The Forts Folle Avoine with its NorthWest and XY companies was the fur trade crossroad between Webster and Danbury. It has been carefully reconstructed to return us today to that exciting stepping stone in state history.

Flowing rivers induced activity because of their accessibility. If you look to the right while leaving Webster, driving north on Highway 35, just before reaching County Road A you might see a tiny dilapidated structure a short distance from the edge of the Yellow River. It is rumored to be a hint of the past of portaging and canoeing, trading and bartering and will stir scenes worthy of thought and imagination of how fur trading encouraged white settlements throughout North America.

Burnett County was named in honor of Thomas Pendleton Burnett. Born in Virginia, Burnett lived in Kentucky where he studied law. In 1829 he moved to Wisconsin and was appointed Indian sub-agent at Prairie du Chien, in southwest Wisconsin on the Mississippi River. A year after he married, Burnett moved to a large farm in Cassville. As a politician, before his unexpected death, he had played a powerful role in the formation of the state. In return, the Territorial Legislature named our county "Burnett" in his honor.

Canute Anderson arrived here in 1854. Anderson, known as The Father of Burnett County, was the lone resident in the area for four years. As Norwegian and Swedish immigrants arrived, they would become the foundation of Burnett County.

In 1855, the St. Croix and Lake Superior Railroad Company surveyed the possibilities of a rail system throughout the western part of Burnett County, and small settlements began to make appearances which encouraged continued growth.

When the adventurous Scandinavians left their homeland in search of a better life, as with all immigrants, it was the undertaking of a lifetime. Swedish and Norwegian immigrants stepped from voyage carriers with dreams tucked deep in the pockets of their hearts and souls and meandered into Granstburg in 1860. When promises surfaced twenty years later of prosperity in Spooner, some of them moved south toward Spooner. Cautious, yet hopeful, these hardy people most likely questioned more than once their decision to leave their Motherland behind and settle in unfamiliar foreign territory.

And, so the story goes...from geologic dismantling and rearranging, through its evolution of unspoiled wilderness, human co-habitation and structure, Burnett County officially began in 1865 as a section of Wisconsin bearing 30,000 acres of mere trickles and streams to roaring waters. As a natural phenomenon, the county we hold in such esteem, as a design other parts of the country could barely fathom, was within reach for all to enjoy.

Because Burnett County had great extremes in temperatures, the growing season was short. The unpredictability of the terrain and its elements was overwhelming to the settlers. With little recourse, they banded together and refused to allow unbearable winters to deter their goals when temperatures plummeted well below what most others could only imagine. Summer heat simmered bittersweet stews or pleasures seasoned with storms, failed crops, and epidemics. Their innocence groaned with optimism and became a common commodity among the newcomers. They rose with the sun and faced each new day's mysteries until the sun slipped beyond the horizon many hours later. Only then did they allow their bodies to rest in the calm of an evening prayer, humbly asking for compensation for their efforts before another day was lost in well-deserved sleep. Lacking the assurances of land developers whose briefcases eventually bulged with promises, settlers took advantage of land claims and explored the unknown of the area. Determination was a necessity. Encouraged by their belief in the Lord, links were established to connect their goals. Little thought was given to how the land had been rearranged 15,000 years before. This new land of hills and valleys, rock formations, cliffs, crevices, gorges, ravines, rushing streams, roaring rivers, dense forests, flowering prairies and views that carried the eye as far as humanly possible was taken for granted and accepted as a gift from the Lord.

Gifts, in turn, offered by the settlers, came in the form of culture as a wealth of Old World tradition steeped in New World pride and surroundings complemented every breath. The important things in life were family, good health, food to eat, and a place to live. If they mixed together religion with aspirations, optimism and intuitiveness, the formula was sure to bring success. They refused to complain about the rocks that surfaced in the fields each spring when none had been visible the year before. What did appear each spring was removed and those of monstrous sizes were left while rows of seeds skirted their shapes. And there were other pitfalls. Trees were so large that only four were needed when building a small place in which to live, however it seemed that no sooner had the structure been completed that it burned to the ground. Frugal as their lives may have seemed, the owner and his friends and family quickly gathered ample supplies of trees that surrounded them, turned them into logs, and built once again. With a stable roof overhead, soil was turned to swallow seeds sprinkled by hands that folded each night in humble prayer.

The Homestead Law of 1862 allowed a settler to reside on and cultivate land for five years at the end of which the land would become his own. Later, the length of time was reduced to three years. Ownership, however, came with restrictions. A homesteader had to be 21-years-old, or the head of a family, a citizen of the United States, or to have declared his intention to become a citizen and couldn't own more than 160 acres of other land in the United States. All were words of encouragement for Europeans who were dismayed with land conditions in their own countries. Civil War veterans also were offered opportunities to obtain government land. Unfortunately, the land was nothing more than sterile sand, failing to ripen the most ambitious seeds. Although droughts seemed inevitable, no setback was too catastrophic to cease caring. Without believing, many had nothing. When personal tragedy occurred, tears were dried and life went on.

Ideally, each settler needed oxen and at least one male and one female farm animal. Successful procreation meant large herds. Settlers also needed to hunt, trap and fish. Again, the Indian became a valuable source of information to nurture their very existence. The hills that surrounded them hid blueberries ripening on bushes waiting to be picked. The heavily laden stems of the wild rice needed relief, and cranberries ripened to a brilliant red. And, like a breast-feeding mother, mature sugar maple trees awaited the tapping of syrup that oozed nourishment for the body.

With the magic of time, this northwest corner of Wisconsin had become beautifully blanketed with majestic pines. Literally an empire, the undisturbed White pine, largest of all pines and coined king of the northern pine trees, took a liking to the sandy soil left behind by the glacier. Lumber camp jobs became plentiful and the magnificent massive-size pines were reduced to ugly stumps by obliging crews who had temporarily deserted seasonal farming. An insensitive lumber monopoly became the state's major industry. Between 1880 and 1910, orders were given by lumber camp bosses to fill every order from every lumber company. The scenery drastically changed as every tree in sight was removed. Carried out with a near vengeance, the end result defied description. When lumber crews moved to other locations, left behind were ugly scenes of muddy fields as far as one could see from the highest of hills. White Pine, Spruce, Hard and Sugar Maples, Yellow Birch, Elm and Oak logs, all reduced by sharpened blades, traveled together on dangerous liquid paths in a westerly direction to the St. Croix and Mississippi rivers, and Lake Superior to the north. When water levels were low, logs created massive jams during the early spring months and, in 1869, 150 million feet of logs jammed the waterways in Chippewa Falls. Once freed, each foot of wood was destined to help build a nation, while the emptiness left behind opened more land to farm.

Investment firms hoping to stimulate growth in the area painted colorful scenes of wealth and promise to potential property buyers. But, it was to no avail. People residing in larger cities could not be convinced that life in such remote areas could offer a sufficient future when advancement already was just a mere heartbeat away from their homes.

Despite the inactivity, homes were quickly built. Convinced that railroads would provide the powerful and swift connections needed for settlements to sprout and thrive in the middle of virtually nowhere, developers continued with their plans. In the meantime, soft-wood replacements of aspen and birch nudged forth to add wisps of new life with a natural return of uncomplicated beauty. Edible berries and plum trees appeared and fields and wild flowers shared the land with rice fields and cranberry bogs. Each new stem of life grew as a gift for those who would follow.

Webster, Wisconsin. What was the purpose of establishing Webster and how did it gets its name? The people who lived in the area needed a base for supplies closer than Grantsburg. It is documented that in 1880, John (Kjelmo) Chelmo, Sr. was the first settler in the Webster area. By the mid-1890s, businessman M. H. Carroll petitioned for a post office. Having no name to attach to his request, he quickly answered that the father of the American Dictionary was a good choice, thus the village with no name suddenly became...Webster with Carroll's wife serving as its first postmistress. Because Mr. Carroll was a man of humble character, it may have been the reason why he did not suggest his own family name for the new village. He was, however, instrumental in creating a self-serving atmosphere by building a general store, restaurant and rooming house that initiated interest for additional businesses. The original general store was destroyed, and another one, built in 1911, served the community for many years and today it is in the backyard of a charming antique shop.

Centuries never tire. As one ends, another quickly begins with new innovations and promise. Life in Burnett County shifted gears, this time to welcome a new era with advancements best described as incomprehensible, unfathomable and overwhelming by those who had survived untold hardships as pioneers.

During the last decade of the 19th century, the Duluth, Red Wing and Southern Railroad discussed plans to establish a rail system from Superior into Burnett County as well as neighboring counties. Unfortunately, plans never materialized. In 1902, the Soo Line railroad entered the picture. Immigrant settlements greeted newcomers who arrived to take advantage of land-staked claims. In the absence of bridges that connected land, ferries provided an invaluable service to the people in the area. King's Ford enabled residents and travelers to cross the Yellow River in North Sand Lake township, and the Pansy Ferry aided those north of Danbury needing to cross the St. Croix River. The railroad would be a welcomed addition.

In 1903, Jackson, Scott and Webb Lake became townships. To complement Jackson Township was the inclusion of North Sand Lake, a truly spectacular receptacle in the state's cache of glacial treasures. Filled with crystal clear, spring-fed water with seepage status, the 962-acre lake reached depths of more than 70 feet with 7 ½ miles of beautiful shoreline. To complement its natural glory, North Sand Lake property would someday be considered choice by those in the future who wished to own a piece of the pie for a wedge of their own *up north* retreat.

Many who served as Jackson Township officers through the years are recognized by North Sand Lake property owners today, with streets and roads bearing their names. J. A. and Ainard Leef, Sylvia Kovarik, Ed Green and Berniece Thompson are just five of many who served townships through the years that have been attached to North Sand Lake since elections began in 1911. Also included was Charles Alden who donated land for the Jackson Cemetery on Alden Road. These roads, often nothing more than suspicious sand ruts with doubts of reaching destinations, and especially unforgiving if carrying heavy loads in carts and wagons, suddenly became fragments of yesterdays. Belief that by layering gravel, clay or sawdust would improve road conditions was worth a try. Other nearby paths were named for early settlers. Although Pratt, Sewell and Mallard Lake roads, along with Leef and Thompson roads remain vital to the ever-growing rural and lake population, the major connection for North Sand Lake is County Highway A, once known as County Road A.

By 1911, night trains chugged their way through Webster during pitch-black early morning hours. Later, round-trip rail activity continued to feed Webster, arriving at more desirable mid-afternoon hours. If townspeople were optimistic about their future, new roads, rail systems and airports would become vital links to their existence. As priorities shifted, appropriations were made available.

Life and its expectations seemed to move along at a faster pace. To satisfy investing firms that salivated thirsty tales to potential buyers, lumbering kept whittling away at whatever was left of the once beautiful regional forests. Frustration plagued the firms with continued disappointment from unexpected lack of interest by the general public.

Searching through back issues of the Burnett County Sentinel, the past becomes an open book. Offering a plethora of documented experiences, the county's first newspaper tells us that on May 4, 1883, an inch of snow helped diminish heavy fires along the St. Croix River. A personal diary revealed that in 1816 ice froze every month and snow averaging two inches in depth blanketed the area during the summer months. Another newspaper entry on May 7, 1908 described a cranberry marsh being created in the St. Croix swamp; that Mrs. Thomas Reed planted grape vines and walnut trees, and that Leopold Schultz was digging holes to plant lots of box elders and apple trees.

In 1912, Webster was platted as a town. Giant steps in the right direction ranged from being first to pour concrete sidewalks to being first to recognize the Federal Farm Loan System, both which pushed Webster far ahead of other settlements. For a land developer, it seemed only right to compile a handbook containing endless lists of promises and glowing descriptions to entice people to move there. A 64-page compendium listing the attributes of Webster and the immediate area was researched, printed and distributed. Labeled as a souvenir filled with Burnett County facts, the soft-cover booklet described the area and its endless opportunities and rewards which awaited those with serious thoughts of relocating. Never once did it mention the Webster area being comprised of tamarack swamps and cranberry marshes. Yet, with a growing population of 500, and being the second largest town in Burnett County, Webster, indeed, had plenty to be proud of.

One of three railroads to serve the county was the Soo Short Line which operated from the Twin Cities to feed the progressive towns of Siren, Webster and Danbury. Because of this modern method of transportation, thousands of inquiries arrived on a daily basis about opportunities Webster offered. The souvenir publication was, no doubt, designed as a marketing ploy of land developers. Descriptions on every page of every ingredient needed to reach a rewarding plateau in life hinted that Webster was an area literally blessed with perfect conditions. Included were pictures telling tales of peacefulness and country beauty that encouraged riches with hard work. Everything seemed too good to be true from the soil to the rainfall, markets and roads, schools and churches, lakes and streams, climate, timber, water supply, crops, livestock, you-name-it and it was yours for the taking if you decided to relocate.

On December 24, 1916, the village of Webster was incorporated. Because many of the homesteaders in the Webster area farmed during the summer and lumbered in off seasons, new businesses became a welcomed and much-needed addition. A school, drug store, medical shelter and hotel were further complemented with religious gathering places as well as the creamery where the drive-in is located today. As Webster grew, so did new listings of blacksmiths, barbers, a shoemaker, contractors, real estate offices, a grocery, bank, saw mill, furniture store, newspaper office, pool hall and candy shop. Positioned along a major highway, plus being a train station was the epitome for Webster and its sister resort town, Spooner, about 30 miles to the east in Washburn County. Webster had become a cozy place to settle by erasing the one-way, two-day trips to Grantsburg one was forced to make for the necessities to survive.

Webster, sandwiched between Siren and Danbury, seemed to have all the preliminary staples to become successful. A bridge was built north of town over the Yellow River, 40 miles of highway were laid and voting took place at the Orange School where a democratic right would give off an aura of importance to those who lived in the area, or were merely passing through. It is no wonder that Webster quickly earned the label Second to None in Progressiveness.

Gears kept shifting. Almost living in the fast lane, Webster witnessed another horizon that seemed to creep in without any kind of announcement. After two decades seasoned with good country life plus transportation to nourish the scenery, the natural gift of glacial remnants began to tempt those from afar who searched for places to fish, hunt and vacation. The abundance of lakes, rivers and woodlands satisfied their dreams. Arriving by rail system or the newly introduced automobile, vacationing visitors settled into the good life of the north woods. When they returned home, most knew that a repeat visit was inevitable. With an awareness that a sparkling gem in the crown of Burnett County had been discovered, they shared descriptions with others who soon tested the excitement of the area. Suddenly, Webster had another winner on its hands. Having been catered to throughout their many phases of life, wealthy tourists wanted to relive the pleasures on weekends, full weeks, and entire summers. They arrived with fishing gear, wives, and children in tow with dogs and cats, and filled lodges, fishing camps, and resorts that sprouted everywhere. It definitely was an eye-opening vacation to write home about.

The local economy began to move at a new pace. While the big cities were making statements of their own during the 1920s, Burnett County continued to establish notoriety of its own. A building boom crept into the woods as cabins and cottages went up overnight in nooks and crannies of the woods and along shorelines. Lodges sporting massive stone fireplaces and communal dining rooms, and resorts of humble seasonal dwellings furnished with wood stoves, iron beds, kitchen sink pumps, and outhouses reached by paths through the woods convinced the newcomer that this was a great experience and one of life's *up north* gifts.

Allure for trips *up north* reached Chicago, Illinois, 450 miles to the south, Duluth, Minnesota, 50 miles to the north, and the Twin Cities of Minneapolis and St. Paul, 100 miles to the west. For those who chose the rail system as a means of transportation, there was the benefit of knowing that the owner of the place where your reservations had been made would be waiting at the depot to drive you to your destination. For those who decided to take to the highways and drive the distance from their homes, there remained one last road that would carry them over sand mixed with gravel. The good life in Burnett County had been nibbled and savored and everyone wanted more.

Promises of springs, sandy beaches, crystal-clear water and accommodation rates of $1.00 to $2.00 per day enticed the masses. If you liked what you saw and decided to purchase property and build your own vacation cottage or cabin, a down payment of $1.00 plus $1.00 per week would snag a $25.00 to $100.00 lot on a sandy shore. Crowned and shaded by trees, bushes and wild flowers, each parcel was a dream come true. Who could resist? Adding finishing touches to the dream was the promise that a cottage would be built for you within two weeks. To garnish the offer were enticing tales passed on by fishermen of their experiences, one in particular describing a party of five men who caught 189 large fish, mostly walleye, bass and a few muskellunge, all in less than a few hours.

Webster was in its glory. Their bank assets trickled over the $160,000 mark and to boost the assets even more were the additions of a lawyer, three physicians, a dentist, pickle factory, potato warehouses, several merchandise stores, hardware, shoe and jewelry stores, a meat market, three land dealers, one of the largest auto garages and repair shops in northwest Wisconsin, tire vulcanizing, a large lumber yard, saw mill, two auto liveries, two hotels, restaurants, a large pool hall, a distribution point for the Standard Oil Company, a branch of Hickerson Roller Mills, a grade and high school and fraternal church organizations. And, underneath it all were telephone wires to carry conversations from town to farm and back. Just as the souvenir book promised, Webster truly was a unique place to settle.

What the city folks gasped and grasped for, locals sighed, having it all at their fingertips every day of the year. Yet, when the Great Depression interjected its many pains, everyone suffered as building reached a standstill. People had no other choice than to stay home just to survive. When the Depression finally ended, optimism once again developed a grand commodity and the lid was removed for more broth to boil over. Entrepreneurs were wild with enthusiasm. The average guy was given a break while the lives of the affluent kicked in as the economy shifted gears again. The good times had returned. New county roads appeared everywhere for an even greater building boom than before.

By 1940, there were 11,382 people in Burnett County. No sooner had the good times arrived than another hurdle appeared in the way. World War II stopped the clock of time and tested the patience of those who had set their minds to develop properties to please out-of-town inquiries from outdoor sports seekers. Patience was, indeed, a virtue that would be richly rewarded in the aftermath when the war ended and life began once again as hammers and saws were removed from storage to spark the new economy.

This time, instead of heading north, south, or east by rail, some vacationers arrived in brand new cars—fancy ones from the big cities, others just as shiny and new, but more humble, each packed with adults, children, pets, fishing gear and food to last a week. It was time to celebrate everything that follows a depression, recession, suppression and anything else in between.

The economy blossomed like a bevy of spring flowers recently showered with love, respect and the sprinkling can of its caretaker. Highways and county roads were alive with four-wheel vehicles and their owners made stops along the way to shop and eat in small towns and villages. To put it in simple terms, life was fun. The air was heavy with hope and we inhaled it with gusto.

By the mid-1950s, the area was doing its best to keep up with the crowds. Vacationers continued to arrive in search of Wisconsin's north wood experiences and resorts burst at the seams. Webster, a town with a population of 549 and a street as wide as any found in a major city, did its best to meet the demands.

Through the years Webster changed. Still small, it possessed the simple staples in life, and then some. Not having grown as decades before had anticipated, its small town touch still kept everyone happy with Johnson's Seahorse Outboard Motors complete with minnows, worms, oars, anchors and tackle. If you couldn't catch fish to eat, you could load up with groceries at Hedbergs, the biggest little store in Webster, Fairway Foods, the Clover Farm Store, Webster Co-op Store and

Creamery, or Everett L. Syberg's Maple Island Products for the highest quality milk, cream and butter. All performed admirably in keeping the locals happy as well as those from the cities.

Lights in the back room of E. P.'s Bakery, where Gandy Dancer Book store is located today, were turned on well before the sun rose each morning to bake "barrel bread" for customers who followed the aroma inside. If you were hungry, but didn't want to cook, you could step into the adjacent shop, the site today of an eye clinic, for breakfast, or soup and sandwiches for lunch. Or you could stop by the Black and Orange Café, grab a bite to eat at Curry's Lunch, have coffee and shoot the breeze with the locals. If your stomach didn't feel good or a head ache began to pound, you stopped at Maser's Drug Store for some Pepto-Bismo or aspirin to ease the pain. If an illness required more than a tablespoon of thick pink liquid or a tiny white pill, you made an appointment with Dr. D. A. Maas by dialing 3311. An ambulance was also just a call away. If fate called, Swedberg's was telephone available to serve the community and surrounding area.

In any town, large or small, there's usually a local watering hole where a beer or two will quench a thirst on a hot summer day. Some had pool tables, like Baker's Inn, or bowling alleys, like B & O Alleys. No matter what your needs, clothing and shoes were priorities. Gambles, the friendly store, was listed in the phone book as Gambles Shopping Center, which, in essence, it was. Owner Lem Collis kept a fine inventory of clothing to wear, food to eat, and meat to roast. When your clothes needed sprucing, Indianhead Cleaners picked up and delivered at the Webster Shoe Store. Yes, there was even a store within the two block business length of Webster that sold and repaired shoes. And, it was worth traveling miles to be greeted with smiles at Kaufman's.

Lorraine's Gift Shop filled those extra-special needs on the spur of the moment without having to drive to another town in search of handmade needlework, custom sewing, and gifts of all kinds. And, if you think there couldn't possibly be room for anything else in town, considering its size, think again. Sub-contractors were available for every job in the book including painting, paper hanging, electrical wiring, refinishing old wood floors, and delivering Skelgas. Adding on or building new or, better yet, drawing plans for a weekend retreat meant visiting Consolidated Lumber or Kringle Lumber and Millwork for everything you needed to get started. When the building or remodeling was completed, Otis Rand hauled away anything you couldn't, and Ray Pardun had enough sand and gravel to fill in all the crevices that surrounded your house. Photographer Henry H. Smach would capture the finished product, or any other moment in your life worth remembering. If the old homestead was ready to fall apart, Brier Brown was eager for a call. So were the agents at Tollander Insurance Agency who drew up papers and documents to protect you and your belongings.

Heaven forbid, should you run out of gas or have car problems and be stranded overnight in a foreign location it was best to be stuck in Webster where the Webster Motel advertised clean modern cabins and shower baths for the public. That was a deal any weary traveler couldn't refuse, no matter what his mode of transportation happened to be. Webster's abundance of service stations not only filled tanks, but also worked on cars. The Mobil station, the Spur Store with food, gas and oil, or Connor's and Paul's were waiting to serve you on the spot. Some service stations offered to keep your fish in their freezers until you were ready to leave town and the Webster Food locker business packed everything in dry ice until you waved goodbye and headed for home.

Fuel businesses kept everyone's lights on at night, homes heated in all kinds of weather, and hearts happy. Just a few familiar names would include heating and plumbing expert "Iggy" Hersant, or Murl Rockwood, also known as Rocky the Plumber who promised that a good job is cheaper in the end. Webster Radio and TV could give you the entertainment you needed to make long winter days and nights and inclement summer hours seem much shorter as well as keeping you tuned in to the rest of the world. Needless to say, there are many others who contributed to the depth of Webster's roots.

The substance of a town begins and ends with religious meeting places, schools, a bank, a restaurant, newspaper, tavern, medical care and a mortician which Webster offered as strength and convenience for its community. Everything else merely strengthens its foundation. Today, 60 years after I first walked the sidewalk in the little town of Webster, it somehow has remained the same size, except for a very slight increase in population and a major addition of new businesses carefully interspersed in town as well as along its outskirts. Managing to care for everyone local and those of us who fell in love with it because it became our seasonal home, it retains its charm with what other towns can only hope to achieve and offer. Today Webster flourishes, not only with its strength from the past, but also with a fire department, an ambulance crew, law enforcement, family clinic, library, a classy grocery store that any neighborhood in any major city would drool over, a drug store, florist, antique shop, DNR ranger station, a café, tavern, fine dining, county fairgrounds, a bank, hearth and home store, hardware, book store, car dealership, radio and television store and a bowling alley, all and much more within two business blocks. A few years ago, Webster laid claim to the only Italian restaurant in Burnett County.

There was a time when we teased each other about not blinking when driving through Webster for fear of missing it altogether, when the truth to the remark is that by blinking you just might miss one of the best kept secrets in Burnett County. And, to boot, for me, in this special small town far from home is the Austin Lake Greenhouse whose founder, Kirstin, grew up in Madison a short distance from our house and whose parents, "Red" and Eleanor Flagstad, were longtime good friends of my parents. There's Zia Louisa's Italian restaurant whose owner, Paul Hansen, I met when he was a youngster spending summers at his grandparent's Hansen's Resort. And Wayne's at the edge of town whose owner, Wayne King, happens to be good friend of one of my husband's Air Force buddies from their 1954-55 Cadet Pilot Training Class, 55-V. What a small world it is in the small wonderful town of Webster.

Those two-lane highways and humble country roads that carried us *up north* from Madison and back eventually became speedy interstates and widened highways to quicken the trip, though still a bit longer than we wanted. When we finally arrived each summer, the cottage, lake and hometown friendliness convinced us that the long drive was well worth every mile. Never was there a question if we should shorten the drive by searching for a lake and a cottage closer to home because we already knew the answer, that our destination of Webster provided us with the best of the best.

Webster and Spooner remain a vital part of my life. They have since the summer of 1945 and will continue until my *up north* visits cease to exist. Spooner may have offered more, but Webster was closer to the cottage and between the two I had everything I wanted or needed.

I remember the white sign poked alongside the road just outside of Webster that read Population 549 and, for years, wondered why the numbers never changed. Did it mean that for every person who died in Webster, a baby was born? As an adult, I still don't have an answer. Although the numbers have increased slightly to 653, it isn't anything of great importance. What is important is a sense of belonging to everything that makes Webster a place I'm proud to call my summer home.

St. Croix Tribal History

The St. Croix Chippewa Indians of Wisconsin belong to the Ojibwa Nation and the Algonquian language family. It is believed that the Chippewa group migrated to the Wisconsin area during the 1600s.

Through the oral tradition, William Warren, Ojibwa historian, recorded that the Ottawa were once one group and lived by the Atlantic Ocean. The Anishinabe migrated from the east to the Great Lakes. During the migration, when they reached the Strait of Makinac, the group separated into three: the Ottawa returned to the east, the Potawatomi went south and west, and the Ojibwa continued west along Lake Superior and north to Canada.

After establishing a camp on Madeline Island on Lake Superior, the Ojibwa traveled the riverways to trap, hunt, fish and gather wild rice and trade with the Sioux. Hunting parties soon established small camps in the Upper St. Croix valley along the St. Croix River.

The Ojibwa continued to trade with the Sioux and French during the 1700s. As the Sioux moved westward, and the French claim of the area was extinguished by the English, the Upper St. Croix valley became known as the St. Croix district. Fur trading continued between the Ojibwa and the English until the colonists gained independence and the area became part of the United States. The St. Croix District Ojibwa became known as the St. Croix River Chippewas.

The United States then began treaty making with the St. Croix River Chippewa. The first treaty was in 1825 and the last in 1854. Although the St. Croix Chippewa ceded their homeland in the treaty of 1837, the Upper St. Croix valley tribe never ceded the right to hunt, fish and gather. The St. Croix Chippewa no longer had a home and the group refused to be moved inland to the Lac Courte Oreilles reservation. They were known as the "lost tribe" and became squatters on their homeland.

The St. Croix Chippewa remained in the river valley until 1934, when the Indian Reorganization Act was passed by the U.S. Congress. The St. Croix Chippewa Indians of Wisconsin were then given federal recognition and small tracts of land within their historic homeland, which was put in trust by the United States. The St. Croix Chippewa became wards of the U. S. government, afforded trust responsibility and tribal sovereignty.

The present day St. Croix Chippewa operate a successful government of the people while retaining the language, traditions, and cultural ways of the many generations of Chippewas before them. The St. Croix Chippewa have entered the 21st century as a strong tribal entity with the teachings of the Anishinabe intact. With this resilience, they have been able to establish a flourishing economy, which provides jobs and education opportunities for the St. Croix members.

Note: The St. Croix Tribal offices are located in Hertel, Wisconsin, between the towns of Siren and Spooner on Highway 70 and have granted permission to include their history in this book.

Having the pleasure of Madison being a mere 45 miles south of the Wisconsin Dells, my childhood was complemented with annual day trips to the Dells, Duck (boat) touring on the Upper and Lower Dells, and exciting evening ceremonials to put a grand finale on the daylong outing. Elderly male Indians who lived in the immediate area walked the small Wisconsin Dells business district in native costume and stunning headpieces to serve as historical ambassadors willing to talk to visitors who also took pictures of them standing with a member of their family. I always felt honored to be in their presence.

Although the terrain of Danbury is much different from the Dells, Indian pride becomes a parallel when the St. Croix Indians of Wisconsin host an annual Wild Rice Pow Wow to celebrate their wild rice harvest. Dressed in native costume of the Ojibwa culture, singers and dancers attend from locations across the United States to compete in the events, including drums, during the festive weekend event in August where Native American food is made available along with arts and crafts.

For additional Pow Wow information, call (715) 349-2195.

Forts Folle Avoine Historical Park

What began about 200 years ago in the area of Danbury when fur traders and hunters established posts in the woods and along waterways, today encompasses 80 acres along the Yellow River as living history where trading posts from 1802 to 1804 have been reconstructed adjacent to an authentic Woodland Indian village.

First discovered during a state archeological dig in 1969, the site is now on the National Register of Historic Sites. Supported by the Burnett County Historical Society, Burnett County PRT and the St. Croix Chippewa Indians of Wisconsin, the Folle Avoine Historical Park, opened to the public in 1989, turns pages and chapters that allow one to enter the life and culture of early Native American residents and Euro-American explorers.

Folle Avoine is a French term meaning "crazy oats," or wild rice. The park, so named for the abundance of rice and its importance as a food staple during the fur trade era when voyageurs and Native American co-existed, is located 2 ½ miles west off State Road 35 between Danbury and Webster on County Road U where tours are conducted by costumed Native American and voyageur interpreters. This is a must for everyone who enjoys and appreciates savoring and understanding the past. Watch for announcements each year of exhibits, lectures, re-enactments, demonstrations, stories and songs, and many other activities offered throughout the expanse of the park and along the edges of the river.

For more information, call 715-866-8890.

Burnett County

People who live far removed from scenic woods and water cannot fathom what we are blessed with in Burnett County. The dream begins with 508 lakes and 30 streams and the Namekagon and St. Croix Rivers, both part of the National Scenic Riverway, flowing freely and unspoiled through the most scenic and undeveloped country in the Upper Midwest. Add 300 miles of well-groomed snowmobile trails, 75 miles of cross-country ski trails and 21 miles of the Gandy Dancer Trail to bike and hike in any kind of weather and you get the feeling that the county is nothing less than a paradise for fishing, hunting, and four season adventure.

Burnett County is located in the northwestern portion of Wisconsin approximately 40 miles south of Lake Superior. It borders Douglas, Washburn, Barron and Polk counties in Wisconsin and Pine County in Minnesota and, at its widest point, extends 36 miles north-south and 42 miles east-west. What this means for me is that North Sand Lake is nearly 300 miles from my home in Madison, Wisconsin, 400-plus miles for those who live in the Chicago, Illinois area, and a mere 100 miles from the Twin Cities of Minneapolis and St. Paul, Minnesota..

The surface waters of Burnett County occupy one drainage system, the St. Croix River. Of the 889 square miles of land and water in the county, the St. Croix

River drains 565.8 square miles. Land areas within the drainage system having no permanent surface waters or drainage outlets comprise 193.4 square miles and landlocked areas with measurable lake surface waters account for the remaining 129.8 square miles of the county's area. The maximum elevation of Burnett County is about 1,460 feet in the southeast corner, and the minimum is 760 feet above sea level.

The most striking land feature of Burnett County is the level to gently rolling outwash plain known as pine barrens which covers all but the southern farming areas of the county. Jack pine is the important cover type on these barrens.

Scattered throughout the area are hardwoods on patches of loams and clays, and brush and scrubby trees in the kettle-like depressions. The original vegetation of the southern farm area was oak or pine, but the second growth timber is largely white birch and aspen.

Present landforms have been shaped by repeated glacial advances and weathering influences of the local climate. A large portion of central Burnett County has been influenced by glacial Lake Grantsburg. Landforms here are relatively level and soils are poorly to moderately drained and composed of well sorted and fine textured sands, silts, clays, and lacustrine deposits. This region extends from Grantsburg east through Siren and Webster to north of Hertel.

The climate of Burnett County is classified as continental with an average annual temperature of 41.4 degrees Fahrenheit. The winters are long, cold and snowy, while summers are relatively short and warm with only brief periods of hot, humid weather. Springs and falls are often short and mixtures of both summer and winter. Mean temperatures drop below freezing in mid-November and freeze-up of lakes follows soon afterward. The average date of the last freeze in spring is May 31, and the first in fall is September 12. Therefore, the growing season averages 104 days. Maximum precipitation occurs in June, however the highest runoff is usually experienced during snowmelt.

Note: This information is on file at the Department of Natural Resources in Spooner.

G. R. Brown Photograph, Eau Claire, Wis

North Sand Lake

Before the days of the fast, multi-lane interstates, people driving long distances on dangerous narrow highways to reach Burnett County on hot summer Fridays who were aware of the quality of their destination never questioned the length of the trip. Madison friends, however, thought we were crazy to drive that far when we lived in an isthmus city of beautiful lakes surrounded by many others. Only those who personally knew about North Sand Lake would understand the reasons for our summer sojourn. Waiting for us was a county with 41,000 acres of water, 508 lakes, two flowages, 10 major rivers, 145 streams and hundreds of miles of shoreline. Not only was Burnett County known as the Fishbowl of Wisconsin and the Sunfish Capital of the World, but secchi disk tests of our near 1000 acre lake continually prove that one could clearly see depths at least 25 below the surface of the water.

Many years ago, we found a postcard with a colored aerial view of North Sand Lake and purchased many to send home to friends and family. Printed on the reverse side was the namc G. R. Brown Co. Route 5, Eau Claire, WI who, most likely, was the photographer. Incredibly beautiful, an enlarged framed print should hang in each of our lake dwellings. Unfortunately, according to the last time I checked, the cards no longer are available.

In the glory of adjectives, North Sand Lake was described on the postcard as clear, deep, spring-fed lake ideal for fishing, swimming and all water sports. The magic attached to those few words has stayed with me through the years which is why I became slightly confused a few years ago to hear a slightly different version of the lake being a seepage lake with no inclusion of springs. Because I've been an active swimmer since 1945, and can attest to the countless springs felt on warm summer days--a sensation a swimmer rarely forgets, I question part of the description. We do know that the lake is rated as the cleanest in the County, and among the cleanest in the state. And, although North Sand is not recognized as a fishing paradise compared to other lakes in the county, be assured that there are trophy fish in its depths. Pictures and stories of my own fishing escapades plus those of others merely reconfirm these convictions.

I remember the late Warren Hansen, whose parents, Barney and Florence Hansen owned and operated Hansen's Resort on the north shoreline of the lake, telling me back in the mid-1950s of DNR testing for numbers and sizes of various species of fish in the lake and a few weighed and measured before releasing were clearly of record breaking sizes. If you've ever asked yourself why the days you spend fishing the lake produce nothing to brag about, it might help to understand the lake, its size and depths, and the weather patterns. Call it a challenge and a test of patience, but believe that there are huge fish in the lake more patient and intuitive than we are at times.

North Sand Lake has been closely watched and stocked through the years by the DNR and in checking through old files I would learn that in 1936, there were 123 large-mouth bass planted. Two years later, they added 3,179,750 walleye, and the following year, 2,000,000 additional walleye fry. In 1940, 400,000 northern pike fry and 1,000,000 walleye fry were planted. Although northern pike continued to be planted by the hundreds of thousands year after year, an additional 1,200,000 walleye were planted in 1944. There were sporadic plantings of bass, but something new happened in 1958 when the DNR introduced 5,000 kamloops trout to the lake. I saw only one taken before they all disappeared. Almost every year since 1961, walleye fingerlings, mostly in the 3- to 5-inch size, have been planted in massive quantities and in the 1990s, with the entry of spring spear-fishing, the St. Croix Tribe also began to stock the lake with walleye.

To respond to a DNR description of North Sand Lake lacking fish cover, local residents, town and county boards, as well as lake property owners tapped the services of The Cooperative Habitat Development Project by building and sinking log crib shelters to improve the fish cover and provide a more healthy environment for the lake's fish population. In a letter dated October 31, 1968, from the Burnett County Department of Social Services to DNR Fish Manager Jack Donatell, Director Thomas E. Keith pledged department help with manpower while, at the same time, described 12 fish cribs already cut and stacked near the road with expectations to reach a total of 16 cribs upon completion of the project.

Keith and his department were concerned, not because of possible lack of manpower, but instead, weather conditions. The year before, log crib shelters were built in knee-deep snow in sub-zero temperatures that prolonged the project. To alleviate the possibility of a repeat performance in inclement weather, Keith asked the DNR if a portable generator could be delivered on sight to make drilling the logs much easier for the men. Other plans were drawn up to build and sink 18 brush shelters in the lake to supplement the shortage of natural fish cover. On November 14, the project began with 10 shelters built on ice near shore. Logs and brush were hauled out of the woods during a five day period, but because the ice was unsafe to work on, and the crew hired to do the work seldom showed up in full force, the project was never completed.

In 1969, a benchmark post was placed on south shoreline property owned by Ray Rubin to record fluctuating water levels on North Sand, Mallard and Green lakes which, at one time, during high water levels years ago, were connected. The benchmark post was done to protect lakeshore areas important to conservation interests in the development of structural (cabins, cottages, and homes) development and manmade shoreline alterations which generally occur during low water level years. This also would serve as a guide in future fish and game management programs for the lakes mentioned.

On March 28, 1969, seven brush shelters were built and sunk in the north end of the lake. Work continued May 9 with 10 fish shelters built by DNR foreman Joe Davidowski the previous November. Unable to sink at that time due to poor winter ice conditions, the shelters were later pulled out by two boats, one on each side of the shelters, and sunk in designated locations.

Pete Moser applied to the DNR March 8, 1973 for approval to conduct cooperative habitat development program by building and installing four log crib shelters at the north end of the lake. The DNR granted permission to do so and stated they would furnish special equipment and supervision.

These are just a few examples from DNR Fisheries Manager Larry Damman that provide us with facts and figures to assure everyone concerned that each situation involving the lake and its fish continues to be handled with professional expertise. A creel survey in 1993 of 3,295 fish in open water showed that the mean length of walleye was 18.4 inches; northern pike, 21.9 inches; largemouth bass, 13.2 inches; bluegill, 7.1 inches; black crappie, 11.8 inches; yellow perch, 9.2 inches; and rock bass at 6.5 inches.

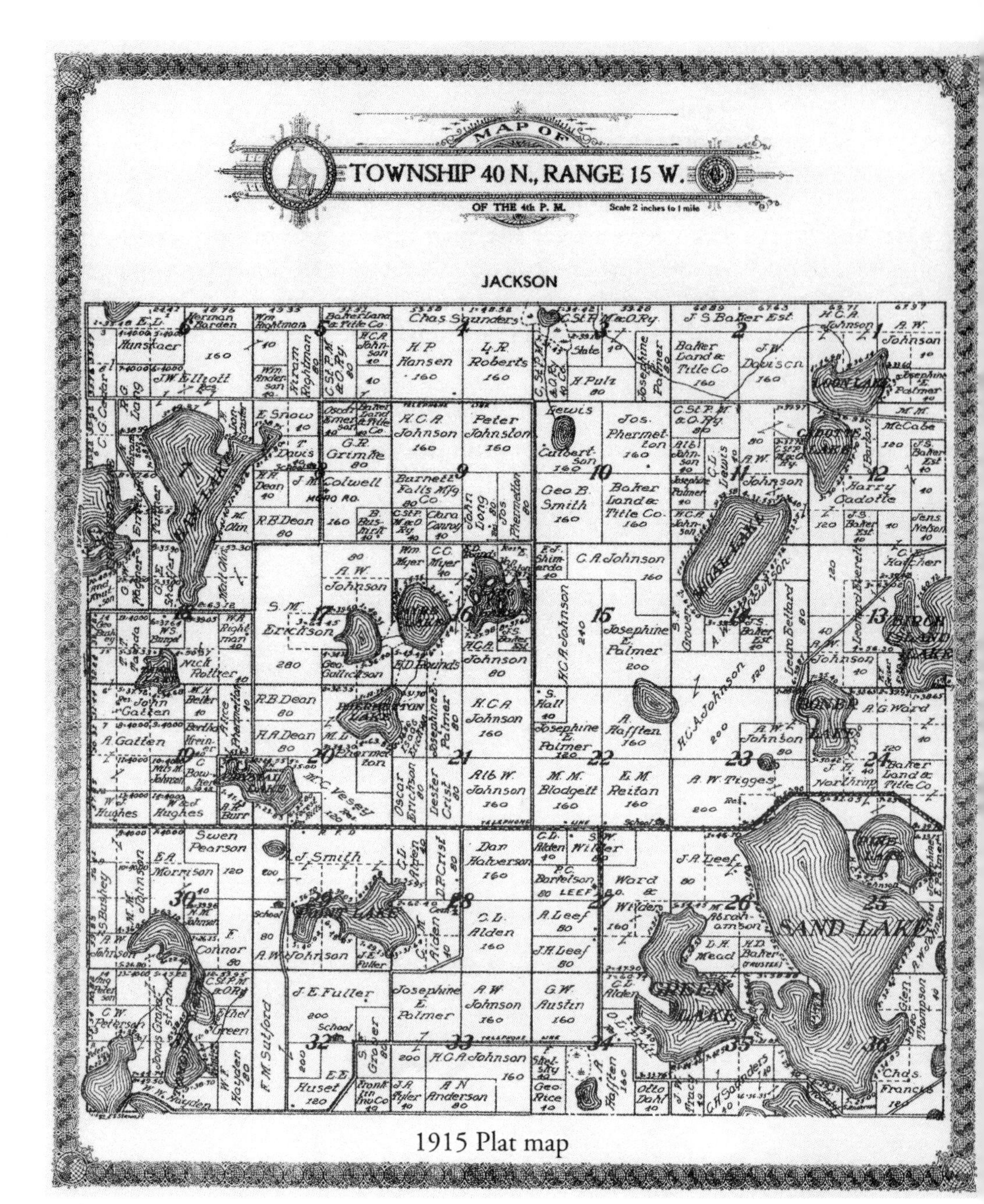

1915 Plat map

Land Abstracts and Memories

There is a story behind every piece of North Sand Lake property. It doesn't matter how insignificant it may seem to some, to a historian it becomes invaluable to an overall picture. As a palette for open fields or farm land, wild flowers or tended gardens, stately trees or berry bushes, dragon flies or butterflies, loons or eagles, white-tail deer or raccoons, or pickerel weeds, lily pads, bulrushes, cattails, bullfrogs, or sandy shorelines, each story or memory becomes a masterpiece of subject matter, unique in its own way.

Land abstracts, however, tell only portions of personal history. Who bought, who sold, how much, and when. The rest is up to memories passed on through the years. Without memories, the past becomes sterile. With them, chapters unfold like genealogical research for all who crave knowing more. Our own abstract reads: *In the mid-1880s, land was granted to the state of Wisconsin for the construction of a railroad from the St. Croix River or Lake to the west end of Lake Superior under the name of Chicago, St. Paul and Minneapolis and Omaha Railway Company.*

By 1902, the United States sold the land to Loren Moody who eventually sold it to a familiar name on many Sand Lake abstracts, Nora Lavell and Anthony A. Lavell, her husband. Another name that will appear on many abstracts is that of Ray Ellis, a kind gentleman who now resides in a nursing home in Siren and admitted that North Sand Lake had been very good to him and his partner, Leslie Tjader, both employed by Lakeside Reality Company. Another familiar name is that of Raymond W. Buggert, Registered Land Surveyor.

Along the way, nature's gifts reward us with humble piers of boards and tamarack tree trunks and seasonal cottages of yesteryear that become interspersed today with imposing docks, spectacular year around homes and weekend retreats that typify lakeshore property owners as a cross section of America bonded together with one common experience, that being in owning a piece of lake property for an *up north* experience.

To gain entry into these scenes, we search, purchase, clear, build, boast, salute, celebrate and nurture. Upon completion rewards are reaped with the beauty of each sunrise and sunset and anything else that complements the experience. To respect what we gain is to dream on forever, never being able to imagine an end to the story.

When I initially gave thought to compiling the past from 1945 to the present of North Sand Lake, my intention was to capture the total scene in 35 pages or less. Sensing a need to ask others to share their own experience added more character and would mean just a few extra chapters. A few became many and the span of time needed to tease their imaginations lasted more than a decade. To everyone who understood the purpose of the project and offered their own reflections about a portion of life too good to forget, it's finally time to sit back, read on, and enjoy. What a ride it has been.

Part I

Thompson Road, unpaved.

Nature never did betray the
heart that loved her.

William Wordsworth
1770-1850

In the Beginning

Barney Hansen was delivering milk in Chicago back in 1942 when he made a decision to shift gears and become a resort owner in the north woods of Wisconsin. He and his wife, Florence, packed their belongings and left the big city for a promise of peace, comfort and tranquility in Burnett County where they purchased land on Fish Lake near County Road H, a short distance from the A & H crossroads. However, because of the country's involvement in World War II, Hansen's plan to build a resort was temporarily interrupted due to a shortage of building supplies, most notably copper tubing necessary for installing electricity.

Determined to make things work, by 1944 Hansen's Fish Lake Resort had become a reality. It was through the local grapevine that Barney would hear about Tom and Cora Cleve's plan to sell their North Sand Lake property. Nothing less than spectacular, the land, once owned by Leonard Chelmo, had been partially acquired by Indiana attorney Oscar Smith, Sr., who in turn sold a portion of it in 1927 to Dan White and Tom Cleve. About to go on the market was a portion complete with Cleve's shoreline house and the small tavern directly behind the house (today's Sandbar). Hansen was interested and arranged to meet with Cleve to learn of more exciting particulars which included 1400 feet of shoreline plus land that crossed over "A" and disappeared into the woods to Little Bass Lake for a grand total of 68 acres. The asking price was $5200.

What the conversation entailed between Barney and Flo that evening during supper is only guess, but an offer to purchase the land was quickly presented and signed on the dotted line making the Hansen's the new owners. With the help of their son, Warren, and the services of Norwegian immigrant Karl Halberg, plans were set in motion. Barney had found Halberg severely beaten along the side of the road one evening and rushed him to town for medical attention. Pledging his service for life to the Hansens, Karl aided in the preparation of a brand new Hansen's North Sand Lake Resort to open during the late spring of 1945. Four two-bedroom cottages, unstained with each cavity exuding the fragrance of raw pine were made available just in time for the summer season at $35.00 per week. In front of each cottage was a humble pier made with boards supported by slender tamarack tree trunks to which a wooden rowboat was tied. That summer of 1945 we spent our first week at the resort in cottage #4.

The following summer, Hansen's resort guests were greeted with a fifth cottage, all five being painted white. Additional cottages were built each year until there were a total of nine lined up along the shoreline to the east of Hansen's house, while No. 10 was built with a different floor plan on the west side separating the house from the small one-room cottage that Karl built and resided in. Years later, the cottages would be painted pastel shades. Evening entertainment drew resort guests and other customers to Hansen's small roadside bar and grocery store. Our pockets jingled with nickels to play jukebox favorites and we danced, sang, laughed and quenched our thirsts with regional brews and sodas when the temperatures climbed. Additions were made to the store and the restaurant offered a limited menu. When Barney Hansen passed away in 1961, the good times down at the store began to change. Florence ran the resort until 1964 when the weight of the job as proprietor became too much for her to carry on alone. Cottages #1 through #9 were put on the market for $4000 each and sold to individual buyers.

In 1956, Art and Ruth Nordstrom and four other couples who were good friends from Eau Claire, purchased an old small cabin situated on one-third of Boner Lake shoreline. Nordstroms fell in love with the area and in 1968, purchased Hansen's house and bar where modern touches were added by removing the bar's outhouse and replacing it with indoor restrooms. After Art passed away and Ruth's health began to fail, the house and bar was sold in 1972 to Ted and Marge Hilgardener. Sharon and John Bachmann would become the next owners and, eventually, the business was turned over to their son, Tom who later sold to Rob Roesell. After a brief few years, Roesell left town and Kevin and Shelly Wear entered the picture. The Wears have been in command of the Sand Bar since February, 2000, and retain its comfort and popularity with their insight, attentiveness, expertise, beverages, pizza, Friday fish fries and other menu items including Shelly's homemade desserts.

The one-room cottage where Hansen's handyman, Karl, once lived, although occasionally rented out after Karl died, sat empty most of the time before being sold and removed from the premises a few years ago. Its front door had opened directly onto dry sand a few steps away from the dampness of the lake's shoreline and served its purpose for the many long years Karl lived there. Cottage #10, rented through the years to vacationers for long and short periods of time, was gutted and extensively remodeled in 2001 by the property's new owners.

The property Barney Hansen purchased back in 1944 became a dream come true for the one-time Chicago milkman who happened to be in the right place at the right time to taste the good life as a bona fide local resort owner on one of the cleanest lakes in Burnett County. Those of us who remember Barney and Flo Hansen and their North Sand Lake resort know what a treat and rare gift it was to spend a week or more there to become a member of their summer family.

It Was a Very Good Year

1945. It was a very good year. World War II was about to end and bubble gum was back on the shelf at Gerhardt's Drug Store. Daddy was 41, Mother was 37 and my sister Elaine was 12. That made me an eight-year-old who loved every waking moment of every day. Uncle Joe had just returned from a fishing trip with friends who stayed at Thompson's Resort on North Sand Lake in Burnett County, wherever that was. Describing the lake, fishing, and a brand new resort that just opened on the north shoreline, he encouraged Daddy to try it for a week. Daddy placed a long distance call to make reservations. Little did we realize that it would become a vacation destined to last a lifetime.

I had never heard of Burnett County before, nor had I heard of Spooner or Webster, but after Daddy made arrangements to spend a week there, I was about to learn what *up north* in Wisconsin was all about. Previous family vacations carried us to the Lac du Flambeau area in the north-central part of the state, but the last time we were there with Mother and Daddy, Grandma and Grandpa Kovacs and aunts, uncles and cousins, I was only nine months old.

Life wasn't quite the same once our vacation plans were confirmed at Hansen's Resort. Lists were found in every room of the house and grew longer with each new day. The small kitchen table radio had to go with us so we knew what was going on in the world during the week. Daddy wasn't a diehard fisherman at the time so he drove a few blocks from home to Berg-Person Sporting Goods on Atwood Avenue to visit Wes LeFebvre, a friend and employee who could offer advice about hooks, lines and sinkers. Mother's trusty pop-out Kodak camera needed ample rolls of film to capture our *up north* experience so she visited family friend, Bill Stoker, at his Hudson Park Pharmacy, another nearby Atwood Avenue establishment. Priorities of my sister, Elaine, who was four years older than me, amounted to bathing suits, sun glasses and bottles of Johnson's Baby Oil to grease up every day for a good suntan. Me? Just knowing that I'd have an inner tube, a flash light, a rubber swim cap and a couple of swim suits was just fine. Throw in my huraches, some shorts and T-shirts for warm days, add tennies, a pair of blue jeans and a sweatshirt for cool nights, plus a skirt, blouse and scarf for Mass on Sunday and a deck of cards to play Rummy, and I thought I had everything anyone my age needed.

On Friday, the day before we left home, arrangements were made to stop the delivery of the newspaper and our mail. After my dog Suzy was driven out to

Our house: 166 Talmadge St., Madison, Wisconsin

Monona Village to spend a week at Dr. Romaker's kennels, Daddy headed uptown to Oscar Mazursky's Market on W. Mifflin St. for something Mazursky had packed for him in appreciation for the choice meat Daddy selected to be delivered there each week. There were two boxes, one with non-perishables and the other with produce and fresh fruit. A stop at Oscar Mayer's employees' market provided a week's worth of meat wrapped with butcher's paper. The next morning, Mazursky's boxes were placed in the space along the back window to fill the car's interior during the afternoon sun with sweet fruity aromas. The last stop would be back on Atwood Avenue at Ole Severson's gas station to check the oil and fill the tank before heading for home in anticipation of the big day ahead.

The next morning, the alarm rang before the break of dawn. By the time we dressed and reached the car parked in front at the curb, Elaine and I became the last two pieces to fit into the back seat. In an almost fetal position with our feet and knees interlocked, we settled down in the two-tone gray Chevy packed tightly without an inch of extra room, for the faraway place of Burnett County. My head rested on a bed pillow Mother puffed up and placed over the arm rest on the left side of the back seat behind Daddy, and Elaine had similar accommodations on the right side behind Mother. We had one stop to make before our plans were carried out to sleep the entire trip and that was to pray on our knees in front of the angel in an arched concrete shelter in front of St. Bernard's Catholic Church in Middleton. The time was 4:30 a.m.

I don't know how Mother or Daddy knew about the statue, but we prayed for guidance and safety on the trip along the narrow two-lane highway. Flat tires or killer traffic odors drifting through the car windows, however, were overlooked. If we weren't inhaling the comforting sweetness from sun-warmed fruit in the back window, we choked on diesel fumes from semi-trucks. Rolling down the back seat windows wasn't an option because the speed-induced wind messed things up, including us. With no air-conditioning, the heat and the intermingling odors, there were many moments that seemed almost unbearable.

Are We There Yet?

WELL ON OUR WAY, THE 300 MILE DRIVE DESIGNED TO BECOME A MID-SUMMER sojourn found us captives in the back seat with eyes closed and minds wondering how much longer it would take to reach our destination.

It was before the era of interstate highways and the trip carried us in and out of countless small towns offering brief looks at rural life with stops for gas or a snack or nickel ice cream cones—strawberry for Daddy, vanilla for Mother, Elaine's favorite, chocolate, and orange sherbet for me. Baraboo. Wisconsin Dells. Mauston. Tomah. Black River Falls. Eau Claire. Although most were places I had never visited before, Wisconsin Dells and its Indian culture was familiar and everything beyond became stepping stones to the cottage. After Eau Claire, a town where Mother and Daddy lived for a short time after they were married, came Chippewa Falls, then Bloomer, a name that made us giggle. Then Chetek. We recognized Rice Lake in name only because it was where the Dahlgrens were from and only then did Daddy convince us that we were getting closer to Spooner. "It won't be too much longer," he said. But, what exactly did that mean?

Awake, we passed time by looking at comic books or playing games. *I Spy* was a quickie to test our cleverness until there were no more new colors inside the car. Counting horses was another game played by looking out our own side window to count horses. Although simple to do considering all the farms along the way, once a herd of cows was passed by, your count of horses was erased and you'd have to start all over again. We'd groan and moan about the game and the time and not having enough room to stretch plus the highway smell. Before long, we'd return to the same curled up position and hope for another quick nap.

Are we there yet? How many times did we ask this simple four-word question? It was beginning to sound like a chant losing its punch. By the time we left Rice Lake, Daddy's response which, up to that time, had been given with a half turn of his head and a smile had dwindled and was minus the smile we loved and took for granted. Leaving Haugen and Sarona behind, we finally reached the tip of the hill to see Spooner in a distance.

At last! We drove down the hill on Highway 63 into Spooner to Walnut Street, turned right and parked for a late breakfast in a small restaurant that I'd remember later as the Topper Café. My breakfast order for a chocolate malt, hamburger and French fries brought a frown from Mother who thought eggs and bacon would be a much better choice, but I won. It was the king of all breakfasts I ever had in my whole life, plus being the tastiest. After the bill was paid, we crossed the street to explore Spooner's other block on the same street in the town's business district. It would lead us to the grocery store at the end of the block. After shopping for staples, the bags were carried out to the car and packed in the back with Elaine and I. By the time we bought pastries and bread at the bakery, we had to sit straight up for the remainder of our trip. Away we went toward County Road A for an additional 20-something more miles before reaching Hansen's Resort on North Sand Lake and a cottage that would be ours for a whole week.

Daddy fixing a flat tire.

l to r, Elaine, me and Mother eating lunch.

l to r, me, Daddy and Elaine in Eau Claire.

We're Here! We're Here!

THE LONGEST TRIP OF MY YOUNG LIFE HAD ENDED. LEAVING SMELLY DIESEL smoke behind on the highway, and clouds of sand and gravel dust from the side country roads, we filled our lungs with pure and clean *up north* air. What surrounded us was everything and more than I could possibly imagine. Instead of walking up the street back home with friends at least an hour after lunch, all of us wearing bathing suits under our clothes, crossing Atwood Avenue and continuing four blocks down Hudson Avenue to Hudson Park and the shores of Lake Monona for a swim, here was a lake connected by a long board to the front door of "our" cottage #4 with soft sand as far as my eyes could see. I wanted to stay forever.

Hansen's Resort, consisting of four unpainted, pine cottages, newly built by Hansen's Norwegian handyman, Karl, were lined up over the sand directly east of owners Barney and Florence Hansen's house. Tied to the sides of the long pier in front of Hansen's place were a few wooden rental rowboats, painted forest green. Each of the four cottages had their own pier which was much shorter and made with slender tamarack trunks supporting flat boards. Attached to each pier was a 14-foot wooden rowboat painted the same shade of green. The beach separating piers and cottages was not landscaped, but instead, a natural blend of soft sandy mounds and long slender weeds that swayed with the breeze.

Back home, lakes surrounding Madison and its isthmus supplied residents and out-of-town visitors in much the same way. With an abundance of parks and beaches, swimming was enjoyed throughout summer except for the peak days of August when dog days kept most of us out of the water. By that time, the water had somewhat warmed and seemed cloudier than the month before which we feared could induce germs to paralyze us with something called polio. On North Sand Lake the water was always cool, never cloudy and looked good enough to drink. And frogs were everywhere.

Cottage #4, like the other three, faced the lake with a front door separating two double-hung windows on each side. Indoors, everything was in a roughed-in state-

Barney and Flo Hansen and "Boy," 1945.

Newly built Hansen Resort cottages.

-no dry wall, insulation, or dropped 8-foot ceilings. Instead, only boards and rafters were exposed overhead while patterned linoleum covered the cottage floor. The front half of the cottage was a combined kitchen and living room with an old round oak kitchen table covered with patterned oil cloth set in the center of the room. A side door separated the refrigerator from the kitchen sink where a hand-pump was screwed

Inside cottage No. 4.

Daddy and me.

into the linoleum covered countertop to bring cold water up from the depths of a well hidden under the cottage. A gathered curtain made with cotton material, hung from a rod that ran the length of the counter to hide the waste basket and a few shelves underneath. To the left of the sink were two gas burners that turned on with the flick of a match, and a metal teapot for boiling water to wash dishes and faces. Instead of a cabinet, enclosed narrow floor-to-ceiling wood shelves were sandwiched between the burners and the front windows to place odds and ends of cookware, utensils, dishes, cups and glasses.

On the other side of the kitchen table and to the left of the front door was a rocking chair and floor lamp. Nailed to the wood framework was a wood shelf with enough space for a small electric radio. An iron-framed daybed pushed against the side windows and a wood stove in the center corner rounded out and balanced the room.

Off the main room were doors to two small bedrooms. Light bulbs attached to the cross beams overhead were turned on by a string that hung directly over each metal double bed. Each bedroom had two windows: one on the side and the other in back.

Fancy it wasn't, but then we didn't expect to find pastel painted wicker furniture and windows draped with chintz. What greeted us was more than sufficient to make our visit comfortable. It was cottage charm in every sense of the word. We didn't care if the silverware didn't match (and it didn't) or that plates were in a variety of

l to r, Elaine, Mother and me, sunbathing on the pier.

patterns or that all the glasses and coffee cups were different sizes. There was no running water, but everything was clean, worked and passed the test. And, besides, each of the three rooms was fragrant with the aroma of freshly sawed pine.

The only thing that took us down a notch was every city person's worst fear. No indoor plumbing meant getting up in the middle of the pitch black night to walk outside through the backyard to an outhouse. Almost as bad was not knowing what lurked in the bushes or trees. Crickets chirped. Frogs croaked. Who knew what else? A chamber pot came with each cottage, but no one wanted to use it so we all braved those middle-of-the-night urges by grabbing the flashlight and waking up someone to go along and then…holding our breath as long as possible until we were finished so we could breathe fresh air again, we'd race back to the side door with a sigh of relief.

That first summer we seemed to be the only ones who drove a car without an Illinois license. Through the next few years, we learned that some vacationers drove even longer distances from Ohio or Indiana. Most, however, were Illinois people from Chicago, Peoria, Cicero, Lamont, and Berwyn. How could I complain about a 300 mile trip permeated with diesel fumes that took only five to six hours when they had to drive an additional 150 miles and more?

The following summer, we were assigned to the new #5 cottage. Although additional cottages would be added in the years to follow, we remained in #5 until the end of the 1964 season when the resort closed.

l-r, Elaine and me walking the shoreline. The edge of County Road "A" is in the background.

Mother walking toward the resort. Kilkare Road is in the background to the left.

Heaven is under our feet
as well as over our heads.

Henry David Thoreau
1817-1862

Up North: *A Father's Summer Legacy*

I'm in love with this lake, North Sand.
Obsessed, some could claim.
Spellbound by its ingredients,
nourished by its purity, depth, breathtaking beauty,
passionate with what is offered when winter snow disappears and
spring nudges through sandy soil before gentle breezes from the south
whisper through willowy pin cherries and young popples
to sketch ripples across the surface,
emotionally awakened when determined northerly winds
collapse white-tipped waves with full-blown fury that commands respect.
I grew up surrounded by lakes,
yet never was mesmerized like this before when drops of
water trickle through the imaginary chambers of my heart,
flushing with excitement...every splash quenches my thirst,
every touch refreshes me, every thought, savored like a
delectable morsel, an indescribable gourmet feast.
North Sand holds my hand like a friend,
guiding me as I wander its periphery like the natives before me.
With treasures awaiting, I wade its crystal shoreline,
fish its weed beds, swim long distances to points, bays and coves,
near cottages, cabins and year 'round homes standing at
attention to guard its magnificence.
And, although the chill is startling at times, the water warms me,
consoles me, embracing me as a reward for cherishing its beauty,
a natural gift of which there is no parallel.
I am convinced there is nothing in life,
no lake within Burnett County to
offer me the same mystique, seasonal pleasures,
fond memories and lifelong rewards as
this up north love of my life,
North Sand Lake.

Catherine Tripalin Murray

Part II

Learning to row with "Boy," 1945.

...it was back then, when docks were piers and cabins were cottages and the seeds to all of this came in a little packet of love that prompted Daddy to make arrangements for me to have a boat at my disposal. For a dollar a day, each rowing adventure would familiarize me for life with the lake and its periphery.

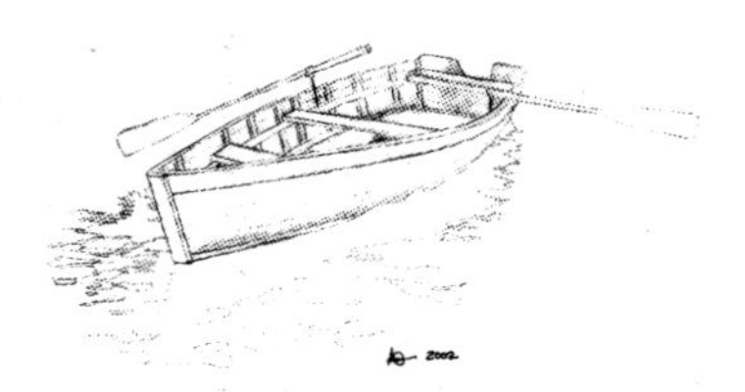

A Rowboat Tour, Then and Now

Before the tour began, rowing was nothing more than frivolous childhood fun. Learning how to row a boat back and forth in front of the cottage was just part of being a kid on vacation with a new toy and no planned future voyage. Solo rowing the entire lake was an entirely different matter that came later as something done on a whim with mystery of the unknown.

The summer of 1945 was an introduction to many things, especially a north woods vacation on a lake with a boat. Once I understood how important it was to use the same strength in both arms to row straight ahead, next was the discovery of how to make a quick turn by pushing with one oar and pulling with the other at the same time. Thinking back, I must have been preparing myself as a skinny youngster about to become an imaginative version of Hemmingway's old man and the sea.

By the time I was twelve, the yen for exploring the entire lake, its weed beds, drop-offs and hungry fish had become a summer quest. With a simple flat-bottom, wooden rowboat, a red boat cushion, some fishing equipment and fishing net, my voyage was about to begin for trolling the circumference of the lake in search of its biggest fish. Would I be successful? Only time would tell.

It was back then, when docks were piers and cabins were cottages and the seeds to all of this came in a little packet of love that prompted Daddy to make arrangements for me to have a boat at my disposal. For a dollar a day, one of the resort's rental boats was rowed down from the main pier to our cottage, then No. 5, by Karl, who secured it to the opposite side of the pier where our own cottage boat was tied. Being somewhat of a tomboy with few fears, the boat instantly became an instrument to use on any given day, according to the weather. As a new mode of operation, rowing whenever and wherever I wanted served as a learning experience on long remembered journeys that would familiarize me for life with the lake and its periphery.

Standing in front of our cottage on the north shoreline, gazing out toward the center of the lake was the onset of new chapters in my life. Points of land and peninsulas jutted out from both the east and west shorelines like fingers. The point far out to the right actually was a double point connected by a concave shoreline. Once I followed course to reach the second and most prominent point, it would be fondly referred to for the rest of my life as The Point. Later, a house would be built on the point with three sides of exposure to the lake. With a sudden 40-foot drop barely beyond the tip of the point, it was one of the crowning mystical glories of lake properties that I fell in love with forever.

In my pursuit of northern pike and large-mouth bass, I engaged the clicker on my rod and reel and trolled with the reel between my bare feet and the rod propped over the flat boat seat in front of me. Starting from our cottage pier, the rowboat tour began in a counter-clockwise direction past the cottages and the resort owner's long wood pier. Adjacent to Hansen's pier was Karl's humble one-room cottage set amid puffs of sand, scattered weeds and trees.

Smith's Shoreline

Extending beyond Karl's place was a narrow strip of lake property running parallel to County Road A acquired by Oscar Smith, Sr. Close to the shoreline was a small unpretentious summer cottage where Smith and his family would spend their summers.

The Indiana attorney first visited the lake prior to the 1920s when a group of fishing friends drove together from their homes in Knox, Indiana to fish Lake Benoit in Burnett County. Referred to as the Indiana Club, they were intrigued with the area and the fishing it provided until one day when Smith discovered North Sand Lake and was so impressed by its size and quality ingredients that he decided it was where he wanted to be during every summer to follow.

Originally owned by Tom Cleve, Smith's property ran along the northwest end of the lake bounded by lake and road plus land on the opposite side of the road which extended far into the reaches of field, woods and a small partially hidden lake (Little Bass Lake), with County Road A hugging the shoreline. Smith's summer trips from Indiana to Burnett County's North Sand Lake were taken in his Oldsmobile with his wife, Irma, sitting next to him in the front seat, while happily squashed in the back seat sat their four children, Amira Catherine (Mulligan), Truman M. II, Oscar B. Jr., and Marjorie (Sundberg). Greeting them was a cottage with no electricity or indoor plumbing. No one seemed to care because it was an *up north* experience on a lake in a wooded wilderness that didn't promise any luxuries of home.

The family remained at the lake during the summer months with Smith periodically commuting to Indiana to tend to his law practice. Later, he was able to enjoy entire summers at the lake with frequent visits from other family members and friends. Through the years, Smith watched the lake shore develop and loom with activity. It was no surprise during a regional resort era that Smith's lake sprouted resorts along its beautiful shoreline of crystal clear water, sand bottom and exceptional fishing. North Sand Lake was definitely worth the long drive from Indiana. Many years later, sons Truman and Oscar, Jr. would build four-season homes adjacent to the family cottage which, today, is owned by Smith's grandson, local attorney Tom Mulligan.

Childhood reflections from the past remind Tom Mulligan of lying in bed at night and listening to wolves howl in the distance. He remembers his grandparents having to travel to A&H to carry water back to the cottage and the fish his grandpa caught at least twice a week that they'd fry and enjoy for supper. Having no electricity meant placing oil lamps at the windows which offered young Tom the entertainment of watching bugs gather until each pane was two inches thick with insects. Other memories include certain times each summer when the road was literally carpeted with leaping frogs. Barney Hansen used bottle caps instead of gravel out in front of his store which made it nearly impossible, if barefoot, for Tom to reach the door. And then…the 1/8-inch biting red ants that crawled around the outhouse to turn visits there lasting more than a few minutes a nightmare worth screaming about. With Tom Mulligan fully appreciating what the lake continues to offer each morning when the sun rises, the length of time the Smith family, now in its fifth generation, has enjoyed their place on North Sand Lake today totals more than 85 years.

Hilltop Resort

Adjacent to Smith's property was a portion of the Leef farm, A. W. Tigges Sand Lake Stock Farm and Chelmo property, before a section was sold to Bob Kazobowski from Chicago, Illinois. Kazobowski worked for the city of Chicago and had three shifts of men working under him. Hilltop Resort became a reality with material transported from Chicago to North Sand Lake by some of his employees who spent short periods of time building the resort before returning home. When it was completed, there were five rental cottages and Kazobowski's home perched at the top of the hill in plain view of the lake. A few of the cottages were built into the steep hill and hung precariously, though supported on columns, while camouflaged by trees and other brush. Steep concrete steps carried resort guests along the side of Kazobowski's home and straight down to the communal pier near a circle of bull rushes and lily pads where young Tom Rypel fished for crappie every summer. Also on the property was a windmill and cistern, both vital ingredients in rural areas and certainly important to people who owned resorts. The windmill extracted water from the ground and emptied it into the cistern before it flowed by gravity through pipes to the back of each cabin. The narrow pipes continued to thread their way through the woods and paths of poison ivy down to the base of the hill where the small lake level cottage was located and where County Road A had at one time crept along the shoreline. Had the road not been moved back, Hansen's

Above: resort windmill

Hilltop Resort, vacant and deserted.

Resort would have been separated from the lake by the county road just as many cottages are today on Big McKenzie.

Hilltop Resort would thrive during the resort era until Kazobowski sold it to his brother. In the mid-1960s, the resort was sold again, this time to Charlie and Irene Lauer, also from Chicago, Il. Lauer wanted to purchase it in its entirety, but the offer was declined. After an agreement was reached as to the owner's terms of what he was willing to part with, Lauer purchased the land and built a two-car garage in the middle of the dirt road that at one time led summer vacationers to the cabins they rented. The garage became a boundary to separate his land from the larger adjacent south portion of the property.

When the excitement and popularity that nourished the lake with resorts began to disappear, Hilltop, as one of seven N. Sand Lake resorts, merely served as a reminder of a time and a place when seasonal visitors traveled from afar to sample *up north* flavors of swimming and fishing in the northern Wisconsin. Much later, in the absence of the Lauers, the land and its buildings suffered years of loneliness and neglect. Lauer's house remained empty, as did the small white cabin next door. At one time, the charming seasonal rental cabin with a screened porch facing Leef Road allowed seasonal breezes to flow through the front room, two bedrooms and kitchen before passing through a wall of open casement windows overlooking the lake. Now it was nothing more than a sad reminder of a flurry of better times. Still solidly supported on the steep sandy hill by concrete pillars, the door was left open and windows were broken by vandals to allow further destruction by the elements and woodland creatures.

The cabin across the road from Lauer's doorstep that was covered with artificial brick siding also was neglected. Inside the partially furnished cabin was a small combination front room-kitchen with an oven that had once successfully cooked food with gas and logs. The cabin at the base of the hill, where cars sporting Illinois, Indiana, and Ohio license plates parked throughout each summer during weeklong visits, no longer rang with the sweet sound of happy vacationers.

The land, its history and the deteriorating dwellings was purchased a few years ago by summer lake resident Dick Kenall and his son, Lee. Unfortunately, shortly thereafter, Dick passed away unexpectedly and, in 2002, the property was sold. After the buildings were removed and the land somewhat graded, a massive, impressive four-season home was built complete with one of the finest views of the length of the lake.

...the southern portion and the Pulsas

The southern portion of land connecting Hilltop Resort was purchased by Mr. Pulsa and his wife, Mary. A huge piece of lake property, it extended from the resort through the field and over to Leef Road where they built a small, modest summer cabin at the edge of the road. Due to the distance from their cabin to the lake, machinery was brought in to plow through a wooded hill near the lake and create a private dirt road wide enough for a large vehicle. Although the Pulsas built a four-season home adjacent to their original cabin in 1958, they sold the 120 acre property to Superior (Wisconsin) Certified Public Accountant Les Olson and his wife, Irja.

Jack and Beverly Spittell

At the time the Pulsas created their own private road to the lake, I was still young and the concept of what was seen by boat made me and others my age staying at Hansen's Resort want to investigate a little more. Forever in search of doing something exciting each day, we pumped up our air mattresses and floated over to investigate. The thrill of the newly opened hill prompted us to pull our mattresses on shore and head for the hill which we climbed to slide down steep embankments of sand mixed with dirt. When we thought we might have pushed our luck to the limit, we all took one last slide, rinsed off in the lake, then climbed back on our mattresses to paddle as fast as we could before our laughter and good time was investigated by the Pulsas. It wasn't until many years later that I became aware of the steep drop-off near their shoreline where the depth seemed to take on the black of the unknown. Today, the beautiful property that had once been a part of the Leef farm and Hilltop Resort is owned by Dr. and Mrs. John Spittell. See: **Over the Rainbow.**

The Olsons

Les and Irja Olson loved their property on North Sand Lake. An earthy person who valued nature, Irja committed herself to utilizing everything it offered and planted an organic garden a short distance from her front door and parallel to Leef Road. Anyone passing by knew immediately that the garden and the gardener both were exceptional and local competition soon brought awards and recognition for her efforts. Irja also pulverized flats of homegrown wheat grass to use as a beverage, and planted perennial ginseng near one of the Hilltop Resort cottages near the Olson property border for the benefit of those who

Irja's two room sauna

Daddy and Mother standing in newly plowed hill leading to the lake on Les Olson's property.

believed in the root and its medicinal powers. Along with her respect of the earth, she valued the lake and is remembered by some as an avid fisherman who enjoyed testing her talent from the shoreline that jutted ever so slightly to a spot where she struggled one day for 30 minutes before landing what was described as being a huge northern pike.

As the victim of arthritis with intense pain, Irja Olson was forced to set aside the things she loved doing most. To treat her condition, Les built a tiny, well-constructed two-room structure complete with fireplace and sauna. A ladder helped Irja reach the highest level of benches Les installed inside. Near the lakeshore, the sauna cabin remains hidden today by full-grown trees and brush.

Les Olson was a talented man blessed with innovative ideas, one of which involved dredging an area at the base of the road the Pulsa's made accessible to the lake to create a lagoon where a pier would be installed to protect his boat from the elements. The pier would remain in the lagoon throughout the winters and be protected from ice shifting during windy spring thaws. During the summer months, the lagoon and flat surrounding land took on the appearance of a combination wildlife sanctuary and well-manicured park.

Although Olson was considered a wealthy man whose land holdings totaled approximately 800 acres in the area, he chose not to install electricity at his place for a monthly savings of $16.00. And yet, generosity was evident in other ways such as the deer farm along Thompson Road that he fenced in and which employed local men as caretakers to protect the deer and other animals that roamed its vastness.

When the doctor told Irja Olson that she had cancer, being a naturalist, she chose to avoid chemotherapy and eventually died. Les sold off 80 acres to Voyager Village and made plans to sell the rest of the property. In 1991, remembering a conversation he had in 1971 with lakeshore property owner Dr. John Spittell, Olson contacted the doctor to ask a few questions. See: **Over the Rainbow.**

One day, back when the property was still owned by Pulsas, my new summer resort friend Lee Katz and I fished for bluegills just off the shore in the same vicinity where

Irja once struggled for half an hour before landing the northern pike. Lee and his parents, Ed and Clara Katz, drove up from Illinois each year to stay at Hansen's Resort the same time we did. Our parents became good vacation friends and Lee and I became equally good fishing pals. That day, nearing the slight southerly shoreline bend, we dropped anchor at what must have been the very edge of the drop-off because no sooner were our lines dropped that we both hooked and pulled up huge bluegills. This continued until we ran out of worms and had to return to the resort. Removing stringers heavily laden with giant bluegills, we regretted not having an extra can of worms, but welcomed the comments from everyone who watched as we stepped from the boat onto the pier.

Moving right along the same shoreline, but around the bend and to the right, into the woods among tall pine trees stood a tall flag pole with an American flag that furled with lake breezes each day to create a sight that made one want to stand up in the boat and salute while passing by. Responsible for the pole and flag was native Ohioan and retired Lt. Col. W. Lewis who had built a place near the boat landing at 408 Leef Road. Every morning Colonel Lewis raised the flag and as night fell, he lowered it. The Colonel's allegiance to his country played an integral role in his daily existence just as his allegiance to the lake was evident when he went door-to-door with information about forming a lake owner's association.

Leef Territory

The public boat landing signaled Leef territory, not only along the shoreline, but across the road and well beyond. It was north woods vastness settled in 1895 by Swedish immigrants Rosina and John Adolph Leef and their five children. See: **Leefs of Leef Shores**

In 1953, grandson Lester Leef married Myrna (Christner) who had grown up nearby on Benoit Lake. The couple moved into the old Leef home on Leef Road in 1963 where electricity had been installed only eight years before and the road, newly paved. Lester wasn't interested in fishing the lake and, instead, in his spare time, opted to do what Myrna casually described with fondness as two-bit farming, raising small crops of hay and soy beans, and keeping a few cows to milk. When Lester retired in 1985 after serving 23 years as Jackson Township Road Supervisor, he and Myrna packed up and moved to Siren where Lester passed away ten years later.

In 1995, about 70 members of the Leef family gathered at the old homestead to celebrate the 100th anniversary of the original Leef family settling on North Sand Lake. Although many stories were shared during the course of the day, Myrna specifically remembered when Lester recalled his childhood days and described Leef family picnics on their shoreline where the public boat landing is located today. It was also the location of their own baseball diamond which extended far out from the shoreline during the unforgettable drought in the 1930s. Back then, picnic fare for the Leef family most likely consisted of fried chicken since Lester's mother raised chickens and sold eggs for extra income.

Grindell's Gold Coast

Property south of the public boat landing inched its way from a low flat shoreline to high wooded peaks where cottages built there overlooked the lake while being protected from Leef Road activity by each narrow winding private drive that zig-zagged around trees to their back doors. At that time, a cottage to me meant a little summer shoreline place with no indoor plumbing, a combined kitchen and front room and two small bedrooms. The cottages built on the wooded hill appeared more like vacation homes one might see in a Better Homes and Gardens magazine to hint of wealth. One was owned by Bob Grindell, an attorney from Frederic whose family summered at the lake. I never met any of their five children, but I do remember them, especially a daughter with beautiful long flaxen-colored hair who water skied behind the fastest boat on the lake. Never before exposed to this type of water activity, I watched in awe each calm day as they passed our pier with her skiing with the greatest of ease. While I was content to row and troll in a humble wooden flat-bottom rowboat, holding my rod and reel securely with my bare feet, the Grindell kids made waves with a different kind of water talent.

Although the cottage became a summer home enhanced by full grown trees and shrubs for the Grindell family in 1952, Bob learned from correspondence he had with the natives that North Sand Lake water level was so low back in the 1930s that ditches had to be dug in the sand banks to move boats into the lake. Through the years, the Grindell children garnered a genuine appreciation for their summer place, its lake, and the good times they shared together as family. They continued to return each year to enjoy the lake with new generations which would blend with the magic of their past.

An Introduction to the First Point

After passing Grindell's place and their closest neighbors, I saw that I was nearing the first point which begins what today is referred to as the peninsula. It would be a matter of minutes before realizing how isolated it was. In simple terms, there was nothing but barren shoreline, weeds, bull rushes and emptiness that would require landfill for future development. When the water levels were extremely high, Green and North Sand lakes merged. Once the lowland was filled, realtors, who had purchased the land from its original owners, sub-divided it to sell. One buyer was Dick Kenall, who with his brother Jim, accompanied their father, Lee, to Devil's Lake in August of 1965 where an established resort was

Nancy Kenall with a string of crappies caught in Back Bay, 1983.

selling its cottages. Not at all impressed, the Kenall's drove throughout the area until they reached Leef Road and a dead end that led to the peninsula. An "elderly" man mowing his lawn at the end of the peninsula informed the Kenalls that the lot adjacent to his property was for sale for $3500. Kenalls countered with the owner of the lot and within ten days it was purchased by Lee Kenall for $3200. Dick Kenall and his wife, Barbara, built a cottage and spent many summers there with their family.

Aftermath of a 1984 storm.

While building their cottage, the Kenalls learned that the elderly man, whose beautiful four season home at the tip of the peninsula (I referred to as the point) and property everyone on the lake admired, was none other than the legendary hockey great, "Moose" Goheen. Goheen was described by Dick Kenall as being a great guy. An ex-hockey player and one of the first to be inducted into the National Hall of Fame at Evelth, Minnesota, "Moose" was also honored as an inductee of the Canadian Hockey Hall of Fame. Goheen eventually sold his lake home to a family that neighbors described as not thoroughly enjoying lake living because of the ages of their small children. After a few years, Goheen's home changed hands again, this time being sold to Dick Ogle. After spending 15 years on the magnificent point, Ogle sold to the present owners.

Another lot just around the point on property facing the southeast shoreline was purchased by Lee Kenall to expand family holdings. And then, years later, Dick and Barbara purchased the cottage next door to them as a place for their grown children to occupy. In the backyard of the Kenall peninsula cottages was an open bay, referred to today as the "back bay" that works its way into a wildlife haven in the opposite end that is referred to by the DNR and others as the *slough*.

The Kenalls have had years of experiences on the lake, both good and bad. The good memories are of great times with their family, gathering and celebrating many occasions with friends and family who returned to shore with fish to clean, fry and enjoy. Interspersed with lake memories is an evening when a nearby chalet-style boathouse burned to the ground. Kenall's also relived the bad times when storms tore away their shoreline, tossed their boats, and twisted their pier. When purple-black skies moved in and threatened to take advantage of their vulnerability, it was lake living at its meanest. With the angry open lake in front and the openness in the back and a single exit on the peninsula road that normally led to seasonal paradise, life on the lake at times posed major problems which included ice damage that greeted them when they returned each spring from wintering in Florida.

Over The Rainbow

Of course, other lots were made available on the point and one purchased before the Kenalls arrived happened to face east immediately next door to Goheen. When Dr. Jack Spittell and his wife Beverly began their search for vacation property within reasonable driving distance from their home in Rochester, Minnesota, the lot was the one they chose.

The Spittells had explored impressive land possibilities along the St. Croix River, yet respected each other's opinion to look further before making final decisions. One day, in 1961, while returning home from a seminar in Duluth, Dr. Spittell opted to take a different route to see what other areas offered. Passing through Siren, he noticed a sign near the roadside advertising Lakes Realty and immediately turned into the parking lot. After introducing himself to realty salesman Ray Ellis, Spittell explained what he had in mind as Ellis listened carefully to terms that would include a nice clean lake. Ellis thought of the peninsula on North Sand Lake near Webster.

Long and narrow, private and secluded, yet perched along a sandy shoreline, the property was well beyond what the Spittells had imagined. Intrigued, Dr. Spittell also learned that the peninsula had once been separated from the shoreline until fill was brought in to make the land safe to build on. Undeniably beautiful, the newly-created strip of lakeshore was endorsed by local realtors as premiere Burnett County lake property. Dr. Spittell returned home and after discussing the property with Beverly, he and a colleague made a decision to purchase 320 feet of shoreline at a cost of $15.00 per foot. Ellis tried to persuade them to purchase the remaining 820 feet for a mere $10,000, reminding them of the property directly behind which spilled into the back bay which was selling for $7.50 per foot. However, because the Spittells had five small children whose educations were highly valued, the two stuck to their initial plan to purchase 320 feet directly on the peninsula facing the lake.

By 1962, only two homes had been built on the point, one at the tip owned by "Moose" Goheen and his wife, and an A-frame owned by the Gene Browns that was right around the corner facing southeast on a finger-like strip of land narrowing to the opening of the back bay. The Spittells were thrilled with their purchase and the vacation home plans they had clipped years before from a Good Housekeeping magazine would finally be put to use. Everything from then on would be coined in the future as a learning experience.

That fall, during Thanksgiving vacation, the Spittell family drove to the lake to check on the progress being made on their summer home only to find no one there. A phone call to inquire where the workers were was answered light-heartedly that

The Spittell Family

front, l-r: Mary and Jack

Second row: Nancee, Peter, Bev with Little Bev, Beverly, Marti and Ellen

Back row: David, Jim, Jack and John

"no one works during deer hunting season." Later, when the Spittells asked about the water quality from the well, they learned that instead of a sample being sent to the State Laboratory in Madison, water was scooped from the well and boiled down to nothing which told the building crew who saw no residue left in the pan that the water was...excellent.

Although the Spittell's vacation home offered a spectacular view of the open lake, not a single pine tree grew along the peninsula. Arrangements were made for Bill Conroy to plant 55 pine trees for a cost of $55.00. Chapters of discoveries awaited the Spittell family with hidden treasures to surface at their feet. Finding arrowheads highlighted many weekends for the Spittell children, yet swimming in the crystal clear lake of such depths from the front yard and beyond posed concerned for Jack and Beverly. Boundaries were discussed and a pact was agreed on: the children were not allowed in a boat, on the lake, alone or with each other, until each one had mastered swimming skills. Only when all five children completed a long swim from their own southeast point to the southwest point on the opposite side of the lake would their passport for lake freedom be approved.

When Dr. Spittell's colleague decided to sell his own portion of the shoreline, the doctor and his wife immediately purchased it to give the family more room to roam. Little did they realize at the time that another major decision waiting in the horizon would create a new treasure at the end of their rainbow.

While enjoying their weekends and extended summer vacations at the lake, the Spittells became thoroughly acquainted with its core and periphery and a certain piece of land bordered by County Road A that included a major portion of the northwest section of Leef Road. To satisfy their interest, Dr. Spittell contacted the owner of the large pine-studded parcel of field and woods that sloped down to 1200 feet of shoreline. At one time, the land had been part of the Leef farm.

Later, it was divided into north and south parcels and given to two Leef sons. The northwest portion would eventually be sold to Bob Kazobowski who built a home and five cabins to debut as Hilltop Resort. The south portion was purchased by a Chicago concrete construction supervisor known as Mr. Pulsa.

At the time Dr. Spittell inquired about the land, it was owned by Les Olson. When Olson's wife died, he decided to sell the property and, in 1991, remembering Dr. Spittell's previous interest, made a phone call and asked the doctor what he planned to do with the land if it became his own. Assured that it would be kept as is, and enjoyed as a family estate, never to be divided or sold as parcels, Olson agreed to sell. In June, 1991, Jack and Beverly Spittell's new treasure came in the form of 40 acres on North Sand Lake which included 1200 feet of shoreline. Olson's letter to Dr. Spittell dated August 17, 1991, hangs, framed, in Spittell's new log home.

Following the purchase of the property, the original Pulsa cabin visible along Leef Road became known to Jack and Beverly as The Studio. Two of the Hilltop Resort cabins on the land were carefully and tastefully remodeled in keeping with the flavor of the early resort era. Renovation included removing paint from floors made with regional Douglas fir. The first cabin, perched from a steep hill among full grown trees, is known as The White House where Spittell family members stay. The second is know as The Brown House. Following the construction of Spittell's new log home nearer to the lake and amid full grown pine trees, The Studio also became a family domain.

The A-Frame

Gene and Etta Brown once owned the lake home my family fondly refers to as the A-Frame. As the last cottage on a peninsula resembling a finger pointing to the opening of the back bay and its natural slough, it is naturally protected with peace and privacy. The A-frame also became a marker for a sand bar straight out from their pier that our family has relished as a favorite fishing spot.

Gene Brown, a River Falls photographer, installed a wood-fired sauna on the beach, then issued an open invitation to his immediate peninsula neighbors to enjoy whenever it was convenient for them. The sauna and good times are remembered with great affection by those who took advantage of the Browns' generosity.

In mid-summer of 1960, Smith and Nonie (Norene) were visiting "Doc" and Beverly Spittell when the Spittells were at their Peninsula Road vacation home. The Spittells spoke of the Browns' cabin being for sale. Within a week Smith and Nonie closed on the property and moved in the first day of August. Although the Browns retained some property at the end of the peninsula, the Champlins purchased that in 1975.

When Smith Champlin retired from ADM Grain in 1972, the family home in St. Paul was sold, allowing them to move to North Sand Lake as permanent residents.

In fact, they were the first permanent residents to live on Peninsula Road. When their telephone was installed in 1970, it was the last phone on a 13-party line. Smith and Nonie lived there until 1986 having made extensive renovations to the house and other buildings.

Smith was a volunteer Deputy Sheriff for many years and active in the original North Sand Lake Association. Nonie was a religious education teacher in the Webster area Catholic churches. They were both in the first group of Eucharistic Ministers at the Crescent Lake Church. Their sons, Michael and Carson, became priests of the Dominican Order.

Weather permitting, Father Mike and Father Carson held Mass outdoors every Saturday evening and, although most neighbors and lake residents who attended were of the Catholic faith, all denominations were welcomed. The only item required of anyone was a lawn chair. During the silence of Mass, an occasional motor boat would cruise by while songbirds flew back and forth from tree branches shadowing the picnic bench altar. Underneath, the family golden retriever rested to create a bit of laid-back, heart-warming religious experience. If it rained, Mass was held in Champlin's garage where the workbench became an instant altar decorated not with statues and flowers, but instead, hammers, saws, fish poles, lures, and deer antlers.

Today, Father Mike reflects on the early days when Carson became a highly respected Cretin High School hockey player being primed to join the 1960 Olympic Hockey Team until he received an interrupting date to begin his seminary studies. And he remembers when he and Carson fished the lake, especially directly off the Point, a spot they referred to as the "secret spot" where the depth quickly plummeted and allowed them both to regularly catch 3 to 5 pound bass on jitterbug lures. Their father took great pleasure in ice fishing, especially in March when he slipped "creepers" under his shoes to carefully reach an area of thinning ice where the crappies ran and the small bobber on his fish pole moved with their light springtime bites.

In the late 1986, declining health forced Smith and Nonie to move to a retirement community in Minneapolis. In less than a year, they were both moved to the Spooner Nursing Home. Nonie died in 1987 and Smith died in 1991. Father Carson died of cancer in 1989.

Their presence, however, remains on the lake where, in 1979, Father Mike and Father Carson founded the Thomas More Center for Preaching and Prayer. The Center is located on Leef Road and nestled in the woods on a hill overlooking the public boat landing. Known in Australia as The Dominican Preachers, their mission has been to provide programs of spiritual renewal to improve laymen preaching within the Catholic Church. St. Thomas More, chosen as patron, was a layman Lord Chancellor of England beheaded under King Henry VIII in 1535. The Center's website is www.thomasmorecenter.org.

Smith and Nonie Champlin, 1983.

Outdoor Mass on the A-frame hill with Father Mike and Father Carson Champlin, 1980.

Hello South Shore!

Left of the opening to the back bay began a strip of nothing to the east. In 1967, Chuck Cashman would build a cottage that peered into the beauty of the slough in back, the back bay at its side, and the openness of the lake before him. It was not quite secluded, yet in total harmony with nature to offer more than the average person could imagine. In essence, *up north* splendor.

Many years later, Roger Larson entered the lake scene when he'd arrive from the Twin Cities with his sister and brother-in-law who had purchased one of Kovarik's Resort cottages along the west shoreline. The short drive from Minnesota and the quality of the lake enticed him to follow their example and before long, he, too, would purchase one of the resort cottages. Weekends became a wonder of enjoyment, especially when he met Pat Heuer, daughter of Len and Rosalie Heuer who had previously purchased Jim and Margaret Moore's cottage five lots from Cashman's place. Roger claims he thought he had everything in the world owning a cottage on the lake and having a girl friend whose parents owned a bar (Mallard Lake Resort) that served beer.

Roger and Pat were married in 1983 and coupled with love and happiness was learning that Cashman's cottage was going up for sale. Larson put in a bid and, in 1986, purchased the property complete with the privacy Cashman once enjoyed and appreciated, plus the location of being down the shoreline from Pat's parents. Convinced this was to be enjoyed for a lifetime together, Larson would eventually replace the seasonal cottage with a beautiful two-story, four-season home.

When asked if there were any special times worth remembering during his many years at the lake, Roger Larson admitted that one in particular took place on July 4, 1976 when the country was celebrating the Bicentennial. In keeping with the historic event, lake shore property owner Clyde Leedberg pulled 13 adult guests representing the 13 original colonies, on water skis behind his purple boat, a sleek water vehicle with a powerful engine that my boys referred to as the Batmobile.

From my mother's diary…

July 4, 1976
Temperature 85 degrees
A most beautiful 4th of July. Lake like a mirror. Lots of action on the lake. Clyde had 13 skiers on his boat. Beautiful to see. Sat on the pier most of the day. Went over to Cathi and Dick's while they worked with fire crackers. A fun evening. Rang the bells at 1 o'clock today from the pier. Others were blowing their car horns and ringing bells. So exciting. In the evening after dark 7 speed boats with white and red lights led a parade on the lake. Beautiful to see. Lots of fire works around the lake and Mallard Lake. A most enjoyable holiday. Perfect weather.
Needless to say, it was a grand celebration for everyone on North Sand Lake.

Roger and Pat Larson are now permanent lake residents and Roger has successfully served many terms as President of the North Sand Lake Association.

Fishing the Isthmus

During my first rowboat tour, I finally reached the sparsely inhabited south shoreline and, ironically, dropped anchor a short distance from shore in front of what years later would become our own four connecting family lots. Visible from the boat were trees and brush, but nothing beyond as there was an ever so slight elevation that prevented an extended view. It was said that when lake levels rose, one could either walk or row through the water connecting Mallard and North Sand lakes. Years later, when the lowland was filled to allow building, the strip was sub-divided and lots were quickly sold. It would become our annual destination after Hansen's Resort sold in 1964 prompting Gordy, my brother-in-law and builder in Madison, to drive to town, learn of the four adjoining lots, and return the following day to purchase them to build three family cottages.

Rubin's Hill

When Ray Rubin was young he vacationed with his parents at Barney Hansen's first resort on Fish Lake. At that time, the southwest shoreline of North Sand Lake was virtually undeveloped, yet Ray was well aware of the quality of North Sand Lake a short distance away. Unbeknownst to him, however, were buried treasures of arrowheads and other artifacts from the past when two Indian tribes lived in the immediate vicinity and battled for the land and water that surrounded their campsites. As with Green Lake, when water levels were high, Mallard and North Sand lakes joined to make wading or rowing a natural and easy chore. Continuing past the swampy lake connection, the land pitched upward with a large wooded hill resembling favorite city parks back home. Owned by Andy Schultz, the hill overlooked the lake and swept south to the edge of Mallard Lake. When Ray Rubin and his wife, Eunice, expressed an interest in purchasing the property, Schultz learned that the young couple did not want the attached Mallard Lake land. Schultz refused to divide it so the Rubins relented and bought the entire package. The year was 1957.

Unexpected surprises awaited Ray and Eunice. Not only did they encounter early spring sucker spawning along their rocky shoreline, but they also discovered an Indian mound on their property near the road which many years earlier had been excavated. Aside from the sacred burial ground, stories about Indians camping on the property they had just purchased was reconfirmed. Because the land was separated by two lakes, the tribe was constantly defending it from other tribes. Other stories passed on to the Rubins by longtime lake resident Glen Thompson included a description of the water level being so low one year that a baseball diamond was found at the base of the hill. It was the same time that the peninsula became an island.

After the Rubins built their own cottage, they became friends of Miss Alva Lavalle, an elderly Rice Lake resident whose name would become synonymous with others who had invested in major landholdings of North Sand Lake property. Eunice Rubin knew that Lavalle owned the entire shoreline from their own hill down to the opening of the slough and across the narrow water entry and tip of the peninsula that continued to the point. When Lavalle learned that the Rubins were interested in purchasing additional property, she promised to contact them if she decided to sell any of her south shoreline property. One day, Siren realtor Ray Ellis knocked on the Rubin's door to inform them of land he had just purchased from Lavalle. Before the transaction was finalized, Lavalle made him promise to contact the Rubins before putting all the property on the market. A portion of the land enabled Ray and Eunice Rubin to plan for the future.

Beginning in their role as property owners of such a magnificent portion of shoreline and woods, Ray and Eunice Rubin mixed a lot of hard work with the same amount of pleasure when building began by tackling each job on carefully planned weekends together as well as during long summertime visits. Laced with heavy doses of enthusiasm, the additional land acquired from Ellis was low and needed fill which Rubins attempted to do with a portion of their hill. Added to beautify the property were hundreds of pine seedlings planted by hand, not only on their North Sand Lake side, but along their Mallard Lake shoreline as well which had become a lovely beach of sand due to what was necessary to create a buildable isthmus.

The young couple enjoyed meeting their lake neighbors and entertained at their cottage on the hill as often as time allowed. When their daughter Renee was born in 1968, family traditions at the lake became even more meaningful. Summer parties and picnics were held outside around circles of rocks that prevented dangers of spreading campfires. When the air grew chilly, or bitter cold, such as one Thanksgiving, a progressive turkey holiday dinner for 22 friends and neighbors was held indoors with the fireplace providing extra warmth. With an unforgettable lake view, it became a Thanksgiving never to be forgotten for a variety of reasons. Thanksgiving Eve, Eunice and Ray peeled mountains of potatoes before placing them in aluminum kettles where they would boil the following day. The next morning, all the potatoes had turned gray and each potato had to be re-peeled. The day after Thanksgiving, the area was hit with an old-fashion winter storm that sent individuals on snowmobiles to make sure everyone in the area was safe. Needless to say, it had become a typical unpredictable Wisconsin north woods experience.

When Rubin's work was completed on the hill, plans were made to build cottages for their parents. On North Sand Lake along the newly purchased flat shoreline property, a seasonal cottage was built for Ray's parents, Eric and Lucille Rubin. On the portion of their Mallard lake property behind them, separated by Mallard Lake Road, a summer cottage was completed for Eunice's parents, Rev. August R.

and Meta Brunn. To prevent any confusion, the triangle of three family cottages were labeled: the Brown House for Ray and Eunice's place; the White House for Eric and Lucille's cottage, and the Reverend's cottage, stained light olive green, was appropriately named the Green House.

Everything that happened during the course of purchasing the hill and years that followed carved sentimental niches for Ray and Eunice. A portion of the woods was cleared to store a jeep truck equipped with a generator and hundreds of pine trees were planted. Mosquitoes mixed with July 4th fireworks each year, but never dampened spirits, S'more parties became sweet reminders of the past, and skating and sledding during the cold months of winter brought out the beauty of seasonal Wisconsin with each sip of hot chocolate and marshmallows to thaw fingers and toes.

Ray and Eunice Rubin's hospitality was unsurpassed and the last party held on their lovely and comfortable wooded hill took place when they returned from Mexico. As a farewell to the lake and woods they had enjoyed for so many years, *Adios Amigo* flyers were hand-delivered to lakeshore property owners with instructions to drive and park along the wooded driveway that led to their place from Mallard Lake road, or how to beach boats on their shoreline without damaging them on rocks in the shallow water.

Before the hill was sold in the early 1990s to developer John Willard, Eric and Lucille's cottage was sold to Curt and Ginny Mommsen, and the flat lot separating Mommsen's from Ray and Eunice's cottage was sold to Rebecca and Steve Yanisch. Visual memories of the past disappeared when the Rubin's brown cottage was leveled one summer and the hill was divided into five lots, one of which would belong to Willard at the base of the other side of the hill next to a lowland separating him from David and Madaleine Lambert's property.

"We took him out for dinner and had a wonderful evening together. He passed away two days later while taking a nap."

Eunice Brunn Rubin

Rev. Brunn and granddaughter, Renee Rubin

Pictures taken shortly before removing the Mallard Lake Road cottage of Ray and Eunice Rubin on their south shoreline hill overlooking North Sand Lake.

Snakes Alive!

As a firefighter in Moline, Illinois, Dave Lambert supplemented the family income as a painter during his days off. One day, while he was doing some work for architect Norm Keller, the two began talking about the trip to Chicago Lambert was planning with his wife, Madaleine. Norm asked Dave if they would be interested in changing their plans and visit property he owned and seldom visited on a lake in Burnett County in northwestern Wisconsin. Also described was a small shed that served as both a boathouse and a cabin where they would stay.

The property, located on the south shore of North Sand lake, was owned by Keller and his wife, Millie, and Millie's sister, Fritzie, and her husband Andy Schultz of Stone Lake. A large parcel of land, it extended across the road from North Sand Lake to the north shore of Mallard Lake and swept up the hill to the east of Thompson Road. Keller further explained that his wife, Millie, wasn't particularly fond of the north woods setting. Although she disliked the annoyance of pesky mosquitoes, the brunt of her dislikes happened one day when she saw a snake slither through the woods. She immediately announced that her days at the lake were over and vowed never to return.

Keller's cabin built in 1952. Lamberts purchased the property and 15 acres.

Young David Lambert, 1955.

When Dave Lambert returned home from his painting job that day he told Madaleine of the conversation he had with Keller and the two decided to cancel their trip to Chicago and head to the north woods of Wisconsin. After spending a week on Keller's land, they returned to Moline and told him how much they had enjoyed themselves. Keller, in turn, offered to sell the property for $3000. It was an opportunity the Lamberts couldn't refuse. Shortly after the purchase was finalized, Lamberts learned that Andy Schultz also owned additional land adjacent to the property and to the west that included another low swampy area and beyond was a large wooded hill separating North Sand from Mallard Lake. Lamberts packed the car and headed north again, this time to purchase the remaining land only to arrive and find a young couple camping on the hill in the woods. Ray and Eunice Rubin were celebrating their purchase of Andy Schultz's property and were discussing plans to build a cottage at the top of the hill overlooking North Sand Lake.

Although disappointed that their mission had failed, the Lamberts, nonetheless, were satisfied with their purchase from Norm Keller and began their succession of summers spent at the lake with their children, David, Jr. and Barbara. In 1979 the Lamberts increased the size of the small combination boathouse-cabin. For 23 years they extracted water from an iron pump a long distance from the cabin

Log privy "mitout a door." Dave's sister, Mary Lambert, 1957.

Madaleine and Dave's brother and their beloved kayak, 1957.

which was about the same distance away as their privy "mitout" a door. When an additional room was added to the cabin, indoor plumbing was installed and the outhouse without a door became history.

Today, film and family scrapbooks remind Madaleine Lambert of the surprises they experienced as lake property owners in a relatively undeveloped north woods area. One episode became known as The Mystery of the Missing Pier. What had been installed during their first summer at the lake had disappeared by the time they arrived the following spring. David built another pier and strongly secured it to the shoreline. Yet, when they arrived the following spring, the pier was gone again. Only after a third pier was built would they learn that piers must be dismantled before winter sets in to prevent destruction when ice breaks in the early spring and shifts in violent patterns from strong winds. They were embarrassed not to have solved the mystery sooner considering that the life along the Mississippi River near Moline, Illinois was far different than North Sand Lake in Burnett County in Wisconsin.

Other memories include the day they packed their brown and white kayak with picnic lunches before setting out from their shoreline to visit the isolated west point that had nary a hint of habitation, and the huge unfamiliar fish a family member caught one day that was carried down the shoreline to Bauer's Deer Haven Bay Resort for identification by Mr. Bauer. In the past, Bauer had rented boats to the Lamberts, so when he saw the fish, he smiled and told them it was nothing more than good fertilizer. It seems they had landed a bowfin, better known by lake fishermen as a dogfish.

The early days of turning off a thick sandy road to an equally thick sandy driveway leading to Lambert's cottage met with disaster more than once. Because of the low swampy land on both sides of the driveway, the soil seemed to suck in the tires of their car when spring arrived, or if rainfall was heavy and lake levels were high. Madaleine recalls the ugliness of bogs that floated to their shoreline when a portion of property now known as Thompson's Bay was dredged for development, and the fright of summer storms that wove paths through the full-grown trees surrounding their cabin. But the land also blessed them with a plethora of north woods beauty when bear, deer, raccoon and other wild animals wandered through to enjoy ripe fruit from an abundance of wild succulence, especially the blackberry bushes, all of which they never would have experienced had it not been for a harmless snake that slithered by one fateful day.

Madaleine Lambert

Below is a letter written by Andy Schultz to his brother-in-law, Norm Keller, after the Lamberts became owners of their North Sand Lake property that included Mallard Lake shoreline.

July 4, 1956

Dear Norm,

*Saw Lambert when he was up. He brought (*bought?*) another refrigerator and wants to get rid of his. Fritz Thompson said he would move it, but when he went there Dave had taken it back inside. The key does not fit the new lock so will wait till you or Dave gets up again.*

You can tell Dave the gas tank costs $14.50, the regulator $8.25 around here. The gas stove originally cost $12.00, but will let the whole works go for $20.00. It doesn't make any difference to me as I'll be able to use the thing too, but this will save him from chasing around

There are no charges pending, had had no expenses.

Weather lately has been nice. Got a 3 lb. walleye the other night. Walleyes are biting right now. Baxter may complain, but he's not as bad as he screams. Baxter reminds me of Gabriel Heatter, if you want to get the blues listen to either one.

When that depression hits you can take $40,000 out of the bank and come up here with me and we'll put it into ammunition and seed potatoes. There's plenty of wood to help us keep warm, the roof ought to last 10 more years, so I guess we can weather the thing out.

Come up and relax awhile.
Love to Millie and Eliot,
Andy

Note: Madaleine is not certain who Baxter was, unless he was responsible for building the shed.

In memory of
Maude Behr,
July 24, 1943.

We loved this
lake, woods, birds
and flowers.

Emil Behr

Emil and Maude Behr

Just around the bend from Lambert's property in the lake's southernmost bay is a treasure of land and history. Exposed, yet private and tucked away in its own pleasure, I discovered it one calm day while trolling the length of the lake. Much later, about 50 years to be exact, I learned about that particular stretch of shoreline and of Emil and Maude Behr who settled there, when I received a letter from Josephine K. Andersen, Luck, whose sister, Mrs. Gerald B. Westlund, once owned the same property with her husband, before the Joseph J. Prestons resided there.

Andersen enclosed a letter written to her sister by Emil on January 5, 1953, and mailed May 11, 1954 from St. Paul, Minnesota, specifically for the interest of future owners of the property which included the exact location of the Behr property and its Indian mounds which, at the request of a recent owner, as well as my own respect for the sacredness of Indian mounds, will remain a secret.

The exterior of the original cabin built by Emil Behr had been covered with corrugated sheet metal and partially hidden by trees near a 450 foot sandy beach that remains one of the most desirable lots on the lake. Its unsurpassed beauty basks in the sun for all to view as the shoreline slowly slips into the lake while its backdrop of deep woods and full grown trees provide a natural shelter of privacy with cool shade. When I first rowed past the property the small structure must not have been in view from the boat and the only thing I remember was wondering what kind of fish were swimming below in the comfort of a protected bay. Because of the distance from the north shore, rowing all the way over there at my age wasn't something I did often.

A few years ago while visiting the owner of the property, I noticed upon entering a new addition of his four season home that remnants of the aging structure included an old wood stove placed against the wall. Stirring memories for a lifetime, the owner shared stories of the meals once prepared on the stove and the warmth wood fires supplied to those who once lived there. He also shared a rumor of many Indian mounds that once had resided on the property and, in Chippewa tradition, had 12 Indians buried in each mound in a standing position with their weapons in the center. To my knowledge, only one mound remains.

When I received a copy of Emil Behr's letter from Andersen, it had been copied and rewritten, as is, for easier reading.

January 5, 1953

When we came to North Sand Lake in November 1926, there were no roads to the lake, only narrow sandy trails from Spooner; some places the sand so deep to the car axle, and so narrow and rutted we could not open the car door. This was in 1927. In the Fall of 1926, we came by railroad to Spooner. Met Mr. Thompson (not related to Glen Thompson on Sand Lake) and Mr. Volkman. They were agents for Northlakes Land Co, from Eau Claire, WI. We looked at several places on Lake McKensie (sic), Webb Lake, Birtch (sic) Island, etc. But Mrs. Behr selected North Sand Lake and just love the place since, at first we bought only the West half, but the following year 1927, we took the entire piece - 25 acres. Mrs. wanted seclusion and by herself. There was no one living on the entire south end. No one on the west side of the lake except Mr. Leif's farm about 3/4 mile back from the lake. On the north was one cabin - I think his name was White. On the east was only Glen Thompson who has 5 or 6 log cabins, and had a few cows and horses and takes tourist and meals at his house during the season. Where the open field is to the east about a mile, there lived Harry Peck and family - 10 girls, one boy. How they ever lived there and raised the children, we could never figure out. It is very poor farming land, for all around that country is only recreation land. But Peck also worked in the woods logging and the boy who was about 20 years old then, was cutting pulp wood all the time. The boy, Gordon Peck, and his friend Ben Green helped me build the cottage, cut brush, clear the land, around buildings, and the road to get in to the lake; cut out the survey line, fence, etc. It took many years of hard work for both of us Mrs. and I. But we enjoyed it - to be out in the woods and our appetite was enormous and sure got good & hungry at each meal, dinner and supper. Together with the pure pine air, we slept at night like a log, so to say.

Most seasons, I could stay July, Aug, Sept. and some seasons when my brother and family were with Mrs. Behr or other seasons my nephew and family were there, I would go home for several weeks in between to go to work while someone was at the lake. I could get off any time as long as I had a man in my place. In them days, help was not so scarce as now. Nowadays, this could not be done. I suppose now the lake property is pretty well weeded up again with brush and young trees. We had to weed, cut brush, trim trees to keep it in some shape. Best to do this in Fall, when it is cool or very early Spring-before the deer flies, mosquitoes come out. Wood ticks are abundant in early spring but about the end of June or early July, they are not bad any more.

It is best to pull young trees if not wanted or two thick when they are young, saves a lot of cutting; also cut brush around stumps, especially oak often it takes about 4 or 5 years for oak brush to disappear if cut each year. Along the wire fence survey line, I would go around each year, remove fallen trees and brush. There is always something to keep one busy-never a lonesome time, fix boats, etc. I intended to get an aluminum boat but they are so expensive. It would be nice to have-no patching, caulking and always ready to put in the water any time I wanted to use it. But I was also afraid someone may take a notion to steal it. Of course for a short distance to St. Paul, it would be nice to have a boat trailer.

We never left things like my Evinrude motor, cameras, field glasses, guns, rifles and valuable cooking utensils and bedding clothes my wife had. If someone was there, we left these things, but to be away for 9 or 10 months, would not be so good. You can be there each week in just a few hours is not so bad.

I had a 2 wheel trailer and the car and trailer was always loaded to the top. Many things we dragged with trailer way up there-like the big heavy range (kitchen stove) one season. Another year, the two rails (iron for gate posts); then again the heavy iron plate for target and all iron old chains and square iron sink, about 50 or 60 pounds. what will not a person do - all when one feels good and peppy.

In later years, well pipe, tools, paint, etc. was bought in Spooner, Webster. During World War 2, cement I got in Minneapolis with the trailer for I could get none in

Webster or Spooner. The basement for the cottage was built by Harry C. Rausch; he built bridges, basements etc. Built in Nov 1945, digging, moving, felling large trees, etc. He has the men and machines so it was easier for me.

Some of the different pine trees, spruce, Norway pine, a few white pine were transplanted by us. You may find some copper or brass tags which I hung on some of the branches near the center on looped wire to allow for growth. The year is stamped on tags. When trees were young, I had chicken netting around trees to prevent rabbits from girdling and chewing the bark in winter. Three blue spruce we brought from Canada when only 10 or 12 inches height. One is near the cottage, and two back of the garage, east of old pond hole. These three trees are from Canada near Lake Nipegon. One season when fishing was bad at Sand Lake - water low and stagnant, we just left and took a trip up there. Trees are not to be transported but they were small, in buckets, or cans and got them home to Sand Lake in care-covered up. Stopped at Little Marias a few days at John Hanson's cabins. Beautiful country up there. End of August, we started back but so cold that potatoes froze in the fields.

Jack pines grow like weeds in some spots, so I pulled them out when small or they would cover everything - especially on the beach. How did you find the water level this year? When we had high water in 1942-43, it reached the high bank along the shore it was the highest since 1926. Water flowed then down Sand Creek which I marked 1/2 mile east of gate - flowed for several years. County put in culvert to leave water to Yellow River south. Water flooded the highway A on north side so the level had to be lowered. One day I was at the creek with my dog - she likes to go for frogs. But fell in the rushing water and pulled into the culvert. I thought good bye, dog; but she came back over the road, wagging and barking, so quick and happy. She was a good swimmer - part Golden Retriever, and loved to be on the boat or in the water.

At first when we came to the lake, we had no well for two years. The water in lake was so clear then - we used that to drink - just go out 50 feet and dip water. Sometimes we got well water from Peck's family. My wife was great friends with all their girls. They brought milk to us each day and Mrs. helped them a lot for they were poor. Now Mr. Peck and wife live north of Webster about 3 miles - 1/2 mile east of Johnson's store. The girls are all well married now. The boy in Army in Europe or up in the woods again. Mr-Mrs. Peck have a nice place now. He made a good deal on his other farm he had near Danbury; after he left Sand Lake and later on had two farms, good land buildings. I wish you could meet him some time. He is an interesting talker; been a woodsman most of his life, and believe he knows the northwest Wisconsin history better than anyone. The Phillips gas station owner - Conners knows where he lives. Mr. Glen Thompson on east shore been up there also many years operating saw mills.

The lake level goes up and down; about 1934-35 during the many years dry seasons, the dust bowl years, it was so low that we could wade across the sand bar a few hundred feet out and had Mr. Glen Thompson come over with his team and scraper to dig a channel through sand bar in order to pull the boat into main part of lake. An old

Indian from Danbury Indian village was over one day and when he saw it - says this was the lowest he ever saw the water level. He said every 7 or 8 years, it goes up or down. After the water level came up a few years after, it was up 12 feet over the sand bar and up to high bank along shores.

Fishing was bad when water low. The fish conservation placed fish protectors all around the lake for fish to spawn. They like weedy places for spawning. The east bay is good for that, but during the dry seasons the weed beds were dry too. When we had the high water, the small pond back of garage was full of water and frogs - fine for fish bait. During dry seasons, all lakes go down. Minnehaha Falls, Minneapolis was dry as a road and the roads in sand were tough to get through loose sand and stuck every few miles. Now it is fun - paved roads almost all the way and good gravel and graded sand road.

In wet weather sand roads are good and few hours after showers, rain all gone and roads packed. If you ever take the road past Mallard Lake to county trunk X, you will find signs if they are there yet. I placed signs at each important turn like this -- HELP PREVENT FIRE and PUT CAMPFIRES OUT. I had before - To Sand Lake or E. Behr, but some kids going through there always shot them up or smashed them. So the first signs were not bothered and may be up yet. I suppose the kids thought the signs were put up by the Road Dept. It is a pretty route that way and comes out by the High School and Grade School on Hwy in Webster.

My wife was raised as a girl about the same conditions as the Peck family. I think it was this that she got so friendly with the Peck's. There were seven children - 5 girls, 2 boys. Lived on a poor land farm near Sparta and Melrose, Wisconsin. Her father was sickly and died young. She was the tomboy of the family, the second oldest and strong and tough. The boys were small and too young. So she helped her father on the farm, cut logs, oak railroad ties, and they burned charcoal to sell. They lived in all heavily wooded country and sandy - in the McCoys Ranch District. Now it is the big Military Reservation McCoys Camps. Mrs. in her younger days played a lot with Indian children, traveling through there in summer during berry time for the woods were full of blueberries, raspberries and many other kinds. We had quite a few blueberries also but a lot died out during dry seasons. Mr. Thompson knows yet where to get them; best also cranberries if you get acquainted, he'll be glad to tell you where to find some. I believe the reason my wife took so to the Indian mound is that she was so much in contact with Indian kids. She must have had a hard life in her young days. Drive ox team for her Dad, had no horses they could afford, for ox teams were best for snaking out heavy logs, braking new land, etc. Then get cows home in all kinds of weather, sometimes late in the night, rain or snow, be wet from head to feet. Dark nights she would hang on to the bell cow that was the leader - start her off and the cow would go home. But to find the cows on a dark night, there were no fences then and cows would wander away for many miles. By listening for the bell cow, they would be found. You see that is why she was so greatly in love with the woods and outdoors. She knew every wild flower up there, the different trees, and medical plants and roots that grown up there for they did not have a drug store right around the corner as we have now. Of course, she learned a lot from Indians also about medical roots, etc. In later years she was in La Crosse as a dress maker. There I met her. The rest you may know how things go.

When we first came to the lake, we just looked the place over - that was in November 1926. It was cold and a few inches of snow on ground. One of the pictures you have, shows this. The water level was not so high then but it had a fine sand beach. Ice in spring break-up usually plows into the beach and spoils it. We only stayed a few hours that year to see the place but did inspect the grounds good.

In early June 1927, we shipped a lot of things - tools, hardware, all the sheets of metal by freight to Spooner. From there, a truck drayman took our things out one early morning. But it took us all day until 4 p.m. to get to the lake. Truck heavily loaded; my car "Nash car" and trailer - all it could hold. Stuck in the sand often - sometimes every half mile. Then dig out, cut brush to pack under wheels, and jack up the wheels to build up brush and boards, planks we had. Sometimes the truck would scrape the sides of bank in narrow trail. We cut more brush in order to get through. But we kept plugging along all day and got there. To top it off, when we got there, just then a big thunderstorm came up. The truckman quickly unloaded, for he wanted to get on the main roads before the storm got too bad.

There we were in a wet strange place, nothing to eat but a few sandwiches we had left. We managed to get up a small pup tent we had for that night. I sat in the tent on chair and tried to get a little sleep that night; and a lantern next to me to keep a little warm for it turned cool that night and wind blowing from northwest over the water. Next day we had more time to rig up our camp for the first summer. Had two tents, a sleeping tent and cots and bedding; and a larger tent for cooking and kitchen, folding chairs, table and gasoline stove. Now we were fixed up real cozy. Even had enough room for meals for our help while building. That day Mr. Peck and his son came over and told us a lot of things and showed us better around the place. The Indian mound then had a large hole dug in the top center about 8 feet across and 5 feet deep but there was nothing in it. Mr. Peck said that some geologist from Madison had been there several years back and dug into it but nothing of importance was found. So several years later when the lake level of water was very low, I had Mr. Thompson and Dave Sewell who lives 4 miles on road past Mallard Lake toward County trunk X - had them both come with their horses and scrapers and fill in the hole in the mound. You may still see the hollow place west of the mound where the earth was scraped out. The large rock was taken out of the lake on the east side where the water was very low and shore dry. A scraper placed under the rock. The four horses had to pull all they could to drag that heavy rock on the Indian mound. The rock is of an odd formation and we thought it would be nice to have on the mound representing the Indian Chief. The smaller rocks we found on our trips to Spooner and Webster when shopping or wherever we happened to go. There was not a rock on the entire place - all sand. Other rocks came from Thompson's shore and gravel pit which he has. The smaller rocks on the mound represent the Indian women and children; the outer ring of rocks, the first line of warriors; the inner ring, the second line of warriors.

To the south of the mound, you can also find where the road or trail used to be. This was also used as a logging trail. Logs in the early days were skidded down the creek south to the Yellow River, then through Yellow Lake, which is the largest lake up there; then out of the lake where the Yellow River goes out again; to the St. Croix and on down the St. Croix River. One time Mrs. Behr and I tried to hike through the woods south to the Yellow River. Mr. Peck told us about 3 miles but we had to give up - all jungles, marshes and mosquitoes. So we turned back - getting dark too - night coming on. You cross the Yellow River on road past Mallard Lake on iron bridge to Co Tr. X. We often went to the Namekagon River about 12 miles north on Co. Tr. H from intersection with Cty. Tr A. This is a pretty river and good fishing. Glen Thompson's son Stuart takes tourists up there on canoe trips down the river to Danbury or where Hwy 35 crosses the river. I think I left some maps of the lake and rivers from up there at the cabin. Or maybe can be had in Webster gas stations, sport goods store, etc.

A few years ago, these were the names of people on North Sand and Mallard lakes -- first on Mallard - Mr. Lykist. He always wore a large cowboy hat. I believe he was from St. Paul. 2nd place was Mr. Jart. He was the one that wore the hearing aid. 3rd place was Winceck - they had a very nice cottage, log cabin, cut siding and glass enclosed porch. Next were the Dietrick's. They were there before we were in 1927 where the open field is and very high bank on Mallard Lake.

On North Sand lake west shore; 1st Ray G. Kennon -- he is a public accountant from Minneapolis. I remember him real well for when we had high water and good fishing, he wanted the lake level lowered by the county board because he built a boat house on his shore and a pier. When the water was high his boat house and pier was afloat and useless but no one signed up to the lower the lake although the county put in a culvert in the road a few hundred feet east of our gate - just enough to drain to keep the water from going still higher and not flood the road on the north side County Tr A. The creek and drain used to be the natural overflow and logging skidway to Yellow River. When this culvert was put in, all worked just fine and every one pleased to keep the water at normal height. I used to have a pier also but gave up the idea for every spring, it was smashed by the ice or else dry or submerged. The place has a good beach and enough rise to land a boat in all kinds of weather or pull the boat on the beach. Where on a pier, it would bang back and forth in rough water and damage the boat. I also wish to say that each year I would go all around the bottom of building to see if all was closed tight and no holes for mice to get in during the winter. I had a rounded putty knife in the tools to press in hair plaster mixed with cement. This would harden in holes and stick there and make it quite mouse proof. We had no trouble with mice for many years. It was nice to get there in the spring and all clean and no damage. You will also find a block and tackle in garage for pulling in boats or for dragging heavy logs out of the way. The two wheel cart was for hauling brush on a pile to an open spot on the beach and leave it there until fall or early winter when there is a few inches of snow and set fire to it. Or a wet season was okay to burn. We would fill the dry brush on the bottom and the green on top and when once started, it will all burn. You must get a brush burning permit from the fire warden. Glen Thompson and Dan Sewell were the fire wardens for some time. Often we had a few pails of water handy and a sprinkle can in case of fire would start running or put fire out for the night in case a wind would come up. Best time to burn was late afternoon and wind from the south so smoke and sparks would fly towards the lake.

On the west shore of the lake next to Ray G. Kennon was Mr. Wagner. I believe he also was from Minneapolis. Kotecki - next from some place in Illinois or Chicago. Then on north shore was only one - his name was White - I believe from Iowa. The last few years John (Behr meant Barney) Hanson's cabins are there. He also has a small store for tourists to get a few supplies and milk. We often went there by boat or road to buy a few things. Then on the west shore coming from Ct. Tr A., I do not remember the first party. He was just building a nice place the last few years I was up there. Then came another part I do not remember. Then Mr. Glen Thompson cabins whose yard makes the sharp turn in the road by this mailbox, Stuart Thompson, Glen Thompson's son, and Stuart's wife Bernice and 2 daughters - oldest about 8 or 9 years now, the youngest about 3 years. Have a very nice house down by the lake, the road to his house branches off to the right about 1/2 mile from the mail box. It is log cabin style, all year round, running water, furnace heat, wood and coal. And knotty pine interior finish - very pretty. Stuart built most of it himself. He is a good mechanic even on cars and machinery; and building, he helped me many a time, even took me home here in Milwaukee when I took sick up there the last time I stayed at Mr. Glen Thompson's house. They are fine people - maybe you will meet them sometime. Then on the east bay, part of Harry Peck's old place was Edgar Kaiser. He built seven cabins but he was of a roving restless nature, a good woodsman. He was from Neillsville, Wisc and moved to the big woods in Oregon to build and operate a tourist camp. They packed their belongings on an old Model T truck. How he ever got out there we all wondered, but his wife was a good sport; she took everything as it came, good or bad. She loved to paint pictures; their cabin was very high on a hill overlooking the lake and she would be painting views. Mr. Kaiser's jalopies were broken down more times than they were running. So Stuart Thompson helped him along often. For several years, the Thompson's also had a mink ranch on their place but prices dropped so for pelts; so they gave it up and so much disagreeable work - also getting old horses for food, grinding meat etc. The further south on Road past Thompson's place is the Deer Farm, as you no doubt know. That was owned by Mr. Swing at first; he was from Chicago and was the operator of 10 or 12 beauty parlors - a peculiar business for a man to be in and take to the woods. The Deer Farm has 703 acres, two pretty lakes in it - Upper and Lower Twin Lakes, private fishing for his friends. One fall season they took out 52 deer but always under supervision of Game Wardens and each deer must be state tagged and each hunter licensed. We often saw buck deer hanging around the fence in the fall. I presume many outside deer are attracted by the deer inside. The last I hear, the place was sold and Mr. Bastine was the owner from Indiana. One year he came up with a pilot in a Piper Cub small airplane and landed in that open field on Peck's old place. That year the field was clear of brush and young trees but we all wondered why a plane should be circling the lake and over the woods. The Game and Fish wardens often came over the lake in planes but always higher up. Maybe you have noticed them at times during the fishing season. Mr. Dale Clark was the caretaker of the Deer Farm the past few years. If he is there yet, I do not know. They had a good all-year house on the place. Mr. Clark helped me clear the yard around the cabin several years ago of large fallen trees after a big storm. One large oak barely missed the building. I could not do this heavy work any more so I had Mr. Clark come over and take out the good logs, to take to Glen Thompson to cut into lumber for their use. The poor wood for firewood. They only took deer out of the Farm when they got too plentiful. Mr. Swing had many loads of baled hay into the place for winter when feed was scarce - also corn and oats.

Kaiser's old place changed hands a few times lately so I do not know the people now there. Mr. Slock (or Skog) is next to the line right over the survey line on the east. His cabin burned a few years ago while he and friends were on the lake fishing. They had an oil or gasoline stove and I suppose the women did not know how to handle it. Gasoline is very dangerous anyhow in a building - in camp or tent, it is not so bad - just throw it out, if possible and let it burn. It was lucky no one was hurt at Mr. Skog's. I believe he is a school teacher or principal in Minneapolis. According to your letter of July 3rd, he is building a new place. It is on the same site. I imagine it is a poor place so low and no drainage. In your letter of August 25, you mention Mr. Skog - teacher from Eau Claire. I believe you are right - I mentioned from Minneapolis. Oh yes I remember him well when his cabin burned. And the man that was over during your vacation from Mallard Lake wears a hearing aid is Mr. Jart.

Well, I believe I will wind up with this lengthy writing and hope I have given you lots of information and history of the place. I only wish I could have wrote better or plainer. You see my eyes are poor and I have to write so large in order to see my own writing. I hope you can make it out all right.

I also enclose some more pictures which may be of interest to you - just keep them - I have duplicates. Oh yes, before I forget, if any time you wish to remove the memory stones for any reason, Mr. Allert can bury them about 2 feet down right where they are. Just make a hole and slide them in. The stones were carved here in North Milwaukee. The brown flat stone is a Tennessee sand stone. The others - a common black n-head. I hauled them up there on trailer in 1944. Maybe I hear from you some time and I hope in this coming year if all goes well as at present, I will be able to come up for a visit this summer and visit old friends up in the neighborhood of North Sand Lake and Webster.

Wishing you all good health and good luck, I remain yours truly,

Emil E. Behr

P.S. If the publishers of Wisconsin Story - Indian Mounds ever get out another edition, I will mail one to you. It is also very interesting of the first white settlers in Minnesota and Wisconsin.

When subsequent buyers settled on the land Emil and Maude Behr had loved for so many years, they not only were intrigued by its location and beauty, and of the original cabin the Behrs had built and covered with corrugated sheet metal, but asked many questions of its past. It is clear with what he attached to his letter of personal experiences settling the land that Emil felt obliged to answer. Imagine their surprise to be informed that there were Indian mounds on the property. To further broaden their knowledge of the Chippewa, or Ojibwa, Indians who had lived and died there, Behr included the following information that he copied from Wisconsin History of Indian Mounds, 1948.

After the glaciers left, the first people came to Wisconsin 10,000 years or more ago. Very likely, they were the hunters who wore animal skins - like the cavemen of the popular cartoons -- to protect them from the icy northern winds. These first Wisconsinites, or their ancestors, are believed to have come into North America from Asia by way of the Bering Strait and Alaska. The white man's history in Wisconsin covers only a little more than three centuries, while the prehistoric inhabitants developed several distinct cultures over many hundreds, probably thousands of years. They left no written history, however, and we can only sketchily reconstruct their way of living from objects unearthed in their cemeteries and former village sites.

These people have been divided into five main cultures -- the old copper industry, the Woodland, the Hopewell, the upper Mississippi, and the middle Mississippi. The Woodland has persisted longest and is more nearly a native of Wisconsin as opposed to an immigrant culture. All belong to that broad division of the human race mistakenly named Indians.

The oldest man-made objects found in Wisconsin are rather heavy copper tools, spear points, knives, axes, harpoons. They were made by the old copper industry folk. Their great age is shown by deep acid erosion not present in the copper tools of later Indian cultures. The Woodland pattern Indians who came into the state probably from Canada between 1,000 and 2,000 years ago at the latest, have left us more clues to their way of life than any other group. Wisconsin and Minnesota seem to have been the center of this culture as the evidences become much greater and then scarcer as one moves down the Mississippi Valley.

Pottery similar to the Woodland type is abundant in Siberia which supports the theory that Woodland pattern had its origin in Asia. The most abundant sources of Woodland relics are their mounds. Wisconsin is particularly rich in mounds; more than 12,000 of them (all are Woodland) have been recorded in various parts of the state. The main centers of them include Milwaukee, Madison, Waukesha,

Racine, Beloit, Lake Mills, Baraboo, Prairie du Chien, Lake Winnebago, and the Wisconsin River. The Indians had a shrewd eye for favorite locations for their Indian settlements. By the time the white settlers had established themselves in the state, descendants of the Woodland type Indian had given up mound building and could not even remember who had built the mounds.

The Menominee are direct descendants. The Potowatomi, Chippewa, Sauk, Fox, Kickapoo and all other historic Algonquin-speaking tribes in the state belong to the branches of the Woodland. The old Menominee Indian reservation differs from other Woodland types in that the dead were buried in pits rather than mounds. Bodies were buried in a folded position, and in other cases were exposed on raised scaffolds until only the bones remained to be buried in pits. The tools of the group, known as "keshema focus" of the Woodland, were heavy crude flaked arrowheads and edged tools polished and grooved, stone axes, and coarse pottery decorated with impressions by cord-shaped tools.

The most distinctive branch of the Woodland was the Effigy Mound group active in the southern half of the state during the golden age of Woodland culture. Their burial mounds were elaborate--some shaped like animals, birds in flight, and rarely men. They also built round and dome-shaped mounds and long straight ones called linear. All were low, seldom over 4 feet high, but sometimes over several hundred feet long. All Indian mounds were burial places and groups of them, cemeteries. The effigy mound is distinctly a Wisconsin development. Lake Wingra at Madison is one rich center of effigy mounds and is particularly noted for a large bird mound with a wing spread of 624 feet. Some 250 mounds of various types have been found in and around Madison alone. A man effigy mound may be seen in Man Mound Park near Baraboo. It represents a man walking and is 210 feet long and 47 feet across the shoulders. On the head are two protuberances, probably representing a buffalo horn headdress, "a rare intaglio depiction" (excavated instead of being heaped into a mound) is in Riverside Park at Fort Atkinson.

The pottery of Effigy Mound people is better than the average Woodland products, and some of it is beautifully decorated. These people were makers apparently of the fluted ax, a tool much prized by collectors. This is a polished stone ax with a groove for a handle to be fitted with broad grooves or fluting on a blade.

In northwestern Wisconsin is found the "Clam River focus" of the Woodland, distinguished by large dome shaped mounds, some of them 12 feet high. These mounds, found particularly in Burnett County, show an unusual burial practice. After exposing the bodies on a scaffold like the old Menominee, they bundled the bones, heaped up a small amount mound and covered its surface with the grizzly bundles. They would then heap on more earth, making a larger mound. Later another layer of bones would be added, and more dirt heaped. Some large mounds contain four layers of bundled bones. The Clam River mounds are of relatively recent origin for well preserved birch bark baskets were found in one, and the fur and claws of beaver in another. Other contents such as the skull of a western mustang pony, and some pieces of charred wood showing marks of a steel axe, fix the time of the mounds construction definitely after the coming of the white man. The Chippewas, the last Indians to live at the site of the mounds, said the structures were made by the Sioux Indians, whom the Chippewas drove away in the seventeenth century into the Dakotas and western Minnesota. Since the Sioux were living there when the earliest white men came, it is reasonably certain that the Sioux were the builders.

Invaders from the South, near the middle of the golden age of the Woodland people, the first of seven immigrant groups from the southeast entered the state bringing distinct culture and higher culture to the Woodland. They were the Hopewellians of the same group that built the famed "Hopewell Mounds" of southern Ohio.

The southerners built relatively large mounds, dome-shaped to hold many bodies in bark lined pits. Their artifices included shaped stone knives and arrowheads of a distinct type and shape, made of such fine materials and rare as quartzite's from the Appalachian Mountains, "hornstone" flint from Indiana, jasper from Ohio, chalcedonies from North Dakota, and obsidian from the Rockies. Among their luxuries were fine pipes and amulets from polished stone ear spool ornaments, beads, pendants and breastplates of Lake Superior copper, button-like objects of silver, conch shells from the Gulf of Mexico, pearl beads, cloth woven from nettle fiber, and pottery of striking shapes and ornaments. The variety of their materials indicates the Hopewell people carried on the extensive "foreign trade" the Mexican influence is shown. Their culture seems to have disappeared a century or two before the white man came.

The ancestors of the present Winnebago were among a later group of prehistoric invaders of the state, the Upper Mississippi people. The Winnebago, when first encountered by white men, were living around the shores of Lake Winnebago and the lower Fox River. These people lived in fairly permanent villages, made high grade shell tempered pottery decorated with geometric patterns, used finely chipped stone arrowheads and other implements and ornaments made of bone and antlers. They buried dead in cemetery plots and built no mounds. Other evidence of the Upper Mississippi culture had been found along the eastern shore of the Mississippi from Trempeleau to Grant counties and in Green Lake and Marquette counties.

And for the kindness of Emil Behr, who spent days recording all of this to pass on to others, we are much wiser to the history and practices of the Indians in Burnett County as well as other areas of the country.

In 2000, an extensive survey compiled by Robert A. Birmingham, state archaeologist in the Division of Historic Preservations and Leslie E. Eisenberg, a forensic anthropologist and coordinator of the Burial Sites Preservation

Indian mound on Behr's property.

Program, both at the State Historical Society of Wisconsin, was documented and published in a book titled, Indian Mounds of Wisconsin. Highly acclaimed by professionals in their fields as the most in depth published study in the past 150 years, the book, published by the University of Wisconsin Press in Madison, Wisconsin, sheds light on very controversial and well-known Indian mounds in Burnett County. Reminding the reader there are more mounds built by ancient Native American societies in Wisconsin than in any other region of North America--between 15,000 and 20,000 mounds, the authors claim that at least 4,000 remain today. Introduced in the 245 page book is William C. McKern who became a staff member of the Public Museum in 1925. McKern began to explore archaeological sites in the state in the mid-1930s, some of which were located in Burnett County. By the early 1940s, he had sufficient information to classify prehistoric cultures of Wisconsin with cultures of similar findings in other states. His findings, as well as those of other archaeologists since that time, are documented at the Burnett County Historical Society and prove not only that the mounds were built in stages, but also prove the presence of the Dakota tribe before being driven out by the Chippewa in the early eighteenth century. The book is a must for general readers and students as well as professional archaeologists and scholars in related fields.

Ike Van Someren purchased Emil Behr's land in the mid-1960s. The family enjoyed endless experiences and rewards of warm summer months each year before temperatures dropped to provide winter thrills for all to enjoy. When Van Someren decided to rebuild the old cottage and add modern conveniences, fragments of the past were preserved to remember the humble beginnings that first sprouted so many years before. In 2000, the property was sold.

Indian Mound
Destroyed, 1897
Restored, 1927
by Emil and Maude Behr,
Milwaukee, Wis

From Corsairs and Saipan to Humble Motor Boats on North Sand

Ed Schnaith

After all these years, I still sigh with contentment when I row into this bay. At one time there was nothing for me to remember besides being optimistic about the quality of fish in the immediate area. Later, I would grow to appreciate the privacy and beauty of the shoreline, the deep woods backdrop that sheltered and protected it from the road, and the mysteries wedged in between. With hindsight, I wish I had rowed there often, yet rowing a boat with skinny arms and no motor didn't allow me to register it as a priority. Years later, a portion of land would be owned and occupied by Ed and Dorothy Schnaith.

Ed was a World War II Navy fighter pilot who flew torpedo bombers, dive bombers and fighters from aircraft carriers. Although he logged 100 take offs and landings in a 10 month period in the Pacific near Saipan, Lt. Ed Schnaith couldn't quite remove himself from bodies of water once he returned home. Following his retirement years later, Ed and Dorothy purchased a newly built cottage on Des Moines Lake in Burnett County. It would become their civilian base while searching for larger lakeshore property on which to build their retirement home. After visiting the DNR to explain what he had in mind, Ed was offered three possibilities that seemed to fit his description of a lake being large, clear and very deep. Typical of military training and pilot briefings, Ed methodically researched and surveyed three lakes in a private plane before making a decision to fully explore North Sand Lake.

Winter had arrived. Overlooking the snow cover, Ed drove up to Glen Thompson's place steep in the woods over the east shoreline. Having been widowed, Thompson lived alone and came out with a rifle and asked Ed what he wanted. Before long, the two were sitting inside Thompson's residence, drinking coffee and chatting about the lake. Learning of Ed's interest to purchase lakeshore property, Thompson told him of a sign attached to a fence near Mallard Lake road on the southern end of the lake and thought the property was owned by man with the last name of Preston. When Ed left, he immediately headed over in that direction. Just as Thompson had described, Ed located the fence with the sign and, after looking over the property, decided to seek out a Land Broker to inquire further about the North Sand Lake property.

Dorothy and Ed Schnaith

The next day, Ed called Charles Tollander and left a message with questions about the land. Tollander returned the call and assured Ed the land was for sale, that he had listed it, but hadn't had a chance to have it surveyed. Ed and Dorothy already were convinced that the lot fit their plans of where to build. Set a short distance back from the water and tucked away in the throes of mature trees and berry bushes, the lake shore lot had a commanding view of the length of the lake. It was everything they had hoped it would be. At that time, the property was owned by a Mr. Preston and a Mr. Weslyn who resided in San Diego and were related by marriage.

The following week, Ed met Charles Tollander at a tavern in Webster to discuss purchasing the land. Ed wanted 200 feet of shoreline and stipulated that the land surrounding it would be included to make certain no one else could build on it. The asking price was $4800. Ed offered $4000 and Tollander accepted. An offer was written, pending a survey. Tollander had to contact property owners next door and three weeks later called Ed to tell him the owners would sell the land with 200 feet of shoreline and include restrictions in the rear to curtail any possibility of future development.

During the winter of 1963, Ed drew plans for the retirement home and building began the following spring with the help of his son-in-law and nephew. Over 100 trees were removed to clear a drive from the road to the lakeshore. Most were regional poplar trees, many being saved for fire wood. A local man from the Doriott family was the bulldozer operator Ed hired and described as doing an excellent job of removing the stumps. Laverne Irons, a local builder, did most of the outside work while Ed worked inside. In 1966, Ed Schnaith retired from the military to settle, with Dorothy, on the south shore of North Sand Lake.

The years that followed found Ed deeply involved in his surroundings. As an avid outdoorsman, he became a spokesperson for certain lake-related issues as well as being a casual overseer of the lake and its periphery. Quickly learning the blueprints of the near -1000 acre lake, its many depths, weed beds and sand bars, Ed mastered the art of fishing during daylight hours and well into the evening when conditions were perfect for walleye. His knowledge and appreciation of his property, the lake before him and the woods that embraced the property triggered a deep sense of how priceless the location was and what was necessary to preserve it. An ecologist by nature, Ed wanted to instill in others the importance of conservation.

Ed's opinions about proposals and possibilities that could affect North Sand Lake and its periphery were, at times, misunderstood. In recent years, he expressed himself again, feeling strongly that the lake had been abused by the advent of jet skis, and was frustrated that many who owned them were oblivious to the precautions necessary by staying away from the lake's shorelines. He tried to impress on property owners who owned jet skis to slow down when they were in the immediate vicinity of loons, stressing that if loons were constantly disturbed, their eggs would become cold and not hatch. He insisted on respect of the No Wake Zones near the entry of the Back Bay and Thompson's Bay. The bottom line was that Ed Schnaith was merely displaying his affection in a parental manner to preserve the lake and the surrounding area for the benefit of future generations.

A few years ago, Ed and Dorothy Schnaith made plans for an addition to their small cozy four season lake home to accommodate their daughter and son-in-law. Although the addition to the rear of the home toward their woods would not have been environmentally damaging in any manner, they were denied a variance which, in turn, meant that many full grown trees had to be cut down before moving their home back an additional 20 feet from its original foundation before the addition was approved. Unfortunately, due to today's stringent policies that have turned well-cared for dwellings into non-conforming structures, the Schnaith's experienced far more than they had anticipated during the remodeling process when each suffered serious injuries on separate days on the premises.

When the addition was completed, and good health returned to both, the couple rested, feeling confident that the remainder of their existence on the lake would be nurtured by family residing with them. When Ed celebrated his 81st birthday he could also celebrate his status as being highly respected by lake property owners, as well as the DNR in Spooner and continued to willingly involve himself in ecological issues. His message yesterday would remain the same in the days of tomorrow: *teach your kids the ABC's of conservation.*

Entering a new chapter in the twilight of Ed Schnaith's life on the lake he loved, and convinced there were more good years ahead along the south shoreline, he would die, unexpectedly, on September 8, 2004. He was 82.

Frank and Sophie Abrahamson

The abstract read: *Conveys land described in caption and other lands. Pursuant to an act of Congress approved April 24, 1829.*

The first transaction on the multi-page document confirms that the United States sold the property to Jonathon Chase in 1886 which was finalized two years later. There were other owners through the years and in 1926, B. F. Faast sold the land to Emil Behr and his wife Maude May Behr. Emil transferred the deed to the property to Maude in 1937. In 1944, the land changed hands again, this time as the estate of Maude May Behr purchased by R. L. Hass who, in turn, sold it to Frank A. and Sophie D. Abrahamson in 1955. After Frank's death in 1972, followed by Sophie's in 1980, the beautiful south shore property was legally transferred to their daughter, Fern Seagren who served as trustee of the estate and chose to remain there, with her husband, James, as a permanent resident after the two retired in 1980.

Frank and Sophie Abrahamson spent years of summers with their children renting the same seasonal cottage at a resort on Mille Lacs, a large lake in Minnesota. As a partner in a St. Paul architectural firm, Frank was well-known for his exquisite designs of classic churches and cathedrals. However, as a licensed architect in five states, time was limited and he was able to spend only weekends at the resort before returning home each Sunday evening to prepare for work the next day.

Through the years, a previous affection Sophie had for Wisconsin continued to grow until one day she decided to inquire about the northwest section of the state. With her daughter, Fern, and son-in-law James, the three visited the Baker Land and Title Company in St. Croix Falls where Mr. Baker described 13 ½ acres with 1000 feet of shallow sandy shoreline that was available at the southern end of North Sand Lake in Burnett County where the water was crystal clear. Intrigued by the description, they traveled to Webster to see if the property was as special as Baker promised. In the dead of winter, Sophie trudged through deep snow to reach a small seasonal cottage perched high on a hill overlooking the ice-covered lake. Visually absorbing the scenery, she returned home with typical Sophie-like authority, anxious to tell Frank of her decision to buy the land.

The Abrahamson's new old cottage on their newly purchased North Sand Lake property, sufficed for a short time before the remodeling began. After adding a basement, the structure was properly winterized. Much of the outside work was done by Sophie, a strong woman who found satisfaction and immense enjoyment in doing the heavy work of laying bricks and stones to beautify the area surrounding the cottage. Determined to protect the property and its lake as a mother protects her children, she became a self-appointed overseer of the land and made certain that others appreciated it as well.

Frank was the easy-going spouse. After five days in the office with intricate designs and detailed drawings, he looked forward to spending weekends cutting trees for firewood, or going fishing. One day in 1962, Frank, another male adult family member and a young grandson pushed away from shore in a canoe to fish in front of the property. They hooked a northern pike so large that it began towing the canoe. Impossible to land, the canoe was eventually beached, and so was the fish, a great northern measuring longer than the height of the young boy.

Frank and Sophie Abrahamson, late 1950s.

It was in the early 1960s when Frank and Sophie sold their home in St. Paul to establish permanent residency on the lake. When Frank died in 1972 at age 87, Sophie chose to stay there alone with Ginger, her Norwegian Elkhound. Being a very able woman considering her age, Sophie faired well. She not only was a great shot who could pick off chipmunks high in the trees, but also slept with a rifle hidden under her bed. One cold winter day, she found herself locked out of the house and walked over to Pat and Lucy Basler's Our Place Resort on Thompson Road near Lakeview for help. Pat remembers how she looked and how cold she was when she reached their front door.

Sophie remained at the lake until 1980 when she died at the age of 87.

Owning such a magnificent parcel of lake shore property creates pockets deep with rewards and drawbacks. A violent storm traveling from Siren one day toppled trees along the way as it wove a path toward North Sand Lake. On June 8, 1993, another destructive storm hit, this time as a seven-mile touchdown roared through Sand Lake and Jackson townships. And, in 1998, Fern and her family watched as high winds zoomed in, toppling one tree after another in domino fashion until six large old trees had fallen with a blink of an eye.

Yet, the good on such a lake usually outweighs the bad and wonderful traditions are established when family stays and new generations continue to arrive. Booya

Fern Abrahamson Seagren-Bowen

parties became popular autumn events at Fern Abrahamson Seagren's place from 1981 to 1986. The first one was an off-shoot of the booya parties they prepared as fund raisers to purchase equipment for the Twin Cities playgrounds. Each draw was huge and their popularity prompted them to bring their booya culinary expertise to the lake. The hearty seasoned stew made with oxtails, beef shanks and chickens had to simmer overnight. The following day vegetables were added. Two hundred and fifty gallons cooked until done in witch-size cauldrons on inside burners. Tables set up in the garage made dining comfortable and eliminated problems if the weather didn't cooperate. Although Seagrens insisted on absorbing the cost, which included bread, many who arrived with the open invitation extended to lake property owners and close friends from neighboring lakes brought desserts in potluck fashion. The last booya party was held in 1986 with 70 new and old friends attending. Despite a garage roof overhead, seating for such a large group found itself inching out in the open with accents of falling colored leaves. Although memories of autumn booya gatherings remain vivid today, Fern's booya recipe remains a guarded family secret.

Property values have skyrocketed on North Sand Lake in recent years. Back in 1959, Frank Abrahamson's records show that taxes on his 13 ½ acre parcel with 1000 feet of shoreline were a mere $135.00. The next year he was shocked by a 40 percent increase. In 1961, because the local schools were being amply financed, taxes decreased by a sizable amount. From then on, North Sand Lake property owners can attest to the fact that...the rest is history. Activity on the lake also has increased and is of great concern today to Fern Seagren-Bowen and her husband, Tom. Fern recalls the $1,000,000 lawsuit drawn up some years ago by Mr. Issacson, the Voyager Village developer who planned to install a private marina at the public boat landing on Leef Road for Voyager Village property owners. Skull and cross-bone posters were printed, distributed and stapled to trees throughout the area, symbolizing death to the environment and lake should Issacson's proposal receive the approval of the DNR and county officials.

After much debate and many heated open meetings packed with opposition, the plan was rejected and the lawsuit never materialized.

The Wehrwein Connection

It seems only fitting that the owners of property at the top of a wooded hill overlooking the length of North Sand Lake are members of the family of the late George S. Wehrwein whose contributions to conservation were recognized in April, 2002, as one of three individuals inducted into the Wisconsin Conservation Hall of Fame. Professor Wehrwein, who died in 1945 after devoting a lifetime to the applications of preserving our natural resources, leaves a legacy that remains a vital part of life on the lake for his son, Austin, daughter-in-law Judy, their children Sven, Paul, Peter and Joanna and precious grandchildren.

Treasures often are found in unpretentious places. Hidden, yet naked to the captive eye with an appreciation for exquisite natural things in life, the small seasonal Wehrwein cottage on the south shoreline couldn't be compared to a single fragment of Rome, Athens, Paris, London or other places Austin visited on assignments and yet, it was so much more. Nestled amid weeds, wild flowers and trees plus a breathless view of the lake, the property was destined to become a much loved family retreat in the north woods.

After years of extensive worldly travels as a journalist and Pulitzer Prize winner in 1953 for International Reporting, Austin and his family sensed something special about their family summer vacations along the Namekagon River near Cable, Wisconsin and decided that it was time to search for lake property of their own. In 1967, after seeing the cottage on a hill and view overlooking North Sand Lake, a decision was made to purchase the property.

The rowdy crew assembled: **Top,** from left; Sven, Mary Ann, Judy, Austin, Dave and Joanna. **Next down;** Peter, Pam, Annie Dog, Paul and Betsy. **Lower;** Ethan, Anna, Zachary, Lucas, Frances, Neal, and Tim—with Jonathan and David in front of them.

The connection with North Sand Lake has provided the best of times from discovering tadpoles to frogs to fish to 7-Up, Oreos and a little red sailboat. The small, but ample seasonal cottage, preserved in its own right, and most likely a fishing shack in its earlier days, became a mansion to the family and is one of many personal gems in the lake's crown…as Austin describes in The Wehrwein Web, his second edition of family history from its roots in Bavaria hundreds years ago to the shores of North Sand Lake in Burnett County…

…the bright yellow, rustic cottage has been a magnet for our family, a happy haven for many jolly gatherings. We bought it in 1967 for $8,500. The three-bedroom cabin on the bluff and the funky boat house on our 267-foot long shoreline have aged with little change. But the properties ringing the clear, spring-fed lake have. The cut-over countryside wasn't exactly a wilderness when we settled in, but it was still thinly-populated open space that seemed wild to us. Now, thanks to the national lake-shore real estate boom, our forested enclave is in the midst of looming suburban "CEO homes," many worth hundreds of thousands of dollars.

The south shoreline did indeed change during the mid-1960s like a cautious perennial waiting for the right time to blossom. Until then, unpretentious dwellings sat lonely through the shoreline area until new vacation sanctuaries began to appear. It was during this time that the Wehrweins of Edina, Minnesota, made a call to area realtor Charles Tollander who sent his young son from town to show Austin and Judy Wehrwein a place on North Sand Lake owned by Oscar Lindgren. Within a few days, an offer was made to purchase the property on a lake they had never heard of before.

The abstract provided Austin and Judy Wehrwein a peek into the past when their lot was platted in 1913--when its first owners were Charles and Sylvia Francis. There were others who owned the property in the years that followed and the Wehrweins surmise that the two twin cabins on their newly purchased land were built during the early 1930s.

Sometime during the next 20 years there were other transfers, one being the Five Lakes Club of Wisconsin mentioned by Fred Dhein in **Chatting with the Locals.** By 1947, some of the names had a familiar ring, one being Henry E. Rahn who owned a small cottage on the adjacent shoreline next to the St. Arnault's of Eau Claire. A year later, Rahn sold to Louis and Cora Slock. In 1953 Slocks sold to Charles and Irene Brown and, in 1958 the Browns sold to Oscar and Dorothy Lindgren whose cottage and land was sold to the Wehrweins in 1967. Wehrwein believes that the adjoining property, now owned by the Leopolds, stayed with the Brown family until the Leopolds bought it in 1968.

When Wehrweins took possession and moved their seasonal clothing and toys to the lake, they became aware of a shoreline resort not in operation at the time. They referred to the place as the farm because of two Holstein cows that strayed onto their property one day causing one of their young children to think the cows were deer. When the couple who occupied the farm moved out, the Wehrwein children, on occasion, would play in various structures on the property which today is owned by the Rohde family.

Austin Wehrwein describes his place on the hill as a museum piece. With Tom and Bobbie Leopold as neighbors to the north, and St. Arnaults to the south, and 263 feet of lake frontage wrapping the base of his lake property, Wehrwein assumed his role as new owner by carefully modernizing the place without destroying its antique charm. The fish house, grand-fathered boat house, and two-hole privy for emergencies only were preserved for all the right reasons while the family made other hidden charm discoveries such as the massive logs that served as floor-support beams resting on nail kegs filled with concrete. It most likely was Oscar Lindgren who had added a porch facing the lake and a wing that included a living room, extra bedroom and a bathroom with a tub. Wehrweins replaced the wood stove with a small Franklin stove, installed a new water system, replaced a few windows and added a front deck, but chose not to winterize. Wehrwein readily admits finding a lake of such quality that he had never before heard of ranks as one of the luckiest things the family has experienced.

Countless memories carry Wehrwein offspring, Sven, Paul, Peter and Joanna, back to their own youthful days when they were packed in the back of the family station wagon that carried them to the lake...when youthful experiences were laden with nostalgic cottage-living discoveries of their own. Paul's recorded recollections are similar to many of ours who were fortunate to spend our early days at the lake. Owning a cottage bred family togetherness of a different kind from what occupied our lives in the city. There were wacky moment times all kids laugh about, and the romance of shimmering sunsets, a drop-off teaming with life and late night loon cries that pierced the air. Each made an impression to last until our minds no longer allow such reflections.

Sven was sixteen when his parents bought the cottage. Thoughts of being separated from friends back home were typical teenage concerns, so many of his summers were spent working as a counselor at Camp Echo in Michigan with infrequent cottage visits during high school and college years. Because eight-year-old Joanna was the youngest, it was difficult to keep up with her other brothers, so swimming became her favorite pastime.

That left Peter and Paul. When Peter was barely into the two-digit age, he would wait for the afternoon breeze before packing 7-Up and Oreos and winding downward toward the water's edge to set sail. Being a lake sailor, his early experiences ran the gamut from sheer enjoyment to cracking the mast partner which, in turn, taught him a valuable lesson for future sailing years. Described as the beautiful little red wooden boat, the Penquin comes complete with the greatest of memories that go hand-in-hand with soda and cookies. Along with mastering nautical lingo and when the water level was unusually low, Peter learned how tricky it was to move the Penquin into deeper water without snapping the center-board.

Paul's escapades include swinging on birches growing on the other side of the fence that protected the Deer Farm from the public. Or playing Lewis and Clark by paddling and portaging from their dock to the Yellow River. Or sending smoke bombs through the culvert on log boats. Try riding bikes from home to the lake. There were breakfasts of the simple things in life like waffles served with real maple syrup and ripe blackberries between swamps past birches. And the time a grown up Paul sailed the family Penquin in moonlight breezes with his 76-year-old grandma, an experience that tells tales of a once little boy who had grown up to admit that... "the cottage renews me and helps make my life a pleasure."

The Wehrwein property, so private in its own way, hidden behind the foliage of the trees that surround it, remained a mystery to me all these years only to learn a few summers ago that Wehrwein had spent a portion of his youth in my hometown of Madison when his father was a Professor at the University of Wisconsin. Even today, he refers to Madison as the Athens of the Midwest—a place where he took advantage of the beauty of the lakes that surrounded the liberal charm of the city.

I also learned that at one time Austin Wehrwein worked for the Wisconsin State Journal, Madison's daily morning newspaper that invited me to write a food column back in 1993, an honor I still enjoy.

What a small world it is, right here on North Sand Lake.

Austin and Judy Wehrwein, 2002.

The Old Francis Homestead and the Leopolds

On the same hill next door to Austin and Judy Wehrwein, where Charles and Sylvia Francis homesteaded and farmed a century ago, stands a small structure as a reminder of the past. Shown on the 1915 plat map, it is adjacent to an enormous spread of property across a wetland on the other side that is owned by Glen Thompson.

Described on the abstract as a single woman, A. C. Hoesley purchased the land in 1952 for $1.00. The following year, Miss Hoesley sold the property to Henry Rahn and Louis Slock who later sold it for $2600 to George, Amy and Betty Lou Brown after Rahn and Slock built a small cottage for the Browns. When her parents died, to settle the estate, daughter Mildred Brown Martin decided to sell the property for $7200 and posted a *For Sale* sign at the side of the road.

It was meant to be. Tom and Bobbie Leopold of Cottage Grove, Minnesota just happened to be in the market for lake property. As they drove around the lake, the couple took notice of the road side sign. Deciding to have their 12-year-old daughter, Susan, accompany them when they met with the owner, the Leopolds and the owners settled down to discuss the property with Susan sitting quietly on a nearby couch. Suddenly, Mildred Brown Martin's little dog jumped up on the couch and bit Susan's ankle. Because everyone was visibly shaken by the incident, Mildred, in desperation, tried to make amends. Apologizing, she complimented the Leopolds as to what nice people they were and said that if her mother had been there to see the dog attack Susan, she would have immediately lowered the asking price to $5,000. The offer was too good to refuse, especially after learning that 1968 taxes were only $70.00.

Tom and Bobbie Leopold's cottage built in 1947 by Henry Rahn. "Mein fishing station" is the table at their back door.

The land and its winding wooded four-tenths of a mile driveway off Thompson Road was far more spectacular than anything the Leopolds imagined when their lake search began. However, despite the cost, there were a few drawbacks. The small pine-paneled cottage wasn't winterized and did not have indoor plumbing. To update living conditions, remodeling meant that the tiny front porch would become a temporary bedroom. During evening storms, rain blew through the screens to soak them and their bedding as water dripped through the roof into buckets placed where they were needed.

It was during the long remodeling process when some of the family's most memorable lake experiences occurred. One winter weekend, the Leopolds and their four children arrived from Minnesota for two days of sledding only to discover the sleds had been left home. For makeshift sleds, they tore up pieces of the old linoleum cottage floor. Another time, the lake seemed to freeze instantly creating a clear satin-like surface which allowed an almost mystical view of fish and vegetation through the ice. They remember weekends when the wood stove quit in the middle of the night and the family huddled together to stay warm. And there was the never-to-be forgotten winter day they were returning to the cottage during a snow storm in a car packed with $100 of groceries when heavy snow and high winds designed drifts across Thompson Road that made it impossible to drive any farther. The only logical way of seeking help was to send the youngest child, a little girl who weighed the least, from the car to Kovarik's Resort for help.

The drama of watching a child walk over snow drifts without sinking has never waned, nor has the excitement of seeing help on the way. It remains one of many favorite family stories that began with a sign posted at the side of the road, a naughty little dog, linoleum sleds, and an old leaky-roofed cottage to blossom into Tom and Bobbie Leopold's beautiful retirement home overlooking North Sand Lake.

l-r: Betty Hendrickson, and Tom and Bobbie Leopold, 2002.

Deer Haven Bay Resort

A roller coaster setting of the south shore dips drastically from Leopold's place to spread across another low stretch of wet land before straining upward again to what at one time was land farmed by Charles Francis and his uncle Glen Thompson's uncle Roy Mowry. The barn foundation still serves as a reminder of the farm and its summer seasons before winter froze the lake and travel across the ice meant riding in horse-drawn sleighs. Many years later, when young Jon Bowman became a regular summer visitor on the lake with his parents, he referred to the property as Bauer's Bay. Out-of-town fishermen who stayed there knew it as Deer Haven Bay Resort, a priceless parcel of North Sand Lake wilderness, woods and water owned and operated by Henrietta and Fred Bauer.

Leaving Eau Claire and city life behind, the Bauers had pulled up stakes to settle into a new lifestyle in a two-story lake house where a small store in the lower level supplied their resort guests with an inventory of staples. Set along the edge of the hill with a spectacular view of the lake, four tiny one-room cabins, each with a screened porch, were lined up a short distance from the Bauer's house. Once owned by the Five Lakes Club for the benefit of members in search of north woods fishing, the parcel now could be described as a 97-acre parcel allowing Bauer's cow, referred to by the neighbors as Wood Cow, to graze in the field behind the house and cabin. Many times, Wood Cow was seen walking along the shoreline that connected nearby properties.

When the water level receded, leaving no water or depths in front to fish, the four cabins remained empty. Cancellations and the absence of vacationers placed a financial burden on Bauer's resort and added stress to their marriage. Frustrated by the situation, Henrietta packed her belongings and returned to Eau Claire. Optimistic that conditions would soon return to normal, Fred stayed at the lake, determined to sit out the drought. One day, after his family grew weary of his refusal to leave, they arrived unannounced and removed him from the premises, leaving everything behind as though he had taken a 10 minute walk with every intention of returning.

Tranquility at the uninhabited resort changed when the County Welfare Program unlocked the doors in an attempt to establish living quarters. However, problems began to surface with an unusual number of cars and trucks entering and leaving the property at all hours of the day and night. Rumors trickled throughout the area that the four little cabins with screened porches originally built for fishermen and their families were being rented out by the hour. What went on behind closed doors became an issue of great concern for the neighbors and before long the premises were vacated leaving the house empty once again, this time for about five years.

Henry Rahn and Louis Slock, both familiar names in homesteading that particular area of the lake, were good friends of Gilbert and Lucille Rohde. Rahn informed

Deer Haven Bay Resort owner's home. Property purchased in 1985 by Gary and Helen Rohde. House burned down Jan. 4, 1999.

Deer Haven Bay Resort Cabins, 1995.

them that the old resort was going to be sold. By that time, the house and cabins were in poor condition having become a popular party spot, especially during the late evening hours. Well aware of the prime location and acreage, the Rohde's discussed purchasing the property with their son, Gary, and his wife, Helen. In October, 1970, the property that once achieved recognition as one of North Sand Lake's seven resorts became a private family domain.

The resort left much to the imagination. Abandoned, the home and cabins had been vandalized by partygoers with one cabin reduced to nothing more than a pile of rubble. Every window on the premises was broken. Paint had been poured down drains, and ceilings were caving in. During the first summer of 1971, the Rohde family used campers as living quarters, relying on an outhouse as their privy. All the necessary fixing and remodeling tasks were handled by family members. When work on the cabins was completed, the family started on the house which would take three summers to finish. In 1974, 12,000 Norway pines were planted in the field where Henrietta's cow once grazed. Before winter arrived 90 percent of the seedlings had taken hold.

Another property transaction took place in 1985 when Rahn, knowing how much the land meant to the Rohde family, plus being assured that the land would remain relatively untouched by future development, sold them an additional 40 acres for a grand total of 137 acres which included 900 feet of shoreline. With each subsequent summer, Gary and Helen and their three sons were rewarded with the fruits of their labor and good fortune. They fished in the summer, hunted during fall, and took advantage of snowmobile trails on beautiful winter weekends.

Ten years later, in 1995, Gilbert and Lucille Rohde sold their interest in the property to Gary and Helen's two oldest sons and daughters-in-law, Dean and Laurie, and Doug and Pam. The Rohde family paradise ended during a brutally cold January 4, 1999 when the temperature dipped to 15 below zero with winds plummeting to a wind chill factor of 40 below. At 5:30 a.m., the furnace exploded sending six people out in the cold. Minutes later, the home was filled with smoke and burned to the ground. Although three volunteer fire trucks answered the call, everything the men needed to fight the fire continued to freeze due to the extreme sub-zero temperatures. Because keys to the cars parked next to the home were lost in jackets left inside, the volunteer firemen had to physically move the cars to prevent the gas tanks from exploding. The aftermath of the life-threatening episode made everyone realize the fragility of life and the security of the house on the lake they took for granted.

The winter nightmare was replaced the following spring with serious discussions of rebuilding. With mutual agreements, enthusiasm and well-planned blue prints including three separate suites, one great room and a pine kitchen to accommodate 20 people, the barren hill was complemented with a magnificent home of logs and stone to take advantage of the shoreline property and its unsurpassed view.

Only the small barn out back remains a remnant of the past, but the field beyond where cows once grazed has become a healthy growth of Norway pines which are being trimmed. In front, looking out to the lake, sand castles appear during the summer months, built by a new generation of Rohde children.

Welcoming the year 2000 meant erasing all reminders of the past except, of course, for the colorful history of Deer Haven Bay Resort and its aftermath which will remain a topic of conversation for many years to come.

Ernest Lieberson on the wood steps at the cottage around 1947 with daughter, Betty, and her cousin, Judy Howald, Ernest's niece, on the left.

Pagano's Place

High on a hill surrounded by stately 60-year-old pine trees overseeing its 200 feet of southeast shoreline sits a small cottage once used by rum runners back in the 1920s. Raided occasionally by Federal Agents when the runners raced for the shoreline and escaped in boats is Betty Pagano's place, oozing with history of the gangster era and the furniture they left behind.

Call it a cabin or a cottage, the place immediately takes one back to a pristine period on the lake we tend to wish would return, if only for a day. With inexpensive second hand full length wood doors installed as walls, the interior is a reflection of an era replaced with modern conveniences. Stepping through the back door you'll find yourself in a small, but convenient kitchen of dark wood. Next to the sink on a wood counter are four marks where the water pump had been tightly secured with four screws. The floor is covered with the original linoleum, ivory with black and red geometric design, yet another reflection of kitchen floors in the 1940s.

Directly off the kitchen is a tiny version of today's great room except that it offers all the charm and even more of what oftentimes is missing from today's elaborate floor plans. A narrow room with a high arched ceiling, narrow beams and a floor to ceiling stone fireplace sports a deer head with a rack and a 1942 tag still attached. North woods charm continues to seep into the adjacent room complemented with unusual size square window panes that wrap around its three sides for a breathtaking view of the lake. Though old, rocking chairs made from slim tree trunks, branches and wicker, look new. Covering part of the original oak and maple floors are handsome old porch rugs with Native American designs woven with slender strips of colored cardboard. It is home to Betty Pagano and in some respects, a museum piece to cherish.

Betty's parents, Ernest and Evelyn Lieberson, taught school in Chicago. How ironic that one of Ernest's students was Warren Hansen, son of Barney and Florence Hansen who would eventually establish Hansen's Resort on the lake's north shoreline. Ernest was introduced to the North Sand Lake area by his colleagues, teachers Ed Hall and Dick Luhman. Hall had a place on Small Bass Lake near Lake McKenzie, and Luhman owned property on Big Bass Lake. One summer day, the three vacationing teachers left Chicago behind and headed to northwestern Wisconsin. While fishing North Sand Lake, a man appeared on the shoreline and called out to them, asking if they were interested in buying the land. Also offered was the empty lot next door for an extra $50.00. Interested only in the little cottage high on the hill, Lieberson declined the offer. By the following year, Glen Thompson had built a cottage for his wife's sister, fondly referred to as "Aunt Ruth" on the choice vacant point that swept down the hill to the water's edge.

Ernest and Evelyn Pagano were excited to have their own place that allowed full summer vacations as a peaceful place far removed from their home in Chicago. Their only daughter, Betty, would grow up in what she referred to as her own little world with summer friends, Carol and Lynda Thompson. She collected agates found along the shoreline, rowed to the point directly across from their cottage to have picnics by herself, and also became her father's fishing companion. There were mornings when she'd wake up earlier than her father and go out in the boat to fish alone. With great fondness, she remembers watching her father return from fishing in his 22 foot wooden boat, low in the water where he sat, with the front of the boat pointed high in the air. She also remembers that bass was the most popular fish on the lake back then and would remain so until northern pike took over. Whatever the catch, to prevent a lingering smell in the cottage, they'd fry the fish in a heavy cast iron pan out back in the garage—the garage where poured cement cracked years before from the weight of the rum runners heavily laden trucks.

Relatives visited during the summer months and cots and folded beds were opened to accommodate company. When summer was ending and it was time to think about closing for another year, wood shutters made to tightly cover all windows and doors were locked in place to prevent break-ins in their absence.

Looking back, Betty also remembers the annual summer storm that came out of the west and caused havoc with their small cottage vulnerably situated along the edge of the hill. When the cottage was first built, measurements were not as accurate as they should have been. Today, if you lay a marble on the floor, it still rolls in one direction. Due to a few other mistakes, the cottage never handled extreme wind and heavy rain as expected.

Those problems were considered to be miniscule as Ernest Lieberson, an inductee of the Basketball Referees Hall of Fame, thoroughly enjoyed, with his wife and daughter, each summer spent on North Sand Lake in a quaint cottage in the land of privacy overlooking a lake that would reward him with years of vacations and fishing thrills. His family is now well into its fourth generation with Betty's daughter, Deb and her four children visiting on occasion.

Urban George Willis with grandsons, Bill and George Caruso

The Summer of '32

It was a long way from Maine to Wisconsin, yet the distance became a mere stepping stone for Urban George Willis that would pave a path to the northwest corner of Wisconsin.

In 1895, when Pittsfield, Maine native Urban George Willis graduated from Bates College and married Amy Dunham Rodick who graduated the same year from finishing school in Bar Harbor, the newlyweds, who will be referred to in this chapter as UGW and ADRW, or "Nana," traveled to Chicago where Willis obtained a job as a teacher. Years later, after hearing social contacts at the University of Chicago speak of Kilkare Lodge on Birch Island Lake in Burnett County in Wisconsin, UGW and ADRW decided to leave behind the summer heat of the metropolis and head north. With descriptions of crystal clear blue waters and lush green forests sounding similar to Maine and its Moosehead Lake that UGW loved as a youngster, the intrigue captured an unforgettable adventure. As time went on and the family grew, thoughts were recorded by Amy Dunham Rodick Willis in a brand new diary which since has become a family treasure.

"Nana and Daddy stayed at the clubhouse or in one of the rental cottages while looking for land, eventually finding property on North Sand Lake where they purchased land from Glen Thompson in 1938." Dorothy Caruso

Summer, 1932

Sunday night we drove along the one way road to Kilkare Lodge. Here we came to comfort, choice people, beautiful expensive cabins—all attributes of a country club made up of city people, on vacation in the north woods. We stayed here for more than a week—fishing better than we found before—good bathing—plenty of lakes—deer were seen at times, in fact, this location seemed more to our liking than anything we had seen. We lounged about the Lodge more than ever before. We sat under the trees, chatting—we played contract (bridge)—we used up a good deal of time, getting ready for meals and reporting for them three times a day.

There were picnics and rides—one day was spent with a guide on Sand Lake. It was here that we came across our camp site. We learned that Sand Lake was the best lake in the Section, that it was deep while many lakes looked as if they were drying up. Sandy beaches were almost all the way around the lake. Yet the shores were high in places and wooded. There were fish, some big ones. As yet there were not many cottages along the shores—this seemed worth further investigation. As soon as breakfast the next day, we drove along Sand Lake. The owner of the land along the shore we were interested in was in his front yard. He gave us permission to prowl about. Our fondest hopes were fulfilled. We selected our spot, then returned to see the owner and talked business. Such fun! A survey was made with the object of planning the lots to allow us the location we wanted. Business was carried on. A trip to Webster to the lumber company results in a call from two enthusiastic young men who helped us with cottage plans.

The Willis Summer Cottage was built by the Webster Lumber Company in 1933. When it was completed, Amy Dunham Rodick Willis and Urban George Willis furnished the cottage and prepared it for the rest of the family to enjoy. In 1936, Amy, or Nana, as she was called by her grandchildren, UGW, their only child, daughter Dorothy Willis Caruso, her husband Felix Caruso, two grandchildren, Ida Jane Caruso and Felix Willis Caruso (now F. Willis or "Bill") along with the maid and baby sitter Elsie, enjoyed their vacation together at the cottage on North Sand Lake.

When the family gathered together again in 1937, the third grandchild, George Rodick Caruso, was in tow. It was during this very hot summer when temperatures soared to over 100 degrees for ten consecutive days that prompted plans to add a front porch where the family could cool off throughout the day and evening from lake breezes. Unfortunately, at the time, the cozy green and white cottage could sleep only three people: Nana, UGW and Ida Jane. The rest of the family retired each evening on real army cots in a white army command tent. Hard, collapsible, and often collapsing, the cots offered a true flavor of camping making it even more exciting during thunderstorms.

Each summer the family visited together at the lake, except for the years UGW suffered serious attacks of poison ivy that kept him in Chicago. Otherwise, during the 30s, 40s, and 50s, he would drive the long distance, always in a new Buick, while Felix Caruso arrived on weekends for a few days, or a full week, transported to Spooner on Northwestern Railroad's Fisherman's Special.

From the very beginning, UGW and Nana insisted the cottage be rustic. Convinced motors were bad for the lake, all fishing was done in a Shell Lake rowboat equipped with two sets of oars. Although there were weeks on end when no one else appeared on the lake, things would change after World War II when the privacy UGW and Nana loved and respected began to disappear.

The original Willis cottage.

In the late 1930s or early 1940s, Glen Thompson built a fourth cabin to the north of the Willis cottage. Thompson also sold a piece of land to the south of the Willis cottage where a cabin was built. The owner was seldom there and kept very much to himself. When he died, Ernest Lieberson purchased the cabin.

As a teacher from Chicago, Ernest Lieberson spent summers at his place next door. He was a good friend of the Willis family and set aside days for fishing and canoe trips with Willis's grandsons, Bill and George Caruso. When the lake was high, it was easy to portage from North Sand Lake to Mallard and Green lakes to fish. There were also trips on the Yellow and Namekagon rivers, the Namekagon being a white water river that offered many challenges to shoot the rapids in a canoe.

Summers at the lake meant everything to the Willis and Caruso families. Bill remembers the first visit in 1936 and the many summers spent hiking and picnicking on the empty beaches of the lake. The year 1945 also stands out in his mind for it was during their return home trip to Chicago an announcement was heard on the car radio that the war had ended. They stayed in Rice Lake the night of VJ Day and people partied all night long.

Through the years, family togetherness continued at the lake. In the early 1950s, Nana died, and in 1956 UGW passed away. Deciding that it was time to modernize the family cottage, Felix had the electric system connected, brought in running water, and added a back porch. Additional land purchased from Glen Thompson allowed

Top: Bill Caruso with a nice bass, 1946.

Bottom: George Rodick Caruso at the pump, 1942.

Felix and Dorothy to enlarge the cottage and make more room for the children and grandchildren. A tub and shower were added, plus a shed so visitors could sleep with a real roof overhead instead of white tent canvas.

When Dorothy Caruso died in 1986, and Felix passed on in 1996, another chapter of North Sand Lake history ended and pages were turned. Because some of the third generation lived in different parts of the country, Ida being on the East Coast and George moving to Arizona, Bill Caruso and his wife, Barbara received the cottage and land to continue the family tradition of spending summers at the lake. In 1997, while preserving the humble cottage UGW built and Felix and Dorothy modernized, Bill and Barbara built a new lake home next door.

Five generations of family have enjoyed the little white and green Willis Summer Cottage and respected the property that Urban George Willis and Amy Dunham Rodick Willis purchased from Glen Thompson back in 1932. Bill and Barbara Caruso and their children, Marguerite Rae, F. Willis, Jr., John Gar, Tom Henry and Jeanne Louise each have countless memories to enrich their lives along with other family members and those of their spouses and children.

A 2001 summer reunion was held at the lake with many in attendance to celebrate the past and present while remembering UGW and ADRW's summer of 1932.

Above: Felix Caruso, September, 1971.

Right: Dorothy Caruso, September, 1971.

Thompson Territory

Immediately beyond the Rohde property, you'll enter Thompson Bay. Waiting to greet you is seclusion within a somewhat hidden man-made bay referred to for years as back bay. It wasn't always like this, however. As a refuge for wildlife, the low marshy area offered growing conditions perfect for cranberry-bearing evergreen plants. Dredged in 1960 by James Stuart Thompson, known by all as Stuart, or more affectionately, "Stu," the back bay project provided additional choices for people in search of lake property. Highly controversial, the scooping of the marsh caused many heated arguments in the area. Although Thompson ran a fence across the opening to the bay to prevent bogs and other debris from floating freely into the lake during the dredging process, the fence was removed late one evening by one or more disgruntled individuals and by daybreak, property owners woke to find a mess washed up on their south shorelines. Today, the bay is entered through a no-wake zone to create a peaceful location for loons and their nests as well as the people who live there.

Thompson Road, named to remember Stuart's father, Glen Thompson, turns south from County Highway A and meanders through open fields and heavily wooded lake property Glen owned and homesteaded. That was back in 1910 when Thompson received a Land Grant for 160 acres on the east side of the lake. To comply with government regulations, he built a one-room cabin.

Described as a gentle-natured man, Glen Thompson was a true entrepreneur in every sense who pursued a variety of opportunities. To help farmers near and far, Thompson owned and operated a steam-reaper. His saw mills were the first in the area and operated out of a small self-built cabin. During this time, Glen met and married Molly McDill of Oberlin, Ohio, and in 1918 their son, James Stuart was born. In 1919, with the help of his Uncle Roy Mowry, Glen built a large two-story family home.

Thompson's Resort and home.

Glen Thompson's mind seldom rested. Along with farming, and gathering cranberries from bushes in the back bay, plus other activities, he also owned a touring boat with side seats that offered comfort for visitors viewing the expanse of the lake. It probably was no surprise to those who knew him that simmering in the back of his mind were plans for a resort. Thompson's large home had become a haven for fishermen from Wisconsin, Illinois, Indiana, Minnesota and other neighboring states. Ever anxious to test the waters of a lake quickly establishing a reputation for good fishing, the fishermen's return each year simply confirmed what Glen already suspected. Further proof of the impact of his own resort was reconfirmed at the end of each day when fishermen docked their boats and carried their catches up the hill to tie to a tree before cleaning chores began. During the early 1930s, Glen's sawmills buzzed as logs were cut to build four cabins on his property. The last one, built by Glen's teenage son, Stuart, was called The Honeymoon cabin.

When Thompson Resort opened in the early 1930s, it came equipped with the enticement of the American Plan. Guests had the privacy of their own cabins, but were fed in the big house on a four-season, glassed-in porch. For $3.00 a day per guest, room and board meant a place to sleep, three family-style meals a day, and a boat. Fishing guides Ollie Taylor and Pete Augustine were in demand in the area, as well as on North Sand Lake and Stuart Thompson decided to join the ranks. Providing a resort with a magnificent body of water made visitors want to stay forever. Year after year, the anticipation of each spring melded with the onset of the daily duties required to run such an operation until the Thompson's discontinued the American Plan and converted the resort to housekeeping cabins.

Many things happened through the years on the vast shoreline acreage owned by Glen Thompson and much of it would eventually involve a young woman by the name of Berniece Keefe. As the daughter of a B & O railroad man who traveled where the company sent him, Berniece grew weary of the number of schools she had attended in Indiana, Ohio and Pennsylvania. Life slowed to a normal pace when they reached family-owned property on the Clam River in Burnett County in Wisconsin. As a new student at Webster High School, Berniece met Stuart Thompson. After graduating, she pursued her dream to become an elementary school teacher and attended a State Teachers' College where she received her degree to teach grades 1 through 8 in rural schools. Many years later, she retired as a Webster junior high school teacher.

The old cliché, like father, like son, pretty much describes Stuart Thompson. He, too, liked to make things happen, one venture being owner of a mink farm. However, his innate enthusiasm for what the location offered began much earlier when he set muskrat traps on the lake. Stuart and Berniece were courting then and, when checking the traps, the two would ice skate from trap to trap. After they were married, a major portion of the property, specifically where Gary and Helen Rohde reside today, would be theirs to enjoy, followed by everything else through the woods and along the shoreline toward Bartelt's Resort, and Kovarik's Resort, more recently known as the Brown Jug before Lakeview Lodge Inn and, today, a private residence. Across Thompson Road from the property was a vast section of land owned by Orrin Thompson (no relative) and his son, Gary. With plans some thought to be somewhat grandiose, Orrin and Gary hired Stuart Thompson to install a fence along the road to prevent deer from escaping from a large lodge they planned to build, complete with a deer farm where guests could hunt white-tail deer. Although individuals continue today to serve as caretakers of the property, the hunting lodge and its promises were scrapped long ago.

Stuart and Berniece helped Glen and Molly run the resort. However, when Stuart's expertise involving major national ironwork projects sent him into the northern part of the country, Berniece and their daughters, Carol and Lynda, traveled cross-country with him. It was during these trips that Berniece played games with the girls about the states, their capitols, what each was noted for with other geographical trivia. Upon completion of each job, the family would pack up and head back to their lake home in Wisconsin.

People came by car during the resort era, but during World War II gas was rationed and many vacationers took to the rails. Jack and Birdie Bowman first visited Thompson's Resort in 1944 by traveling from Chicago on a trip that seemed to take forever. Back then, when one traveled by train, one was expected to dress in proper attire. Thus the Bowman family traveled the distance wearing clothes not necessarily conducive to comfort. When they finally arrived at the depot in Spooner, Jack, Birdie, and their sons, Jon, Kent and Brent, sighed in relief as they stepped from the train to hear last names called out by resort owners interspersed through the crowd, waiting to drive their guests to vacation destinations. After every name had been called but theirs, they watched as Glen Thompson strolled up and said with a smile, "You must be the Bowmans." Relieved at being claimed, the

Bowmans shook hands with Thompson, shared greetings, piled in the car, and headed to the lake leaving a cloud of sand and gravel dust behind them for another journey, this time a mere 25 miles. When the war ended, and rationing became history, trips to the lake for the Bowmans were made in the family car. Still a lengthy time-consuming 450 miles, the family didn't seem to mind as much providing the clothes they wore were comfortable.

Glen Thompson

Although walleyes were non-existent, not being natural to the lake, Jon Bowman remembers the abundance of northern pike, largemouth bass, crappies and other panfish. The daily limit was seven bass and seven northern pike. Jon's days of fishing the lake as a youngster parallel mine and his stories are endless treasures of fishing adventures through the years. It's too bad we didn't know each other back then to combine our knowledge of when and where and how to fish as fishing along the Thompson Bay shoreline was an area I seldom explored as a youngster. By the time I could operate a motor, I had already established my own favorite spots. Jon's many fond memories include the old red army siren Glen Thompson used each day to alert resort guests who were out fishing that meals were about to be served. The noise of the siren was so shrill that all the youngsters in the immediate area argued each day over whose turn it was to wind it and for what meal.

Stuart Thompson and his northern pike. Looking on is Charles Francis, Glen Thompson's nephew.

The Bowman family stayed at Thompson's Resort every summer until 1957 when they purchased Stuart and Berniece Thompson's first home. Today the Bowman name is synonymous with others who have established lake seniority with special memories attached to each year. Well into

Thompson Resort cabin

their third generation on the lake, Jon Bowman and his wife, Rosemary, purchased in 1979 property adjacent to the Thompson home that his parents owned, and amid what impressed him as a youngster. Planning for the future, the Bowmans gave much thought to the design and construction of their retirement home. Its extraordinary beauty is complemented by a wrap-around deck and gazebo-in-the-sky. The Lake Tahoe pitch of Thompson's woods allows family and their guests to ride seats on an electrical steel lift that carries them down to the shoreline and back up without straining a single muscle. As a young boy, Jon had not a care in the world when his family vacationed on Thompson territory. Today as a retired psychologist and permanent resident of the lake, Jon plays a vital role in the health of the community as well as the rehabilitation of Siren residents in the aftermath of the tornado that destroyed a portion of the town in June, 2001.

Proof that wild animals visit often is evident in one framed picture in Jon and Rosemary's home that was snapped inside looking out at a black bear clinging to a tree trunk within reach of the deck railing. In the backyard, a scene from yesterday graces their property with a small dwelling built years ago as a garage by Stuart Thompson. Remodeled into a cabin by Percy and Adline Seinko in the 1950s, with additional renovations through the years, the one-time garage today is a charming cozy retreat that serves as a guest home for Jon and Rosemary's visiting friends and family. The lovely large Thompson home, filled with chapters of a past that could fill volumes is owned by Berniece Thompson's grand niece through marriage, Pat Ries Hernandez, who resides there with her husband, Fritz.

After Molly died, Glen attempted to operate Thompson's Resort by himself. With help from Berniece and her daughter, every waking hour seemed to be spent in the kitchen preparing food and baking bread. Most of the resort guests stayed a single week which allowed a repeat menu week after week without boredom for their guests. When the era ended for Thompson, one by one, the cabins were sold. His nephew, Clarence Francis and his wife, Mary, purchased one of the cabins in 1965. For the next three years, the couple were persistent in having Glen stay with

A lake view from the top.

them. It was during this time that Glen shared his remembrances of the early days. He told them how he and his Uncle Roy Mowry ice fished for northern pike and traded the frozen fish in town for beef. He described the building of his two-story house and of the trips to Spooner and Webster and how important it was to keep an ax in the car because trees often fell across the roads during storms and needed to be chopped and removed before travel was continued. He also remembered in great detail the northern pike that surfaced near his boat one day that was so large it almost seemed to be the length of his boat. Although an undeniable metamorphosis has taken place on North Sand Lake since 1910 when Glen Thompson began to homestead there, memories of him being a man of integrity, insight and kindness have never changed since his death in 1968.

About ten years ago, an elderly woman stopped by to revisit the Thompson property where her family vacationed in the late 1920s and early 1930s. After driving the long distance from Indiana, she recalled meeting Glen Thompson through a friend in Spooner. On another occasion the woman arrived with a female travel companion to stay with Molly and Glen. The next day the two friends rowed a wooden boat out on the lake. When night fell, they became lost. Catching glimpses of a light moving back and forth, the girls followed it to discover Glen on the shoreline swinging a lantern, hoping to guide them back to shore. She remembered, with poignant memories, a pristine lake and virgin forest surrounding it.

Before reaching Thompson's Resort, at a point of open water just past Thompson Bay, is a bend that sits on a shallow sandy swimming area. It is a picture perfect scene one might find in any magazine featuring cabin life in the north woods. Although in the past the cottage was painted red, today its gray color blends nicely with stems, branches, tree trunks and foliage surrounding it. A few years ago, Betty Hendrickson informed me that the dwelling on the eastern point was referred to as "Aunt Ruth's" cottage. Mollie Thompson's sister, Ruth, bought the point from Glen where she and another teacher friend, Edna Krick, had a cottage built there.

Mr. Bannit, a guest at Molly & Glen Thompson's resort, helping Birdie Bowman hold her fish.

Betty and Bert Hendrickson used to drive from their home in Eau Claire to visit the St. Arnaults, their Eau Claire friends whose cottage was on a flat shoreline strip prior to the elevation of the Wehrwein-Leopold property near Rohde's. Although the cold, windy, rainy weather during the 1963 Labor Day produced a miserable weekend, Bert and Betty still wanted to own property on the lake. In 1964, they became owners of the Thompson cottage on the east point. Lots of repairs were necessary—screens, roof, and much more--but the $4000 asking price was almost too good to be true.

Once Betty Hendrickson settled in as a lake property owner, she became fascinated with stories of the past shared by those who remembered the drought decades earlier when the lake level receded so drastically that shorelines seemed to expand by the day. On weekends, sandy beaches were often blanketed with Prince Albert tents, pitched by people who planned to spend a few days on the lakeshore. Cows also benefited from the low water levels as they walked back and forth across the exposed sand bar between the east and west point to graze, a situation that forced Glen Thompson to install a confining fence with posts, many of which today still remain in the lake.

I remember rowing as a youngster one July afternoon with nary a breeze to ripple the surface and distort the view of the shallowness below me when I noticed a strip of sand under the boat, between the points. I had never seen it before and have never seen it since then. Today, I wonder if it was the same area where the cows walked. I remember questioning the depth and wondering how the water could be so shallow there with a pure sand bottom and no weeds. Tempting as it was to slip over the side of the boat for the experience of swimming there, I opted not to and instead hung my head over the side to study the shallow water and blue gills that swam by.

Through the years, Betty Hendrickson made discoveries of her own. One day she watched an eagle swoop down to grab something from the water that was too heavy to lift. Forced to remain in the water instead of flying away, the eagle used his powerful wings like oars in a forward motion to reach the shoreline where he dragged whatever it was from the water, then picked away at a well-earned feast. Hendrickson also is very familiar with the red stones, or Lake Superior Agates, found along her shoreline.

In 1982, Glen Thompson's son, Stuart, Berniece's husband, died from a cancer that began early in their marriage when he worked around asbestos in the ship yards. Today, Berniece, in every sense, is the North Sand Lake matriarch. Reflecting on the past, Berniece recalled Stan and Jean Bulka who built a cottage on one of Thompson Bay lots. Stan loved the property and purchased a pontoon that would provide many enjoyable trips touring the lake. The pontoon was properly named...Thompson's Navy.

Birdie Bowman's catch of the day, sometime after they bought their place in 1957.

Note: To erase any confusion that may occur beginning with Pagano's Place, Betty and Bert Hendrickson own the gray cottage on the east point that was built yers before for "Aunt Ruth." The flat land supporting the cottages stretches up the hill to Pagano's place and to Caruso's and the Willis Summer Cottage before blending into Thompson Resort property and the Bowmans.

Bernice Thompson

Jon & Rosemary Bowman at their guest house, 2000.

Emma Bartelt and me, with four unidentified children, 1955.

The Last Resort

Emma Bartelt, a peach and a firecracker of a woman, was small in stature, always smiling, yet spirited enough to own and operate a resort. Just around the bend from the stately Tahoe-like stretch of Thompson property lies a beautiful sandy beach that once framed a rather unpretentious resort. Void of small structures lined up on the shoreline in single file, Bartelt's Resort sported small white cottages zig-zagging a path from the water's edge to the woodsy park-like setting, each in view of Mrs. Bartelt's home. Although a few were partially hidden from the lake, all four cottages had lake access in a nice cozy half-moon setting that looked straight out to the deepest section of the entire lake. Two hundred feet southeast of Kovarik's Resort (later The Brown Jug, Lakeview Inn, and Lakeview Lodge), Emma's resort had humble beginnings. The first cottage was converted from a garage, while the second one is thought to have been a chicken coop. At one time, blocks of ice cut from the lake during the winter months were stored in one of the structures in preparation for the warm months of summer.

As with the other six resorts on the lake, the same vacationers returned year after year, making each summer a reunion of seasonal friends with a few new ones added to the list. In 1965, Emma Bartelt sold the resort to Illinois residents "Shorty" and Marie Edwards who changed the name from Bartlelt's Resort to Our Place. A tea kettle came with each cottage and the old outhouse remained "out back" just in case there was an occasional indoor plumbing problem.

The resort is where the Barut family from Illinois would eventually stay. In the beginning, Bob Barut remembered stories his grandfather had heard about

Marie Barut with a stringer of blue gills and "sunnies."

Bob Barut, center, sister Wendy, upper left; Sister Julianne, upper center; Mike Burdick, lower right; brother Mitch behind him; brother Kent, lower left; fall, 1969.

Bob Barut and his dad, 1969.

catching "big northern pike in a crystal clear lake in northern Wisconsin." The Barut family decided to head north to investigate North Sand Lake and stayed at Hansen's Resort along the north shoreline which backed up to County Road A. As soon as they arrived and looked into the water from the end of the resort's long main pier, they saw the bottom, just as grandpa promised. Bob was four-years-old then and remembers the deep clear water at the end of the pier as being scary. He also remembers the good times he had playing on the resort's sandy beach, the nickel he tried so hard to pick up in the bar only to learn that it had been nailed to the floor, and the ride he was given in Warren Hansen's Chris Craft as big as a car with a throaty rumbling sound. And owner Barney Hansen's private club, Barney's Blarney Bunch, when guests who were initiated into the club had to kiss the Blarney stone. Barut claims that his now deceased grandmother, Marie, who was initiated the evening of July 21, 1961, never forgot the experience and enjoyed telling about it through the years to friends and family.

The brief number of Barut summer vacations at Hansen's were filled with great nostalgia for the youngster. When the resort closed at the end of the 1964 season, and each cottage was sold to individual buyers, the family searched for another place to stay. Wanting to remain on the same lake, they drove over to Our Place and became regular summer guests there.

Marie and Shorty Edwards, 1969.

Pat and Lucy with children Rebecca, Sarah and Aaron, 1971.

Pat Basler and 36 inch northern pike.

Enter Pat and Lucy Basler who had dedicated themselves to an international volunteer service in the Orient. During their seven year service involvement from 1963 to 1970, they met and married and three of their four children, Rebeccah, Sarah and Aaron, were born. When the Baslers returned home, Pat taught school in Bloomer for one year before moving to Webster to teach in their school system where Lucy would also teach. In 1971, both were convinced that owning a resort on a nearby lake would be a nice change of scenery so they bought Our Place, retained its name, continued to teach during the day, and ran the resort in the evenings, on weekends, and during the summer months. When the Baslers hired someone to have Emma Bartelt's house lifted to add a basement underneath, it was evident that seven other structural additions had been made through the years. They also discovered that the original foundation was made up of logs, still in excellent condition.

In 1977, a fourth child, a son, Adam, was born. Although Pat and Lucy had great times during their tenure as resort owners, they made a decision in 1983 to sell the beautiful 12 acre lakeshore property. Totally void of any serious real estate activity at the time, the land was divided into separate parcels, some being sold to those who at times occupied the cottages as vacationers, like Bob Barut and his father who purchased one of the parcels and built their own place in 1988. Thus, the final chapter of the North Sand Lake resort era ended.

Most resort owners sell and move on. Not so with the Baslers. Loving the land as they did, they decided to stay. Today, Pat and Lucy Basler remain on the property that rewarded them with many years of special times. Residing in a dome-shaped home christened Athani House I, they are set back from the lake, yet surrounded by the beauty of colorful and productive flower and vegetable gardens touched by sun filtering through the leaves of full-grown trees. And there's more. The Baslers also have provided a spiritually unique experience for others in a quiet place called *Sacred Grove* where you can sit and rest a spell while collecting your thoughts. All you need to do is walk in because *Sacred Grove* is in the woods and welcomes you at any time.

Sacred Grove
Come ...
walk the labyrinth.
sit and enjoy the old trees.
hike the ridge.
explore the paths
throughout the Sacred Grove.
If you
want to know
God
better,
you should
take a walk with
God -
- a 4 year old

Hidden from Thompson Road is a labyrinth where one can walk within a circular rock-lined path measuring one-third of a mile from beginning to end. The labyrinth was built by the Baslers as a path of prayer--where one can be alone to meditate and make a connection with God. When your walk is completed, you can rest on one of the nearby benches. A short distance away, and within view among the Jack Pine forest, is a small newly-built, one-room structure, appropriately named Athani House II. Although there is no electricity or water on the premises, it is a perfect place to spend time absorbing the beauty of the woods and the solitude of nature. A stone's throw from the Athani House II is a modern outhouse complete with a tiny double-hung window and two skylights allowing the outside to slide in. To spend a weekend or overnight at Athani House II, alone or with another, reservations are required and donations, accepted. From the excitement and activity of North Sand Lake, to the peacefulness hidden beyond and tucked deep into the woods, this place promises to rest your soul. For more information, call Pat or Lucy Basler at (715) 866-7798, write to them at 3437 Chenoweth Drive, Webster, WI 54893, or contact them, via e-mail, at lucynpat@sirentel.net.

Witt's and Kovarik's Resorts

Sign on Thompson Road

Located just north of Bartelt's Resort was Witt's Resort, the two being separated by a spread of sand with some rocks to sugar-like sand. As with many resort proprietors at the time, Mr. and Mrs. Witt resided in Illinois before heading to the north woods of Wisconsin where they quickly transformed themselves as locals. Their resort with six cottages, heated by wood stoves, allowed their guests to cook on three-burner, counter-style stoves. Out in back was a single outhouse—one side for men, the other side for women. New and returning guests were eagerly awaited each summer by the Witts until Emma Witt became a widow and the work load of operating a resort became overwhelming. After much thought, a decision was made to keep the resort open only to help those who happened to stop by in search of a place on the lake to rent for a week or two. Emma was happy to oblige.

Before long, Emma realized that she no longer wanted to remain on the lake by herself. The 69 acre parcel extending from the lake to Thompson Road and across to Pine Lake, six cabins and a large lake home were put up for sale.

Moving day for the resort's new owners Joe and Sylvia Kovarik and their five-year-old daughter, Judy, was mixed with emotion and excitement Sylvia will never forget. It was October, 1958, and the area was ablaze with beautiful and comforting autumn colors. Suddenly, the temperature dropped and snow fell, carpeting everything. Was it an omen or a lesson that weather in northwestern Wisconsin is forever fickle and prone to surprises? Making the best of an unexpected weather change, the move was finally completed. Yet other adjustments were necessary. Although they had the modern convenience of indoor plumbing, the house was heated by a large wood-burning furnace. Unlike anything they faced in their home back in Illinois, the following year they treated themselves by installing a gas furnace in the house and added gas heaters in each of the cabins.

Joe Kovarik's first year running Kovarik's Lakeview Resort was hit-and-miss. Emma Witt left behind no list of previous renters which forced Kovarik to rely on people who stopped by at random. Their new friends, Barney and Flo Hansen who owned Hansen's Resort on the north shore, sent the overflow of vacationers without reservations to fill Kovarik's vacancies. After business caught on at Kovarik's Resort, apartment size gas stoves and inside toilets were installed for added comfort in each cabin. Too busy to fish, Kovarik made another major change by adding 40 feet

Joe, Judy and Sylvia Kovarik

Two of Kovarik's six cottages with their home on the far right (formerly the Brown Jug and Lakeview Inn).

to the lake front portion of his home. Included was a bar and fireplace to create a gathering place for their guests and local people who stopped by for light refreshments and fellowship. Fishing contests were held in the winter and, because Kovarik was a musician in his own right, arrangements were made for jam sessions featuring local musicians during the spring months.

Much more of the unexpected would occur besides the heavy October snow they encountered in 1958 when ten years later Joe Kovarik was returning late one evening from performing as a drummer with a local group. His car struck a deer and went into a ditch. At 6 a.m. someone drove by and called for help. Joe Kovarik died at 2 p.m. that afternoon. Once again, the burden of a widow owning and operating a resort repeated itself. Sylvia Kovarik sold the cabins to individuals, but kept the bar open until the following year. In 1970, the Kovarik home and bar was sold to Richard and Pat Brown and what was left of Kovarik's Lakeview Resort became The Brown Jug.

Judy Kovarik, 5, with big large-mouth bass.

Several other owners entered the picture after Rich and Pat Brown sold their popular place and today, after extensive and expensive remodeling as Lakeview Lodge, the structure was purchased again, this time as a private residence. In the interim, an attempt was made to turn the woods behind the resort into a campsite. Although all of the full grown trees were prematurely cut down, due to great concern shared by lake property owners, and after many meetings with attorneys and county and township boards, the plan was vetoed. Restrictions made years ago to prevent campers and trailers from parking on North Sand Lake property continue to be honored today, however it was too late to prevent a beautiful, full grown wooded area sandwiched between Thompson Road and the lake from being destroyed.

Leach's Little Cabin on the Hill

Emily and Glenn Leach built their first cabin in 1953 on cement blocks measuring a 20 x 20-feet square. With the help of Ray Husen, owner of Husen's Resort on the northwest shoreline near A, the primitive shell built high on a hill overlooking the lake from its eastern position was initially lighted by bottled gas lanterns. Before water was furnished to the family by a hand-built well pump, the lake water was so clean that Grandpa Holesky, Emily's father, would row the boat out a ways from shore to dip his cup for a quick cool drink to quench his thirst.

Although the landscaping was nothing more than a jungle of poison ivy and poison oak, the Leach family relished the privacy of being at the very end of a dead end road.

Initially painted red and white, it wasn't until the cabin became all white that someone would tell how lake fishermen had used their "little red cabin" as a marker.

When Emily and Glen Leach began their search for a family cabin they noticed an advertisement in the St. Paul newspaper. Placed there by a real estate agent in Siren, WI, the thought of owning property on a lake triggered their interest. Emily remembers the first day they looked at property on Green, Mallard and North Sand lakes when the temperatures rose to an intensity that forced them to stop by the small bar at Hansen's Resort for refreshments. Barney Hansen, owner of the resort on A at the north end of North Sand, had been painting in preparation for summer business. He welcomed an opportunity to take a break during which time he described to the weary searchers a large piece of lakeshore property that had been on the market for a long time. So long, in fact, that each year Hansen was asked to post a For Sale sign for it in his bar.

Hansen showed Emily and Glenn a large map of North Sand Lake and the land for sale, and also the letter he had received from a Mr. Dagget, attorney for the Archdiocese of St. Paul in Minnesota. Father Hemming, who once owned the land, had passed away and willed the land to the Archdiocese. At one time, years before, a long strip of land that skirted the lakeshore was owned by the railroad whose plans were to lay a rail system that carried logs cut from the land immediately surrounding the lake. When that no longer seemed feasible, the property, which spanned a reported 3500 feet of shoreline, was purchased and equally divided by Father Hemming and Father Baskfield, two Catholic priests from the Twin Cities area.

Much time passed after Fr. Hemming's death before the Leaches decided to purchase the property. When they did, discovered were plaques measuring about 12-inches square painted with over-size letters J.M.J. nailed to trees. The Jesus, Mary, and Joseph signs were left on the trees by the Leaches until the elements rotted the wood and fell apart.

The brightly painted red and white cabin with Grandma Holesky at the window holding Leach's seven-month-old son, Chuckie.

Emily and Glenn Leach enjoyed knowing the deceased Father Hemming's good friend, Father Baskfield, and his dog, Lola. Father Baskfield's cabin was a small, one room summer shack lighted only by a lantern. His northeast point met a sandbar in front that extended well beyond the shoreline to provide ideal swimming conditions along the flat sandy shallow bottom. Void of anything remotely close to cabin luxuries, Father Baskfield's lake retreat must have been his heaven on earth as he'd leave his post in St. Paul on weekends and drive to North Sand Lake for rest and relaxation. During those special weekends, he'd spend time reading in his "divine" office, hang out with his friend, Warren Hansen, and enjoy a bottle of beer whenever he was thirsty. When Father Baskfield became a Monsignor, he sold his land to Warren Hansen.

When Glenn Leach was first looking for lake property, he thought that 500 feet of shoreline would be more than ample. But Mr. Dagget refused to divide Father Hemming's land blessed with 1500 feet of shoreline. Later, when Father Baskfield became a Monsignor, he wasn't sure if the Leaches could afford his adjoining land, which is the reason he sold it to Warren Hansen for $3600.

Although the land was very low and at times portions seemed to disappear into the lake, Warren Hansen, son of Barney and Flo Hansen, made plans to develop it by clearing the property, sub-dividing it and selling parcels to build on. A contract was made in the area to clear the land, however when the job was completed, Hansen was shocked to find that every single tree on the land had been removed, leaving the once beautiful wooded area extending from the shoreline void of any growth other than weeds and roots. I remember looking at the land from my boat one day and was shocked at how unnatural it looked and was saddened at the lack of communication between Warren and person or people he had hired. About the same time, the Leaches purchased two to four thousand pine trees from the Department of Natural Resources in Madison, WI and offered many of them to Warren to plant and help fill in his land.

Winters at the lake were described as being desolate, yet, as deserted as it seemed, each weekend was eagerly awaited to pack and head to the cabin. Ice fishing in front of the Leach cabin was excellent. One night, the Leaches and their friends set ten tip-ups with lights, then went to Kovarik's Resort to mingle with other winter visitors. When they returned to their cabin, all the tip-up lights were glowing. Amid the bright glow on the ice, they attempted to pull in their lines only to discover that all were tightly snarled together due to a huge northern pike too large to pull through the ice. Once hooked, the fish swam in circles, snagging the other nine lines to set off each light. All lines had to be cut, including the one with the northern pike.

Many other things happened through the years, one in particular was the day Emily witnessed a lightning strike on the lake which created a spray of water unlike anything she had ever seen. Another lightning strike occurred in 1971 when they were nearing the completion of their second weekend retreat. The new building caught on fire and suffered extensive damage. A third lightning strike hit two big trees, one of which remains. All in all, their land and the little cottage on the hill became one of great pride. Today, the Leach family celebrates four generations on North Sand Lake.

Emily Leach

Husen's Resort

A few years ago, Mrs. Ray G. Husen was reminiscing about a bright fall day in 1948 when she and her husband first saw North Sand Lake. Sharing fond memories with me of a time and a place a half century ago, she told me of the day a real estate salesman in Grantsburg mapped out a drive for them to see a variety of lake properties that might be of interest to them. Remembering how impressed they were with the clear water in North Sand Lake and its sandy beach, they decided it was exactly where they wanted to be and purchased the property before sunset.

The following spring, Ray Husen and his brother-in-law, Raymond McDaniel, drove up from Illinois and pitched a tent for sleeping quarters while they began work on what would become Husen's Resort. Although the weather was reported as being very cold, two days later, their cabin was finished. They returned home to prepare for the next trip north when Mrs. Husen would accompany them in a car crammed full with necessities. Because the Husens were in awe of the tall white pines and other trees brilliant with spring green foliage that surrounded them, they made certain that as many as possible would remain standing, especially the large pines. Four additional cabins were built with small wood stoves for heat. The experience of becoming settled way up in the north woods had already become a very rugged venture with lots of hard work and by nightfall, they'd collapse in bed, exhausted from their efforts.

Considering the amount of work that needed to be done at the lake, and having a family back home, trips were made between work and school schedules. Roy Husen loved his newly purchased lake property. When Mrs. Husen's parents came up to stay with them, her father also quickly adapted to the land and took great pleasure in cutting wood for everyone there. If there was any time left for relaxing, it was spent fishing with catches described as being plentiful.

The original road on the property nearly met the edge of the lake so Husen had to bring in a road grader to redirect it in the opposite direction and connect with a road to the rear of the property. When completed, plans were made to bring electricity to the site. Initially denied by the electric company, Husen informed them that if they did not respond to his request, he would bring in his own electricity and prevent anyone from bringing in additional lines that would cross his land. By 11 a.m. on a Saturday morning in early June of 1949, the electric company bowed to Husen's demands and made certain that each cabin had turn-on switches and pull-down strings for a modern touch to the somewhat isolated north woods existence. When a gravel pit employee arrived to cut a road to the lake and remove countless stumps left behind, a nice beach was created for the people who stayed at the resort. A ramp to the resort's shoreline seating was built by Husen for the benefit of their guests.

During the years as seasonal residents and resort owners, the Husen family grew, and so did the guest list. A fifth cabin was built and an addition was made to their own place which gave them much needed space. Each year they eagerly awaited the return of summer when seasonal activity kicked in and friendships were made with new guests while returning guests were reunited like family. They'd tell stories and laugh together about the night a bear scratched its back on the family's cabin, and the time a skunk crawled underneath and "perfumed" the entire area—a mere smattering of memories, yet each tale a treasure that became more special with time.

Summers on the lake for the Husen family developed into rewards beyond words, their lives richly blessed by location and the people who stayed there. Forever, unfortunately, was not meant to be. When Husen's children grew older and developed other interests back home in Illinois, and the enthusiasm necessary to keep going each day began to wane, they knew it was time to sell the resort. Cabins were sold to individuals, the property was divided and, what once was known as Husen's Housekeeping Resort, was referred to as...Husen's sub-division.

Husen's Resort and shoreline.

The Interim

By the time I passed Husen's Resort in the direction of A where traffic paralleled the shore and bull rushes that would later beckon fishing with Richard Harrison, Hansen's Resort was beginning to look more like a mother whose outstretched arms were waiting to welcome tired little me back home. Nearing the speck of a pie-shaped parcel sandwiched between the shoreline and A became clearer with each weary row and I could hardly contain myself knowing that within minutes I'd be back at our pier. Lacking the same strength or zest I possessed when the lake tour began, relief beyond words flushed through my mind. I knew that I'd have to be careful to hide my emotions while refusing to admit the excursion around the entire lake had become slightly more than I had imagined. Considering my young age, it would take everything I had left to pretend that I was just fine...even though I wasn't.

Thinking about all of this a half century later brought to mind a more recent tour in 1996 when I ventured out alone from our place on the south shore as a 58-year-old grandma in a paddleboat using my legs instead of my arms, and ended up wondering if I might expire before I returned. Granted, I was much older and wiser, and far stronger, yet the innocent late-in-life voyage on a sunny calm summer day when I hoped to cover approximately seven miles of shoreline by myself didn't include the possibility of a breeze that rippled the surface of the water about the same time I approached the north shore to complete half of the trip. As I was rounding the corner near Kilkare Road, rowing in a clockwise direction, the slight breeze shifted to a strong wind blowing against me and introduced major waves to contend with.

Although the rest of the trip home wasn't as enjoyable as the first half, I still found myself returning to my youth and the late 40s and early 50s when I rowed past areas of scattered rental cabins, cottages, woods, and sandy beaches void of the tremor of today's activity, except for the sound of a few small fishing boats tied with rope to wood piers with old automobile tires as bumpers. Heading into the waves, I was reminded how everything had changed including me and my mode of transportation. Instead of wood piers inching into four feet of water, metal piers jutted out to deeper depths. Many piers had heavy metal lifts that kept boats out of the water to protect them from storms and waves in the owner's absence. And a number of piers were literally laden with toys like the slow easy paddleboat I peddled to the much faster water vehicles equipped with the power to buzz like crazed bees from a disturbed hive. Unlike the simple black inner tubes we floated on, tubes took on a new look in bright yellows and blues of humongous sizes in the shape of trampolines. Also, and in abundance to satisfy the needs of people who wanted more than a quiet canoe or rowboat ride were pontoons the size of mini-cruise ships to accommodate entire families or groups of friends. A stone's throw from the shoreline that once led natural paths to cabins and cottages now were landscaped shorelines with perfectly positioned trees and gardens to spectacular dwellings referred to by some as weekend retreats.

I noticed a short distance from the end of a pier near A, a beautiful seaplane secured by heavy anchors that kept it in place before the next lift-off, depending on the direction of the wind, to skim tree tops before disappearing into the wild blue yonder of Burnett County and beyond, all of which became...food for thought.

As I continued paddling, trying to steer with a somewhat fickle handle, I smiled, remembering the seaplane ride I took as a young teenager one summer. Departing from Hansen's Resort main pier for a mere $15.00, I saw for the first time the lakes and ponds resembling puddles from the sky that were hidden in the woods surrounding me for miles around.

The remainder of the trip was becoming more difficult by the minute. The daydreaming and solitude and beauty of the lake had turned me into some kind of idiot to anyone watching from land, wondering what I was doing out in weather like that, in a paddleboat, by myself. It seemed, at times, that I was getting nowhere fast until I passed another pier, then another, and another. By the time I reached Lakeview Inn I knew that optimism had been my salvation. I was convinced that if I could make it across the lake to Hank Clement's point, I could hug the peninsula shoreline and still be somewhat protected from the wind while making headway back to my cottage on the south shoreline isthmus.

When I finally reached our cottage, it was almost impossible to lift my legs over the side of the paddleboat and all I could think of as I rolled over the boat into inches of water was a cold A&W root beer.

I must not have looked too desperate as Dick came off the porch hollering..."And where the heck have you been?" He told me that he had been up and down the shoreline asking neighbors if they had seen me and when they all answered no he became even more concerned. Briefly, after describing my adventure, its poor timing and how thirsty I was, he turned and went to the garage for a cold can of root beer from the refrigerator where pop, beer and worms are kept cold for the right moment and this, definitely, was one of them.

Meanwhile, shifting back to my rowboat tour decades earlier, I was nearing the warden's cottage and the mysterious place next door.

The Warden's Place

Stanley Swenson worked as a Game Warden for the DNR and lived in Spooner. In 1953, Swenson and his wife, Marcia, purchased an old one-room cottage on the narrowest strip of land along the north shoreline pointing toward Kilkare Road. Described on the abstract as Parcel 2, the land was adjacent to Hansen's Resort property with the exception of another old cottage in between. Swenson's place and the next door cottage sat on the edge of a shoreline heaped with billows of soft sand. With help from Swenson's sons, Gaylen and Allen, the structure had been lifted and placed on roller logs to move to Parcel 1. By continually shifting the position of the logs, the cottage was turned halfway around so the open porch faced the lake. Nancee Swenson remembers her father-in-law describing years later about the condition of the dwelling when he purchased it and that inside was a brass bed and mattress under which a machete was hidden. In the center of the small one-room cottage was a small wood stove with a brick chimney extending straight up and through the peak of the roof.

The Swenson family remodeled the cottage and used it on weekends when the weather cooperated. A dedicated game warden, Stan fished only when the catch of the day would be prepared and enjoyed the same day. Because weekends at the lake never seemed long enough for Gaylen and Allen, the boys rode their bikes from Spooner during summer vacation just to swim and fish at their cottage before heading back to complete the 50 mile round trip.

In 1962, after a serious confrontation with poachers who left him badly beaten, Stan moved his family 300 miles to the south-central part of the state and the Norwegian community of Stoughton, Wisconsin. He continued to serve as a Game Warden for Dane County, retired in 1962 and died in 1970.

Meanwhile, back on North Sand Lake during the mid-1960s, the Swenson cottage was modernized by installing indoor plumbing and electricity. In 1973, Allen Swenson and his wife, Nancee, purchased the property from the estate. As one of few older cottages on the lake with a three-season porch, the Swenson family summer retreat exudes yesterday's charm with tucked away nostalgia.

The Old Gray Weathered Cottage

There are mysteries in the trees and woods that surround us as well as in the depths of the lake, but this old gray weathered cottage has become the biggest mystery of all.

Before I continue, you should know that the warden's cottage and the old gray weather-beaten cottage were, at one point, thought to be the same. However, my mind carries me back to two side-by-side cottages, the worst of the two disappearing within a year of my presence at the lake. Never would I have imagined years later, when asking lake and immediate area residents about the owner or occupant of the cottage, no one had an answer except the Hansen's who claimed they had heard that someone stayed there one winter and froze to death.

Everyone I asked seemed oblivious to what I was talking about and where it was, yet I remember it as vividly as having seen it and entered it five minutes ago. To dispute the belief that it might have been one cottage, later remodeled, I have

The mystery cottage

Daddy and me

No one seems to remember this small weather-beaten cottage but me. Taken by Mother in 1945, these pictures are proof of what we discovered during our first summer at Hansen's Resort down the shoreline to the left.

pictures to prove, thanks to a magnifying glass, of two different roof lines, one white and one dark gray in the background taken during the summer of 1945. I knew then, without question, that the Warden's place and this old sad-looking dilapidated cottage at one time had, indeed, been side-by-side neighbors.

It was 1945 and our first year at Hansen's Resort with their four newly built unstained cottages were in sharp contrast with what had been weathered a short distance down the shoreline toward the east. Adding even more mystery was the rumor shared by the Hansens that a man froze to death there during the winter and his only survivor was an institutionalized daughter. A name was never attached to the story making it a perfect mystery to solve for Nancy Drew.

A few days after we arrived and checked in at Hansen's, Mother, Daddy and I carried our camera down the shoreline from our #4 cottage. Circling the old cottage, we noticed how close the back door was to A. At one time tightly secured, the padlock had been broken and was hanging from the latch. Carefully, we opened the door to peek inside. Having absolutely no plans to enter the place, what we saw made such an impression that Daddy and I walked in and looked around.

Hearing that someone froze to death the previous winter didn't surprise us and we wondered why anyone who knew the area and the brutality of cold and snow would have stayed there during the winter months. There was no insulation. Single wood boards served as the only walls, inside and out, with blue skies and gray-blue water seen through openings between various planks. A double brass bed had been pushed into a corner and hanging from one of its brass posts was a pair of trousers and a suit jacket. Near the small wood stove in the center of the room was a table with paint, brushes, pencils, a sketch book and other art supplies with additional supplies balanced on the rafters directly above. An oatmeal pan sat on the burner and a container of oatmeal, a can of coffee and glass jars filled with white sugar and flour were inches away. Feeling uncomfortable about being inside where we didn't belong, we turned to leave when we noticed a large rough hewn wood barrel behind the door. Packed inside with coarse straw-like packing material were layers of beautiful Haviland china decorated with tiny delicate pink flowers and a wisp of a gold edging. Unable to take pictures inside without a flash attachment, we relied on our memories to preserve what we had seen. When we arrived the following year for our second visit at the resort, the old weather-beaten cottage was gone.

While gathering information at the Burnett County Historical Society for this book, I learned that Earl and Aline (Millette) Clark, whose parents had settled much earlier in Jackson Township, married in 1936 and built a little cabin in 1938 on the acre of land given to Aline by her Uncle Simon Millette. Their cabin was located on County Road A near Kilkare Road on North Sand Lake. The Clarks lived there until 1941 at which time they moved to Quebec, Canada when the property was sold to Frank Ridgeway. This, of course, stirred even more questions in my mind. Was it possible that the old gray cottage I remember so well and the cabin built by the Clarks were one and the same? Was it Frank Ridgeway or a member of his family who succumbed during the bitter cold winter months? I spent many hours on different days at the Government Center near Siren trying to fit pieces together until 2002 when I decided to try one last time only to be told that County death records no longer were available to the public. My pleas and explanation to the woman at the desk that my previous historical projects had been recognized with awards by the State Historical Society of Wisconsin and this project was a fund raiser for the benefit of the North Sand Lake Association were to no avail.

And so, I am hoping someone who reads about the old gray weathered cottage will have a few answers for me to include in the next printing of the book. In the meantime, the mystery remains unsolved.

Part III

...with pockets full, hands and arms laden with poles and bait, a net and two boat cushions, we wove our way through the woods on a narrow path still damp with early morning dew. Waiting for us on the little lake tucked in the woods behind our cottage was serenity and good fishing at its north woods finest.

Cottage Life at the Resort

Treasure Map

I love this map. Drawn with a pencil and dated 1945 means that it was my eight-year-old impression of Hansen's Resort having four cottages available during their first season on the lake. By some stroke of Motherly-love luck, the map was saved and now hangs in my cottage as a reminder of my first summer on North Sand Lake.

If you've already noticed, not only is treasure misspelled, and Sand Lake shown as Sand Land, but the north and south locations of the shorelines were incorrectly written. Well, I was only eight at the time. The drawing also shows a cottage to the left of the four resort cottages and another one next door where I was sure a treasure could be found, thanks to the glory of a childhood imagination.

Most likely, the person in the only boat on the lake was Daddy as it was his favorite fishing spot. As for the small box-like shapes behind each of the four cottages, don't confuse them as cars because they were the outhouses we used. Although I didn't draw a short pier with a boat in front of each cottage, I did include Hansen's long weathered pier with a bench at the end where I often fished.

Hansen's house accurately shows stairs leading from the front door, lakeside, as well as a back door that led to the back door of the store, as drawn. And, although the resort had a single gas pump, I don't remember it being where I drew it, but at least one was available. Over to the right is another pier, a clearing of trees with a house at the top of the hill. Appropriately named Hilltop, Bob Kazobowski's resort was perched there, yet only one of its buildings is visible. That major road running from west to east is none other than County Road A.

Hansen's Resort fish cleaning house was situated about where Moser's garage and bait shop is today. And, yes, as shown, there were paths leading through the field and woods and beyond to Little Bass Lake, not shown on the map.

At the time this was drawn, I was not yet aware of the shape of North Sand Lake as the extended points which are so much a part of the lake's design on both east and west shorelines as well as the back bay, are missing. However, once I was old enough to explore by rowing beyond our immediate shoreline, those discoveries were made and never forgotten.

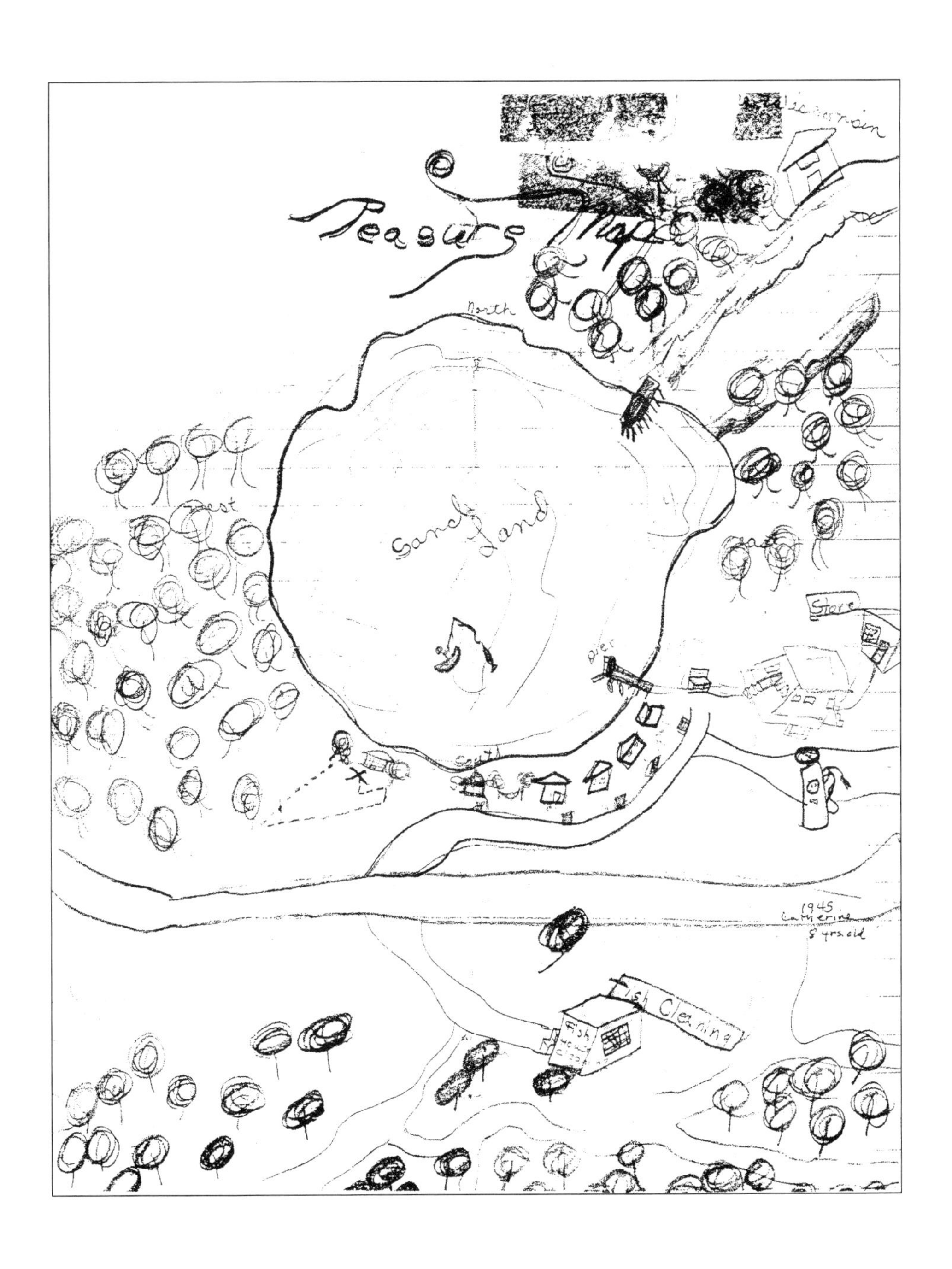
North
Sand Land
pier
Store
Fish Cleaning
1945
Catherine
8 yrs old

Frogs

Catching frogs wth a coffee can.

The darling little creatures were everywhere. Although I never was sure just when they'd make their appearance each summer at the lake, it seemed their numbers became abundant shortly after we arrived near the end of July. In fact, there were so many frogs that no one felt guilty about using them as bait.

There could have been more than a few different kinds of frogs along our shoreline, but those I remember best were either dark green in color or the brighter green pickerel frog with circular black patterns covering everything but the belly. They hopped around like they were in the prime of their life adding *up north* intrigue to the shore in all kinds of weather.

The frogs became my friends. After breakfast each morning I'd run the short distance from the front screen door to the water's edge to see how many were hiding under the rowboat if it had been pulled up and left on the shore the night before. One shove to dismantle its position and at least a dozen frogs would scatter for boat cover, or dive into the water. If I wanted to catch a frog, I had to learn a few methods of finesse and was intrigued by how they tried to camouflage themselves among multi-colored stones in the water.

With hours spent learning their daytime habits, castles were made by packing a squatty coffee can with damp sand before carefully turning it over. Surrounding each castle were moats made with stones and sprigs of weeds and wild flowers for decoration. Once completed, the least active frogs were placed on a throne at their respective castles. Confinement usually lasted less than a minute before escaping my command.

On my 13th birthday, Daddy gave me a Montgomery Ward *My Buddy* tackle box and a West Bend rod and red reel. I waited patiently from my October birthday to the following July when I could use my new fishing equipment for the first time. Remembering bits and pieces of stories established fishermen share with others, it seemed natural for me to grab a frog, hook it through its lips and cast after I had rowed a short distance from the end of the pier. One cast and Bang! I was in awe that a 16-inch bass hit immediately and quickly sat down and rowed back to the pier holding the rod and reel with my feet for Daddy to remove the fish from the hook while I was hooked for life. As a fisherman who rowed holding the rod and reel between two feet as a convenient and comfortable way to troll, the method would remain as part of my mode of operation for years until I graduated to a spinning rod and reel.

By the time I was 16, fishing no longer held the same childhood mystique nor did the lake with its weedbeds of various depths in various places. I knew where to go and what to do in any situation and felt comfortable fishing alone. It was also a time when I learned much more about the frog. My three-year high school homeroom also happened to be a biology room which triggered another plateau of interest in biology that swelled to new proportions with the purchase of a dissecting kit. The silky skinned frogs with webbed toes that attempted to elude me at all times suddenly offered me new pleasures.

I learned that frogs captured worms, mosquitoes and other insects with their sticky tongues for succulent meals, at the same time being easy prey for mammals and reptiles. It was an example of…survival of the fittest. Aside from that, dissecting frogs became a passion. Snipping around their ankles and wrists, plus making a careful slit down the belly, I played doctor-scientist by carefully removing their skin, studying their intestines and watching their hearts beat. Suddenly, out of sheer innocence and intrigue, my friends, the frogs, became my victims.

I never felt guilty about what I was doing because I thought of each operation as a class project. However, those educational moments of performing surgery on the shoreline would haunt me many years later when frogs became a rarity at the lake and the one or two I'd see each summer were appreciated in a much different manner than when dozens greeted curious me each morning after breakfast.

Above: With Boy, looking for frogs.

Right: Daddy and me with the first northern pike I ever saw, 1945.

Mother

Bench at the end of the long pier in front of Hansen's home. Looking west in the background is Karl's one room cottage.

Piers

Each cottage had its own pier and wooden rowboat. Although short, the piers were sufficient, yet crudely built using small tamarack tree trunks as posts to support its wood planks. In 1945, when Hansen's Resort first opened for business, the piers were high off the water, perhaps due to the water level of the lake or inaccurate measuring. Later, they seemed to get longer and lower making it much easier to get in and out of the boat.

While I spent much of my time swimming, boating, and playing with frogs on the shoreline, my sister, Elaine, devoted herself to lying on a towel at the end of the pier for more privacy. A peek around the window shade was the first thing she did each morning to check the weather. If it was gloomy, she complained. If the sun was shining from a cloudless sky, she was happy as a lark. Slippery and shiny with Johnson's Baby Oil covering her body, she spent most of the day soaking up the sun for a tan that would make everyone envious back home.

I never thought about getting a tan, yet spending my days on the shoreline made me darker by the hour. Tanning naturally without the use of creams or oils and without effort must have irritated Elaine as she pointed out the difference one day by referring to me as being a dark, muddy brown compared to her rich golden shade. Okay, so who cared…? I was eight and she was twelve. I liked frogs and she liked boys. Mother didn't want me to get so dark, but to change that she'd have to keep me indoors all day and that wasn't even worth discussing.

Because the end of our pier was in water too shallow for anyone to dive except Daddy who called himself a shallow diver, Elaine and I often walked down to

Above: Hansen's Resort shoreline

... and pier.

the resort pier which extended well beyond ours to make diving less dangerous. I couldn't dive so it didn't matter to me. I didn't know how to put my head in the water without getting water in my nose, so instead I'd lie on my stomach on the pier and dangle a line with a hook and a worm in front of small perch that congregated on the lake's sandy bottom under the pier. Perch were a rarity on the lake so seeing them was a thrill for me.

Elaine, on the other hand, wanted nothing to do with fishing and dove into eight-foot depths at the end of the pier with the greatest of ease. She had beautiful form. With legs kept straight, knees together and feet pointed like the ballerina she was back home, it was poetry in motion. All of it was done without pinching her nose or wearing a pink rubber clamp like me. However, unlike Daddy who dove shallow and stayed under so long we never knew where he was, Elaine would surface within seconds and use graceful disciplined strokes to return to the pier for another dive while I kept my eye on the small perch below.

Barney's pier offered memorable times, whether sitting, sunning, fishing, swimming, diving, or boarding a plane for a $15.00 flight and aerial view of the immediate area. The only thing that could interrupt our enjoyment was lunchtime which meant much more than a quickly made peanut butter sandwich. Mother treated us each noon to a large platter lined with crisp lettuce leaves. Arranged on top were sliced tomatoes, Oscar Mayer bologna, salami and their Family Brand with sliced Swiss cheese fanned creatively for sandwiches we could make on soft white bread from the Spooner Bakery.

A Happy Trooper

Frogs and piers. Swimming and fishing. How much more exciting could it get? Other treasures were within reach and waited to be discovered on a daily basis. It was pure and simple with the awareness and intuitiveness of a youngster who was in love with everything.

Age didn't matter, nor did it ten years later when I was eighteen. Everyday, rain or shine, alone or with cottage friends, made waking up in the morning a moment to celebrate and before falling asleep at night my mind would automatically pour through what I had experienced and learned during the waking hours. And, in surplus was an imagination that carried me away at the blink of an eye. With no television, hand-held battery-operated games or water toys with engines, seconds ticked away and chugged along at different paces with non-stop fun and games that left no room to brood or complain about anything. Life was wonderful. It was a ten year period of being dependent on parents who had created a family vacation allowing me to enjoy it to the fullest as one might have a wonderful dream and not want to wake up for fear of losing it forever.

Because of the distance from home, we never had to worry about unexpected company and overnight guests. Instead, we enjoyed new friends who stayed in the other cottages. If friends back home liked what they heard from Mother and Daddy, they, too, reserved cottages for the same time we were there so everyone had fun together, yet appreciated the privacy of having their own place. Needless to say, it was a winning formula.

Grandpa Kovacs and his grandson, my cousin Billy Kovacs.

After Grandma Kovacs passed away in March of 1946, Grandpa came to live with us. When we headed north each summer, Grandpa packed his suitcase and temporarily moved in with Uncle Bill, Mother's brother. One summer, Uncle Bill drove to the cottage with his son, my little cousin Billy, and Grandpa. I cannot remember if they spent the night with us, and if they did I have no idea where we all slept as it would have been too long of a trip to turn around and return home the same day. Another time, Uncle Joe, Daddy's brother, drove up with his son, my little cousin, Joey, and they, too, must have spent the night. However brief, it was fun to share time at the lake with family members. Otherwise, if people from home stopped by to say hello it was because they were renting cottages at resorts on nearby lakes or passing through the area.

Mother and Daddy's nephew, my cousin Joey, 1958.

It's Gonna be a Hot One...

The chill of the lake made its own daily statement during summer hot spells when smaller and shallower lakes warmed to what we all referred to as bathtub warm. It didn't seem to matter how high the temperature climbed as North Sand Lake may have warmed slightly on the surface, but below was enough to make the sweat on your brow disappear in a second or two, especially when swimming directly over one of the lake's countless natural springs.

Due to window placement on all three sides of the front section of the cottage, a nice cross ventilation blew through the entire three rooms. But, let's face it—whether you were lucky enough to haul a fan from home, had a hammock tied to two trees, a refrigerator filled with lemonade, beer and pop or a freezer with Popsicles and ice cubes, the best place to be was in the lake. Not on the lake or near the lake, but in it and for as long as possible.

I remember one of those hot days when Daddy sat on the pier after a refreshing swim and dipped two washcloths in the water to lay over each thigh to keep cool as a shield from the sun. This went on for a major part of the afternoon. When the towels had warmed from the sun, both were dipped again in the lake and placed over his knees and under the hem of his bathing suit.

At the time, it probably felt refreshing, but by nightfall, Daddy was in pain with a sunburn that made him walk funny the next morning. When his thighs began to blister, he drove to Spooner to see a doctor, and returned home with ointment and orders, as we expected, to stay inside or in the shade outside.

Mother and Karl's dog, Boy.

Daddy in the hammock.

Because of his good health, it seemed strange for a doctor to place limits of what he could and couldn't do. The only time we saw anything affect him was during a fall season back home when the family picnicked at a city park surrounded by woods. Daddy picked a huge bouquet of beautiful white berries on stems with green leaves for Mother to put in a vase on the coffee table in the living room. When itchy pimples began to appear on his legs and arms, followed by huge oozy blisters, he made an appointment to see his doctor who identified from pictures that Daddy had been in direct contact with poison ivy.

Meanwhile, back at the lake, the only other method of relief during hot spells was to spend time down at the store where air conditioning cooled the senses and the skin while we socialized with our cottage neighbors and sipped our favorite beverages. We'd go home for supper, then return to the store where the place was jumping with jukebox tunes until closing. Don't let anyone tell you that these were anything less than great big times. There was no pool table to occupy the hours spent there, or machines to play, or any other forms of mental stimulation other than just being with each other and finding enough to laugh and talk about hour after hour, night after night. The next morning, the lake was waiting for a repeat of the day before, and so were we.

If it looked like rain, life changed when we headed for town.

Elaine, me and Mother

An evening down
at the store.
Back row, l-r,
Barney and Karl.
Far right, Daddy.

Far left, Mother
and Daddy dancing.
Far right on the bar
stool, Flo Hansen

Fred's Cafe would become Topper's, our favorite Spooner restaurant.

Rainy Days

Cold, windy and gloomy rain days may have depressed some, but not us. That first year in #4 meant getting our feet wet as to what cottage life was all about. The following year, nestled next door in #5, where we stayed every summer from then on, the cottage became our own little summer home. Daddy warmed the cottage with a wood fire before a damp-day breakfast of orange juice, oatmeal, toast and cocoa with marshmallows. After water was pumped and heated for dishes and they were washed and put away, we'd play Rummy, Dirty Clubs or Monopoly. Once the excitement of winning mixed with the agony of defeat subsided, the only thing left was to get in the car and go somewhere, anywhere.

A little town on a big street, Webster, population 549, didn't have much to keep us occupied for hours. Nine miles to town did, however, treat us to a short, two block business strip of household staples on a street much wider than most streets in major cities. Brief stops may have included the general store, corner grocery store, two hardware stores, a drug store, restaurant, bakery, bank and gas station. Webster remained a compassionate lifesaver and made us feel at home.

The slightest hint of a full day of gloom turned a rainy day destination in the direction of Spooner, about 23 miles from the cottage. Daddy considered some rain days to offer the best fishing, but he never complained about our own frivolous needs to go to town, visit the stores, and spend a little money before returning to the cottage. Once we became acclimated to the route, he fished and Mother drove.

Spooner had two business blocks filled on both sides with stores to visit and browse. Any place was a good place to start, but somehow we usually began our tour at the corner drug store at the very heart of town. We were always in need of postcards, film for the camera, a movie magazine or two, and another bottle of Calamine lotion to treat tiny, itchy skin eruptions that refused to disappear from the limbs of the unfortunate few. Inexpensive gifts that we all assumed were made by a nearby Indian tribe drew me like magnets. Tiny beaded coin purses, belts, and pine jewelry boxes shiny with shellac, I pleaded, were all I ever wanted...besides the deerskin moccasins I never got.

There were small stores along the way, each providing a necessity in life. Windows of the jewelry store confirmed that all Spooner brides were well taken care of from an engagement ring to a shower and the subsequent wedding. At the end of the block, on each corner, were hotels built years before for the convenience of visitors who arrived on trains at the depot across the street.

We walked by taverns, but never went inside despite the view through the windows along the sidewalk of mounted deer heads hanging from knotty pine paneling. Added to the mystique was the rumor that the 1920s Chicago gangster Al Capone used to frequent one of the taverns many years before. Since children, at least us, didn't enter taverns back then, I knew I'd have to wait until years later to walk in and see for myself what decorated the walls in each place besides stories of intrigue.

A few doors away was Smith's, a gift shop totally unlike anything we had back in Madison. Considering the difference in population numbers, the shop was like entering a fairyland of colored glass, antiques, classy knickknacks and trinkets one wouldn't expect to find anywhere other than in a big city. Every conceivable inch of display space seemed to be occupied with treasures, tastefully arranged. We were in awe of everything and, as a result, spent lots of time whispering and being careful while looking, touching, and oftentimes, buying.

When our visit to Smith's ended, we continued peering into windows of adjacent stores until we reached Topper's, our favorite Spooner restaurant. A hamburger, French fries, and a thick chocolate malt was a perfect lunch as far as I was concerned and all that was needed before spending a few more hours in town. After visiting the corner clothing store with an inventory of quality stylish apparel, we'd cross the street and continue our walk. Browsing and peering a little more, we reached the bakery in the middle of the block where baking aromas made our mouths water. Sights of freshly baked bread, donuts, pies, cakes and cookies, plus seafoam candy made us realize each time we visited that the bakery was another Spooner treasure. Why soft, sweet pillows of white foam candy slightly studded with pecans should look so delicious after a filling lunch only a youngster could answer. Buying a small bag to nibble on was a special treat for all of us, especially me. I had a sweet tooth.

Our last stop would include both grocery stores at the end of the block across the street from the movie theater. After we'd glanced up at the marquee to see what was playing at a movie theater in Spooner, we'd walk through the department store before returning to the car to arrange our purchases and head for the lake.

There were, at times, visits to the fish hatchery on the outskirts of town where we were always in awe of the size of both musky and northern pike. The state had built the hatchery in 1913 and it offered us a chance to see giant fish swimming while protected from hooks, lines and sinkers and the most able of fishermen. There were 13 ponds for raising fish at the time which, now and then, were spotted and pulled from the water by herons and other strong large birds in search of a quick meal.

Considering how long it took to drive to Spooner and back, by the time we reached the cottage, no matter how often this was repeated through the years, we were always satisfied about how special a rainy day could be.

Rainy days often produced chilly nights which meant a fire in the wood stove. One night, as I stood with my back to the stove to feel warmth before jumping into bed, the hot metal proceeded to scorch my pale pink quilted nylon tricot bathrobe. Another lesson learned.

Our cozy cottage

A woodstove warmup

Mother and Daddy

Mother and Daddy on the steps of the old Catholic church, near A & H.

Sunday Morning

Sunday usually began with a hearty breakfast at the round kitchen oak table. When everything had been cleared, washed and put away, we'd dress in our cottage church finest which meant skirts, blouses and scarves for Mother, Elaine and me, or hankies with crocheted edges to cover our heads. Daddy's summer church attire was a nicely pressed short-sleeved light-colored, light-weight cotton shirt and summer trousers with neat creases. Mother and Daddy wore dressier shoes while Elaine and I slipped our bare feet into sandals, huraches, or penny loafers.

The Sacred Heart Catholic Church was located on H just a long block from the A&H intersection. Quaint and charming and nestled in the woods like a picture on a card, with Crescent Lake serving as a backdrop, was the little church we fell in love with. Actually, it seemed more like a chapel. Its interesting past began in 1905 during a Thanksgiving snow storm when a Bishop and a priest were returning to Spooner after visiting Indian Missions and became lost with their horses. The holy men were rescued by Peter Durand and Peter Tetrault who took them to the Durand home where they warmed and rested after a meal before setting out once again for Spooner. As they boarded the train, they promised to return.

Nine area families opened their homes for Mass and, in 1908, land for a Catholic Church was donated to the Diocese of Superior by the Omernik family. In 1910, a mission church was dedicated to St. Monica before completion and then was destroyed by a storm. Parish members returned to the drawing board, this time contemplating a reduction in the size of the new building. By 1927, the little Crescent Lake Church with bi-monthly Masses was feeling growing pains due to the popularity of the area as a summer vacation spot. An addition was inevitable.

Although the exterior of the church appeared to be a humble country place of worship, the interior seemed elaborate to me--what one would hope to find in the confines of a chapel. Beautiful statues and paintings inside represented everything hauntingly holy. On the other hand, kneelers, unlike padded ones back home, were difficult for little knees to kneel on and probably even more difficult for the elderly. Barely off the floor, the hard, unpadded wooden kneelers kept me so low that I couldn't rest my arms over the pew to pray the rosary. Yet, we were endeared to every inch of the church for it represented all the things our religion worshipped while complementing it with special hometown touches. Before each Sunday morning Mass, a female parishioner would walk in proudly carrying beautiful bouquets of flowers, gathered that morning from someone's garden, no doubt her own, to place on each side of the altar.

Another hometown touch that we especially enjoyed usually took place about five minutes before Mass began, if the assigned server failed to show up. The priest would walk down the short aisle toward the altar before turning around to face those of us sitting in pews and ask if someone would fill in as server. One Sunday morning no one volunteered. Suddenly, in the silence of the moment, Daddy raised his hand. I remember looking at him in amazement, knowing that he hadn't served Mass for as least 40 years. I wondered how he could remember everything he did as a young boy when he served Mass at St. Joseph's in Madison's Italian Greenbush neighborhood. Fortunately, or unfortunately, he wasn't needed as just about the time he was leaving the pew to approach the altar, the young missing server ran up the front steps and entered the church. Out of breath and hurrying down the aisle, he smiled in an apologetic way before tending to his duties.

And yet another touching rural hometown scene was the respect women and children received when the small church filled to capacity. Without being asked, men would leave their pews and go outside to stand next to the open side windows to attend Mass at a different angle, returning inside only to receive Communion.

When the Sacred Heart Church showed signs of another population increase of vacationers and new property owners, the drawing board came out again. Plans for a new church were accepted in 1958 and work began as our charming little summer church that seemed more like a beloved chapel was torn down to make room for a new, modern air-conditioned structure built by the son of one of the original parish families. Also disappearing were the beautiful statues and ornate interior. Although the new church met the demands of a new era, I will always remember and forever miss the little one with the huge double-hung side windows that pushed up high for the men who stood outside to celebrate Mass with those of us inside.

After another addition was built in 1978 due to the ever-expanding population, the church with many names became known as the Sacred Hearts parish.

We never questioned going to church on Sunday while on vacation. Attending Mass made us feel good inside. The rest of the day was like any other as cottage life and its wonders resumed.

Mastering The Dropline

Many years ago, in the second decade of the century, my Hungarian-immigrant Grandma and Grandpa Kovacs settled in Madison where Grandpa eventually would become caretaker of Tenney Park, located on the city's north eastside along Lake Mendota. The picturesque park was accented with lazy lagoons stretching for blocks, with the Yahara River flowing under other bridges of other streets to connect Lake Mendota with Lake Monona on the other side of the city's isthmus. Locks balanced the water level to allow ease in boating from lake to lake. The beauty and lushness of Tenney Park encouraged people to swim in Lake Mendota, stroll or picnic during the summer and skate on its frozen lagoons during the winter months.

Being surrounded by water, the location enhanced Grandpa's fishing and when time permitted, found him out on Lake Mendota in all kinds of weather with his handmade dropline. After rowing over weed beds he grew to know like the

garden planted in his backyard, he'd stand in his small wooden boat and, in cowboy fashion, swing the end of the line complete with leader, sinker, bait and bobber high over his head in a circular lasso-style. He released it when the line had gathered enough speed to sail a good distance from the boat. Only then would he sit down and watch the bobber.

Lake Mendota was known for its huge northern pike, but garfish also inhabited the lake and Grandpa was remembered as someone who often walked home from work with a rope slung over his shoulder, carrying a "gar" so long that its tail dragged behind on the sidewalk.

Daddy paid heed to Grandpa's fishing expertise so it was no surprise, as newcomers to North Sand Lake back in the 1940s, that Daddy purchased cane poles for the family and added his own handmade droplines for bluegill fishing. Made from a simple piece of wood wrapped with line, leader, lead sinker and hook, you could easily stick it in your back pocket or tackle box before carrying worms and a net to the boat.

The droplines that Daddy made became an endearing item attached to fond memories for me to savor through the years. Not only did he make new ones through the years, but his method instilled a unique fishing freedom I've always enjoyed. By dropping the line over the edge of the boat to whatever depth I felt was appropriate, it was a matter of seconds before the fish began to bite. If they didn't, the line would be pulled in while the boat was rowed about ten feet to a new location. Perched on the boat seat with the wood part of the dropline positioned under my thigh to prevent unnecessary tangling, my right arm would rest on the side of the boat as the line quickly dropped from the weight of the lead sinker. When I felt it hit the bottom, or noticed slack in the line, I'd pull the line up a little and drape it over the tip of my index finger to feel the slightest nibble. A quick jerk of the hand was the only thing necessary to hook a fish. Fishing off the bottom enabled me to catch a bullhead now and then, or perch which were seldom seen or caught on the lake. I also caught dogfish (bowfin) on my dropline, or northern pike just as Grandpa once did, but normally the line was used only for panfish.

Before Daddy sold his cottage in 1989, he made six more droplines for me, one of which remains in my tackle box that only I use. The other five are kept in an empty coffee can in the garage for family members. Humble dropline fishing is perfect to do from the rowboat, but not so perfect from the pontoon unless you want to sit on the floor of the pontoon which is not at all comfortable for any length of time, especially if you're not a youngster.

Daddy, being ambidextrous, added an extra dimension to his bluegill fishing by using one hand for the dropline and the other hand for his cane pole, both at the same time. For him, it was like clockwork.

Daddy and his 36 inch, 12 pound northern, 1952.

l-r: Daddy, Elmer and Alice Sepke, me and Diane

Mike the Fisherman

Although fishing never played a role of any importance for Daddy back home, it became a daily ritual at Hansen's Resort. Considered a privilege that was never abused, fishing on a lake of such quality created a craving for Mother Nature's gifts.

With each vacation spent at the resort, favorite fishing spots were quickly established.

Straight out from the Warden's cottage was the first place Daddy usually headed for in any kind of weather. Before mastering the use of a drop line and a cane pole at the same time, he'd begin by dropping his line and catching a small bluegill. This was used to bait the heavy hook of the rod and reel. He would then slide the bobber to the right length and throw the rod and reel line out before setting the clicker. Only then would he carefully insert the hook on his dropline down the center of a worm to fish for keepers before training his eyes to keep track of the bobber for big fish action.

We all learned through big fish trial and error coupled with Daddy's stories and those shared by others that it was a good idea not to get too excited if the bobber suddenly disappeared. Experience and patience taught us that by jerking the line too quickly it could scare away the attacker. The second time the bobber went down for more than just a minor bob usually meant the attacker was in the process of cleaning the fish of its scales. This was the time to carefully disengage the clicker because when the bobber when down for the third time, the attacker was turning the fish to swallow it, signaling it was time to press your thumb to the line on the reel and set the hook. To allow no slack during the time you reeled in the fighting fish, you needed to let it tire itself by allowing it to run. To do this you slightly released the pressure with your thumb before beginning to reel again. It was a good time to talk to yourself while hoping the fish wouldn't tangle in a thick weed bed, or worse, wrap the line around the anchor chain which would help the fish snap the line. If you brought in the fish too fast, you'd almost need someone else in the boat to help with the landing net as northern pike are strong and can be a nightmare for the inexperienced fisherman to land.

Other times, you might have so much bluegill action that you forget about the bobber only to look in the same direction of where it was the last time you checked and realize it is gone. Then you have no choice but to put the drop line down, take the rod and reel line in your fingers and give it the tiniest of tugs just to feel if there is any movement at the other end. If you feel fairly confident that something is hooked, you take the clicker off, press your thumb to the reel and jerk the pole while beginning to reel in at the same time.

And so it was, one cold, dreary, windy, wavy, rainy, miserable August day back in 1952 when Daddy went out in the boat to fish. When he returned, he had just finished a 30-minute struggle with the biggest northern pike we had ever seen. Maybe not by someone else's standards, but to us a 36-inch, 12 pound northern was a trophy fish.

Behind the resort cottages and across A to an area where Moser's built their service station many years later, Hansen's Resort had a simple fish cleaning shack. It replaced a high, crudely built wood table which had previously served the purpose just fine, complete with flies and bees. Within the confines of the new fish-cleaning quarters with a roof overhead and screens to keep the bugs out, Daddy cleaned the monster fish with the help of Elmer Sepke, from Berwyn, IL who was staying in #10 with his wife, Alice. Also closely watching was Diane Semrad, my girlfriend from Madison who was spending a few weeks with us.

Instead of cutting the fish into steaks or strips, it was cleaned, left whole and frozen for Mother to stuff and bake when we returned home. After the head was set out to dry, I kept it for years without it emitting too much smell from its resting place, on a shelf in the garage. Studying at random its mouth of razor-sharp teeth, I realized what kind of damage a northern of that size could do to fingers or hands if the fisherman wasn't careful.

Above: Daddy and me cleaning fish across the road from the cottage.

Left: Mother

Gone Fishin'

Clipped from a Burnett County newspaper a few years ago was a column meant to carry the reader back in time with previously written reflections of what life was like decades earlier. Triggering the imagination to reconfirm what was assumed by many through the years, the following information appeared in an August 24, 1933 issue: *Fishing in the Sand Lake that lies northeast of Webster, along County Trunk A, Glueheisen yesterday caught a northern pike weighing 30 ½ pounds and measuring 46 inches in length.* I read it twice and nearly jumped out of my shoes. I knew it! I just knew it! All these years I've been defending the magnificence of the lake and its ingredients with my convictions that there were, indeed, trophy fish, both in its depths and shallow waters, to make fishing on any given day a challenge. And, there it was, announced by the media. It also provided a nudge to remind those who fish the lake and can't seem to find the right spot on the right day, then complain for days, to keep trying. North Sand Lake is nearly 1000 acres in size with depths of more than 70 feet, with mysteries most of us will never solve. It is not an easy lake to fish, but the big ones are lurking there.

I remember the local fishing guides who were available to hire for half or full days. Although Glen Thompson's son, Stuart, from Thompson's Resort along the east shoreline, guided now and then, guides most familiar to me when I was young were Ollie Taylor, Pete Augustine, and young "Peanuts" Pratt who I didn't hire, but fished with because we had become summer friends. Each time Daddy fished with Ollie or Pete, he'd spend the entire supper hour sharing stories of the day that made you want to grab your tackle box and pole and head for the boat. When Daddy bent to my pestering to go along and asked one day if I'd wanted to join them, I jumped at the chance.

l-r: Daddy, Peanuts Pratt and Gordy, 1958.

Pete Augustine met us one calm, sunny, summer morning at the resort pier. After packing the boat with all the essentials, the three of us headed over to an area just past Les Olson's place and in view of the public boat landing and the Colonel's American flag. As soon as the motor was turned off and pulled up, Pete began to row with slow, quiet strokes while glancing back and forth over his shoulders until he was satisfied with the location. After patiently instructing us with advice about bait, how to hook it, the depth to fish, speed to reel and angle to net, the fishing began. Because nothing was happening, he rowed a little farther until the action began and continued with northern and bass hits and catches. When it was time to return to Hansen's, the motor was dropped back into the water and we headed back to shore for a lunch of hamburgers at the resort's restaurant and bar. Daddy asked Pete to join us for lunch, but he declined with a smile and chose to sit at a table by himself. At 1 o'clock, we returned to the same spot on the lake and fished until mid-afternoon when it was time to call it quits for the day. The number of hits and fish caught during that time shifted my enthusiasm into high gear.

Thinking that I had just learned everything there was to know about fishing, I fell asleep convinced that the next day I would go fishing by myself. After breakfast I rowed from our cottage to the same place with the same fishing pole, the same bait, using the same techniques and caught…nothing. Not even a bite. Years later I would better understand and appreciate the knowledge and expertise of guiding and the mystery of a formula I never would learn.

One day "Peanuts" and I motored out to a spot near the southwest point he described as being very deep with good fishing. It was a gloomy windy day and

one my mother probably would have preferred me not venture out in a boat, but I did and promised her I'd be careful. Peanuts maneuvered much like Taylor and Augustine, locating *the spot* while rowing around in circles and back and forth until he sensed the boat was within the range of good fishing. All of this was done without depth finders and any other battery operated fishing equipment. While Peanuts assured me the weather was perfect for fishing, the anchor dragged with the waves and refused to hold us until we gave up and returned to shore with nothing to show for our efforts. I remember the spot being out in front of where Dr. and Mrs. Spittell built their first cottage.

That particular spot was just around the point from another fishing experience I had with Daddy on another miserable day of bad weather when we had been trolling back and forth along the shore from the back bay to the point. When the wind picked up and a few rain drops fell, we knew we'd better head back to the cottage as soon as possible. While Daddy rowed past the A-frame, I trolled with the rod and reel he had given to me on my 13th birthday. Using a small perch for bait, I held the pole until we were almost to the point when something hit my line with a vengeance. Because of the weather, I set the hook immediately as Daddy put the oars down and grabbed the net, encouraging me to be patient. Whatever I had at the end of my line was big and definitely would require help landing. Still, I was shocked when the fish, a huge northern pike, was reeled in close enough to the boat for Daddy to net. I had heard enough fish stories in my youth, seen some beauties fresh from the lake as well as those mounted, but when I saw the fish I knew immediately that it was pretty close to the 26 ½ pound northern that was caught by Ed Shipanik and mounted to hang inside the resort store. As the boat inched toward shore, Daddy leaned over to scoop as much of the fish into the net as he could when the monster flipped, broke the line and dropped off the rim of the net to disappear deep into the grayness of the waves. In the meantime, my fishing hat blew off my head and was carried away with the wind on the waves.

The first fish caught with my new rod and reel.

I did what most teenage girls would do and that was to sit down, hang my head and shed a few tears. As we hit the point and open water, the waves doubled in size. Daddy battled the wind and rowed until he reached my hat about the same time I realized I'd better forget about the fish I lost and concentrate on getting back to the cottage. As waves pounded against the side of the boat, we were pushed to the western hilly shoreline and ended up at Robert Grindell's pier where we tied the boat and climbed steep wooden stairs to reach their summer home. Thank goodness someone was there. Although we were drenched with rain, the Grindells were very kind and invited us inside so Daddy could call the resort to have someone run down to #5 and tell Mother to drive to Grindell's Leef Road driveway and pick us up. The boat remained at Grindell's until the storm passed. Since that day, and in the years ahead when we owned property on the south shore, I've been fascinated with the peninsula and possibilities that other fish the same size, and bigger, lurked below and continued to elude most fishermen.

Every year, two men arrived at Hansen's to stay in #1 for a week to fish the back bay for bowfin, which we all referred to as dogfish, a non-edible scavenger that wasn't worth preparing to eat because of all the bones. But it was a good fighter, was great fun to catch, and made a powerful garden fertilizer. If you happened to hook one and it broke your line, there was no need to fret. However, if you did catch one, you were required by state law to slit its belly and throw it back into the lake as food for predators, or use it in your garden. The two men chose to carry them all back to their cottage each day to dazzle us all with the numbers caught and the size of each one.

Bill and Polly Stoker and their kids, Carlene, Pat, Tom and Bill, were our good friends in Madison who decided to spend a week in #4 at the same time we were in #5. Bill was a pharmacist at his Hudson Park Pharmacy on Atwood Avenue, a few blocks from our house. He was also an expert fisherman who traveled often to Canada to fish lakes there. It was great to have them next door until one day when the fun ended after Bill hooked something too big to pull close enough to the boat to see exactly what it was. You have to remember that Bill caught northern pike in Canada that were larger than anything we had seen on North Sand Lake. This time, the battle seemed endless. Doing everything he could to keep the fish from

Above: l-r, Daddy, Polly Stoker, Mother and Bill Stoker, 1955.

Left: l-r, Polly Stoker, Grandpa Kovacs, me, Billy Stoker, Daddy, Pat Stoker and Bill Stoker, 1955.

diving deep into the weeds, Bill battled for an hour until the line snapped. When he returned to his pier, shut off the motor and tied the boat to one of the posts, Polly knew by the scowl on his face that something had happened that wasn't good. She watched him march up the plank over the sand and to the cottage, open the door and slam it hard enough to let everyone know that he wanted to be left alone and not have to answer any questions.

The next day, he opened up during breakfast and confessed that he had never had a fish on his line like the one he lost the day before. He felt justified in being angry that the big fish scored a victory.

Cooking T-bone steaks on a makeshift grill, Mother and Daddy, 1959.

Daddy frying the fish he caught and cleaned for the resort guests.

Entertaining at the cottage: l-r, Alice Sepke, Polly Stoker, Mother, Clara Katz, Ella Ellendt

Back: Elmer Sepke, Bill Stoker, Ed Katz and Ed Ellendt, 1956.

Little Bass Lake

Hansen's Resort property crossed County Road A and disappeared deep into the woods where it met Little Bass Lake. Secluded, accented with a marshy shore, pickerel weeds and an old wooden row boat, this was one of the best kept secrets in the immediate area. The boat belonged to the resort and when Daddy learned of its availability for those who stayed at Hansen's, he had Karl, their caretaker, reserve it for him early each morning.

Daddy faced pretty much everything in life with gusto and once he had a taste of fishing the little lake early in the morning before anyone else was awake, it became his own secret domain. Little Bass Lake was shallow and on rare occasions froze out during an especially brutal winter. After restoring itself, fishing again became worth getting out of bed early for, and that's exactly what Daddy did. Every morning he'd be up about 5:30 because of a biological alarm that stirred him back home on work days as well as weekends. If there was a chill in the air, he'd make a fire in the wood stove to warm the cottage before the rest of us crawled out of bed much later. After a short trip to the outhouse directly behind the cottage, he'd pack up his fishing gear and head across the road before vanishing in the woods and the path that would lead him to the lake where the boat was tied.

Held over one shoulder by a strap was a boat cushion which freed both hands to carry a long handled landing net, his rod and reel, a cane pole, tackle box and can of worms. A gray sweatshirt worn over a white T-shirt seemed to be the only thing he needed for warmth that early on most days, otherwise, in case of rain, he wore a parka. The rest of his attire seldom changed from either tan or gray wash trousers, a hat and dark brown leather shoes protected with galoshes from paths laced with morning dew.

Because there was no motor on the boat, rowing was the only mode of operation and he did so in a methodical manner so as not to disturb the fish in this paradise where only occasional sounds of nature pierced the air. By nine o'clock, not only was breakfast waiting, but fishing on the hidden lake seemed to have run its course for that portion of the day. After tying the boat to a wood stake pressed deep into the dampness of the shoreline, he'd gather all of his belongings before returning on the same paths that wound through the woods to where the field began with the cottages in view. Added to the load was a stringer of bass or northern or both, and often, very large.

They were special private times for Daddy and sometimes for me if fishing had been particularly good and I'd go along the next morning. I remember it being a place where our conversations were whispered. I also remember only one cottage on the small lake, that being at the far end on its north shore, although I never saw anyone on or near the property.

With fishing gear in tow, I hiked alone through the woods one day from another angle, found myself at the small white dwelling slightly back from the shoreline and decided to try my luck fishing out in front. After baiting my hook and throwing out the line, the bobber would immediately disappear due to what I eventually surmised to be a very hungry turtle. That, plus being alone, somewhat concerned me. I decided that I had had enough and began to thread my way through the woods to the south where a connection was made with the worn path that took me to the end of the woods and the openness of a field. After crossing A, I walked toward #5 to unload my gear and reconnect with family.

I've often wondered, since then, if I would be so brave today to willingly lose myself in the woods, a place, as a young girl, I had little or no fear of.

Those early morning fishing escapades amid the solitude and privacy of Little Bass Lake continued to add intrigue to Daddy's early mornings during his 19 years at the resort and eventually became memories that were impossible to duplicate.

With all the fish Daddy caught, cleaned and froze from both lakes, hundreds were used each year for a fish fry held on Barney and Flo's lakeside lawn for all the people who were staying at the resort during that particular week. Fish were fried in heavy cast iron pans placed on a makeshift grill, low to the ground, over a wood-fueled fire. It was fun for everyone, especially Daddy who was proud to have furnished the fruits of his daily fishing escapades.

Karl

Daddy returning from Bass Lake.

Kilkare Road

There seemed to be more than a tinge of magic attached to every day at the lake that wasn't absorbed at the time. As questions surfaced years later, we attempted to recapture the same experiences without much success. Youngsters have a unique way of exploring the unknown being innately equipped by enjoying each moment without hesitation or interruption. Insects, weather and any other possible deterrents were usually dealt with void of fear. That wonderful invincible attitude we possessed prevented ruination of innocent episodes like walking a major portion of Kilkare Road barefoot and returning with nary a care or complaint. It was 2.1 miles of pleasure from A to a sharp curve where we either turned around and headed back, or meandered just a bit longer.

Back then, Kilkare Road was sandy-soft underfoot and seemed to be in the middle of nowhere. A handful of vacation friends staying at Hansen's with their parents decided one day to take a walk for a first hand investigation of what the road was like and where it would lead. Innocuous from the beginning to the end, our conversations and laughter along the way would be music today to anyone's ears. Toss a rock. Throw a stick. Pick a wild flower. Pull a weed. Hear a noise? Stop breathing, look and listen. Was it a chipmunk? A bird in flight? Squirrels scattering? A snake? A raccoon or skunk? Hold your breath! Worse ever, a bear? Better yet, a deer?

Was it possible that such an adventure on a hot summer day could be void of mosquitoes, gnats or deer flies? Looking back, I wonder where pesky insects were hiding. Or was their absence due to moments of innocence of our ages? After all, the long walk took place during that flying insect interim between July and August which in adulthood could mean a bona fide… nightmare. Maybe the insects really did annoy us, but being kids, we didn't pay the same attention to such annoyances as adults might. Was it possible when a random car passed by that we never coughed or rubbed our eyes when road dust filtered through the air? And why were we never concerned that strangers might be lurking in the shadows of the woods? We never thought about that or wearing hats or sunglasses or using mosquito repellent. It was intrigue mixed with youth that made the long walk back seem shorter than it really was.

They were such special times in our young lives and surprises made them even better. When we reached what we presumed was the end of the road, before a sharp curly curve where the golf course begins today, there before us was a stone fireplace propped alone on property overgrown with weeds. Walls of a building that once surrounded the fireplace apparently had disappeared during a fire. We conjured a scene in our minds and questioned how tragic the fire might have been, why the fireplace was still there and, as casually as turning around to head back to our cottages, changed the subject once again, leaving the fireplace propped in the weeds behind us.

Kilkare Road, early 1950s.

Lee Katz and his friend, Frankie.

More than half a century later, the Kilkare scene remains vivid in my mind due to a good memory and stories shared with Barefoot Annie whose family summered on Birch Island well before my time. It was a popular north woods vacation spot where big city people, back in 1915, began to enjoy seasonal sojourns to Point Kilkare on the northwest side of Birch Island Lake. C. E. Hatcher was the builder and owner of the lodge, its cabins, and the adjacent Kilkare Farm. Multiple sales transactions occurred through the years, one made in 1924 by Grover Elmore. Many years later, the property was purchased by Wisconsin land entrepreneur N. E. Isaacson who developed what we know today as Voyager Village. As a reminder of the past, Elmore's home remains along the Voyager Village par three golf course.

Kilkare Resort had more than a few lives. After the lodge burned to the ground, it was reconstructed. Was it possible that the fireplace in the weeds and woods belonged to the old lodge? When Chicago magnate Walter Johnson of the Johnson Candy Company fame purchased the property, his employees vacationed at the resort, free of charge. One of the original resort cabins was eventually sold to Grant DeNormandy, another wealthy Chicago businessman whose fortune in the Windy City was made in the dry cleaning business. Later, DeNormandy and his wife, Evelyn, built a home on the same portion of land which was accessible only by boat. After his death in a car accident that occurred between Chicago and Birch Island, DeNormandy's wife remained on Birch Island before selling and moving to a lake closer to Hayward.

DeNormandy's widow was known by locals as being an interesting person whose Birch Island estate was furnished with priceless antiques. My parents were invited to the elaborately furnished home one evening after striking up a conversation with her at a local restaurant. They enjoyed their visit and the evening would become one of their most uniquely interesting *up north* experiences. Although I never had an opportunity to meet Mrs. D., I witnessed something with a few of my summer friends that remains today as another lake mystery.

It was a warm, mid-summer afternoon when we were fishing from our rowboat near the warden's cottage on A when a car slowed down and parked at the edge of the lake. We recognized the lone occupant and driver as Mrs. D. and watched from the boat as she made her way down a sandy embankment before stopping to dig a hole in the sand with her hands. After placing something in the hole, she replaced the sand, patting it with her hands to cover any hint of something being buried. Not once during that time did she look up to see if anyone was watching. When she had finished, she returned to the car, drove slowly toward Kilkare Road, turned and disappeared.

If there was anything I could kick myself for today, it would be my failure to row over to the burial place and, out of sheer nosiness, satisfy my curiosity. With typical youthful inquisitiveness, we created scenario that included either a gun or jewelry or money. Later, an adult tampered with the excitement of our imaginations by suggesting that it could have been an article of clothing sprayed by a skunk that needed entombing. Not appreciating anything that sensible, the scene remains a mystery that only Mrs. D. could solve.

The last time I walked Kilkare Road with cottage friends was during the mid-50s when Lee Katz and I veered from the rest and wandered through the woods in the direction of Bass Lake. There were few cottages or cabins to give us a sense of direction, but before long we realized that we were approaching an old house or cottage most likely occupied at certain times of the year, yet deserted at the moment. Lying at the base of a tree near what we assumed to be the far edge of a backyard was a huge moose rack. Having no previous knowledge of moose roaming the area, I felt that I had discovered a collectible. Although somewhat damaged by the gnawing of sharp-toothed animals, the rack was beautiful and I carried it back to our cottage, then hauled it back home to Madison as a gift to my high school art teacher for classroom sketching. Until graduation in 1956, the rack remained perched on a class room cabinet as a daily reminder of one of my cherished Kilkare Road adventures.

Webb Lake

Among Daddy's youthful passions were sports, reading about King Arthur and his wife, Guinevere, Sir Lancelot, Knights of the Round Table and, in the Sunday comic strips that we all called the funny paper, *Prince Valiant.* Thrown in for good measure were poems or readings he referred to as Anglo-Saxon that he was forced to memorize and recite as a student at Central High School in Madison where he graduated in 1925.

What would this have to do with a place about ten miles through the woods called The Cabaret at Webb Lake? Well, by fast-forwarding to the 1950s, it was where we'd go on summer weekend nights when a three-piece homegrown group of musicians would set up in a small alcove to entice locals and vacationers like us to dance the night away. It was a great experience to mingle and besides, I loved the décor. Bar stools were tree trunks with the sawed seats shellacked to prevent slivers and wear. Behind the bar hung locally caught fish, mounted to remind everyone who entered just how good fishing was in the area. On the wall behind the bar stools were more mounted fish and a large bulletin board layered with randomly thumb-tacked business cards for customers to study for a variety of reasons.

One night, Daddy was nearly danced to death by Mrs. Fontaine who owned Oak Lake Inn. She was a huge woman in weight as well as height and the sight of her dancing with Daddy, being about 5' 8" and 150 pounds, was one to behold. Daddy, being a champion dancer from the late 1920s, could keep up with her as she, too, was a great dancer, but Daddy being the gentleman he was couldn't refuse her requests to dance because he felt it would be rude. At the end of each dance, he'd glance at us and roll his eyes as he walked her back to her chair before the next song began, hoping she'd be tired and want to relax which never happened until the chair broke as she sat down, sending her rump first to the floor. Everyone gasped, but being a good-natured woman, she laughed, picked herself up and Daddy, sweet Daddy, found another chair for her to sit on. It was a perfect time to end the evening and say goodbye.

Otherwise, on any other evening, when the waltzes and two-steps ended and instruments were packed away by the musicians for another week, we'd pile into Daddy's car and head back to the cottage. Before too many silent minutes had passed, Daddy would begin his recitation of Anglo-Saxon with words ending in iths. With the windows rolled down to let the warm evening summer air pass through the car in the pitch blackness surrounding us, depending on what portion of the moon was showing, the *willith, nillith, prillith* verses continued while Daddy carefully maneuvered the car to avoid a skunk here, a deer there. The only other sounds were those of the rhythmic midnight hums of north wood insects.

While the entertaining continued with *ith* verses and a mischievous vein or two of laughter in between, we'd all wonder if this was the night he could get beyond one particular verse that always ended like an ellipsis leaving our thoughts stranded. Years later, after Elaine had married, the ellipsis served as a signal for my brother-in-law Gordy, the proverbial Norwegian Lutheran with blond hair, blue eyes, and a smile that could warm a monster's heart, to begin loudly singing "Jesus Loves Me" through the open car window on his side. Mother, Elaine and I, sitting semi-squashed in the back seat, giggled at his exuberance because he was, in many ways, a quiet person who wouldn't ordinarily perform in such a way. Giggling, too, because we had grown up hearing and singing the hauntingly beautiful Gregorian chant as Catholic school students. And what was this "Jesus Loves Me" music that he sang with such conviction like a kid at a southern Baptist revival who was nourished on grits and sunshine? After Dick and I were married, he was added to the car and the unrehearsed fun we had together on the way home from Webb Lake.

We'd laugh at Daddy because he was that incredible type of a person who could find humor in something he tried and somewhat failed at, which added humor to teasing Gordy about his songs. Before long our laughs pierced the solitude of the midnight hour until we'd arrive back at the cottage to retire after yet another great evening together. How I wish, today, that we had secretly recorded one of those short trips back from an evening of music and dance at The Cabaret in Webb Lake.

One night, right after we returned and had locked the cottage door, we heard a loud tiger-like screech that took our breath away and made us stand still wondering what was happening. Everything seemed to vibrate from heavy galloping around the cottage before the screeching and the rumbling ended when, whatever it was, ran away. Assuming it was a deer being chased by a bobcat, I wondered about that possibility many years later when I witnessed a cougar crossing Alden Road.

Kissing the Blarney Stone gang, l-r, Karl, Barney, Mother, Flo Hansen, and Elmer and Alice Sepke.

Kissing the Blarney Stone

One reached North Sand Lake adulthood at Hansen's Resort during clandestine evening meetings held down at the store. Invitations were made to special individuals to become a member of the Blarney Club of which I knew absolutely nothing about. Mother and Daddy were members, but never spoke about it in my presence. Clueless, I felt honored that summer of my 16th year to be notified of being selected to join. It didn't take long to sense that my ever-protective mother had her doubts about me being initiated which made the thought of joining the club even more intriguing. Being the happy-go-lucky guy Daddy was, he chuckled through a kitchen table discussion of to be or not to be until Mother finally gave in and agreed that I could join.

Kissing the Blarney Stone in Ireland is said to bestow eloquence on all who dare. Not knowing what it had to do with Burnett County, I sensed that it was somewhat of a big deal at the resort and I'd have a membership card to flash with no dues to pay. Initiation took place only during the summer months when the season was in full swing and a person worthy of the honor was selected by Barney Hansen, the Norwegian owner of Hansen's Resort. That was it.

A day after the announcement was made, word quickly spread throughout the enclave of the resort, making sure everyone who already was a member would attend. After supper dishes were washed and put away, we walked down to the store and were warmly greeted with broad smiles from everyone there. There was excitement in the air and I continued to thrive on the mystery of it all.

In front of the large reach-in floor cooler against the wall was a wood platform on which a large wood chair with arm rests added a touch of a humble throne. Not remembering having seen either platform or chair before in the store, my mind raced as Barney, wearing denim overalls and white T-shirt, walked in with Flo at his side. When it was assumed that everyone had arrived, Barney stepped from behind the bar, lifted his hands to quiet the crowd, and told them the initiation was about to begin for me to become a member of their private Blarney Club.

Mother and Daddy were standing front and center as I was led to the throne and asked to sit down so Flo could blindfold me. When she finished, someone on each side of me placed a hand on my arms and lifted me to a standing position on the platform before grabbing my shoulders to turn me around and around. When I became dizzy, they moved me backwards to the throne where I sat down again. With the blindfold still in place, I was asked to lean forward to kiss the Blarney Stone. Naively thinking of something like a rock, the surface instead was warm and soft with a deep crease down the center and a putrid smell. My blindfold was removed and there, standing slightly stooped over in front of me, was the backside of Barney who seemed to be quickly pulling his overalls back in place. At the same time, everyone, including Mother and Daddy, started clapping, shouting, laughing and congratulating me and…that was it. I had become a North Sand Lake adult by kissing Barney's rump, only it really was Flo's folded arm made stinky with a good dose of Limburger cheese. Not only had I become a bona fide member of the Blarney Club in less than five minutes, and remained the center of attention throughout the evening as well as continued celebrity status the next day, but finally understood why Mother felt a need to protect me from something she wasn't sure her "little girl" could handle.

The Blarney Club card, signed by Barney Hansen, was placed in my billfold and carried with great pride for years to come. It meant that I could mingle with adults at any time in the store because of my club adult status. Although somewhere, through the years, the card disappeared, shown here is Marie Barut's card as a Blarney Club member, shared by her son, Bob, to use in this chapter.

Leef Shores and the Empty Chelmo Silo

It was a hot August day in the late 1940s when Mother, Elaine and I decided to take a walk down A to explore Leef Road. The sand and gravel road that turned off County Road A seemed to bury our feet in fine sand making it difficult to walk due to the dry conditions. Leef Road may not have extended to Mallard Lake Road as it does today, but instead seemed to be more of a private dead-end path perfect for taking our time in the warmth of the hour.

Along the road grew raspberry and blackberry bushes blessed with sunshine during much of the daytime hours. In shady areas poison ivy grew in abundance. A polite invasion of someone else's land is always accompanied by intrigue and through the stillness of the afternoon we spotted an old gray house hidden by full grown trees and dense brush just past the Olson property and across to the west side of the road. We would learn later that the house belonged to the Leef family for which the road was named.

The Leef family immigrated from Sweden in 1896 and played an integral role in the history of North Sand Lake and its northwestern periphery. John Adolf Leef and his wife, Rosina, left Sunrise, Minnesota and arrived in Jackson Township in 1896 to homestead on the northwest side of North Sand Lake with their children, Henning, Edwin, Oscar, Ellick, and Rose, with daughter Hilda remaining in Sunrise. Although John Leef was a dairy farmer, he was particularly proud of the sawmill he owned and operated and the native timber cut into lumber for building. As a concerned parent, John and Rosina realized a need for a nearby school and, for the convenience of their children, established the first Leef School in the upstairs of his sawmill woodshed. Later, a few miles south of Mallard Lake, a North Sand Lake school would begin serving area children. Prominent and highly respected, John A. Leef served his community well as Township Chairman in 1915, Town Board Chairman in the mid-1920s, and also as a member of the Leef School Board.

Many years after my initial barefoot stroll on a sandy Leef Road, I met with one of J.A. Leef's grandsons, Ainard, to learn more about the immediate area and its past. Ainard and his wife, June (Chelmo) welcomed me into the kitchen of their Pratt Road home in October, 1994, to be interviewed for this book. Their Pratt Road property, originally designated as railroad land for future development, was purchased in 1910 by Ainard's father, Adolph "Edwin" Leef. Ainard and June had grown up together as Ainard's grandfather owned the Leef Road property to the North Sand Lake's northwestern shoreline, extending to A and included land to the immediate left and June's father owned the farm property and woods on the other side of A which encircled half of Bass Lake and ended at Kilkare Road.

When Ainard's grandfather homesteaded the North Sand Lake property in 1896, it consisted of 186 acres and one-half mile of lakeshore later referred to as Leef Shores. There was no access to Leef Road back then and what we know today as A was described by Ainard as being nothing more than a wagon trail. In the late 1930s, with WPA manpower, the township furnished teams of horses and wagons to build Leef Road. Ainard remembers when some of their Leef Road farm property near the public boat landing was in the water, and during a serious drought the water level receded to such extremes that the shoreline became a baseball field for the Leef boys and their friends. Another severe dry spell prompted them to play baseball at a new field near A and Kilkare Road where a marsh is prominent today. Back then, Leef and his friends referred to it as The Meadow.

In 1915, June Chelmo's parents, Leonard and Ethel (Franklin) Chelmo, purchased 200 acres from A. W. Tigges which included an ample portion of the north shoreline extending across A from the Leef farm, through half of Little Bass Lake and over to Kilkare Road. In the 1920s, Oscar Smith, Sr., a practicing attorney from Indiana, purchased property from Chelmo that included North Sand Lake property so he could build a cottage for his family. Smith offered his boat to June and her oldest brother, Lyle, and the two had many good fishing experiences on the lake. June remembers a spot on the lake that was so shallow it seemed almost island-like where she could easily watch fish swim under the boat.

When asked years later about the Smith property, Oscar Smith, Jr. recalled having no electricity, no indoor plumbing, and because water from the well had a strong taste of iron, the Smith family drank water from the lake. There were only three cottages on the lake in 1931 and with little activity, bathing suits were seldom worn. Oscar Smith, Sr., sold a portion of his property to Tom and Cora Cleve who built a house on the shoreline (located today behind the Sandbar) before eventually selling the land to Barney and Florence Hansen to establish Hansen's Resort.

As with other homesteads, a portion of property on the Leef farm was reserved as a burial place for family members. In the late 1930s, the Leef property was divided among J. A. Leef's four sons: Adolph Edwin, Karl Oscar, and Alfred Ellick divided the northern section, and John Henning was willed the southern portion of 106 acres with 1320 feet of shoreline. Adolph Edwin sold 23 acres to Walter Pulsa, and Karl Oscar sold 23 acres to Bob Kazobowski who used the lakeshore portion to establish Hilltop Resort. Roger Leef, his wife, Mary, and their two children who are fifth generation Leef family members, reside in the original Leef home still partially hidden and protected by nature's growth that separates it from North Sand Lake and Leef Shores.

As a child, Ainard often fished the back bay and the southwest shoreline with Uncle Henning, especially the far western end of the shoreline where they waded with 10 foot cane poles and caught countless bullheads and dogfish. Because the roadsides were alive with frogs and toads, there was always an ample supply of bait to interchange with worms and grasshoppers. Ainard claims the entry into the back bay was abundant with other species of fish, but admits that it was fun keeping busy and catching any kind of fish rather than catching nothing at all.

During my visit, June Chelmo's memory captured the time Glenn and Molly Thompson held School Board meetings at their resort on the east side of the lake. If Leonard Chelmo planned to attend a meeting during the bitter cold winter months and June accompanied him on the horse-drawn wagon or sleigh trip across the frozen lake, he'd make certain that her feet were kept warm by bricks or iron that had been heated on the wood stove. Also remembered were experiences during other seasons and a day back in the mid-1920s when a storm quickly moved in. Frightened by its intensity and dark clouds, her father ran as fast as he could carrying her in his arms while hollering to his sons to follow to outrun a tornado that was, literally, at their heels. They all survived, but the storm destroyed their silo in the field on the other side of A.

While June was sharing this story with me, my own memory returned to a summer experience of back in the late-1940s when Mother, Elaine and I ventured through the woods across the road from the resort to follow the path that Daddy walked early each morning to Little Bass Lake where he fished from a flat-bottom boat. Because the south end of the lake was low and marshy, the three of us left behind the area where the boat was tied and meandered through the dampness to dryer land on the other side of the lake where we scaled a hill of full grown trees carpeted with berry bushes and ripe fruit. On the other side of the hill was an open field of waist-high weeds literally alive with butterflies.

The excitement of searching for anything and everything in foreign territory rewarded us as we came upon a clearing in the middle of the field and a deep round concrete circle filled with metal and glass. An oven. An ice box. Pots and pans. Broken dishes. A wash bucket. Looking rather innocent and inviting for the curiosity seeker I was, I poked a stick at things in the deep dry well and just as I was lowering myself into the cavity, Mother yanked me back saying something like, "Catherine, don't you dare!" Good thing she warned me because when I tossed a stone into the center of the circle of junk, frogs jumped and snakes slithered everywhere from their shaded hiding places.

I never forgot the fun we had exploring that day, and many times later I searched, to no avail, for the stone circle dropped into a field of weeds. Forever bewildered by its presence as to what it was, how it got there, and why it was in the middle of nowhere, I was elated to hear June's story about the storm because I realized then that the wide dry well was the foundation of Chelmo's silo, destroyed by a tornado, forgotten with time. The mystery had been solved.

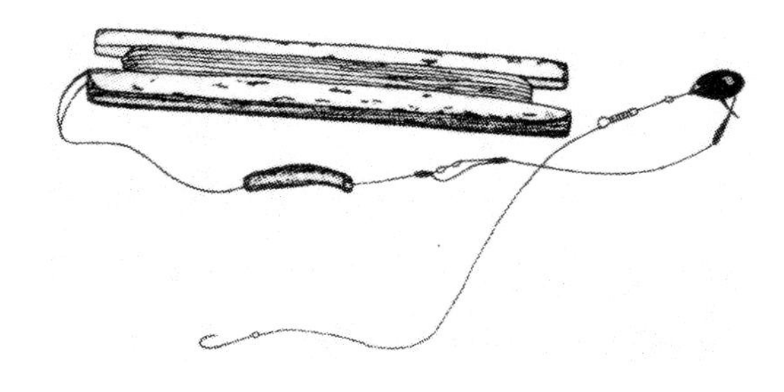

With my best friend, Diane.

Diane

As I grew older, though still a teenager, summers at the cottage remained as important to me as those spent as a youngster. I really didn't care what was going on back home as long as I could be *up north* at the cottage. However, when I reached eighth grade, I asked Mother if I could invite Diane Semrad, my longtime best friend, to join us. By then, Elaine had graduated from high school and was attending the University of Wisconsin in Madison. Having a summer job kept her back home which meant the double bed in my cottage bedroom was all mine with plenty of room for someone else.

I first met Diane in third grade at St. Bernard's Catholic School. The church yard was across the street from Semrad's house, and up the street and across the tracks from ours. The proximity of our houses allowed us to meet before school and gather again after supper when we'd sit on neighborhood curbs under the street lights to play street games with other neighborhood friends. We recorded ourselves singing Hit Parade songs a few blocks away on Atwood Avenue at Irv Goff's Music Company and were surprised we sounded so nasal on record. We filled spiral notebooks with pencil drawings of fictional mystery book covers, tried to act like Ava Gardner, imitate Frankie Lane and cleverly rearranged the first letters of the first and last names of well-known entertainers...Srank Finatra, Back Jenny and Lanky Fraine to name just a few.

We sang Gregorian chant together, prayed the rosary together and every morning, with our good friend Carol Weber, hung our heads over the front pew during Mass to watch for any centipedes that might appear on the Communion steps. At the same time, we hoped the nun was paying less attention to us and more attention to the priest at the altar. Otherwise, we'd feel a sharp poke telling us we'd better shape up fast...or else. I remember feeling shocked to learn that someone hid a roll of

Relaxing in the best lake in the county.

At night, down at "the store" with Mother, smiling, sitting second from the left at the table. Standing behind her, me, left, and Diane, right.

toilet paper behind the life-size statue of the Blessed Mother, and was also surprised to find empty wine bottles in the convent garbage can.

Aware of how temperamental girls can be at times, Diane and I never had a disagreement. We just giggled our way through every grade and every school-related and social experience. We ate curly-cue French fries together at Ward's Hungry! Hungry! Hungry! drive-in across from Lake Monona, sipped malted milks at the Ice Cream Shop across from East High, and doubled for our Junior Prom. Although I had wonderful friendships with other girl friends, she became part of the family because every morning for four years she stopped at our house on the way to school so we could walk together. Unfortunately for Diane, I was never ready on time. Four long years of arriving at 7:30 in the morning meant sitting on the davenport in our front room, waiting for me to get my act together. If there was any reason for her to be upset, it should have been for that alone, yet she never complained.

Diane's family didn't take summer vacations like we did so having her join us through the years was two-fold. We explored our surroundings and took advantage of doing together what I did alone every other summer—swimming, sunning, floating on air mattresses, fishing and hiking. The most fun, however, was being down at the store each night when everyone staying at the resort gathered together for good times. If some cute local boys happened to stop by the store, they'd find a way to mingle with the crowd to get closer to us during which time my parents kept their eyes wide open to catch a glimpse of anything that didn't meet with their approval. One night, a couple of college guys stopped at Barney's to have a few beers. When they asked if we wanted to go outside and fool around (which meant nothing more to me than hanging out on the premises) the expressions on my parents' faces signaled a big emphatic "No" and that was the end of that. We were 17, survived the intermittent disappointment, and after the guys left we just went on having a good time inside with all the resort people.

It would be impossible to spend a week together having fun without some kind of glitch and it happened one morning when we were the first ones to open our eyes, then stayed in bed whispering so we didn't wake Mother and Daddy. The inside of the cottages had the same unfinished look as they did the first year the resort opened. There was no insulation, dry wall or paneling, which created a charming raw appearance in each shoreline dwelling. Over the bed, from wall to wall, two pine beams crisscrossed in the center where the light box was secured with a bare bulb and long pull-string attached. We decided to take the long silk scarves we brought along to wear during Mass on Sunday and tie one end of each scarf around the beam while the other two ends were tied to one of our big toes. When we were finished, we laid back and started to laugh. The stupidity of it all made us laugh even harder when we discovered that we were unable to sit up straight to untie our toes. Laughs turned to giddy hysterics of how stupid we felt and would look when Mother would have to be called in to rescue us. When she opened the door and saw us, me with my right leg and Diane with her left leg straight up in the air with toes neatly tied to silk scarves, Mother shook her head, smiled and said, "Oh, you girls" before untying us and saying, "what did you do that for? "

We remained the best of friends after graduation. The following year, Diane was a bridesmaid in my wedding. When she married and moved away, we continued to correspond during the holidays. In writing, we'd recall our flawless friendship and how foolish and innocent we were about many things, chalking it up to part of growing up.

The reminiscences and laughs ended a few summers ago when Diane called me at our cottage from her home in Louisville, Kentucky to tell me she had cancer. A short time later, she passed away.

Dinner at Perry's (today's Channel House, Siren), l-r, Daddy, Emma and Ralph Roman, and Mother

Cottage Characters

Most of our cottage friends were average people like us. A few hinted of some affluence, but only with the cars they drove, while others we just weren't sure about. One thing we did have in common was enjoying the resort and the lake which was evident each night when everyone gathered down at the store to party.

It was a wonderful assortment of people, each unique in their own way. One who stood out more than the rest was a tall, gangly, bespectacled and balding man (often without teeth) who we knew as Ralph Roman. Each summer, Ralph and his wife, Emma, drove up from Peoria, Illinois at the same time we were there and a few summers they stayed next door in #4 cottage which made the walk back and forth between our cottages convenient for many reasons.

Ralph was a joker, a self-made comedian ready to capture an audience at any given moment. You could tell he had been like that his entire life and he wasn't about to change just because he was getting older. Ralph's attire at the cottage was a white, sleeveless, scooped-neck undershirt worn with gray wash pants. Considering his physical appearance, that alone created a memory. Emma, who wore house-dresses, and shorts only during hot spells, was constantly after him to behave himself, but it never worked. Ralph was so funny that he had us laughing all the time about… nothing.

We never knew when he was telling the truth or a fib. One day, he confessed to Mother and me that he had performed in the past as a clown, but also was one of the actors on the Fibber McGee and Molly radio program, namely Mr. Wimple. After our mouths dropped, it seemed only natural to shake off the shock and ask for his autograph which came later in the form of a note, some of which was, and still is, legible. Written during the first half of the 1950s, aged Scotch Tape marks remain.

From that confessed moment on, Ralph seemed to get funnier by the day. Although Mother and Daddy liked their privacy, they never minded when he opened the side screen door and walked in uninvited because they knew he'd have them both laughing within minutes. When the weather was conducive to sitting outside, chairs were set up along both sides of the narrow front sidewalk connecting the cottages for friends to gather for a late afternoon cocktail party. Ralph liked his martinis, as did many others back then, and every hour spent together made us mention more than once that someone should be filming and recording what was happening. While Emma continued her efforts to keep Ralph from making a fool of himself, the rest of us sat back and enjoyed his antics and efforts to stay as funny as a clown and the radio character he once was. The more we laughed, the better he performed. Every joke and every laugh ignited a bigger flame.

Because "Mr. Wimple" didn't want anyone else at the resort to know who he had been professionally, he asked Mother and I not to mention his involvement with the Fibber McGee and Molly program. I don't know how Emma found out about the tales he told us, but when she did, she went through the cottage roof. Was it because of a pact the two had that the professional secret was not to be shared with people they met on vacation? We weren't sure. We thought the first confession was harmless. It took a long time before Ralph made another confession, this time to tell us that he had fibbed and really wasn't Mr. Wimple. Shocked again because by that time we were totally convinced that he was and yet, we laughed and forgave him purely because by that time a summer friendship highly seasoned with laughter and good times had evolved.

Did we laugh for two years for nothing? Hardly. Ralph Roman was our summer friend and a cottage character we would never forget.

Alice, Elmer and Kilroy

The lake was beyond anything we could possibly have imagined, the cottages were cozy and fragrant like a pine forest because of the unpainted pine boards used to build each one, the store where we hung out after supper offered nightly entertainment with beverages to drink and music from the juke box. Yet, the people we became acquainted with added the finishing touch. In fact, many of us became such good friends that weeks the following summer would be reserved at the same time for somewhat of an annual reunion. One couple who stands out the most in my mind was Alice and Elmer Sepke.

The middle-aged Sepkes from either Berwyn or Cicero, Illinois, always stayed in the # 10 cottage located on the other side of Hansen's house behind the store. The one-bedroom cottage had a different floor plan from the rest that were lined up along the shoreline on the other side of Hansen's and was sandwiched between the Hansen's and Karl, the resort handyman whose small one room cottage was on the opposite side and close to the shoreline. Sepke's may have thought that #10 offered a little more privacy besides having only one bedroom. Although they had no children, a little white poodle and a big black shiny Buick seemed to be their rewards in life.

Alice and Elmer were totally unaffected by status or material things except for the Buick which was Elmer's shining star. He kept it polished at all times and parked it where nothing would offend it in any way. We never knew what Elmer did for a living, but thought he might have been a truck driver. His hands showed wear. He had a thin mustache, piercing gray eyes and a space between his two upper front teeth. He also had a great big heart. Elmer never said much, but you knew if he liked you. In turn, you welcomed his friendship. He was also a diehard fisherman who returned to the lake each fall with Alice to fish in cooler weather.

Alice's daily attire was a patterned cotton house dress worn with white anklets and white oxfords with chunky heels. At times, when the temperatures rose, she might slip into a pair of shorts, but otherwise it was a dress by daylight and slacks in the evening. She spent each day with her hair set with bobby pins and her head wrapped with a pink hair net of thick, silky-pink threads tied at the nape of her neck. Wearing a matching pink bow, the poodle was her constant companion which she cradled in her arm.

Before suppertime, Alice would remove the hair net, pull out the bobby pins, fix her hair and prepare supper. When dishes were done, minus the dog, Alice and Elmer walked through the yard to the back door of the store where all the resort guests and their kids gathered. Although the store sold bread, ice cream and other staples, it also had a bar, bar stools and a jukebox. For a quarter, the jukebox played five favorite tunes while people talked, laughed, danced, drank beer or pop before slipping another quarter in the slot for five more tunes. When it was time for the little ones to go to bed, a parent, usually the mother, would walk back to their cottage with the children, tuck them into bed, then return to the store where the music and laughter continued to sift through the pines while everyone else fell asleep. There was no reason to worry about them being alone, or whether to lock their doors. And there were no fears about them sneaking out. They knew better.

One night, as a young teen who was allowed to stay up later than usual, I noticed as I left the store to head back to the cottage that someone had used their finger to draw a picture in the evening dew that coated Elmer's big black shiny Buick parked under the lights behind the store and near their own cottage. Drawn in a comical way on the trunk was a strange looking bald-headed man with a funny looking face and a long nose that hung over the fence he obviously was standing behind, grasping with his fingers. Not being at all familiar with the drawing or the words "Kilroy was here," Daddy explained to me as we walked back to the cottage that it was a humorous character leftover from World War II. After all these years that particular scene and the calm of the late August night air remains so vivid in my mind that Kilroy and Alice and Elmer will always be a fragment of resort happenings and people too good to forget. Later I would learn that it was Elmer himself who drew Kilroy on the trunk of his car on his way to the outhouse.

I don't know if Elmer ever fished back home, but he loved getting out on the lake and usually fished alone. His daytime and fishing attire was the same: dark gray work clothes, a Fedora-style hat, and a cigarette at the corner of his mouth. One miserable stormy day, Elmer went out on the lake and by nightfall had not yet returned. Alice was frantic. She came over to our place, paced back and forth, cried, and kept looking out the front window hoping to see a hint of a light from a boat in the pitch blackness of the night. Conditions were too awful for anyone to go out in search of him and the situation left us all with an empty and helpless feeling. It was about 10:30 when Elmer finally returned, oblivious to anyone's concern, including his wife. The relief of seeing him alive made Alice forget about how worried, yet angry she had been and the next day, everything was back to normal.

Although cottage friendships were refreshingly wonderful and annually nourishing, once the resort closed, summer plans drastically changed for everyone. Our summer family of friends went in many different directions and the only time we saw Alice and Elmer again was one day when they stopped by Mother and Daddy's cottage on the south shore a year after it was built and once, just to hello, when they passed through Madison on their way home in the fall.

Elaine's Friends and a Visitor from Norway

He was young, handsome, tan and well-built, yet no one seems to remember him except five 16-year-old teenage girls, one being my sister, Elaine, and me. The blonde, blue-eyed Ainard Neygaard (spelled phonetically because no one on the lake claims to have known him although he must have been a summer guest of someone on or near the lake), arrived in July of 1950 when Elaine's longtime school friends Carlene, Jean, Pat and Sharon spent a week with us. He was also very polite and flirtingly delighted to meet five pretty girls his own age who were sunning themselves on the shoreline in front of our #5 cottage. It took only a few days before he became a pest.

In the beginning, the girls were thrilled to meet someone their own age of the opposite sex and the flirting became somewhat mutual between giggling girls who seemed determined to make the foreign visitor with the heavy accent feel welcome. But, by the third day, the girls decided they had had enough and wanted to be left alone with their beach towels, sunglasses, and glass bottles of Johnson's Baby Oil to induce beautiful tans. So, they talked less. Giving him the silent treatment wasn't successful, nor was their attempt to avoid him. To fill the gaps of silence, he'd show off his body and strength by doing handstands on our pier. When he needed to do

Pat Sutter, Sharon McMahon, Jean LeFebvre, Carlene Stoker and Elaine Tripalin, 1950.

more to turn their heads, during a handstand he'd slowly lower his body until it was parallel with the water. It was a feat that normally would have impressed anyone. Apparently, the impressions from similar calisthenics performed back in Norway meant nothing to the girls from Madison.

By the fourth day, the girls ran from window to window pulling down the shades if they caught a glimpse of him walking down the shoreline toward the cottage. Before venturing outdoors, each girl would peek from the windows to make certain they could go outside and not be bothered. Yet, their efforts continued to fail. During one of their carefully guarded conversations, he must have overheard them talking about a dance that was being held a few miles down the county road in a small roadside inn because shortly after we arrived that evening, in walked Ainard.

Back then, dances in rural farm communities meant a large imaginary doughnut-like circle on the floor for couples to follow while moving in the same direction. Clockwise two-steps kept a nice flow on the dance floor with no bumps, grinds or toe-crunching. Chairs pushed against the walls were resting places to return to at the end of each dance to chat with family and friends before returning to the circle once again.

Although the lights were turned low, it was impossible for Elaine and her friends to fade away in the shadows against the dark wood paneling and Ainard, wearing clean, crisp, perfectly pressed clothes, approached them ready to dance. He was turned down by everyone except Carlene who started to feel sorry for him and accepted, stood up and followed him out to the circle where the two moved awkwardly in the same direction as the locals. Watching all of this and being compassionate like Carlene, I felt sorry for him and would have been happy to dance with him, but I was only 12 and I'm not sure Mother would have approved.

The evening ended earlier than planned because the girls were anxious to slip out and disappear for the rest of the night. We packed ourselves into the car with Mother and Daddy and roared back to the cottage with the girls frantically planning how they would avoid him the next day. If the picture taken of all of them together on the shoreline that first day or two hadn't disappeared through the years, you'd see him on this page as a handsome, tanned Norwegian teenage boy who was just trying to befriend a bunch of fickle 16-year-old girls. Maybe, with a picture, someone would recognize him as the young relative who visited them back in the summer of 1950.

Ed Shipanik, Sr. with his 45 inch, 26 ¼ pound northern pike, 1952.

The Shipanik Gang

If you are convinced after numerous attempts through years of fishing the depths of North Sand Lake in search of the big ones, to no avail, and that the number and size of the fish on any given day are nothing more than fables, read on. In fact, some tales are so exciting you might want to grab your pole and head out to your favorite weed beds for a trophy fish.

It seems only right that this chapter includes visual proof. But first, as an introduction to the pictures, let me tell you about the Shipanik Gang, a large happy family that headed north from the Chicago area every summer to occupy all ten cottages at the same time at Hansen's Resort. This group just loved to have fun. So much so that

Ed Shipanik and wife, Emily, with their sons, Gene on the left, and Ed. Jr., on the right.

we were always thankful our reservations didn't overlap with theirs. For when the Shipaniks moved in, there wasn't much space left for anyone else.

I never met the Shipaniks back then, but heard a lot about them. Our paths never crossed because we rented the last two weeks of July and first two weeks of August, and they came up the first two weeks in June and the last two weeks in August yet it seemed natural to refer to them as the Shipanik Gang. Because our vacation schedules didn't jive, I missed out on all the excitement that crept along the north shoreline like powerful electrical currents connecting each cottage from sunrise to well past sunset into the midnight hours.

Florence Nicelwizc wasn't a member of the Shipanik family, but she was one of their close friends who made the annual summer sojourn. On September 30, 1994 she wrote a few memories to North Sand Lake property owner Art Solberg about the past while mentioning Ed Shipanik's wife Emily and others.

Dear Art,

I visited Emily about a month ago and she is looking good, but can't walk too well. We were reminiscing and talking about Sand Lake and all the good times and years spent there and the 26-pound northern pike and the 10 ½ pound walleye, both mounted. Those were the days.

I'd like to put some stories together about Hansens, Husens, Kovariks and original owners, the Kazubowskis from Chicago who bought the property and farm across the road. He and my father-in-law, John Nickelwizc, went to look over the property when they were buying on Sand Lake. That must have been in the 1930s or sooner. Then Hansen bought. We came out with Hank, Ed, Paul, Joe, and Joe and Edna Chick and the

Mike Shipanik with his grandfather, Ed. Sr., and a 5 pound bass caught during Ed. Sr.'s last trip to North Sand Lake.

Bowers, the Dalburgs. Still in contact with Dalburgs, as Emily and I are the only two left from ten cabins of people at Hansens.

Note: *Hansens, Husens, Kovariks and the original owners, the Kazubowskis* (Kazobowski) pertain to the lake's resort owners. Her mention of the *farm across the road* meant property on the other side of A that meandered down to reach the shoreline of North Sand Lake which the Kazobowskis from Chicago purchased to establish their Hilltop Resort. Hansens would not buy the shoreline property for their own resort until 1944.

Ed and Emily Shipanik and their sons, Ed, Jr. and Eugene with Emily, Shipanik's brother, Father Paul, and the rest of their relatives and friends did, indeed, make their mark at Hansen's Resort. Ed, Jr's son, Mike, the first grandson of the family, today enjoys the offerings of North Sand Lake with his children, Matthew and Katie, Shipanik fifth generation. Mike and his wife Rebecca now own Art Solberg's lake home, and recently shed light on the hilarious shenanigans of the Shipanik Gang who vacationed year after year at Hansen's Resort.

Every year, the entourage of Shipaniks and their friends would leave Chicago in the middle of the night and drive across Illinois/Wisconsin state lines in a northwest direction toward the Burnett County portion of Wisconsin. Many hours later, and well into daylight, paradise could be seen as they reached the top of a hill on County Road A to view the north shoreline of North Sand Lake. Hansen's were anxiously awaiting each smiling passenger with open arms and ten sets of cottage keys to turn over for the next two weeks.

And that's when the show began, for the fun-loving Shipaniks immediately prepared to return to Spooner to pick up the rest of the group that would soon be arriving by train from Chicago. Everyone dressed in wild outfits and costumes before getting in their cars to drive back to Spooner where they'd park, form a parade and march through the Spooner streets and two-block business district on Walnut St. that took them directly to the railroad station. Along the way, people in town who wondered what was happening joined in the parade and when they reached the train station, Joe, who had dressed like an Indian, put his ear to the track to listen for the train before announcing its arrival. A short time later, as family members and friends stepped down, they were shocked to see a mass of familiar faces interspersed with the hospitality of strangers to greet them.

Practical jokes were the Shipaniks' forte making their lives spin around as often as possible during their stay…like the time the State Police issued a bulletin for a missing beer truck and its driver. Both were eventually discovered at Barney's (Hansen's Resort) in fair condition. It seems that the Shipanik gang met the delivery man at the bar the day of his delivery and kept him there, slightly inebriated for a few days until the entire stock left on the truck was consumed by all. This joke and the fun it created cost everyone involved the value of the undelivered beer—a small price to pay, they all agreed, for the fun they had and they laughed about it for weeks. The beer truck driver, however, was not laughing and in trouble with his wife as well as his employer. But it was all in fun, the Shipaniks insisted.

Always clowning, Ed. Sr. and brother-in-law, Joe, dressed for a trip to Spooner carrying a giant "spoon" typifying a favorite northern pike lure.

With memories like these, plus countless others, who could ever forget these people? Everything they did was on such a grandiose scale that it shouldn't have surprised anyone that someone in the group would catch a huge northern pike off the end of Hansen's Resort pier. It was the big fish story of 1952 and could have been plucked from a Jack Lemon-Walter Matthau *Grumpy Old Men* movie scene. As one of those past experiences one wishes today had been filmed from start to finish and, if it had, the beginning scene would show Hansen's long weathered wood pier with a bench at the deep end where one could cast a line, then sit down to relax, and wait. That, unfortunately, would have been too placid for Ed Shipanik, Sr. who walked to the end of the pier with no intention of relaxing. Instead, he cast out his Dacron 40 pound test line with a bluegill at the end as bait before strapping the old steel rod tightly to the pier so he could play some early evening Pinochle with his cronies in cottage #1.

Ed's fishing philosophy was that the bigger the bobber, the better it was because the bluegill used as bait wouldn't be able to pull the bobber under water like the boy who cried wolf. No need to get excited about nothing, he claimed. This philosophy came in two parts and Part Two meant that once the bobber disappeared, it was time to light a cigar and only when the cigar was half smoked would he set the hook.

This time was different. The date was August 19, 1952 and it was late in the afternoon. Although occasionally glancing out at his giant 4-inch round bobber, Ed concentrated more on his card playing until he thought he heard his Shakespeare reel buzzing and when he looked up and through the open front screen door, noticed the bobber had disappeared. Running outside, he let the screen door slam as he ran toward the end of the pier with no idea how long the bobber had been under. His fishing philosophy suddenly had no meaning. He grabbed his pole and set the hook for the battle of his life. Doing everything possible to prevent the fish from wrapping the line around one of the posts of the pier, he knew it was imperative to tire it out before bringing it in to net. He was mad that he had spent so much time inside playing cards when he should have been more attentive to his line. With Pinochle being the last thing on his mind, Ed struggled to no avail. Realizing the possibility of losing the fish without seeing it, he was forced to return to the shoreline and enter the water where he and his brother-in-law, Joe, eventually beached a 45-inch, 26 ¼ pound northern pike. By that time, a shoreline of relatives and friends who had witnessed all or half of the battle were already celebrating the capture of a trophy fish.

The fish was carried into Barney's store and placed on a bed of ice in the main bar area where everyone ordered a beer to toast the catch. Well into the evening, people continued to stop by to see the fish and now and then, just when someone would lean over for a better look, the fish would suddenly flip, scaring and scattering everyone. It was just one more reason for the whole gang to laugh and toast once again.

For 12 years after it was mounted, the giant northern remained a conversation piece over an archway in the store. When Hansen's Resort was completing its last year as a resort in 1964, Ed Shipanik, Sr. expressed an interest to buy the total package, but his wife, Emily, felt differently, not wanting to be that far away from her grandchildren. The fish was removed from the bar and taken home to hang on a wall in Florence Nickelwizc's recreation room next to a 10 ½ pound North Sand Lake walleye, also mounted for posterity.

Today, the northern pike graces a wall in Mike and Rebecca Shipanik's North Sand Lake vacation home, an appropriate place since it was caught by the grandfather who taught Mike how to fish and always reminded him that if he respected the lake and its heritage, the lake would return favors. And grandpa was right. Today, Mike is an outstanding fisherman who treasures using his grandfather's rod and reel and whose largest northern pike taken from the lake weighed in at 17 ½ pounds and largest bass tipped the scales at 6 pounds. Mike's other fishing experiences on the lake include catching and releasing over 50 largemouth bass and countless northerns on any given day.

Shipanik stories continue and when Mike was a youngster, a Mepps Spinner was removed from his arm at the Spooner Clinic, a place where his Uncle Gene was taken years before when he was Mike's age to have a Johnson Silver Minnow and Pork Frog removed from his eyelid. Years later, while fishing, Mike called to a nearby loon by making cooing and clicking sounds before the loon suddenly turned and swam over to his boat. After being treated to a few minnows, the loon decided to stay close to Mike for the rest of the week. Every year that followed, when Mike arrived at the lake and began his cooing and clicking sounds, the same loon would swim up to his boat. When Mike's grandpa told him that he was "looney," it merely reinforced that Shipanik humor was still alive and well.

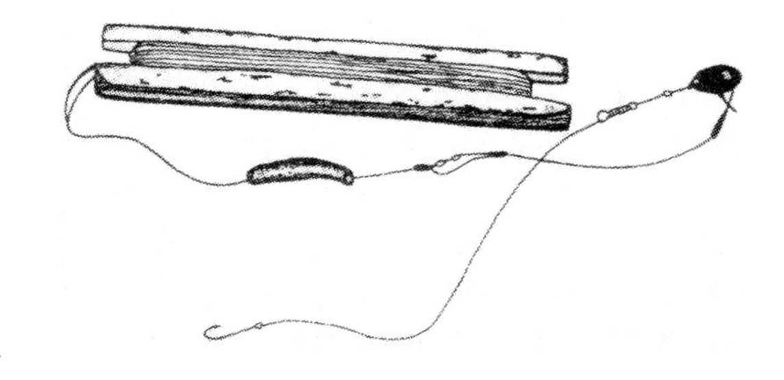

Behind the Scenes

As time went on, things began to change. Mother and Daddy's summer vacations at Hansen's Resort increased to five long wonderful weeks in cottage #5 while vacations for Elaine and I grew shorter. Although our stays became somewhat sporadic, we still entered the dates of each visit under our names printed in pencil on a stud in our bedroom as well as in the outhouse out back.

I married and had my first baby, Michael, in October, 1958. Elaine married and had her baby, Tom, in June, 1959, giving Mother and Daddy their first two grandsons and the beginning of the family's third generation on North Sand Lake.

After my divorce, Michael and I spent a week at the lake each of the next two summers with Mother and Daddy. When Dick and I married in June, 1962, the three of us stayed for a week with Mother and Daddy. One evening, after having a great time partying down at the store, Dick and I returned alone to the cottage and had no sooner turned out the lights than a racket of banging pots and pans began with hooting and hollering at our bedroom window. Having never experienced anything like it before, it took a few minutes before realizing that we were subjects of a full blown shivaree with Mother and Daddy included. After a chorus of noise and laughter that must have traveled the shorelines of the lake in that late evening hour, they all returned to the store again, leaving us alone with honeymoon-like memories neither of us had anticipated in that way, shape or form.

The following year we all rented cottages at the same time, Elaine, her husband Gordy, and their son, Tom, in one cottage, while we spent a week in #3 with Michael and our two-month-old, Bill, and Mother and Daddy being alone in #5. The next summer, Dick and I and the boys stayed in # 8. Pregnant again, this time with Bob, who was due Christmas Day, but waited until January 9th. Whether days were cold, cloudy, or rainy, the sun seemed to rise each morning because we were all together again, each family in their own cottage, yet a few doors away from family headquarters.

With all the wonderful years and treasured memories to build on, one can only imagine how sad it was to learn that the summer of 1964 would be our last year at the resort. Barney had passed away a few years before and operating a resort by herself was too much work for his wife, Flo. Her decision was to close the resort at the end of the summer and sell the cottages to individuals. Convinced our summers would never be the same, we sat around the kitchen table in #5 for serious family discussions.

There is an old Italian saying that nothing lasts forever, but we didn't want it to end like that. We refused to give up the lake of everyone's dreams, but weren't interested in buying enough resort cottages to keep us all together. Other resorts were checked out, but it was the lake we found to be irreplaceable. Forget the long distance we drove from Madison and all the lakes along the way. Call it stubbornness, but the

High noon in cottage No. 5.

At the end of a day...

real problem was that we all were spoiled. Out of sheer desperation, we decided to rent a few cottages on Oak Lake. The next day, Elaine's husband Gordy, being a builder back in Madison, decided to drive to town to see if there were lots available on North Sand Lake and learned that four adjoining lots on the south shore of the lake were for sale. Call it being in the right place at the right time, or a gift from above, it was meant to be. After the family agreed, Gordy immediately purchased all four lots for $1800 each to begin a new chapter in our lives.

The best of times were about to become even better.

Part IV

During this post-war era and well into the 1950s demands were multiplying for cottages and cabins. Ainard Leef, already experienced in the art of construction, and Pat McNeal, having learned carpentry from his father, paired up as Leef and McNeal Builders.

Chatting with Locals

The Buyers and Sellers

While interviewing lake property owners for this book and studying their land abstracts, certain names kept appearing, two being Ray Ellis and his good friend and real estate partner Les Tjader. Both worked for Lakes Realty Company in Siren and were actively involved in listing and selling a substantial amount of vacation property in the area, especially on North Sand Lake. It was a warm August day in 1999 when I first visited Ray Ellis to talk about the past, the lake and how that information would aid my research. His willingness to share what he could, accompanied warm smiles with each sentence, all of which was deeply appreciated.

Born in 1918, Ray Ellis was celebrating 81 years of living a good life in Siren and at The Cove, his residence at the time. Tall, happy and healthy, Ellis chuckled when I asked him if he had ever fished North Sand Lake. He admitted that he hadn't, but always passed along to prospective buyers the best of the fishing tales he had heard from those who did. When he did find himself in the middle of the lake, it was during the winter months while landing on the ice as the pilot of a Stinson Voyager equipped with skis. After serving in the military during World War II, Ellis took flying lessons available through the G.I. Bill of Rights and the 100 flying hours he logged in the Stinson was in one of four planes owned by Lakes Realty. Needless to say, these proud moments and recollections remained vivid in his mind.

Although Ellis and Les Tjader also owned a construction company that built roads and paved airport landing strips, Ellis readily admitted that North Sand Lake had been good to them by making life financially easier. He remembered when wells were manually excavated and how much quicker it was for new property owners to gain occupancy if he could convince them that drilling would speed up the process. He also remembers Les Olson who owned a portion of what once had been the Leef farm, and of the picnic Olson held on his property back in the 1950s for everyone on the lake as well as those who were interested in becoming property owners.

Forever intrigued with the peninsula, which is referred to in this book as the Point, I learned that hundreds of acres back then were owned by Alva Lavell of Shell

Lake. At one time, she promised to contact Ellis first if she planned to sell, and he hoped she wouldn't forget. He knew that once people were exposed to the beauty and clarity of the lake, lots would quickly sell. He also recalled that a doctor and a newspaper man from Osceola owned a considerable amount of property of the other side of the peninsula.

About a year after Ellis initially contacted Lavell, she called to inform him that she was going to sell the lakeshore peninsula property which could be reached only by rowing a boat. When Ellis acquired the narrow strip of land, arrangements were made to have a bulldozer bring in fill to connect it to Leef Road and to make the land suitable to build on. Raymond W. Buggert, local Registered Land Surveyor, had been assigned to survey the property. With his wife, Mildred, accompanying him, he rowed a boat to reach the peninsula while their dog swam alongside the boat.

Before putting closure on our conversation that day, Ellis also talked about purchasing Kovarik's Resort after an accident took the life of owner Joe Kovarik. Although the resort cottages were individually sold, the bar remained open and was operated by Kovarik's widow, Sylvia, whose living quarters were located at the rear of the building. **See: Kovarik's Resort.**

Another familiar name during this time was Charles Tollander who lived in Luck. Tollander started a Land O'Lakes branch in the area and traveled often in the ice cream truck to make deliveries along the way before reaching Webster. Sensing an interest in real estate throughout the area and potential vacation land boon, Tollander decided that he wanted to be a part of the action.

In 1955, Tollander moved to Webster and within the year had sold his first property on North Sand Lake. With cabin, the price was $8500. Although resorts liberally speckled many lake shorelines in the immediate area, people who rented cabins and cottages each summer were beginning to see the attributes of owning a place of their own. The market had not yet exploded, and wouldn't for a while, yet the possibility was on the verge of happening and those who were savvy to the market also speculated that it was just a matter of time.

Tollander remembers his first lake property investment. It was in Union and he bought 16-acres of land at $5.00 per acre. He sold it the next week for $10.00 an acre. Next stop was Birch Island where he paid $1.00 per foot and sold it almost immediately for $4.00 per foot. Especially lucrative was his specialty of buying resorts and sub-dividing the land. Oftentimes, his partners in these ventures were Ray Ellis and Les Tjader. He also recalls Ainard Leef and Pat McNeal buying and selling North Sand Lake property. And there was the never-to-be-forgotten day when Tollander visited property on one of the many Bass lakes in the area which had just gone on the market for $16,000. It was too good to pass up and he wrote out a check for the full amount before returning home to call the bank. Tollander's concern was that he didn't have a dime to his name. The bank president listened and calmly told him to come in the next day. Tollander recalls that this was often the way things were done back then in small hometown communities.

It is fair to say that had initials been drawn into cottage foundations along the North Sand Lake shoreline, the letters RE, LT, CT, AL and PMcN would merely confirm the activity Ray Ellis, Les Tjader, Charles Tollander, Ainard Leef and Pat McNeal created years ago by gut reactions that made them the buyers and sellers of lake property in the immediate area.

Ollie and Lolita Taylor

Native Americans were our natural conservationists. The Indian loved his land and what it offered and blueberries, maple sugar and wild rice became natural staples to use as bartering power. Lakes and land provided food and pelts. Although most of their settlements remained permanent, tribes were apt to move on in search of other locations when supplies waned.

When lumber camps shut down and crews changed locations in other wooded areas, small dwellings left behind became homes for members of Indian tribes. The most ideal locations, however, were those along lake shores where fishing was good, ceremonials were held and the beat of drums echoed miles away. Many things changed when French and British traders arrived in Wisconsin as some of the foreign traders were nothing more than intruders who stripped the Indian of their survival. As the culture of the American Indian began to disappear along with their traditions, heritage and dwellings, the heart beat of the community was silenced forever.

Many years ago an area where the Great Lakes of Huron, Superior and Michigan met was referred to as the Sioux. It was there that Native Americans searched for the Megis, a small shell they believed to be a religious symbol. It was also where Indians gathered when migrating from the Atlantic coast before moving on to the Straits of Mackinac and the Madeline Islands which they considered to be their ancestral home. Following the water of the St. Lawrence Seaway, the Brule River became a vital waterway as the Indians portaged down to the St. Croix River to reach the land that surrounds us today. The area filled their needs with wild rice, fish and game and other dietary staples.

The Native American who lives in this area today is a descendant of the St. Croix Band of Lake Superior Indians. Referred to for years as the Lost Tribe, they refused confinement at a reservation. In 1924, the Indians of Burnett County became United States citizens. Today we know them as the Ojibwa.

Ollie Taylor, a Native American who was called Shawlin, or South Wind by his father, lived in the immediate area and was respected by all who knew him. His family

Ollie Taylor

arrived here around 1802 and homesteaded near the narrows, a connection that joined Lower Clam and Clam lakes and where it is believed family members were buried. Ollie was born in 1899 in Bashaw Valley where early rice camps were his family's salvation. By the age of 16, Ollie had become a fine fishing guide and trapper and was employed by Rose Christianson at Big McKenzie Lodge. Later, he would work for Mr. Willoughby, and Renaldo "Ren" Pratt, former manager of the Kilkare Lodge and Big McKenzie Lodge. A man of few needs who never reached for the material things in life, Ollie Taylor considered the outdoors as his tabernacle.

North Sand Lake was Ollie Taylor's favorite place to fish for large-mouth bass. He charged $5.00 a day to guide and years later, received $15.00 for full days that began at 4 a.m. and ended well into dark after the day's catch had been cleaned, layered on ice, and packed in butter barrels to ship by train to Chicago where most of the vacationing fishermen resided. His favorite lures when fishing for northern pike and bass were live field mice he carried in a loose brown paper bag. With no hook placed through any part of the mouse, rubber bands, instead, wrapped tightly around its front and back legs to secure it to a small piece of plywood where a hook was attached.

Ollie didn't portage with a canoe as his ancestors once did. His modern mode of transportation through the woods from lake to lake was an old Model T. Although he usually guided one day at a time, there were hard core fishermen from big cities who wanted the most from their fishing trips to the north woods of Wisconsin and searched for the best guide to hire, oftentimes for weeks on end.

After experiencing and recuperating from two heart attacks, Ollie was guiding on a lake one day when he felt ill. A few days later, at age 67, a third attack took his life. Ollie had been a happy, highly respected guide with simple wishes. The outdoors he so loved nourished him as a fishing guide and trapper during a career that had spanned 51 years.

Ollie's wife, Lolita, was a descendent of the Conner-Spooner families and very proud of being 1/8 Native American. The Connor family arrived in this country from Ireland in 1740 and in 1884 homesteaded at Connors Lake near Devil's Lake and County Road A. With a smile to warm anyone's heart, Lolita thrived on good memories and continued to speak to groups anxious to learn about local history. She also relished sharing stories of growing up there, of how vital wild rice was to her family and the delicious offerings it provided after soaking all night long. As a child, she loved picking blueberries in the wilderness, a special treat that ended when school began.

After graduating from high school, Lolita pursued an education and received a Bachelor's Degree in Education from the University of Wisconsin-Superior. She was a member of the Fond du Lac Band of Lake Superior Indians and married Ollie Taylor, a tribal leader of the St. Croix Band. The couple had two sons, Patrick who is deeply involved in tribe leadership, and Eugene, now deceased.

Chatting with Lolita Taylor, 2000.

Lolita Taylor not only taught school, but also worked in Adult Basic Education as a teacher and director for the Wisconsin Indianhead VTAE District. She is the author of *Ojibwa: The Wild Rice People and Native American Contributions to Progress* and devoted herself to a seemingly endless variety of educational projects. After completing her longtime career as a school teacher in the Webster school system, she retired in 1973 at age 65. A beloved, well-known active senior citizen, Lolita remained in the home near Hertel that she and Ollie shared together for so many years.

Lolita Taylor has been recognized by the Smithsonian Museum in Washington, D.C. for her memoirs, and her name appears on a plaque on the Honor Wall of the National Museum of the American Indian. At age 95, she continued to work on *Travel Back in History on County A*, a compilation documenting her ancestors and her own childhood spent near Connors Lake.

Lolita Taylor loved every aspect of history and storytelling that played a major role in her life and enjoyed passing legends on to countless children to become a legend in her own right. I feel honored to have spent an afternoon with her in her kitchen as she graciously shared her own past while encouraging me to complete this book about part of mine.

Lolita Taylor died March 8, 2004 at age 95.

Pete and Vi Moser

Mention the name and a light flickers in the minds of most everyone in the area which begins with Voyager Superette, its former owners Pete and Vi Moser, and their children Judy, Jim, Jerry, Janice, Jack, Jean, Jolyne, Jeff, Joy, June and Jay.

For me, it also reflects a time when a bunch of cute little blond-haired children arrived at Hansen's Resort about 10:00 a.m. on Saturday mornings with their mom, who cleaned cottages for Barney and Flo Hansen before guests arrived during the mid-afternoon hours. While Vi moved from one cottage to the next, the little Mosers stayed outside and had a great time swimming and playing in the sand in front of each cottage so their mother could keep an eye on them to make sure they were having fun and behaving at the same time.

At that time, the only grocery items available to resort cottage guests were the staples on shelves inside Hansen's small store/bar where guests gathered in the evening. What wasn't stocked there meant driving to A & H or into town, Webster being the closest distance of about 10 miles. When Barney died, and the small two-bedroom cottages were individually sold, Flo Hansen sold the property across A to Vi and Pete Moser. It was not purchased with a business in mind, but the Mosers were acquaintances of Hansen's son, Warren, and liked the area so much that the idea of owning property across the road from North Sand Lake was like a dream come true. It was 1968 and the open land of sand, gravel, dirt, weeds and wild flowers from County Road A that led through the woods to Bass Lake in the unseen background was about to change.

Pete and Vi Moser were married in 1942. With every intention to settle down in Webster and raise a family, their plans changed when Pete went to work for the Great Northern Railroad in Superior, 50 miles north. In 1952, the family returned to Webster with many little ones in tow. Pete entered the logging and construction business and worked as Road Supervisor for Jackson Township. When well-known state land developer, N. E. Isaacson, acquired a vast holding of wooded property bordered by A, Kilkare Road, Birch Island and Long Lake Road to develop a community called Voyager Village, Pete and his son, Jim, became responsible for nearly all the driveways in the development.

In 1969, Pete and Vi moved into their new home designed with a walk-in basement that faced A. Managing a small convenient grocery store for Voyager Enterprises Corporation had never entered Pete's mind and there much work to do. Although a liquor license was acquired, people who visited the store seemed interested only in loaves of bread and containers of milk. By 1972, it was obvious that an extended foundation was necessary to meet everyone's need. By adding shelves and coolers, the walk-in basement became Voyager Superette.

Lingering in their minds were plans the two often discussed about building a two-story motel and a launderette behind their house with the woods as a natural backdrop. Because of the proximity of the lake across the road, and drainage requirements, the idea never materialized. Instead, they built a service station complete with gas pumps outside and tanks inside for live bait. Today the station serves as their son Jim's construction business headquarters.

Having a small grocery store so close to North Sand Lake quickly spoiled those of us who remember the years when there was little or nothing readily available to satisfy whims of hunger and thirst for those who lived or vacationed in the immediate area. Suddenly, instead of bread and milk, there was a great inventory of items available to purchase just minutes away, merely by walking, riding a bike, jumping in the car or arriving by boat at the pier behind what we've known for years as the Sand Bar. It was convenience at its best, and with a smile. People stopped by early in the morning to grab a newspaper and chat. With groceries stocked for three daily meals, gas for cars and boat tanks, ice cream and Popsicles to slurp on hot summer days, beverages to chill for picnics and parties, and later, videos to keep everyone occupied when the weather was less than perfect, the Mosers worked hard to keep their customers happy and satisfied.

As Voyager Village continued to expand, affordable wooded campsites sold with restrictions that camping was allowed only for a five year period. The camping boom created an overwhelming amount of business at Voyager Superette. People were coming and going from early morning to late evening hours for many items, especially ice. Although there were two ice machines on the premises, the store couldn't seem to stock enough ice to satisfy all of the campers and Pete or Vi often found themselves driving to Spooner for surplus supplies. When they returned, campers would be waiting for pieces chipped from the heavy ice blocks.

Unfortunately, the good times began to wane. When the five year camping contracts expired and each property owner was expected to build, most of them put their property up for sale. The decline in business came close to ruining Moser's Voyager Superette.

Pete and Vi Moser

Years went by and days seemed longer than ever before. When health problems began to surface, Pete and Vi Moser realized that it was time to take a break. As Pete's health deteriorated, Vi became his nurse who cared for him with the same love and affection they shared with each other during their 59 years of marriage. His rewarding life as a husband, father, grandfather, great-grandfather and friend was nearing an end.

Pete Moser's life had embraced the joy of fishing, hunting, farming, and gardening. For a few hours of sheer relaxation, a good Western movie was always welcomed. He was forever proud of his family, his accomplishments in life and the business he and Vi successfully operated along the edge of A across from North Sand Lake's north shoreline. In death, he was honored with a procession led by a fire truck from the Jackson Volunteer Fire Department, an organization he helped to establish, to the Jackson Cemetery where he was buried with full military honors.

Pete Moser passed away August7, 2001 at the age of 79.

Bill Conroy

When I learned that my friend Ed Schnaith was a good friend of Bill Conroy, I asked if he would accompany me to Conroy's home so I could interview him for my book. A few days later, after arrangements had been made, Ed picked me up in the afternoon and the two of us headed toward Bill Conroy's home to hear the lifetime local resident, who served Burnett County as Coroner and Deputy Sheriff, share bits and pieces of the past.

Bill Conroy and good friend, Ed Schnaith, 1995.

Conroy was highly respected by the townspeople and others throughout the county and it didn't take long for me to understand why. A big man with a warm smile and gentle manner, Bill comfortably settled into his favorite chair and began to describe his friendship with the Indians that flourished through the years from an incident that had occurred many years before. I learned that his father, Dan Conroy, occasionally stopped by their camps to drop off a side of beef with other food items. Other times, he'd pick blueberries with them in the woods.

If Dan Conroy needed extra help at his logging camp, he'd hire local Indians.

With logs branded DC, the Conroy dam was built on Lang Lake, so named for Bill's grandfather. When the dam swelled with three feet of water, it was opened to carry other logs to the next lake or body of water until they reached the St. Croix River. It was also a time when roads were nothing more than wide paths of dirt and sand and often blanketed with hay all the way to Superior to prevent ruts from forming. Bill shook his head in amazement when recalling the day his father walked from the old Conroy homestead near A to Grantsburg to tend to business. He returned home carrying a large sack of flour on his back.

Webster was described by Bill Conroy as an area being not much of anything when he was growing up. Yet, he vividly remembers a dry spell that left the water level on North Sand Lake so low that one could walk 200 to 300 feet from the shoreline before reaching water. Also visible during that time was a prominent sand bar. He estimated that it took about 20 years for the water levels to return to normal and when they did, lake water covered some roads along its periphery. He also remembers the day Les Olson asked him to build a dock. Bill couldn't read blueprints, but accepted the job anyway. The dock ended up being three feet too high. Anyone interested in getting up on the dock needed a set of steps to do so. A few years later, the dock was under water and the tiny Jack Pines that covered the area in the 1930s were lost. During that time, North Sand and Mallard lakes became one body of water.

Dry spells created other scenes to be remembered. Fred O'Brien cut hay where Green Lake is today, and farm animals grazed in the area we know today as Thompson Bay. And, the finger of lake property we all know as the point or peninsula was a steep hill before "Moose" Goheen built his own place. Land use restrictions were virtually non-existent back then and the hill was leveled to accommodate the construction of other seasonal cottages and vacation homes.

Before our visit ended, Bill asked if I knew that County Road A just past Leef Road once swept down to run along the water's edge and past Kilkare Road. A portion of the road still exists today, hidden by trees and other growth near the base of a deserted house on the hill that once was a part of Hilltop Resort. Had the road remained as it was back then, the cottages Hansen's built for their resort would have been separated from the lake by the county road just as many cottages and homes are along a strip of Big McKenzie. Conroy also described the huge parcel of lakeshore property on Leef Road and A, today owned by Jack and Beverly Spittell, and then moved on to another massive portion of land Olson once owned along Thompson Road where he was hired by Olson to feed the deer on a deer farm enclosed by wire and, in certain places, wood fences to prevent their escape.

The hours spent with Bill Conroy opened another door of North Sand Lake's past and each recollection was enthusiastically recorded as soon as I arrived back at the cottage.

Bill Conroy passed away at the age of 90 on April 3, 1999.

Theman Danielson

Theman Selmer Danielson and his wife, Madonna, welcomed me into their lovely two-story home on North Lakeland Avenue in Webster on a warm sunny afternoon, September 6, 1996. The home, built in 1940 by Robert Magnason with oak from the property, originally operated as a general store that supplied items for loggers, as well as a meat market for the people in the area. Living quarters were on the second floor. When the Danielsons purchased the home in 1946 for $4000 with a down payment of $500, it came with nearly two feet of water in the basement.

Madonna and Theman Danielson, 1996. A portion of Webster's first post office is seen in the background.

Although Theman Danielson was well into his 90s when I interviewed him, his mind was sharp, his smile was genuine, and he was anxious to open the chapters of his life which began with a memory of his father who moved to the Webster area a century earlier in 1896 from Belgrade, Minnesota. The family farm, settled in Oakland near Lake Viola, was where Theman was born November 15, 1900, the tenth child of Norwegian homesteaders, Ole R. and Mathilda Danielson. Sensing my enthusiasm as a historian, he continued to reflect on the past for the next few hours and, as each recollection unfolded, a bonding experience with other longtime Webster resident was formed.

After attending a tiny country school next door to the family's log home, Theman enrolled at Webster High School in 1916 and saddled his horse each week for the long ride to town where he would stay with people before returning home for the weekend. Because meals were never consumed with his Webster hosts, Theman prepared food for himself in his room. When he entered 11th grade, his father bought property in town and built a one-room house with a wood stove to serve as his son's home away from home until he graduated from high school.

While attending Webster High School, Theman became a member of the school baseball team and many times traveled to North Sand Lake to play against the Sand Lake team. Games were usually held on Sundays and he remembers in particular the Taylor brothers as members of the lake team. Both were outstanding in their positions, Ollie as catcher, Lawrence as pitcher. With a twinkle in his eye and a honest nod of his head, Theman admitted there was no doubt in his mind that both talented Taylor boys would have played today for the Minnesota Twins.

Back then it seemed that every town had a baseball team. Uniforms were purchased by each town and baseballs cost $1.50. At that time, Webster High School was located on the other side of the street from today's school. Classes were held on second floor, and elementary grades occupied the first floor. After the school burned down, a new school was built across the street.

Theman recalled a Mr. Compeau from Montana as a great teacher of sports. When Compeau came to town to purchase groceries, Theman was assured of a ride to North Sand Lake to play ball. Otherwise, transportation was by horse to a baseball diamond described as probably being fully grown today with trees. But at one time, the diamond, remembered as very flat land in the low swampy area near Kilkare Road on the same side as Voyager Superette, was separated from the lake by the county road. He also recalled a dry spell that left water levels "somewhere around those in 1918 when baseball games were played well beyond the shoreline of Yellow Lake.

Hunting, of course, occupied a vital role in everyone's life and after spending a morning hunting in heavy deep grass near the lake's edge, one could head for home by noon with a day's limit of pheasants. Theman's brother, Stuart, was an accomplished outdoorsman and paid by logging companies to guide. One year he shot 27 moose, 7 deer and 3 bear.

The sand road to Sand Lake had crooked dirt ruts and steep ditches. One day Theman received word that the Sand Lake team wanted him to join them for a game. His father was using the horse and, because Theman had no means of transportation, two men were sent to pick him up. They were so intoxicated that the trip became a daytime nightmare. Theman sat in the back seat of a car whose top folded back like a convertible. Every time the car got stuck, Theman was thrown clear of the vehicle. The driver would have to shift the car in reverse while the other two pushed it back on the road. By the time they reached the Sand Lake diamond, the game was half over.

Another time, Theman and Stuart Thompson spent the day fishing along the east shoreline of North Sand Lake near Thompson's resort. Using rods and reels, flys, spinners and bucktails, they caught a great number of northern pike and large mouth bass. When asked the size of the northerns, Theman casually replied, "Oh, about 8 or 9 pounds each," sizes he claimed were common back then. The fish were taken to shore, cleaned and fried for a picnic.

Lafayette Connor was Theman's good friend and the two spent many good times together. Connor's father was a surveyor and Theman's father was good with the axe, and the pair often went together when Connor's father had work to do. Theman remembers his father telling him that when he moved from Minnesota to the Webster area, he pulled a covered wagon carrying his wife and their five children. The last four or five miles of the trip were completed only by chopping through the woods to make way for the wagon and its four horses. When they finally reached their destination the wagon came too close to the edge of Johnson Lake and tipped over. No one was hurt, and the wagon was pulled up and out of the ditch.

Danielson's stories continued to flow with ease as Madonna and I listened. He was proud to have lived a lifetime in Webster and in their home for 53 years. His thoughts returned to his graduation in 1920 and his enrollment in the college in River Falls and Moody Bible Institute in Chicago, IL. He described his affiliation as an officer with Gideons International and his service in distributing thousands of Bibles throughout Burnett County and the world. Not surprising was his belief that God had walked with him throughout his life.

In looking back, and in every sense, he was a true entrepreneur. Among the long list of markets he explored and the businesses he owned and operated, including his primary business, the Danielson Insulation Service, working as a guide hunting and fishing at the Blueberry Hill Resort near Danbury was particularly enjoyable. He also owned a wholesale blueberry business as well as a Christmas tree business. And he was very proud of the resort he helped to launch back in the 1930s in Minnesota. Just when I thought there wasn't a stone unturned, his mind shifted to baseball to tell me of the teams he played on, the positions he played, his athletic prowess and sheer delight in everything it involved.

As our conversation was nearing an end, Theman asked if I would mind leaving by the back door so he and Madonna could show me the location of Webster's first post office. A mere toss of a pebble from the back door was an old-fashioned pump—another inkling of yesteryear in the yard of the first house built in the early 1900s in the small town of Webster I've grown to love. Beyond it was the small garage-like structure where mail was received and sorted before delivering.

After Theman retired at age 88, he and Madonna continued to enjoy the beauty of winter from their home on Highway 35 and when summer arrived, savored the warmth of the sun and gentle breezes that drifted through open windows and doors. With the increased traffic in front, he was reminded each year that others were discovering the pleasures of Webster and the area's many lakes.

Theman Selmer Danielson died December 15, 2000 at the age of 100.

In 1999, the Danielson home was sold to Roger and Vicki Tollander, owners of Cashco Lumber directly across Hwy. 35 who established Aunt Thelma's Antiques, Collectibles, Quilt and Craft Store. Today the historic home, owned by Merle and Marilyn Meyer, is open daily as Emily's Luncheon restaurant.

Lafayette Connor

When Lafayette Connor celebrated his 100th birthday on March 29, 2000, the town of Webster celebrated with him. Highly respected in the community, Connor had remained an active senior citizen and was looking forward to a grand party being planned for him a few days later. A declaration that April 1, 2000 was Lafayette Connor Day was presented to him by Webster Village President Allen Steiner at the Webster Community Center with St. Croix Tribal Chairman Lewis Taylor, Senator Alice Clausing and Representative Mark Pettis in attendance with Connor family members and many local friends. Complementing the occasion were displays of treasured pictures from family scrapbooks.

Visiting with Lafayette Connor, 1994.

Lafayette Marquis Connor invited me into his Webster home to be interviewed for this book. The living room spoke of his talent with many Indian-themed oil and acrylic paintings he had completed through the years, and a small authentic hand-crafted birch bark canoe that hung, suspended, from the ceiling. At the same time he brought into view his 20-year hobby of making hand-sewn deerskin gloves, he proudly stated his heritage as being one-fourth Chippewa, one-eighth each French and Irish from his father, and the other half from his Norwegian mother. He claimed that his mother's native language was what he had first spoken because his father once worked at a lumber camp where all employees happened to be...Norwegian.

Connor's memories focused on to an era of Burnett County which he claimed was desert-like terrain requiring centuries of cultivation by the Woodland Sioux before taking on a personality of its own. From his own wealth of experiences, he recalled as a child that Webster was nothing more than a cranberry marsh and a store. Home was a log cabin on Austin Lake Road where he lived with his siblings, Ruby, Pearl, Rupert and Dewey, and their parents who farmed the land overlooking the Yellow River and Connors Bridge. Lafayette explained that the Woodland Sioux, as migratory farmers, were the first settlers who arrived each spring to plant corn, beans and squash. Mentioning the first roads Native Americans made with a V-shaped apparatus pulled by horses, he referred to them as paths curved to make the shortest route to each destination. When asked about his first recollection of Burnett County wilderness, he recalled the day in 1905 when he went to Grantsburg and saw log cabins and the people who lived in them standing outside.

Lafayette Connor's father, Darius, and his uncle, William, were half Ojibwa. Darius was a County Surveyor from 1916 to 1946, having learned the trade from William who was Lolita Taylor's grandfather. In his notes, William wrote that he was elected path master in the spring of 1886. He went to West Marshland to vote and had the county surveyor lay out a highway in an area near Leef Road to Clam River to enable teams to pass through.

When Lafayette was a young child he and his brother, Dewey, accompanied their father to North Sand Lake where Lafayette served as his father's chain bearer, the chain being used to measure land. When people began to purchase lake property in the 1920s, his chain duties became even more demanding. Mention 1918 and Lafayette would tell of a fire in the black swamp dirt that smoldered for a year. It was during the flu epidemic and because of the health problems it caused in the community, many people died from smoke inhalation.

As a consummate reader, Connor's education beyond the sixth grade was achieved with books. Through trial and error, he became a barber in 1916. He and his wife, Marie, lived in other states and the years from 1927 to 1951 were spent barbering in Chicago. When they returned home to Webster, Lafayette worked with his son, an engineer, to establish Forts Folle Avoine near Yellow Lake. In 1994, Lafayette donated his 70 foot pine tree for Webster's outdoor Christmas display. After a tree crew removed 30 feet from the bottom of the tree, it was hauled to its holiday resting place in the center of Webster's Main Street.

During our conversation, North Sand Lake was often mentioned. The Connor family could not afford the expense of fishing equipment, yet their simple homemade items provided suitable gear. By using branches from maple or birch trees, grub worms or sunfish were cut into pieces to be used as bait. Fishing was very good back then, according to Lafayette, especially when water levels were high and Green and Mallard lakes connected with North Sand Lake, allowing them to fish all three lakes from canoes without having to portage. There were also tales of tragedy, one involving a lumberjack who tried to cross North Sand Lake with his team of horses and full load of logs when the ice broke. As far as Connor knew, everything remained at the bottom of the lake.

To encourage tourism during the early 1920s, the insecticide DDT was dusted from a plane and...all the birds died. He shook his head in disbelief at the end result of good intentions and was convinced that the dusting also affected fish on certain lakes, ponds and streams as well as shoreline reptiles.

As with the others, it was an honor to spend a few hours listening to Lafayette Connor share remembrances of the past.

On April 11, 2001, Lafayette Connor passed away at the age of 101.

Pat McNeal

Pat McNeal remembers a time when almost no one lived on North Sand Lake. Except for the Leef family, Glenn Thompson, Tom Cleve and a few others, the lake and most of its shoreline could best be described as pretty close to being untouched.

McNeal was familiar with the lake during all seasons and remembered the narrow strip of land separating North Sand Lake and Mallard Lake. During dry spells the strip became a damp makeshift road. When the water levels were unusually high, ditches along each side filled with lake water. Yet, what may have appeared for some to be land unworthy of anything, especially family picnics, was not the case at all. In fact, Pat McNeal and his family and friends settled on dry patches for Sunday outings on the isthmus, or bundled up for the breezes that quickly passed back and forth from one lake to the other. While the men fished from the south shoreline before cleaning and frying fish in heavy cast iron pans over open fires fueled by twigs, branches and logs, the women unpacked picnic baskets filled with their homemade specialties. During the winter months, McNeal and his good friend, Ainard Leef, cut ice from the lake. The ice was taken to ice houses, packed in saw dust and stored for area residents, restaurants and bars. When someone needed ice, a message was sent or a phone call was made and an old truck would soon be making the delivery.

Memories such as Pat McNeal's open interesting chapters for those of us who arrived on the scene many years later. One particular Sunday in 1939 when McNeal was 13 years of age, he was about to embark on an experience he'd never forget. Not thought of as being too young to row from Tom Cleve's place on the north shore of North Sand Lake all the way to the south shore where the picnic was in progress, Pat and two visiting cousins from Prescott borrowed Cleve's simple wooden boat and rowed across the lake, taking their time while Pat sat in the back of the boat and trolled with his rod and reel and Daredevil. After reaching the south shore they joined in the family picnic. Later, the three boys pulled the boat from the shore and started their return trip with Pat resuming his position in the back of the boat to troll. Just as they were about to round the point, Pat snagged something well below the water's surface. Now knowing if he had hooked one of the cribs he heard had been dropped in the general vicinity, he attempted to work the line free when he felt something moving on his line and realized he had a fish.

The wind was picking up as is often the case when one reaches the openness of the lake, and heavy waves pounded against the boat. It took time to pull the fish closer to the boat and just as young McNeal made some headway, the fish splashed and made a run. Realizing he had a fish too big to land without a net, Pat's cousins prepared themselves to hit the fish with an oar, a feat not as easy as they had hoped. Finally, after two or three more times of reeling the fish close to the boat, the boys connected and made a direct hit, stunning the fish, allowing all three to pull the 47-inch, 23 pound northern pike into the boat.

Pat McNeal achieved family hero status that day, and again when a picture and article appeared in the local newspaper. He is shown here holding the fish after it had been gutted.

When World War II ended and McNeal returned home from military service, he helped his father, Leon, build a small cabin nearby that would eventually be owned by Tom Rypel's father. He also helped his father build The Lone Pine, a County Road A bar named for the lone pine growing near the back of the property. The bar opened August 6, 1946 and became a popular place for locals as well as seasonal visitors and temporary summer residents. Today it is known as the Crow Bar.

During this post-war era and well into the 1950s demands were multiplying for cottages and cabins. Ainard Leef, already experienced in the art of construction, and Pat, having learned carpentry from his father, paired up as Leef and McNeal builders. For the next 29 years the two were responsible for much of the building and remodeling of existing structures on or near North Sand Lake, one being a home for a man everyone knew as Colonel Lewis, a retired Army Lt. Colonel from Ohio. The home was built almost adjacent to the public boat landing on Leef Road. In Lewis's yard was a tall flag pole where an American flag furled every day of every year, serving as a symbol as well as a marker for people on the lake. Another home the two were responsible for building was Frank Preiner's home on the sandy south shoreline of Mallard Lake. It was at the base of the hill that held the Dietrick homestead which had belonged to Mrs. Preiner's parents. See: Mallard Lake.

McNeal and Leef, two prominent and well-known names in the chapter of locals, made a difference in the North Sand Lake area.

Pat's good friend, Stan Rypel, after a day of fishing on North Sand Lake, 1952.

Pat McNeal

Fred H. Dhein

At age 92, Fred Dhein agreed that the only things left in life were the memories. With that, he proceeded to retrace a time and a place when an unexpected visitor would stop by a resort without a reservation, then wait patiently for the resort owner to begin making calls to other resorts in search of accommodations elsewhere. With directions in hand, the visitor would be sent along the way, fully appreciative of the respect resort owners had for each other and the lodging that had been secured for the night, all in the name of north woods friendship.

Fred Dhein was born November 2, 1908 in Minneapolis, Minnesota to William and Estella (Westfahl) Dhein and raised in Madison, Wisconsin where he graduated from Madison East High School. Years later, in 1943, he would move to the Town of Scott and become the owner and operator of the Five Lakes Club Resort on Oak Lake.

Fred Dhein spent the major portion of his life across the road from Oak Lake. Spry at 92 when we first met, Dhein effortlessly turned back the pages of time to 1907 when area lake property was purchased by wealthy Chicago businessman James Norris in search for a quiet place where he and his wife could enjoy retirement. Because the small lake was surrounded by oak trees, Norris decided to call it Oak Lake.

Lobby at Five Lakes Resort, Oak Lake

James Norris's plans were of grandiose scale. His lake Chateau, built in 1912, came equipped with luxuries local people could only imagine. Sadly, any additional long range plans failed when both Norris and his wife died seven years apart during the 1920s. In 1927, Mr. H. W. Stricker purchased the land and brought in wealthy Chicago families to vacation and form a club by paying $300 to lease the property for life. Dining and recreation rooms were added to the Chateau and a large structure on the premises that previously was home to Norris's hybrid Anacona hens was converted to a lodge for guests. Greeting them in the lobby of the lodge was a fireplace built with area rocks to warm early mornings and late evenings when temperatures dropped. Additional bathrooms were added for the convenience of those privileged to stay on the premises. Detached outdoor cabins were also built. Additional property was purchased on Oak Lake, Upper and Lower Twin Lakes, Birch Island, and North Sand Lake to create amenities for members at the new Five Lakes Resort.

Five Lakes Resort cabin

The resort flourished. After many years as a vacation destination for the wealthy that arrived in Spooner on Fridays on one of two weekly trains called Fishermen's Specials, the resort owner died. The Five Lakes Resort property lost its opulent status and gradually became somewhat deserted.

William Dhein purchased the resort in 1943 and opened it a year later with the help of his son, Fred. The Dheins were familiar to the area having spent family vacations at Ivan Johnson's Resort on nearby Des Moines Lake. Fred had been working in Henderson, Kentucky and was anxious for an opportunity to return to Wisconsin. Shortly thereafter, he met Marion LaPage Sebilsky Boyer in Spooner and the couple married April 1, 1949. They would operate the resort until 1969 when Fred decided it was time to retire. Being a resort owner had rewarded him in many ways. With the help of his good friend, local fishing guide French-Canadian Pete Augustine, Fred also learned to guide and oftentimes introduced his resort guests to North Sand Lake, a place he described to them as a beautiful lake with plenty of fish.

The fish caught on North Sand or Oak lakes were cleaned, packed on ice thickly blanketed with wood shavings, and stored in any of the 15 ice houses in the immediate area. The ice houses were built with double walls filled in between with shavings to act as a natural insulator to prevent the ice from melting. When the weekend drew to a close and guests packed up for return trips home, their vacation catches were removed from the ice houses and readied for the long trip ahead.

Friday night fish fries back then were not as we know them today. Instead, the resort's American Plan menu provided hearty and excellent meals prepared by Fred's wife, Marion, and her staff for breakfast, lunch and dinner served at the same time each day. A friendly deer allowed in the dining room walked from table to table in search of food and never failed to arouse guests, especially the youngsters. Another enticement to stay at the resort was shoreline skeet-shooting and golf. For those who preferred more privacy with a place of their own, a dozen one, two and three bedroom log cabins were made available, amply heated by wood stoves and complete with indoor plumbing of chemical toilets.

When Dhein was asked about fishing today and the noise from new lake recreational machines, he shook his head and reminded me that fish do not have ears, but they do react to vibrations. He described today's fishermen with fast boats and powerful motors that roar into quiet sections of lily pads as being disappointed at the lack of

Fred Dhein, 2001.

instant strikes, oblivious to the fact that by the time their first cast is made, the fish have already moved on to a quieter place.

The years had been good to Fred Dhein. Highly respected as a good man with many friends, Dhein not only could boast of having a road named for him a short distance from his home which, at one time, was the resort warehouse on the edge of a sprawling 9-hole Five Lakes Resort golf course across A from Oak Lake Restaurant, but there's also a Dheining Room at JoMama's Corner Café at A and H. At age 92, he vividly recalled many things, especially March 2, 1981 when he and Marion were returning from Webster and noticed a thick cloud of smoke in the distance. The closer they were to home, the more massive and intense the cloud became. A raging fire was burning to the ground the Five Lakes Resort he had once owned and operated for so many years.

Marion Dhein died January 11, 1986. In the twilight of his life, widower Fred H. Dhein rose early each morning to have coffee at Jo Mama's before crossing the A & H intersection to Boone's to meet his good friend Bob Scalzo where the two played ample rounds of cribbage.

Fred Dhein passed away June 30, 2002, at age 93.

Bob Scalzo

I didn't know Bob Scalzo when I was young, but had heard his name mentioned many times by Daddy. It wasn't until about ten years ago that we met when I introduced myself to him during a flea market held at A & H corners. I knew, however, all about Scalzo's small store where County Roads A and H crisscrossed—a place, especially many years ago, one could reasonably refer to as Salvation Corners. If your car was running low on gas, Ethyl was waiting to fill your tank. If you needed pancake mix to keep the kids happy on a cold rainy morning, boxes of mix were lined up on a shelf like a platoon of soldiers. How about bread for bologna sandwiches at noon? Milk for supper? Ice cream for a late night treat? Cold beer on a hot day? Potato chips? Pickles? Bait for the big ones? Or a newspaper to keep you in touch with the outside world? Bob Scalzo made certain his inventory, whether in view at room temperature on wood shelves or buried in the depths of chilled coolers, kept customers happy and satisfied any day of the week.

Many years ago, perched at the peak of a mound dividing two county roads, A and H was nothing more than a barren four corners with Alfred Trombley's house along the side of the road. Trombley built a small store front in 1933 and installed two gas tanks. On the other side of the road, where Boone's is located today, was the Scott School playground. Otherwise, it was just plain wilderness with hints of *up north* woods.

After the store was destroyed by a fire in 1942, Chicagoan John Sherrard purchased the property in 1946 and rebuilt on the foundation. Vaughn Steele built a small

A place to shop after Trombley's store on the other corner burned down. Byrne's Store followed before it became known as Scalzo's A & H. Today we know it as A&H Country Market.

store with gas tanks for himself on the third of the four corners and in 1957, when Steele decided to sell Steele's General Store, Bob Scalzo purchased the business we know today as A & H Country Market. Stocking all the necessary staples plus live and artificial bait prevented spur-of-the-minute trips to town over bumpy gravel roads that spewed sandy dust in all directions. A & H seemed to be just up the road for most of us.

Bob Scalzo was not a product of early area farm settlers. His parents, born in Conflenti, province of Catanzaro in southern Italy, sailed for America and settled in Canada. Upon learning of plentiful railroad jobs available in Burnett County in Wisconsin, they packed up again, this time heading for Spooner where Bob was born on January 24, 1922. The Scalzo family lived in Spooner's Little Italy—described by Bob as being on the other side of the railroad tracks with about 15 other Italian immigrant families.

During the early 1930s, despite the plummeting effects of the Depression, those who could afford vacations exited from reality in the cities and headed to the north woods of Wisconsin. Every Friday, the passenger train called Fisherman's Special left Chicago with city folks anxious to fish hundreds of miles from home. When the train arrived, resort owners from Washburn and Burnett counties were waiting for those who had booked reservations at their area resort cabins, cottages, and lodges and required transportation to reach their final destinations. The seasonal weekend and week-long fishing jaunts created much excitement for Spooner residents as well as for their young children.

As a youngster, Bob Scalzo hung around the train depot, anxious to talk to black porters. One porter, John Morris, told fascinating stories during weekend layovers about life in the bustling metropolis of Chicago in Illinois. When the Fisherman's Special pulled out of the depot on Monday morning, Scalzo awaited its return on Friday so he could hear more tales of big city adventures.

Back then, many roads leading out of Spooner meandered through the countryside and alongside lakes and adjoining woods were narrow and sandy. Two cars meeting, headed in opposite directions oftentimes created problems. Kilkare Road jutting from County Road A happened to be one path referred to as a "road" when Scalzo began delivering newspapers to vacationers from Chicago and the Twin Cities. Tips were virtually non-existent, he recalls, shrugging it off as a result of the country's depressed economy. His employer was Spooner resident Amos Miller who drove a Model T truck carrying papers to be dropped off at resorts and lodges, or sold after Mass on Sunday at the Catholic Church on H near A & H, a location Scalzo was privy to. Initially, Scalzo went along with Miller for the thrill of riding in a moving vehicle, but before long asked for a salary because of the amount of time he spent on the route. Chicago Sunday papers sold for 15 cents, while all others cost a dime. After some pestering, Miller agreed to pay Scalzo 25 cents a week. There was much activity from A & H and beyond and at one time, in the town of Scott, there were 32 resorts and 278 cabins. Jackson Township's resort activity had not yet reached anyone's expectations.

Another delivery route for Bob Scalzo was Grover Elmore's Birch Island place at the end of Kilkare Road, and the Kilkare Lodge just around the hook of the bend and into the woods. Managed by Ren Pratt and his wife, the property later was sold to Mr. Walter Johnson, wealthy owner of the successful Johnson Candy Company in Chicago. However, the immediate area had its ups and downs and Scalzo recalls how the drought affected Birch Island in the late 1920s and early 1930s when the lake was nothing more than a large puddle surrounded by cattails. When asked about individuals, he quickly mentioned Mack Taylor, in his opinion the finest baseball catcher ever, and brother of local Indian fishing guide Ollie Taylor. Another person Scalzo remembered was Ivan Johnson, known throughout the area for his snowshoe dance performed at Webb Lake, today's Cabaret on County Road H.

In 1957, in the same area where young Bob Scalzo hopped rides years before on a Model T truck to deliver newspapers out in the boonies, he reentered the A & H corners as owner of a grocery store with gas pumps. In the backyard, white-tail deer were kept in a large fenced area for the benefit of vacation people to view, feed and, possibly, pet. In 1972, Scalzo sold the store and moved across the road into his new building named Outpost that allowed him to furnish his customers with a wider variety of items for hunting and fishing.

Today, although retired, Bob occupies a strip of concrete every Saturday in the Outpost parking lot where his fold-up tables hold a variety of items, flea market style. He and his wife, Mary Ann, who passed away a few years ago, enjoyed their home on H in the immediate area and planned to stay there for the rest of their lives.

Needless to say, A & H no longer is a mere crisscross in the woods. The once seemingly lonely corner today bustles from morning till night. Besides Catholic and Lutheran churches less than a block away, the community is blessed with a Volunteer Fire Station. Still the heartbeat of the corner, A & H Corner Market that keeps everyone well fed with fresh produce, meat and beverages, is also respected for their venison processing. Purchased from Bob Scalzo in 1986 by Gary and Mary Haas, the Haas family is proud of the addition of their hunter-friendly business.

Swooping down the hill on the other side of the road with woods as a backdrop, Jo Mama's, the former Corner Café, serves homemade food so delicious you'd think you were back in Grandma's kitchen. Other businesses in the immediate area include a wood and carpentry shop; Bamboozles, a recently remodeled bar offering a limited menu, cocktails and occasional entertainment and, in the woods behind A & H Corner Market, a popular new restaurant and bar called The Shop. Just a blink away is a bank and Dock's Unlimited where boats can be purchased and stored, and motors repaired. At the opposite end of the building is the Cat's Meow, a beauty parlor that takes care of the things we cannot or don't want to do ourselves. Three real estate offices will help you find the right *up north* place to relax, unwind, and call your own. The Senior Center, once a vital link in the area, continues its good intentions as a gathering place to play cards, enjoy noon lunches

Bob Scalzo and his wife, Mary Ann, 1996.

and attend evening meetings. Unfortunately, in the shade of adjoining aged oak trees, the emergency medical service closed it doors a few years ago, much to the dismay of permanent and seasonal residents.

Because A & H has become our own little village in the woods, we say, in Italian, Mille Grazie Bob Scalzo, for paving the way!

A & H Corner Market...today

Although A & H is part of Scott Township, it's also considered vital for Jackson Township people and those who live or vacation on North Sand Lake. For 18 years, Gary and Mary Haas have worked overtime to keep all their A & H Country Market customers smiling. Remodeling and additions through the years have kept in pace with the growth of the area and, although phases oftentimes become costly, what has been done to the little market at the crossroads becomes yet another gift for those who rely on what the Haas' offer.

Last year, new siding spruced up the exterior. Yet the building has retained its small town charm while taking on the look of a rural America not quite so isolated in the woods as in the past when traffic was at a bare minimum. Coin operated beverage machines positioned outside near the front door offer quick picker-uppers to locals, vacationers, and anyone just passing through, especially on warm days. There's even a ramp for the handicapped. Inside you'll find new coolers for dairy products, meat and neatly arranged produce. During the spring and early summer planting periods, annuals and perennials are set on tables in the parking lot saving gardeners trips to town. When August arrives, you will find delicious locally grown produce and freshly picked sweet corn inside.

The selection of food items has grown through the years and today there is a good selection of alcoholic beverages as well as daily newspapers from near and far. Over the small checkout counter hangs a huge northern pike, about the size I hooked twice and lost both times. It is, undeniably, the dream of every fisherman who visits the area to snag a northern of this size before returning home. If you are luckier than I've been and aren't a bona fide catch-and-release person, Haas' son, Gary, Jr., who has a taxidermy service to preserve your catch, offers a guarantee for a lifetime of applause from family and friends. To help you reach those goals, the Hass family now carries live bait and tackle to cater to the whims of all fishermen.

Later in the fall, sights are set on deer hunting and, although the deer herds in some southern areas of Wisconsin have been affected by CWD (chronic wasting disease) thus curtailing the hunt and subsequent supply of meat as rewards, Burnett County has had no problems and the number of deer killed and processed continues at A & H on a full-time basis during hunting season. The 30-plus years of Haas family expertise is known and respected throughout the area as well as in other states,

A&H proprietor Gary Haas.

which is evident as hunters who have brought their deer and bear to be processed return year after year.

I've often wondered what we'd do without the A & H Country Market during the summertime and can only imagine how important it is to everyone in the community during the winter months when the weather, at times, becomes typically brutal in the north woods of Wisconsin.

On September 28, 2005, 62-year-old Gary Haas passed away.

Peter J. Augustine

Pete Augustine and Ollie Taylor were good friends and fishing guides with admirable reputations and a vast knowledge of what to do, how and when, especially on North Sand Lake. I once fished with Pete Augustine, but just once was never enough. Daddy had the luxury of spending an occasional day with Pete to learn as much as he could about fishing the lake. One of those days, I accompanied them. I didn't know much about Pete at the time, but heard that he was an Indian guide, like Ollie Taylor, which greatly impressed me. Later, I would learn that he was not of Native American ancestry, but possibly, French Canadian. Pete loved the outdoors and the fishing, hunting and trapping it provided him as an accomplished guide and someone resort owners called on to guide their vacationing guests.

Pete was born in St. Paul, Minnesota to William and Pauline Wallas Augustine on January 12, 1903. The family moved to the Town of Scott, Burnett County in Wisconsin on May 4, 1910 when Pete was seven years old. It would be his home for the rest of his life except during World War II when he served in the military.

When Pete died on July 23, 1987 at age 84, it was a loss to everyone in the community and anyone who had been privileged to know him. Two of those who served as pallbearers were Fred Dhein and Cliff Heverly, both with Oak Lake roots, Dhein as the owner of Oak Lake Resort, and Heverly, whose cottage was located on Oak Lake and was an accomplished cohort in the local fishing guide scene. Another pallbearer was Attorney Oscar Smith, Jr. whose father, Indiana attorney Oscar Smith, Sr., purchased property and built on the north shore of North Sand Lake where his family would spend entire summers beginning back in the 1920s.

Complete with military honors, Pete Augustine was buried at Sacred Hearts Cemetery in Scott Township.

A day's catch on North Sand Lake for Bill Stoker, Pete Augustine and Daddy, 1954.

Pete Augustine, 1983.

Jo Gelher Robinson aka Jo Mama

Also known as Jo Mama, her restaurant with the same name could be described as pure pleasure at the A & H crossroads. But it wasn't always there to serve good food with tender loving care. Many years ago, the humble corner in the middle of seemingly nowhere became a breather for those who lived in the immediate area. Not only was gas available, but trips to town were reduced because of the grocery items provided on the spot. With the ever-increasing number of vacationers appearing on the scene each summer, its crisscross was like finding water in the middle of a dessert. The difference, of course, was the location, smack in the woody Wisconsin wilderness of...*up north.*

County roads A & H met and meandered years before Al and Margaret Gelher arrived. A talented individual, Al Gelher enthusiastically attempted many things in life. Living each day to the fullest, he knew that if he didn't explore his ideas he would never know if they would be successful ventures or miserable failures. Down the road, this philosophy was gathered and carried along by his daughter, Josephine.

The year was 1959. Al and Margaret Gelher left behind a succession of profitable restaurants in Minnesota for Wisconsin's northwest woods. A & H still hinted of being in the boonies when the couple purchased property on Hanscom Lake and built Gelher's Resort in 1965. Two years later, Al built a gas station where the land swooped down from the A & H intersection into a protective shell of full grown trees. By adding a tiny restaurant, Gelher's Corner Café was quickly inhaled by locals and vacationers like a breath of fresh air. During this time, Al was reaching well into his 70s, yet worked around the clock as waiter, cook, bottle washer and gas station attendant. In 1970, with the work load becoming increasingly too heavy to handle, ownership changed hands when Duane and Shirley (Durand) Muller bought the café and changed the name to A & H Corner Café.

In 1978, Gelher's daughter, Josephine, returned to the north woods to manage her parent's resort. By 1993, she became the new proprietor of the café and appropriately changed the name, as a reflection of herself, to Jo Mama's. Although she wishes she could have predicted herself as a restaurant owner by purchasing the café directly from her father, she is happy to be there in his spirit. Today, the shy little girl who was unable to respond to being called on by school teachers, averages 80 hour weeks surrounded by old and new friends behind the scenes as well as out front while mingling with customers. Except for closing Christmas, Easter and Thanksgiving, time spent on the premises adds up to about 400+ hours each month. Needless to say, it is obvious that Jo loves what she is doing.

Looking through the years of preparing meals for her family, plus bartending and cooking at The Brown Jug, Voyager Village, Lumberjack and the Sandbar, the last three remaining as popular local establishments, Jo could easily write a book as

Jo Mama, Jo Gehler Robinson, 2000.

well as a cookbook or two and, hopefully, some day she will. In the meantime, she remains satisfied preparing and serving her home-cooking to everyone who walks through the door and, aside from the well-known professional athletes, and regional out-of-town politicians who have dined there, Jo claims that her dream would come true if Oprah Winfrey walked in.

Special touches added by Jo Mama begin early in the morning. Return home to the big city and you won't find anything that will nourish your body and rest your soul like her Walt's Special or Jo Mama's Omelet served with biscuits light as a feather. Noon favorites might include turkey dumpling soup and Barney's potato rolls. Cream pies are made from scratch, oftentimes with fruit picked in the nearby woods. And there's bread pudding—another Barney-the-cook recipe left behind when Barney returned home to Indiana.

Slice bread in halves. Stagger in five rows, placing 8 halves in each row. Sprinkle with raisins. Cover with 10 slices of bread. "Politely" scald 10 cups of milk. Add 2 cups of sugar, 2 tablespoons of vanilla and 22 beaten eggs. Pour over bread and "sink all bread real good." Sprinkle top lightly with cinnamon and nutmeg. Sink all bread again. Bake at 350 degrees until no liquid is left inside, approximately 35-45 minutes. Makes three 9- x 13-inch pans.

Note: "Sinking" means to place a platter over the bread during the assembling process to make sure the liquid is absorbed.

Paul Hansen

I would be remiss if Paul Hansen wasn't included in this chapter. Although young Paul may not be a bona fide old-timer, he is the grandson of Barney and Florence Hansen who owned Hansen's North Sand Resort, and the son of Warren Hansen, Barney and Flo's son. Needless to say, Paul Hansen has very deep roots and a good solid niche carved in North Sand Lake history and belongs in "Chatting with the Locals."

Paul and I first met when he was a skinny young kid spending the summer with his grandparents at their lake resort. Norwegian on his father's side and Italian on his mother Mary's side, although he definitely looked more Norwegian, Paul was immersed in being Italian which gave us much to talk about besides the lake, fishing, swimming and the woods surrounding us. His days were spent along the length of the shoreline in search of something to do, fishing off the end of the long pier in front of his grandparent's pier and, at night, spending brief moments to mingle with the rest of us down at the store.

Raised by his Italian mother and Italian grandparents, Paul would learn that food was meant to be a celebration that had no boundaries. So, it was no surprise many years later after his father's C & S Café in Webster became Paul's restaurant that he would continue to follow in his father's footsteps by expanding his world and open *Zia Louisa* (Aunt Louisa), Burnett County's only Italian restaurant. We are happy to report that the rest, as they say, happily, is history.

Little Paul Hansen with a huge North Sand Lake northern pike.

With engrained knowledge of exactly what makes Italian food so special, Paul utilized his Italian background by using his Great Aunt Louisa's pizza dough recipe to reestablish it as a *Zia Louisa* signature item, aka the house specialty. By the end of the first year, for starters, Paul and the restaurant would toast to sales of 10,000 pizzas. Paul flips and twirls each circle of carefully stretched dough just like the old Italians did in New York City. That was back when pizza was first introduced on a huge scale to the public following World War II, to keep up with the demand of the servicemen who had enjoyed it while based in Italy. Being Sicilian, I relish the thought that Paul keeps canned anchovies on hand to decorate my pizza orders as well as those ordered by other anchovy aficionados.

Zia Louisa's menu features many other items from appetizers to sandwiches to entrees, each prepared and served with great pride. Complementing the interior are black and gold lace curtains to remind him of the window treatment at his Italian grandparent's home and the joy he experienced living with them.

Aside from food, Paul is also a walking book of local knowledge with an extensive collection of jokes customers have shared with him in the past that he somehow manages to mentally store and recite with a dry sense of humor, word for word. This is a trait most likely inherited from his father, the Warren Hansen humor that made me giggle as a teenager, especially when he teased me about all my (16) bathing suits.

Although Paul resides in Webster, a portion of his heart belongs on North Sand Lake, a place where he knows every weed bed, each depth of the lake, the fish that were caught, those that got away, fishing methods, and what bait should be used on any given day, depending on the weather that is moving in, moving out, or temporarily settled overhead. He's also a great cook and master at making excellent pizza especially tasty, especially with...anchovies!

With my good friend, Paul Hansen, at Zia Louisa's.

Part V

l to r, Bill, Mike, Bob and Tom, 1981.

Using metal wiener spears from the 1940s, the magic of marshmallows toasting to a golden brown over a bonfire of twigs and branches added a glow to life at the cottage as a finishing touch and perfect way to end a day ... up north.

Up North Food

Time is of the essence when one arrives at the lake. With all of the natural beauty that awaits us, gourmet recipes quickly take a back seat to easier and quicker nourishment in life like boxed macaroni and cheese, instant oatmeal, and small square waffles that go from freezer to toaster. Grilling hamburgers, hot dogs, brats, chicken and steaks outdoors keep the stove top clean while the eight-hour-plugged-in-slow-cooker takes the drudgery out of cooking on perfect days when there are better things to do in the lake, on the lake and relaxing either in the shade of the oak tree, or in the warmth of the sun. After hours, late night dessert comes in the form of marshmallows toasted golden brown under the stars, over a crackling bonfire.

While canned gravy should be considered a staple, some brands of commercial spaghetti sauce are almost as good as your mom used to make. Canned spaghetti with sauce that most Italians wouldn't allow in their homes suddenly becomes a treat for youngsters who haven't yet acquired a taste for the real thing and Campbell soups are stacked precariously for an easy noontime grab. It's a different way of life and it is to be savored for the moment as well as forever.

Although life can shift gears to become a breeze in the kitchen, what waits outside is another matter. Short simple handmade piers with car tires painted white perched on pier posts to prevent knicks on the sides of wooden flat-bottom boats and 6 hp engines for trips anywhere on the lake where the fish might be biting, find brand new toys to bewilder or confuse the old-timer. Long piers (now referred to as docks) on wheels, canopies, extensions for pontoons, lifts for speedboats, and those noisy machines that pierce the air like a disturbed hornet nest suddenly remind us that time stands still for no one.

Despite all of the obvious changes and mechanical doo-dads beyond our front doors, food remains one of the simple pleasures in life. Boxed, canned, fresh or frozen, the preparation of what we eat *up north* depends on who's in the kitchen and how long the cook wants to stay there. It doesn't matter how quiet or noisy the time or the place is, eating is the all-time common experience. Without it, living would lose its luster.

This chapter reflects the good tastes shared by people who own a piece of the North Sand Lake pie. It also includes Mother and Daddy's favorites. Each recipe, regional or otherwise, whether simple or complicated, is a special one that has been prepared time and time again to please families and satisfy cravings to make mealtime experiences an *up north* occasion to remember for a lifetime.

The Store aka "Barney's" in 1958, and years later known as the Sandbar.

Sandbar

The Store. The Sandbar. That wonderful old place with a cache of history wedged between the seams and cracks of the foundation. Everyone who stepped in as owner after the Barney and Flo era would agree that volumes of memories should have been documented for those of us who salivate for the reflections of the past on North Sand Lake.

Mine, of course, began in 1945 when I was eight-years-old and the small building alongside A was merely referred to as the store or Barney's by those of us who rented Hansen Resort cottages. Small, humble, and packed with good times and good people, during the day it provided a quiet, laid back atmosphere where a loaf of bread and a quart of milk could be purchased, cold beers were enjoyed, and pop, candy bars and ice cream treats were waiting in the freezer for the youngsters. After supper, the store removed its mask and became the resort's entertainment center where the noise level increased as families gathered to add a finishing touch to the interior. It was a great place to hang out anytime, but especially after supper dishes were put away for another day.

Barney Hansen wore denim overalls and a white crewneck t-shirt with sleeves. He was a large man, handsome and with a smile that matched Flo's whose gentle ways soothed the crowds. I remember how impressed they were one day when, as a teenager, I dropped a coin in the juke box and solo-danced the Jack. Never having seen it performed before, but popular back in Madison during the Bebop days, they couldn't figure out how I could twist my legs and feet in different directions to the beat of the music without tipping over. Their son, Warren Hansen, was especially intrigued and teased me for the rest of the years we stayed there by saying, "Hey, Cath, do the Jack."

When Barney passed away, we tried to keep things jumping at the store, but it wasn't the same. As hard as Flo tried, we all questioned how much longer the good times would last. Although Warren was there to help as much as he could and spent a lot of time in the kitchen, the 20 years that Hansen's Resort graced the north shore was about to end.

Others who would move into Hansen's house and operate the store were Ted and Marge Hilgardner, remembered for the homemade chili they served, Linda and Ed Nordstrom, and Sharron and John Bachman who owned the property from 1983 to December 31, 1995 before their son, Tom, stepped in. The Sandbar's kitchen was small when Bachman's became owners and only hamburgers and French-fries were served. After remodeling to expand the kitchen, they added soup, baskets, and other food items to the menu. A family room was added on to the main house and because they were refused a variance to build a garage adjacent to the house, the Bachmans were forced to buy 50 feet of shoreline from Oscar Smith, Jr. so a garage could be built on the other side of their lake property to the west. A back room of the Sandbar was turned into a gift shop before Tom removed the antiques and gifts to establish a video room.

The next owner, with his mother in tow, was Rob Roessel, whose background included the Hollywood movie industry and production of *Grumpy Old Men.* Rob arrived with innovative ideas for a new look at the Sandbar while organizing never-before North Sand Lake regattas launched for sailing enthusiasts from near and far. With ideas to turn the Sandbar into more of a roadside dining spot, musicians were hired from the Twin Cities to entertain on certain weekends during the summer months. The idea offered a new twist and electrified evenings with standing room only for a newer generation of customers who drank and tapped their feet while we old timers sat back and savored each familiar note.

When Roessel moved out, Kevin Wear, with an extensive food preparation background plus being a former Voyager Village chef, stepped in with his own ideas of expert food preparation. The menu was mouth-watering, as were the meals that, on occasion, were designed as gourmet dining with fixed prices. Those of us who appreciated his culinary expertise applauded his efforts and remained eager for repeat performances of delectable magic served on the north shore of the lake. The following year, Kevin and his special friend, Shelly, married. Their Friday night fish fries drew scores of locals and vacationers to enjoy a new reign, new atmosphere and an exceptional wait staff that would quickly become a favorite place to hang out.

Unfortunately, in April, 2006, the Sandbar we all loved was torn down.

The Sandbar

The little roadside bar along the edge of County Road A has come a long way since I spent portions of each day there since 1945 when our vacations first began at Hansen's Resort. Barney and Flo Hansen made everyone who walked through the door feel welcome whether they were eight years old like me, or "the locals."

After Hansen's became a chapter of local history, the store/bar/restaurant changed hands many times and today remains in good hands with Kevin and Shelley Wear overseeing the operation, food preparation and presentation, delicious Friday night fish fries and occasional gourmet fixed price dining. Kevin has had extensive training and experience as a chef at various locations near and far and we're all happy he's on the lake for us to reach by foot, car, bike, pontoon or other water vehicles. With his usual casual demeanor, here is a recipe from his repertoire of delicious recipes that Kevin proudly shared with these comments... 'exact amounts are used for baking! Cooking is instinct! Have fun!'

Shrimp Mamakos

Flour
Olive oil
Shrimp
Fresh Garlic
Sambuca liqueur
Heavy cream
Pasta
Grated Parmesan
Green Onion

Heat skillet and enough olive oil to coat the bottom of a skillet.
Dredge shrimp in flour and place in hot oil.
Brown shrimp on both sides.
Add garlic and Sambuca--standing back as it will flame up.
Add heavy cream to cover.
Bring to a boil and cook over low heat until desired thickness.
Place over your favorite pasta, top with Parmesan cheese and green onion.
Drink leftover Sambuca on ice.

Favorite *up north* recipes from appetizers to desserts and everything in between

Daddy, 1988.

Instant Vegetable Dip

Twenty years ago, when I played tennis twice a day and exercised in the club's fitness center, my food intake was somewhat monitored for obvious reasons. This recipe was shared by the aerobic instructor in answer to a request for a tasty, low calorie dip for raw veggies. You can make it within a minute, dip your vegetables and enjoy every single crunch without any guilt feelings.

2 tablespoons mayonnaise
2 tablespoons low fat plain yogurt
1-2 teaspoons ketchup

Note: Another quick trick for saving the waistline is picking up a package of dry Salsa mix in the produce department at Wayne's in Webster. All you have to do is add chopped fresh tomatoes and onions and you'll have some of the best salsa you've ever tasted

Bleu Cheese Meatballs

This recipe came with a Nieman Marcus cookbook. I serve them as an appetizer, but they'd be equally enjoyed served as an entrée. What's leftover is reheated the next day with great results. If you like bleu, or Gorgonzola cheese, which could be substituted, you'll enjoy these many times in the future.

¼ pound bleu cheese (or Gorgonzola)
¼ cup mayonnaise (not fat free)
2 tablespoons Worcestershire sauce
1 tablespoon dry mustard
1 teaspoon salt
¼ teaspoon pepper
1 egg, beaten
½ cup milk
2 cups Corn Flakes
1 pound ground beef

Crumble cheese.
Add mayo, Worcestershire, mustard, salt, pepper, egg and milk.
Crumble Corn Flakes and add to mixture.
Add ground beef and combine.
Shape into 1-inch balls.
Brown in oil and serve warm.
For best results, chill mixture for two hours before shaping meatballs.

Makes 2 ½ dozen meatballs

Marinated Mushrooms

Here is a too-good-to-be-true appetizer made with the snap-of-a-finger and forwarded to me by Bob Swanson, Sun Prairie, who dabbled with it until it was perfect. With minimal preparation, the quality and flavor of the finished product is outstanding.

1 tablespoon balsamic vinegar
½ teaspoon Hellman's Dijonnaise mustard
¼ teaspoon salt
1 garlic clove, pressed
2 tablespoons extra-virgin olive oil
8 ounces fresh mushrooms cleaned and sliced or cut in half depending on size
Freshly ground black pepper to taste

Combine vinegar, mustard and salt in small jar. Shake well.
Add garlic and olive oil and shake well again.
Put mushrooms in glass or plastic bowl.
Add marinade and blend.
Season with black pepper.

Serve right away or let chill in the refrigerator for about 30 minutes.

Crispy Sweet Sand Lake Dills

Berniece Thompson puts her money on this recipe. Described as the "best you ever tasted," these pickles begin with a quart of dill pickles and promises to occupy a small portion of a morning or afternoon of a day when you want to be productive and the weather isn't nice enough to venture outside. Rewards will follow. Serve these anytime, but also as an appetizer cut in crosswise chunks with toothpicks like they do in Milwaukee.

½ cup cider vinegar
¼ cup mixed pickling spice tied in thin cloth
1 quart sliced dill pickles (if whole, slice 1-inch thick)
3 cups white sugar

Place vinegar and spices in a good size glass jar that can be sealed.
Drop in pickles. Pour in sugar, but do not mix.
Screw on lid.
Refrigerate for 10 days.
When you are ready to make a second batch, just add 1 cup sugar to the pickling liquid.

Brandy Slush

Years ago, a cookbook of favorite recipes was compiled by the Crescent Lake Ladies of Sacred Hearts of Jesus and Mary Catholic Church on H, just beyond the corners of A & H. Discovering the book in Mother's collection, I found many recipes had been submitted by North Sand Lake property owners and church members such as Emily Leach whose simple recipe we all should have on hand to quench our thirsts when the temperatures continue to rise during mid-afternoon hours.

2 cups water
4 tea bags
7 cups cold water
12 ounces frozen orange juice
12 ounces frozen lemonade
2 cups sugar
2 cups Brandy or
Vodka
Ginger-ale

Boil 2 cups of water and add 4 tea bags; steep.
When fully steeped, remove tea bags and add cold water, orange juice, lemonade, sugar and liquor of your choice.
Mix well and freeze. To serve, mix half slush and half ginger-ale.

Cosmo Slush

Last year, I discovered the Cosmopolitan and manage to enjoy one twice each week. A delightful modern martini, it is now in slush form thanks to Betty Crocker, complete with its low fat status. This, too, is perfect for entertaining at the lake, having something cold and delicious already prepared in the freezer, especially when company arrives.

6 oz. frozen (thawed) limeade concentrate (from 12-ounce can)
3 tablespoons powdered sugar
2 cups citrus-flavored vodka or orange juice
1 cup orange-flavored liqueur or orange juice
4 cups 100% cranberry juice blend

In blender, place limeade concentrate and powdered sugar.
Cover and blend on high speed until well mixed.
Add vodka and orange liqueur.
Cover and blend until well mixed.
In 9 x13-inch glass baking dish, stir limeade mixture and cranberry juice until well mixed.
Cover and freeze at least 8 hours until slushy.
Stir before serving in martini glasses.
Serves 14

Note: For better flavor, Betty Crocker suggests using 100% cranberry juice, not cranberry juice cocktail

Goombay Smash

Although the scenery is different on North Sand Lake, it's okay to pretend on a hot summer day that you are vacationing in the Bahamas by sipping one of these.

2 ounces light rum
4 ounces coconut rum
4 ounces pineapple juice
2 ounces orange juice
"touch" of grenadine

Mix, pour over ice, and garnish with a cherry.

Sweet Maria (La Dolce Maria)

If you love dessert, but don't want anything as heavy as cake or pie, try a little liquid with fewer calories, but packed with treasured flavor. It's right up there on Cloud Nine. Mamma Mia! Salute!

1 ounce Amaretto di Saronna
1 ounce sweet cream
1 ounce vodka

Shake well with cracked ice.
Strain and serve in a champagne or martini glass.

Favorite Hot Cocoa

When we were little girls, my sister, Elaine, and I had tea parties using a children's set of dishes given to her by Daddy's mother, Caterina, our Sicilian grandmother. Cocoa was made with Hershey's unsweetened cocoa and served by Mother with a marshmallow on top in small china cups on saucers decorated with pink rosebuds. Years later, when I was married and had three little boys in the house, tea parties were non-existent, but when cocoa was made, it was just like Mother used to make, complete with marshmallows. I know that cocoa served in a cottage on a chilly morning, or even at bedtime, is quicker to make with small packets of instant cocoa, but it will never take the place of this recipe, found after Mother passed away, handwritten on a card in her dark green metal recipe box.

¼ cup plus 1 tablespoon Hershey's unsweetened cocoa
½ cup sugar
Dash salt
⅓ cup hot water
1 quart milk
¾ teaspoon vanilla

Combine dry ingredients in saucepan.
Blend in water.
Bring to boil over medium heat, stirring constantly.
Boil and stir 2 minutes.
Add milk, stir and heat, but do not boil
Remove from heat and add vanilla.
Beat with rotary beater until foamy, optional

Makes about 1 quart.

Single Serving

1 tablespoon cocoa
2 tablespoons sugar
Dash salt
1 Tablespoon water
1 cup milk
½ teaspoon vanilla

Follow directions above.
Beating with a rotary beater is not necessary.
Adding a marshmallow is optional.

Hot Chocolate Malt Mix

I don't know about you, but malted milks made me feel better when I was little and sick and wasn't the least bit concerned about my waistline. Here is a quick and delicious hot drink with that wonderful flavor of malt from the past.

2 cups non-fat dry milk powder
¾ cup sugar
½ cup cocoa mix
½ cup chocolate malt mix
¼ cup powdered non-dairy creamer

Mix all ingredients in large bowl and blend well.
Store in a tightly covered container.
Yield: 4 ½ cup mixture which makes about 16 6-ounce servings
To prepare a single serving: Place ¼ cup mix in a cup. Add ¾ cup hot water. Stir to blend. Add a dollop of flavored whipped cream if desired.

Voyager Village Aebleskivers

In preparation for the annual Labor Day weekend, Voyager Village residents form a committee to organize a Craft Fair that draws exceptional artists from near and far. It also features a used book sale, steamed corn on the cob, a raffle, lunch, homemade pies and their signature item, Aebleskivers. Pronounced Eebel-skivers and Danish in origin, which represents much of the region, past and present, they are baked in skillet-like irons with concave receptacles and sold two for a dollar. The golf-ball size gems, served with apple sauce, jam, maple syrup or all three are considered a pancake and gourmet ethnic treat for me and others who devour them in an open field that once grew corn along County Road A.

8 eggs, separated
¼ cup sugar
1 teaspoon salt
4 tablespoons butter
4 cups (1 quart) buttermilk
4 cups flour
2 teaspoons baking soda
1 teaspoon nutmeg

Beat egg yolks with sugar, salt and butter. Add buttermilk.
Mix together dry ingredients and add to buttermilk mixture.
Fold in beaten egg whites.
Drop a dollop of the rich batter into each of the seven cup shaped wells of the iron and bake briefly on the stove top.

Barney's Potato Rolls

Jo Mama's Corner Café

Here is another favorite café recipe left behind by a cook named Barney. Don't let the size of the recipe scare you. It is a treasured recipe that will provide enough to put in the freezer for unexpected company.

9 cups water
6 potatoes (2/3 cup instant)
6 cups sour milk or buttermilk
2 cups sugar
6 ounces butter
4 tablespoons salt
12 cups flour
9 tablespoons yeast
24 to 27 cups more flour

Heat first 6 ingredients to 120 degrees. Add remaining ingredients. Let rise. Punch down once.
Form rolls and bake at 350 degrees.

Wild Rice Pancakes

As a youngster, Tom Rypel fished the area in front of Hilltop Resort on North Sand Lake with his father about the same time I fished the shoreline in front of Hansen's Resort. We didn't know each other then, but our paths crossed 55 years later at Roamer's Inn during a book signing party that owners Pat and John Angell arranged there for me. Tom and his wife, Kathy, immediately became our good up north friends who we looked forward to socializing with during the summer months.

For 20 years, this recipe was prepared and served by the Burnett County Dairy Breakfast held annually on a Saturday morning in June and became one of Rypel's favorites which Kathy was anxious to share with me. In 2003, the day before Thanksgiving, Tom, a former Dean of the Marquette Dental School and practicing dentist in the Milwaukee area, left his beloved cabin built by Pat McNeal years before near Bushey Road, in search of a buck before dark. Although his quest was successful, he died of a heart attack after dragging the buck toward his pickup truck parked in the woods.

1 cup flour
½ teaspoon salt
1 tablespoon baking powder
1 tablespoon sugar
½ cup cooked wild rice

continued

Wild Rice Pancakes *continued*

- 1 egg
- 1 cup milk
- 2 rounded tablespoons sour cream
- 2 tablespoons melted butter, room temperature

Sift dry ingredients. Beat egg, milk and sour cream until smooth. Stir in melted butter. Pour pancake amounts on hot grill and heat until golden on each side.

Note: This is also a good recipe without the rice.

Chokecherry Jelly

Chokecherries are tiny dark purple-red berries that make picking tedious, but the resulting jelly makes it all worthwhile. The jelly can be spread on toast, pancakes, waffles, English muffins, hot rolls and biscuits. Growing on delicate trees in woods, roadsides and riverbanks, both berry and tree are a pleasure to have nearby to appreciate as a regional gift. This recipe was submitted by Stan Hathaway, Governor of Wyoming, for The Republican Cookbook, published in 1969.

- 3 ½ pounds chokecherries
- 3 cups water
- 6 ½ cups sugar
- Fruit pectin to jell
- ¼ teaspoon almond extract

Pick, wash, and stem ripe chokecherries.
Add water to cherries, bring to a boil and simmer, covered, for 15 minutes.
Squeeze out the juice.
Measure 3 cups of juice into a very large saucepan.
Add sugar and mix well.
Place over high heat and bring to a boil, stirring constantly.
Add fruit pectin.
Bring to a full, rolling boil and boil 1 minutes, stirring.
Remove from heat and add almond extract.
Skim off foam with a metal spoon and pour quickly into glasses.
Cover at once with hot paraffin.

Grape Jam

I'd be remiss if this grape jam recipe wasn't included in this chapter. I can remember Mother laying newspapers on the kitchen table in preparation of making jam each September and I have carried on the tradition, only with a different recipe.

I found this one years ago in Bea Smith's Great Lakes Cookery book and have had such great results that I wouldn't think of trying any other. Smith's popular weekly column once appeared in the Traverse City Record Eagle and the Charlevoix County Press, and her books, including Four Seasons Cookbook, published in 1993, have become a treasure of regional recipes interspersed with nostalgia and folklore. This recipe is printed as is from the Great Lake's Cookery book.

It's jelly making time and I always advise to use the directions on the package of pectin when making jams and jellies.

Following their directions makes for foolproof preserves.

However, I am going to give you my old-time recipe for grape jam.

This always has been successful through the years for me and brings out the true flavor of the grapes.

Be sure the grapes are ripe.

Measure purple grapes and add to each heaping cupful measuring 1 ½ cups grapes to 1 cup sugar.

Place both the sugar and grapes in a preserving kettle and heat slowly until the juice starts.

Mash and cook for 20 minutes, stirring to avoid burning.

Press through a sieve while hot and pour into sterilized glasses and seal.

This jam is easier to handle if made in small quantities.

My handwritten notes in Smith's cookbook to make a single batch are as follows:

Fruit as directed plus 5 cups sugar for one batch. This will make nine 4-ounce glasses or five 8-ounce glasses. The best!

French Toast

My boys just loved this recipe when they were young and claim today I don't make it often enough at the cottage, and they're right. It is another exceptional simple and delicious breakfast recipe.

2 eggs, beaten
2/3 cup milk
2 tablespoons sugar
¼ teaspoon nutmeg
½ cup flour
½ teaspoon salt
Butter

French or Italian bread, cut thick works very well, however any type of bread will do just fine.
Beat first 6 ingredients and dip bread in mixture, coating well.
Melt butter in heavy pan and fry until golden brown on one side.
Melt additional butter and brown other side.
Serve with soft butter and warm syrup.
Note: Sprinkling with powdered sugar adds yet another special touch.

Cari's Egg Strata

When we first acquired four lots on the south shore back in 1964 and built on three of them, the fourth lot was saved for Gordy and Elaine's son, Tom. However, years later, it was sold twice, the third time to Dick and Carol Langdok from Minnesota. Their lovely lake home today bursts with activity when their children and grandchildren arrive to spend weekends together. Although everyone has weekend chores, Cari is in charge of Sunday morning breakfast and this has become the family favorite.

7 slices of white bread
½ pound shredded cheddar cheese
½ pound shredded American cheese
Ham, as much as desired
8 eggs
1 quart milk
1 teaspoon salt
½ teaspoon pepper
1 teaspoon dry mustard

After cutting the crusts from bread slices, lay bread on bottom of 9 x 13-inch pan. Layer with both cheese and as much ham as you'd like.
Mix remaining ingredients together and pour over top.
Refrigerate overnight. Bake uncovered at 350 degrees for 1 hour.
Let set for 15 minutes before serving.

Schmarren

When the north wind blows toward Ed and Dorothy Schnaith's place on the south shore, one might be treated at lunchtime to this recipe passed on to Dorothy many years ago by her mother. Schmarren was served in my mother's Hungarian-German household for breakfast on chilly mornings when she was young. Either way, for breakfast or lunch, it's ethnic comfort food, especially for those who remember enjoying it during their childhood days.

1 eggs
1 pint milk (approximately)
¼ teaspoon salt
Flour
Crisco, or other shortening
Sugar

Mix together eggs, milk and salt.
Add enough flour to reach the consistency of a dumpling (about 2 ½ cups).
Melt shortening in heavy skillet to about ¼-inch deep.
When hot, add mixture cutting constantly with two knives until nice and brown and in small pieces. Serve sprinkled with sugar.

Wild Rice with Hickory Nuts and Feta Cheese

My friend, Terese Allen, also claims that her favorite way to eat wild rice is mixed with crumbled bacon and strips of omelet for breakfast or lunch. Man-o-win, the Ojibwa Indian word for wild rice, takes on many ethnic flavors whether using oranges, soy sauce and ginger roots, or mixed with feta cheese and hickory nuts. This may seem fussy for a cottage food, but considering the regional ingredients of wild rice and hickory nuts, it might become a jewel in your recipe collection.

1 cup wild rice, well rinsed
1 teaspoon salt
1 tablespoon butter
½ cup finely chopped onion
⅓ cup hickory nuts
⅓ cup crumbled feta cheese

Combine wild rice, salt and 3 cups water in pot.
Bring to boil, reduce to low heat, cover and simmer until done to your liking.
When rice is about three-quarters done, heat butter in small skillet over low flame. Add onions; sauté until tender.
Raise heat to medium, add nuts and cook until they are toasty.
When wild rice is ready, drain off excess liquid, then heat until grains are dry.
Stir in onion-nut mixture. Transfer mixture to bowl; sprinkle with feta and serve immediately.
Makes 4 to 6 servings

Willis Cottage Recipes

Steeped in history, the little white seasonal cottage with a lattice-wrapped base built in 1933 by Urban George and Amy "Nana" Willis became the site of family pride and traditions when special cottage recipes were enjoyed through the years, then passed on to grandson Bill Caruso. Although the cottage was recently sold, aromas of the past continue to filter through porch screens and trees that wind down to the shoreline from Caruso's new seasonal home next door. These aged family recipes with ingredients most have on hand were carefully recorded at the cottage by "Nana" for future family gatherings.

Cornstarch Pudding

3 tablespoons cornstarch
1 quart milk
2 or 3 eggs, separated
Pinch of salt
3 tablespoons sugar
Vanilla extract
Cut up fruit (oranges, bananas, etc.), sweetened with sugar

Dissolve cornstarch in some of the cold milk.
Mix in well-beaten yolks, salt and sugar.
Heat the rest of the milk to scalding and add to mixture.
Boil 4 minutes, stirring continually.
Add flavoring.
Pour over fruit sweetened with sugar in casserole dish or other serving dish.
Make meringue recipe with egg whites and pile on top.
Brown lightly under broiler.

Corn Fritters

6 small ears of corn, uncooked
Salt, pepper, butter
Milk, if necessary
1 cup flour
1 teaspoon baking powder
2 eggs
A little sugar

Scrape corn carefully into bowl so no parts of husks get into mix, but all the corn milk does. Mix in rest of ingredients. Fry by spoonfuls and eat hot.

Flapper Pudding

1 cup butter
1 ½ cups sugar
3 eggs
1 ½ pounds vanilla wafers, crushed fine with rolling pin
1 large can crushed pineapple, well drained
Whipping cream

Cream butter and sugar. Add eggs, crushed wafers and drained pineapple.
Mix thoroughly and let stand in refrigerator overnight.
Garnish with whipped cream.

"Nana's" Fish Chowder, Camp-Style

Lean salt pork (or bacon), about ¼ pound
1 large onion
Water
3-4 medium potatoes
1 can milk
Fresh fish, 3-4 bass or 2 big northern pike
Salt
Oyster crackers

Cut salt pork that has lots of lean meat in it into tiny pieces (about 1/16- by ¼- by 1-inch).
Fry gently over slow fire, watching and turning constantly, taking out pieces as they get crisp and done, and pouring off some of the excess fat.
Cut onion into small pieces.
When pork is done, sauté onion gently, being careful not to burn or brown.
Put into kettle. Add enough water to cover sliced raw potatoes.
Cook a little. Add pieces of fish. When almost done, add milk and heat to a simmer.
Water should be cooked almost down, or some poured off.
Canned milk makes a fine rich chowder.
Salt cautiously to taste, because of the salt pork.
Have crackers ready.

This is very good warmed over.

Blueberry Walnut Streusel Muffins

Before the rail system was introduced to the area, connections were made by stage coaches. When the Northern Pacific Railway to Grantsburg was completed in 1884, it became a popular route with a round-trip fare of $4.20. Blueberries picked in the area were also shipped by this new method of transportation, thus labeling the route the Blueberry Special. I can't imagine a summer at the lake without serving these, slathered with butter to enjoy with coffee early in the morning on the screened porch. This happens to be my favorite blueberry muffin recipe.

1 ½ cups flour
2 teaspoons baking powder
½ teaspoon salt
4 tablespoons softened butter
½ cup sugar
1 egg
1 teaspoon vanilla
1/2 cup milk
1 ½ cups fresh blueberries

Stir together first 3 ingredients. In a larger bowl, cream butter and sugar until fluffy.
Beat in egg and vanilla.
Stir in flour mixture alternately with milk;
fold in blueberries dusted with additional flour.
Grease muffin cups or place a paper baking cup in each of 12 large muffin tin cups. Spoon batter into cups, filling about ½ full.
Mix together and sprinkle with streusel topping.
Bake at 400 degrees for 25 minutes or until done.
Allow to rest for ten minutes before removing from pan to cool on wire rack.

Topping

2 tablespoons melted butter
2 tablespoons packed brown sugar
¼ teaspoon cinnamon
¼ cup chopped walnuts

Six Week Bran Muffins

You are expecting company. You'd like to treat them to something special in the morning to enjoy with coffee without going through a lot of trouble. Perhaps you'll serve these at the kitchen table. Maybe on the pier. Or shoreline in a beach chair. Wherever, this is as quick and delicious as any homemade muffin recipe can be and will become one you'll use often.

2 15-ounce boxes of Raisin Bran
3 cups sugar **See: Note**
5 cups all-purpose flour
5 teaspoons baking soda
2 teaspoons salt
4 teaspoons cinnamon
2 eggs, beaten
1 cup salad oil
1 quart buttermilk
1 large can fruit cocktail, drained

Mix cereal, sugar, flour, baking soda, salt and cinnamon.
Add beaten eggs, oil, buttermilk and mix together well.
Fold in drained fruit cocktail.
Cover tightly and refrigerate.
Do not stir again.
Fill greased muffin tins about 2/3 full.
Bake at 400 degrees for 15-20 minutes.
Properly covered, dough will keep in the refrigerator for 6 weeks.

Yield: 6-7 dozen

Note: I use 2 cups white sugar and 1 cup light brown sugar)

Blueberry Bread

If you don't happen to have muffin tins, make this instead. It is wonderfully moist and next best to blueberry muffins… or maybe even better.

1 ½ cups all-purpose flour
1 ½ teaspoons baking powder
½ teaspoon salt
½ cup softened butter
1 cup sugar
2 eggs
1 teaspoon vanilla

continued

Blueberry Bread *continued*

1 teaspoon grated lemon peel, optional
⅓ cup milk
1 to 2 cups fresh blueberries
2 teaspoons flour

Mix together first three ingredients.
In a larger bowl, beat butter and sugar until thoroughly mixed.
Add eggs, vanilla and, if desired, grated lemon rind, and beat until blended.
Stir into butter mixture a small amount of mixed dry ingredients, followed by a small portion of milk.
Stir to blend, then repeat until adding the rest of the milk.
In another bowl, dust berries with 2 teaspoons of flour before carefully folding into batter.

Grease the bottom of a 9 x 5-inch loaf pan and turn batter into pan, baking at 350 degrees for 45 to 55 minutes, or until bread springs back when touched lightly.

Allow bread to cool 15 minutes before turning out on rack to cool.

Note: If desired, sprinkle top of baked bread with sugar immediately after removing from oven, or before baking sprinkle batter in pan with streusel mixture of ¼ cup sugar, 2 tablespoons flour and 1 tablespoon butter.

Banana Bread

The plight of the banana in our cottage ends in a loaf pan when, on warm summer days, bananas seem to ripen with the blink of an eye. So, it's a good thing we all like banana bread, especially this recipe, because it doesn't require anything you won't already have in the pantry.

1 cup sugar
½ cup shortening
2 eggs
2 ½ medium mashed bananas
½ cup cold water

2 cups all-purpose flour
1 teaspoon baking powder
1 teaspoon baking soda
¼ teaspoon salt

Cream sugar and shortening.
Add eggs, bananas and water.
Mix together dry ingredients and blend into banana mixture.
Bake in a greased 9 X5-inch loaf pan at 350 degrees for 1 hour, or until done.
Can be baked in three small loaf pans for about 35-40 minutes.
When cool, sift powdered sugar in a small strainer to cover bread.

Note: Chopped nuts and dates can be added.

Pumpkin Bread

This recipe is prepared and served at the John Hancock Inn in Hancock, New Hampshire. Once I tasted the intensity of the flavors, I knew I'd never experiment with another pumpkin bread recipe. For those of you who spend autumn at the lake, try this. You'll love it.

1 ½ cups sugar
1 ½ cups packed brown sugar
1 cup oil
3 eggs
1 16-ounce can pumpkin
3 cups all-purpose flour
1 ½ teaspoons ground cloves
1 ½ teaspoons ground cinnamon
1 ½ teaspoons ground nutmeg
½ teaspoon ground allspice
1 teaspoon baking soda
½ teaspoon baking powder
½ teaspoon salt
¾ cup raisins, chopped dates or walnuts See: Note

Combine sugars and oil.
Beat in eggs, one at a time, and pumpkin.
Combine flour, spices, baking soda, baking powder and salt; add to pumpkin mixture.
Stir in fruits or nuts.
Pour into two greased 9 x 5-inch or one 9 x 5-inch and two 7 x 3 ½-inch loaf pans and bake at 350 degrees for about 70 minutes for larger loaves, or 60 minutes for smaller loaves.

Note: I like a combination of chopped dates and walnuts.

Rhubarb Bread

The old-fashion pie plant: forever forgiving rhubarb that rewards us with excitingly juicy desserts each spring despite how little nourishment or care the plants require. There are many rhubarb bread recipes, but this one is particularly good.

1 ½ cups light brown sugar
⅓ cup vegetable oil
1 egg
1 cup buttermilk
1 teaspoon vanilla
1 teaspoon salt
1 teaspoon baking soda
2 ½ cups flour
1 ½ cups fresh rhubarb, diced

Mix first 4 ingredients, then add vanilla.
Mix together dry ingredients and add to first mixture.
Mix well and fold in rhubarb.
Pour into two well-greased 9 x 5-inch loaf pans.
Sprinkle with topping.
Bake at 350 degrees for 60 minutes or until done.
Cool. Remove from pans.

Makes two loaves.

Topping

½ cup light brown sugar
1 tablespoon butter
½ cup chopped walnuts
1 teaspoon cinnamon

Rhubarb Kuchen

Mother was a great cook and this was one of her favorite rhubarb recipes.

Daddy already had rhubarb plants in his garden and once I established plants in my own cottage garden, I felt that almost everything else was minor.

One summer Dick's nephew, Greg Murray, had just completed his first tour of duty as a Marine during the first war in Iraq. While returning home from California, he decided to stop at the lake before heading home to Ohio.

On a warm sunny afternoon we walked around Mallard Lake and spotted two lone rhubarb plants way out in the middle of a weedy overgrown field which, most likely, at one time had been someone's garden. We returned with a shovel and traipsed through the weeds so Greg could dig deep to free the plants from the field to plant in my own garden. I think of him each spring when the plants begin to nudge their way through the sandy soil.

1 ¼ cups sifted all-purpose flour
½ cup butter
1 tablespoon sugar
½ teaspoon salt
1 teaspoon baking powder
1 egg
2 tablespoons milk
3 cups rhubarb, cut in 1-inch pieces
¾ cup sugar
2 tablespoons flour
2 tablespoons butter

Blend first five ingredients with fork or fingers until creamy.
Mix egg and milk with fork and stir into flour mixture.
Press into a prepared 8 x 11-inch or 9 x 9-inch pan.
Spread rhubarb over top of dough.
Make streusel topping with remaining sugar, flour and butter with fork until crumbly.
Sprinkle over rhubarb.
Bake at 350 degrees for 1 hour.

It's wonderful served warm with coffee, or as a dessert with a small amount of whipped cream.

Mallard Lake Resort Chili for a Crowd

Long ago, when water levels rose, North Sand and Mallard lakes were joined. In fact, a former Mallard Lake Resort owner remembers hearing that Mallard Lake was referred to as North Sand Beach. Stanley Burner bought Mallard Lake Resort in 1959 and stayed there for about twelve years. When Barbara and Gordon Johnson purchased the resort in 1998, they found this recipe among other items left behind by another former owner of 13 years, Carl Hanson, who now resides in Voyager Village. A week at the lake wouldn't be complete without a kettle of chili to simmer, serve, reheat or freeze for another day and is perfect when the gang arrives because everyone knows that it will taste even better the next day. Today, the popular destination operates all year as Mallard Lake Family Resort and Campground. Along with modernized cabins on a beautiful sandy beach, there are 50 seasonal RV sites on 30 acres, overnight camping accommodations, a restaurant and lounge, executive seasonal sites, and many other amenities.

8 – 10 pounds ground beef
4 large onions, chopped
2 #10 cans dark red kidney beans, drained and rinsed
2 #10 cans tomato sauce
4 1-pound cans tomatoes
1 tablespoon salt
2 tablespoons pepper, or to taste
2 tablespoons Tabasco Sauce
6 tablespoons chili powder

In a large kettle, brown together meat and onion; pour off grease. Add remaining ingredients and simmer 2-3 hours.

Mother's Chili

Although chili has a thousand faces, the one your Mother made when you were growing up ends up being your favorite for life. And, this is it.

3 slices bacon
½ cup chopped onion
1 garlic clove, minced
1 pound ground beef
1 16-ounce can red kidney beans, drained
2 8-ounce cans tomato sauce
1 16-ounce can tomatoes, cut up, with juice
½ teaspoon chili powder
¼ package Lipton's dried onion soup mix
Salt to taste

Cut bacon in 1-inch pieces and brown in heavy sauce pan.
Add chopped onions, garlic and ground beef and brown. Drain grease.
Add remaining ingredients and simmer, covered, about 20 minutes.

Bluegill or Crappie Chowder

What a shame it would be if this was left out. Found in a local paper more than once and saved for obvious reasons, it is a slight diversion from using northern pike in chowder and should become everyone's favorite cottage/cabin/home fish chowder recipe. I wish I knew whose recipe it was so I could given them credit and hope they don't mind that I added my own Notes.

- 5 large white potatoes
- 1 large onion
- 2 garlic cloves
- 3 celery stalks
- 1 green pepper
- 1 cup milk
- 1 cup stock (See: Note)
- 3 tablespoons butter
- Salt and pepper to taste
- ½ cup water
- 3 tablespoons flour
- 2 pounds cleaned, diced bluegill
- 2 tablespoons melted butter
- ½ cup heavy cream

Finely chop potatoes, onion, garlic, celery and green pepper.
Add to milk, stock and butter and season to taste.
Bring to a boil and simmer about 1-2 hours.
About 30 minutes before serving, mix together and add ½ cup water, 3 tablespoons flour, fish and melted butter.
Simmer for 30 minutes.
Remove from heat and stir in heavy cream.

Note: Fish bouillon is available in most stores and can be used with water as stock.

If not available, bottled clam juice can be used as stock.
Chopped fresh parsley also is a nice addition.
If you don't like green pepper, leave it out.

Cottage Creamy-Corn Chowder

This will take the bite out of a chilly day when the wind blows from the north and white-tipped waves crash on shore.

- 1 cup chopped onion
- 2 tablespoons butter
- 1 cup peeled, chopped potato
- 2 cups boiling water or chicken broth
- 1 teaspoon salt
- 1/8 teaspoon pepper
- 2 cups cream-style corn
- 1 ½ - 2 cups milk
- Fried bacon

continued

Cottage Creamy-Corn Chowder *continued*

Sauté onion in butter until tender.
Add potatoes, water, and salt and pepper.
Cook over medium heat until potatoes are tender, about 20 minutes.
Stir in corn and milk.
Bring just to boiling and serve garnished with crumbled fried bacon.

Serves 6

Note: A small can of kernel corn, drained, or a small amount of frozen corn can be added for a thicker chowder. If too thin, thicken with instant mashed potatoes.

Mediterranean Fish Soup

You can make this ahead, refrigerate or freeze, then reheat in a heavy covered saucepan or skillet in just 10 to 15 minutes with no loss of fresh-cooked flavor. Although the recipe is vague in calling for "frozen fish fillets," I've used northern pike, bass or bluegills.

1 large onion, chopped (1 cup)
½ cup chopped celery with leaves
1 large garlic clove, crushed
2 tablespoons butter
2 cans (16 ounces each) tomatoes, cut up
½ cup dry white wine
½ cup minced parsley
1 teaspoon salt
¼ teaspoon each pepper and thyme
1 package (1 pound) frozen fish fillets, thawed or partially thawed, cut in 1-inch chunks

In large saucepan, sauté onion, celery and garlic in butter until tender.
Stir in tomatoes, wine, parsley, salt, pepper and thyme.
Cover and simmer 30 minutes or until fish is opaque and flakes easily with fork.
Serve with crusty bread.

Makes 4 to 6 servings

Note: If desired, sprinkle each serving with additional minced parsley

Bean and Hot Dog Chowder

When I first saw this recipe in an old 1968 hot dog cookbook revised in 1983, I had a feeling it was one most children would like for lunch or supper any time of the year. Then I discovered that grownups liked it, too. Reminding me of wagon train food served out on the prairie under the stars, it was also perfect for cabin-cottage-campouts around an up north bonfire roaring under the same stars.

Serve in bowls just as you would thick chili con carne with saltine crackers, biscuits or homemade bread. Although it is supposed to serve six, depending on how hearty the eaters are, in our cottage it would easily serve eight.
With a few changes, here is my rendition.

6 hot dogs, cut in ¼-inch slices
2 tablespoons butter
½ cup celery, sliced ¼-inch thick
¾ cup onion, thinly sliced
¼ cup green pepper, finely chopped
2 28-ounce cans pork and beans, undrained (See: Note)
2 8-ounce cans tomato sauce
½ teaspoon salt
¼ teaspoon pepper
1 teaspoon brown sugar

Place sliced hot dogs and butter in a large soup kettle over moderate heat.
Sauté the hot dogs until they just begin to brown.
Add celery, onion and green pepper and continue to sauté until onion is limp and transparent.
Remove pieces of pork from the beans and discard.
Add undrained beans to the hot dog mixture.
Add tomato sauce, salt, pepper and brown sugar and mix well.
Cook for 10 minutes longer or until heated through.

Note: I used what I had available in my pantry which was a 28-ounce can of plain "original" baked beans and a 28-ounce can of baked beans seasoned with bacon and brown sugar and it worked out just fine.

Fresh Tomato Soup

By the end of summer, our sandy soil gardens should reward us with ripe red tomatoes. Although the plants might suffer from the miserable yellow leaf rot, the fruit remains juicy and is anxiously awaited. That is, of course, if the deer haven't already feasted on the stems, leaves and fruit like they did in my garden during early summer. However, if you are lucky enough to harvest more than you can slice and eat in a day, try this simple, yet delicious recipe from Kathy Rypel.

continued

Fresh Tomato Soup *continued*

- ¼ cup butter
- ½ cup chopped onion
- 1 cup water
- 6 medium tomatoes, peeled and diced
- 1 tablespoon minced fresh garlic
- 1 ¼ teaspoons salt
- 1 tablespoon sugar
- ¼ teaspoon thyme leaves
- ¼ teaspoon pepper
- 1 bay leaf
- Sliced lemon for garnish, optional

In a 3-quart pan over medium heat, melt butter and cook onion until tender, about 10 minutes. Stir in flour until blended, then gradually stir in water.
Add tomatoes and remaining ingredients, except sliced lemon.
Heat to boil, then reduce heat and simmer for 30 minutes.
Serve in bowls and garnish with lemon slices.

Stuffed Green Pepper Soup

If you are successful in keeping the wild animals from your garden, here is another great soup that will soothe your soul and warm your toes when the temperatures begin to dip in September. It was given to me by my Pennsylvania Italian friend and cookbook author, Barbara Vaglia McCalley and is especially hearty served with thick crusty Italian bread

- 1 ½ pounds ground beef
- 1 medium onion, chopped
- 6 cups beef broth (49-ounce can)
- 1 28-ounce can crushed tomatoes
- 1 can tomato soup
- 1 cup ketchup
- 4 large green peppers, chopped
- Salt and pepper to taste
- 2 cups cooked white rice

Brown ground beef and onions; drain off fat.
Add beef broth and bring to a boil.
Add tomatoes, soup and ketchup and season with salt and pepper.
Cover and simmer 2 hours, stirring occasionally.
Add cooked rice and serve.

Wild Rice Soup

Tom and Kathy Rypel spent many hours each year harvesting wild rice together in early fall from a canoe in shallow lakes where the grain grew in abundance. As a result, their wild rice recipes are also in abundance. When French explorers first arrived in our area, they referred to the aquatic grass grain as ***folle avoine*** *which meant "wild oats." Control of wet lands and the wild oats would become the reason for countless Indian tribal wars. Tom and Kathy enjoyed many bowls of this hearty soup when they spent time together at their cabin in the woods.*

⅔ cup uncooked wild rice
2 tablespoons butter
1 tablespoon minced onion
¼ cup flour
1 quart chicken broth
⅓ cup shredded carrot
⅓ cup diced celery
⅓ cup sliced fresh mushrooms
1 cup or less Half & Half (cream) See: Note
2 tablespoons dry Sherry
Fresh parsley

Prepare and cook rice.
Melt butter in 4-quart pan and sauté onion. Blend in flour.
Gradually add broth and cook, stirring constantly until smooth and slightly thickened. Stir in cooked rice, salt, carrot, celery and mushrooms.
Simmer 5 minutes.
Add cream and dry Sherry.

Note: Although consistency will differ, milk can be substituted for the cream.

Pink Ambrosia

When Jack and Birdie Bowman first arrived on the lake in 1944 to spend their vacation at Thompson's Resort, they knew immediately that it was a place they'd return to year after year from their home in Chicago. In 1957, the Bowman's purchased Berniece and Stuart Thompson's home on the shoreline woods of the lake resort. It became a family affair in 1979 when their son, Jon, and his wife, Rosemary, purchased the adjacent lot. One of Birdie Bowman's favorite recipes is refreshingly delicious any time of the year, especially during the warm summer months.

3 ounce package of strawberry Jell-O
8-12 ounce container of small curd cottage cheese
8 ounce container of Cool Whip
15 ounce can of drained crushed pineapple

Mix together and chill in the refrigerator.

Note: Any Jell-O flavor can be used.

Cranberry Delight

Sharon Johnson and her mother, Marie Mackey, love this recipe and thought the rest of you would enjoy it as well. Hand-written on a tablet designed with a butterfly, dragonfly, cardinal, frog, raccoon, black bear and moose, the recipe lends itself well to any meal prepared for family or company visiting the north woods.

2 cups cranberries, ground
3 cups mini-marshmallows
½-3/4 cup sugar
2 cups unpeeled apples, diced
1 cup seedless grapes, cut in half
1-2 cups whipping cream, whipped (no sugar added)
Pecans or pistachio slivers

Combine cranberries, marshmallows and sugar.
Chill overnight.
When ready to serve, add apples and grapes to mixture.
Fold in whipped cream.
Sprinkle with pecans or pistachio slivers.

Raspberry Jell-O

Sharon and Eldon Johnson purchased Mother and Daddy's cottage in 1989 and immediately became a member of our family. I was invited over one day for a Johnson family gathering and tasted a Jell-O salad that put a smile on my face. When I asked for the recipe, Sharon smiled, too, as she is the first one to admit that she's not a "Becky Homemecky" and spends as little time as possible in her cottage kitchen. However simple, it happens to be a cottage winner, especially because of my passion for red raspberries.

Small package of raspberry Jell-O
1 can raspberry pie filling
1 cup hot water
Cool Whip

Prepare as directed on package using one cup of boiling water to dissolve Jell-O. Instead of adding the cup of cold water, stir in pie filling and stir until blended. Pour into a serving container and refrigerate.
Spread with Cool Whip and serve.

Note: Let your mind create other possibilities with other flavors.

Sicilian Potato Salad

I'd be remiss if I didn't include this recipe as one Daddy greatly enjoyed. I made it one day a few years ago and shared it with my lake neighbor Ginny Mommsen who since has made it many times for her friends and family in St. Croix Falls. Featured in one of my cookbooks, the recipe was initially found in an authentic Sicilian cookbook and since then I have added a few touches of my own.

2 pounds small potatoes, preferably redskins
1 pound tender green beans
3 green onions, 3 inches of head only, sliced
2 tablespoons chopped fresh basil
1 teaspoon oregano
½ teaspoon onion salt
½ teaspoon garlic salt
½ teaspoon black pepper
¼ cup olive oil
3 tablespoons red wine vinegar
1 cup red cherry tomato halves
Juice of half a lemon
Salt to taste
Sugar, optional

continued

Sicilian Potato Salad *continued*

Boil potatoes until firm, but tender. If desired, leave unpeeled.
Immerse in cold water to stop the cooking process, remove, dab dry with paper towels and allow to cool.
Boil beans to same consistency, rinse with cold water and cut in half.
Cut potatoes into bite-size chunks.
Combine all ingredients except vinegar, tomatoes, lemon juice and salt.
Refrigerate potato mixture.
When ready to serve, add mixture of remaining four ingredients, and a pinch of sugar if too tart.

Note: If desired, additional dressing can be prepared and added.

Serves 6 to 8

Simply Delicious Creamy Coleslaw

I found this recipe in a small cookbook purchased at the antique store in Webster. One mouthful and we knew it was a keeper. All you need is some deli-prepared coleslaw from Wayne's and the rest is a snap.

1 pound deli-prepared creamy coleslaw
1 package shredded cabbage for coleslaw
4 or more green onions, chopped, using some green
1 can (16-ounces) Mandarin oranges, drained well
Handful of salted peanuts

Place prepared coleslaw in a large bowl and fold in additional shredded cabbage to the amount desired.

Mix in onions, oranges and peanuts and place in the refrigerator until ready to serve. If Mandarin oranges are not available, drained pineapple chunks can be substituted.

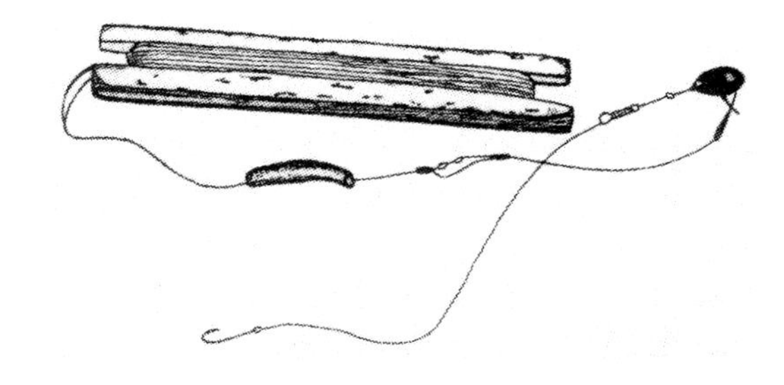

Steve's Tomato Salad

Steve Yanisch is the first to admit this is not his own creation, but one found in his Silver Palate Cookbook. What matters is how we moaned with pleasure with each bite one evening while having dinner on his screened porch. Along with being a great cook, Steve fishes the lake he knows like the back of his hand and generously implements his MO as a catch and release fisherman. His wife, Rebecca, tends to her breathtakingly beautiful flower garden that draws applause from neighbors as well as anyone walking or driving by. Certainly, both have become gems in the ever-growing crown of North Sand Lake. Meanwhile, back in the kitchen and after November 2004, the mouth-watering aromas wafting through the screens of their lake home (hopefully in my direction) will become even more enticing after Steve completes a cooking class in Tuscany, Italy.

And, just an added note: if you don't have a protected place with good soil to grow tomatoes up north, stop by Joe Klecker's place on Norman's Landing Road where juicy tomatoes and much more grow in abundance in his garden for you to purchase.

6 large ripe summer tomatoes
1 red onion
¼ cup basil puree (See: Note)
¼ cup black or Kalamata olives
⅓ cup olive oil
Dash red wine vinegar
Salt and pepper
5-8-ounces chevre cheese (See: Note)

Core tomatoes. Cut into wedges. Julienne the onion.
Add all ingredients except cheese.
Refrigerate 1 hour or let sit 30 minutes before serving.
Turn over tomatoes and add cheese in pieces.
Can be served in a bowl or on a lettuce leaf.

Note: Basil puree: blend a handful of fresh basil leaves with a tablespoon of olive oil in food processor.

Chevre (shehv-ruh) is French for "goat" and is a pure white goat's milk cheese.
Store tightly wrapped in the refrigerator up to 2 weeks.
When chevre takes on a sour taste, it should be discarded.

Raspberry Vinaigrette

You may have to drive to town for a few of these ingredients, but it will be well worth the extra miles. There are some things in life that one discovers one no longer wants to live without and this recipe happens to be a winner. For years I've used packets of Good Seasoning Italian dressing to make my own salad dressing and that will never change. However, for a slightly sweeter and lighter taste perfect to toss with Romaine lettuce and other tender greens, try this. It is superb!

1 cup olive oil
1 cup corn oil
¼ cup raspberry spreadable fruit (jam)
⅔ cup Alessi white balsamic raspberry blush vinegar
Salt and pepper to taste
3 tablespoons chopped shallots
3 tablespoons chopped fresh parsley

Mix together thoroughly and store in the refrigerator.
Shake well before using.
Excellent with tossed Romaine lettuce and other tender greens tossed with grape tomatoes, green onions, and other salad vegetables.

Serves 12-16

Garlic French Salad Dressing

This is another favorite shared by my Sun Prairie friend Bob Swanson who carefully worked with it until he rated it high enough to forward it to me as a newspaper food columnist. It is especially nice if you are interested in preparing a small amount of dressing and not enough to feed an entire family.
I can guarantee that you will make this more than once.

3 tablespoons salad oil
2 tablespoons ketchup
1 tablespoon balsamic vinegar
2 teaspoons sugar
¼ teaspoon fresh pressed garlic
Dash or two of Angostura bitters

Combine all ingredients in a jar.
Seal with a tight lid and shake vigorously until well blended.
Store in refrigerator 2 to 4 hours for flavors to develop.
Dressing should be used within a day or two while the garlic flavor is still fresh.

Note: I use olive oil. Also, the bitters are not essential, but they do add flavor.

President Reagan's Macaroni and Cheese

Assuming that everyone has macaroni on hand, the only non-staple ingredient necessary to make this a winner is grated sharp cheddar cheese. Although kids today seem to prefer macaroni and cheese from a box, this becomes a special treat for the rest of us who like an old-fashion, hometown touch from scratch. Whether you are Democrat or Republican, ya gotta love it.

½ cup macaroni
1 teaspoon butter
1 egg, beaten
1 teaspoon salt
1 teaspoon dry mustard
1 cup milk
3 cups grated cheese, sharp

Boil macaroni in water until tender and drain thoroughly.
Stir in butter and egg.
Mix mustard and salt with 1 tablespoon hot water and add to milk.
Add cheese to macaroni, leaving enough cheese to sprinkle on top.
Pour macaroni into buttered casserole; add milk and sprinkle with remaining cheese.

Bake at 350 degrees for about 45 minutes or until custard is set and top is crusty.

Sweet Corn Kernels

The wife of a Dane County corn farmer shared this recipe with me years ago while chatting at her husband's produce stand at Warner Park on the north side of Madison, near our home. It is an excellent no-fail freezer method of preserving the freshness of sweet corn. Because it is already buttered, all you have to do is thaw and heat. Each year at the cottage, I buy about six dozen years for this recipe. Don't buy a utensil to scrape corn from the ears as a sharp steak knife does a better job.

6 cups of raw corn
1 cup water
¼ teaspoon salt
3 tablespoons sugar
1 stick butter

Bring water, corn and salt to a boil.
Cover and boil gently for 6-7 minutes.
Remove from heat and add stick of butter or margarine.
Cool and pack with juices in freezer bags or containers.

Note: 8 ears of corn usually yields about 6 cups of kernels.

Best made as a single recipe.

Mother's Green Pepper Omelet

*Called **frittata** by Italians, this was served often when we were growing up, especially on Fridays when Catholics were not allowed to eat meat. Mother worked with this until Daddy thought it reminded him of what his mother used to make. He loved it and so did the rest of us.*

2 tablespoons oil
Small garlic cloves, chopped fine
2 medium onions, sliced thin
2-4 green peppers, sliced thin
3-4 eggs
½ cup milk
¼ cup Italian bread crumbs
¼ cup grated Romano cheese
Salt and pepper
1 teaspoon freshly minced parsley, or ½ teaspoon dried parsley

Pour oil in heavy 10-inch skillet and sauté garlic, onions and green peppers slowly until tender.
Whisk eggs and milk together and pour over vegetables.
Sprinkle with crumbs and cheese and salt and pepper to taste.
Add parsley on top.
Cover and cook slowly until set.
Cut in wedges and serve warm.

Baked Stuffed Peppers

This recipe is from way down yonder in New Orleans where Italian immigrants arrived and settled more than a century ago. It is also where Daddy rode a box car to from Madison in 1927 to reach a Catholic college nearby where he would attend and play football on a scholarship. There are a variety of ways to personalize this recipe as you will see.

6 sweet bell peppers, any color, cut in half
2 tablespoons olive oil
1 medium onion
1 pound ground chuck
2 garlic cloves, minced
2 tablespoon chopped celery
1 tablespoon minced fresh parsley
1 cup Italian bread crumbs
½ cup grated Parmesan cheese
Salt and pepper to taste
Spaghetti sauce

Cut peppers in half and remove core and seeds.
Steam until somewhat soft, but still firm.
Sauté onion over medium heat.
When translucent, add meat and cook until brown.
Add garlic, celery and parsley. Cook 1 minute.
Add bread crumbs and cheese, saving some for topping.
Remove from heat and stir.
Fill each pepper half and place in baking dish.
Stir remaining cheese and bread crumb mixture in oil or butter.
Sprinkle each pepper to make a light crust when baked.
Make a tent with aluminum foil.
Bake at 375 degrees until done, approximately 30 minutes.
Serve with spaghetti sauce.

Makes 12 filled pepper halves

Note: Additions can be made, a few possibilities being anchovies, fennel seed and/or Italian sausage

Stuffed Bell Peppers-Syracuse Style

Years ago, a reader of my newspaper column asked for a stuffed pepper recipe that didn't include meat or rice, but instead stuffed with breadcrumbs like an east coast Italian friend prepared. When your pepper plants reward you sometime in August, try my friend Ross DePaola's mom's recipe from Syracuse, New York. You'll be glad you did.

4 large green, red and/or yellow bell peppers (red being the sweetest)
3 cups dry breadcrumbs
½ cup grated Parmesan cheese, plus additional cheese for the topping
1 teaspoon garlic powder
1 teaspoon dried basil
4 tablespoons olive oil
Salt and pepper to taste
4 tablespoons prepared marinara sauce, plus additional sauce to cook peppers in (see notes)
½ cup raisins

Preheat oven to 350 degrees.
Cut peppers in half lengthwise and remove stems and seeds.
Mix remaining ingredients together in a large mixing bowl.
If mixture is dry, add a little more sauce.
Place marinara sauce in bottom of large baking pan and thin with a little water.
Fill each pepper half with filling mixture.
Place filled peppers in the pan and cover with additional Parmesan cheese.
Cover pan with a lid or aluminum foil.
Bake 45 to 60 minutes, or until peppers are tender.
Any leftovers are delicious reheated.

Note: Marinara sauce is a regular meatless spaghetti sauce to make this vegetarian fare. Also, be sure to use raisins as they add a true Sicilian touch.

Rossario's Asiago Potatoes

My friend, Ross Parisi, owns an Italian restaurant in Monona, a Madison suburb, and serves this on occasion. If you haven't been introduced to Asiago cheese to date, it's about time you are. Having a wedge at all times at the cottage and back home in Madison is a must, either for slicing to serve with wine, grating, or for sauces. This is a favorite of many of our friends.

6 large potatoes
1 tablespoon butter
1 heaping tablespoon flour
2 cups milk (or less)
4 ounces Asiago, grated
½ onion, chopped
2 tablespoons chopped fresh parsley
2 tablespoons chicken bouillon or 3 cubes bouillon
½ cup grated Romano cheese

Peel and cut potatoes; cook till fork-tender, not mushy.
Melt butter in saucepan over medium heat.
Add flour and stir; cook till bubbly.
Add milk and cook, stirring constantly, until sauce boils and thickens.
Add Asiago and cook, stirring constantly, till cheese melts.
Transfer to baking dish.
Add onion, parsley, chicken bouillon and grated Romano cheese.
Pour sauce over all.
Mix well. Cover loosely.
Bake at 350 degrees for 30 minutes.

4 generous servings

Jack Spittell's Grilled Northern Pike

This is about as simple as typing the recipe which makes it even more intriguing and inviting. When Jack describes the outcome, he does so with his eyes closed and a smile on his face which means that it is...absolutely delicious.

Northern pike
Hellman's Real Mayonnaise
Lemon Pepper seasoning

Fillet and remove skin from fish.
Rub flesh with mixture of mayonnaise and seasoning.
Cover and refrigerate for a few hours.
Grill both sides until flesh easily flakes with a fork.

Pickled Fish

When Pat and Lucy Basler were proud proprietors of the Our Place Resort, Lucy was equally proud of this recipe which she eagerly shared with resort guests. The recipe slogan was, 'Catch 'em at Our Place, Pickle 'em at your place!'

Soak fish two days in salt brine (enough salt in water to float an egg)
Drain, rinse fish, and cut into thin strips.
Pour enough white vinegar over fish to cover.
Let stand for two days.
Drain and discard vinegar.

Mix together

- 2 cups white vinegar
- ¾ cup sugar
- 2 tablespoons mixed spices

Cool liquid and add ½ cup white wine. See: Note

Alternate layers of fish, thin slices of onion, and thin slices of lemon.
Fill jars with liquid and seal, removing some of the spices.
Place in the refrigerator.
They are good to eat in 3 to 4 weeks.
If they taste salty, they haven't aged enough.

Note: Lucy often eliminates the white wine and claims they are still delicious.

Poor Man's Lobster

I clipped this recipe from Chet Newman's Burnett County Sentinel column On the Wild Side for the next North Sand Lake northern pike you happen to land this summer, or any other time of the year. Passed on by Dave Burke from Scott Township, Newman called it a simple and tasty recipe for northern pike, and he was right.

- ⅓ cup salt
- ⅓ cup sugar
- Water to fill a large pot
- Melted butter
- One northern pike

Bring water with salt and sugar to a full rolling boil.
Put in the fish fillets, turn off the heat and let stand for 15 minutes.
Dip fish in melted butter and enjoy.
Those who want even more of the lobster flavor can add dill to the boiling water.

Up North Fish Bake

Back home in Madison lives an outstanding cook and cookbook author friend who writes free lance for various publications. When I saw her Wisconsin Fish-lover's Paradise column with this recipe, I knew it was a must for this chapter. It can be prepared in foil for one-dish campside cooking, but also works well in a 350 degree oven.

Terese Allen, thank you!

3 large potatoes, scrubbed and thinly sliced
1 large onion, thinly sliced
Salt and pepper to taste
2 cups sliced zucchini or mushrooms
2 tablespoons chopped fresh herbs of your choice, divided
(or 1 tablespoon dried herbs)
1 ½ pounds panfish fillets
2-3 tablespoons butter, cut into bits

Prepare campfire or grill. Butter a large foil baking pan.
Spread potatoes and onions in the dish and season with salt and pepper.
Cover tightly with foil; place on grill close to coals and cook 20 minutes.
Layer zucchini or mushrooms over partially cooked vegetables.
Season lightly with salt, pepper and half the herbs.
Cover and continue to cook 10-15 minutes.
Layer fish over vegetables; dot with butter and remaining herbs;
Season lightly with salt and pepper.
Cover and bake 10-15 minutes, or until fish is tender.

Serves 4

Pirate Pie

Sharon Johnson's mother, Marie Mackey, clipped this StarKist tuna recipe from a magazine at least 25 years ago and often made it for supper for Sharon and her sisters, Jackie and Georgeann. It's one of those flavored remembrances that one carries through life and remains special enough to repeat during weekends at the lake to return to the past with a new generation.

2 6 ½- ounce cans of StarKist chunk-style tuna
3 eggs
4 ounce can sliced mushrooms, drained
1 medium tomato, ¼-inch slices
4 slices American cheese
1 envelope instant mashed potato mix (See: Note)
1 tablespoon chopped fresh parsley

continued

Pirate Pie *continued*

Drain tuna. Beat eggs, slightly and add to tuna.
Add mushrooms and half of the parsley.
Place in bottom of a 9-inch Pyrex pie plate.
Top with tomato slices.
Cover with 3 cheese slices.
Prepare instant potatoes using ½ cup less of liquid.
Spoon thick mashed potatoes over cheese.
Cover with remaining cheese cut diagonally in half.
Bake at 375 degrees or until potatoes are light brown and cheese melts.
Cut into wedges. Garnish with remaining chopped parsley.

Serves 6

Note: If envelopes of instant mashed potatoes are not available, make your own mashed potatoes.

Parsley Parmesan Chicken

Jon and Rosemary Bowman live in a beautiful home that blends with the Lake Tahoe essence of the property. Both retired, they reside there year 'round and prepare many special seasonal and regional recipes. When asked if they would share a favorite family lake recipe, they generously shared this one.

¼ cup bottled Italian salad dressing
3 to 3 ½ pound broiler-fryer, cut up
1 slightly beaten egg
2 tablespoons water
½ cup grated Parmesan cheese
⅓ cup fine bread crumbs
2 tablespoons snipped parsley
½ teaspoon salt
½ teaspoon paprika
⅛ teaspoon pepper

Pour salad dressing into 9x13-inch baking dish.
Add chicken and turn to coat.
Cover and refrigerate for 4 hours.
Drain and reserve dressing.
Combine egg and water in plastic bag.
Combine cheese, bread crumbs, parsley, salt, paprika and pepper.
Dip chicken in egg mixture then shake in crumb mixture.
Place in baking dish, spoon remaining dressing over all.
Bake at 350 degrees for 45 to 50 minutes.

Serves 4

Chicken Booyah

Like Thompson Road's Fern Seagren Bowen, Appleton's Post-Crescent food columnist Carol Hanson, has fond memories of summers in northern Wisconsin at a cottage on Lake Michigan when the family prepared a huge kettle of booyah to simmer all day over an open fire. When it was done, bowls and crackers were passed around picnic tables with mugs of cold beer. Hanson generously shared this recipe for Food Editors' Hometown Favorites, a fund raising cookbook compiled by MADD, Mothers Against Drunk Driving, and edited by Barbara Gibbs Ostmann and Jane Baker for the Newspaper Food Editors and Writers Association Inc.

5 pounds stewing chicken, cut up
1 ½ pounds beef stew meat
¼ pound lean pork, cubed
½ pound dried navy beans, soaked overnight
½ pound split green peas
2 cups canned whole tomatoes
4 cups diced carrots
2 ½ cups diced onions
3 cups diced celery
½ lemon, peeled and cut into pieces
8 cups diced potatoes
4 cups shredded cabbage
4 tablespoons butter
Salt and pepper to taste

Place cut-up chicken, beef stew meat and pork in a large soup kettle.
Cover with cold water.
Slowly bring to a boil. Skim.
Simmer 1 hour.
Add drained navy beans, green peas, tomatoes, carrots, onions, celery and lemon.
Cook about 3 hours, or until chicken is very tender.
Add potatoes, cabbage, butter, salt and pepper.
Simmer 30 minute.
Note: During cooking, it will be necessary to add cold water to keep meats and vegetables covered and to ensure a soup that is not too thick.

Makes 4 gallons

Cottage Goulash

Mother's mother, my Grandma Kovacs, was a cook in a rectory in Germany before she married Joe Kovacs. That was before the turn of the 20th century, back when good cooks seldom recorded their family recipes for posterity. When they arrived here, that didn't change. So, when Mother was married, there was nothing for her to work from and Old World recipes suddenly took on an American touch. This was not the delicious Hungarian goulash Grandma used to make that Mother raved about, but it is a recipe we grew up eating and loving. When I became a mother, I called it Halloween Goulash because it was what I made for supper before the boys went out trick or treating. It's another tasty dish with few ingredients to prepare at the lake.

3 pieces of bacon, cut into ½-inch pieces
1 medium onion, chopped
Oil
1 pound lean ground beef
½ of a 7-ounce box of Creamette elbow macaroni, cooked
1 can Campbell's cream of tomato soup (See: Note)
Salt and pepper, optional

Brown bacon and onions in tiny amount of oil.
Add ground beef, brown, then drain.
Add cooked macaroni and soup.
Fold together and heat through.
Season, if desired.

Note: Depending on the amount of macaroni used, have an extra can of tomato soup on hand to supplement the dish with approximately 1/4-1/2 cup more of the condensed soup.

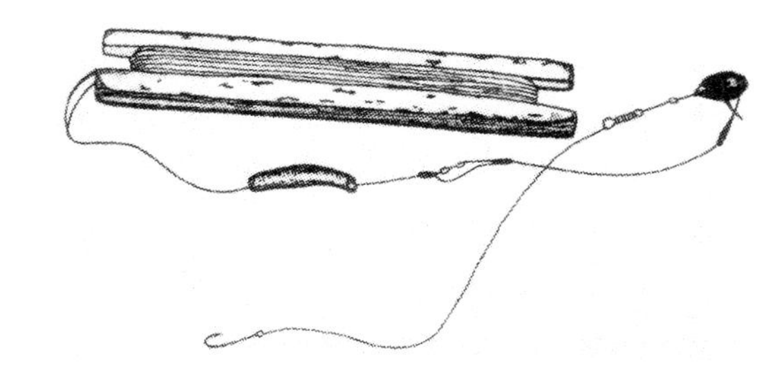

Coney Island Casserole

We already know this is up north food that will please the little ones in the family, and also be enjoyed by adults, especially those who can remember the excitement of summer months spent many years ago out east at the beach resort on Brooklyn, New York's popular Coney Island. This is a no-fail recipe that can easily be personalized with your own adaptations.

1 tablespoon oil
1 pound hot dogs, chopped
1 pound ground beef
2 15-ounce cans tomato sauce
1/2 cup olives, sliced
1 small onion, diced
Pinch of oregano
Salt and pepper
3 quarts boiling water
1 tablespoon salt
2 cups elbow macaroni
¼ pound sharp cheddar cheese, grated
Salt and pepper to taste
Olives for garnish

Heat oil in large skillet.
Add hot dogs and brown on all sides.
Remove from skillet and set aside.
Add ground beef to drippings, stir and brown.
Drain excess fat.
Stir in hot dogs, sauce, sliced olives, onions, oregano, salt and pepper.
Set aside.
Bring water to a boil and cook macaroni with salt; drain.
Add to meat sauce and toss.
Put grated cheese across top and turn into a 2 quart casserole.
Bake 40 minutes at 350 degrees.
Garnish with olives.

Serves 4 to 6 to 8

Make Ahead Chow Mein Casserole

Wild Rice with an Oriental twist appears on page 132 in a delightful fund raising cookbook, ***Wild Rice from the Folle Avoine,*** *recently compiled by the Burnett County Historical Society and Friends of the Burnett Community Library. With the addition of soy sauce, water chestnuts and bean sprouts, plus having to prepare and refrigerate the casserole up to 24 hours prior to baking makes it easy company fare you'll be proud to serve.*

1 ½ pounds meat loaf mixture (ground beef, pork and veal)
3 cups cooked wild rice
2 tablespoons butter or margarine
½ cup chopped onion
½ cup chopped green pepper
⅓ cup soy sauce
2 cans (10 ¾ ounces) low sodium cream of chicken soup
2 tablespoons grated ginger root, or less
1 can (8 ounces) sliced water chestnuts, drained
1 can (14 ounces) bean sprouts, drained and rinsed
6 ounce package wide-style chow mein noodles

Brown meat loaf mixture in skillet; drain.
Add to cooked wild rice.
In same skillet, melt butter;
sauté onion and green pepper until tender (about 5 minutes).
Combine soy sauce, soup, ginger, water chestnuts and bean sprouts.
Stir in meat mixture, onion and green pepper.
Pour into greased 3-quart casserole.
Refrigerate, covered, up to 24 hours.
Heat oven to 350 degrees.
Bake, covered, 45 minutes.
Uncover; sprinkle with noodles.
Bake until heated through, about 15-20 minutes longer.

Mother's Sauerkraut and Wieners

Having been born in Hungary, Mother's method of preparing sauerkraut and wieners must have been slightly Americanized along the way by my German grandma as it is the only one of its kind I've ever seen prepared in this manner with these ingredients. It definitely is a cold season meal and although I seldom make it anymore, I love it to death. You may substitute rope sausage, or kielbasa, but make it this way first to get the feel and taste of Mother's ethnic efforts. It is so simple, so good and so hearty

3 slices bacon, chopped
1 garlic clove, chopped
1 medium onion, chopped
1 can or jar (16 ounces) sauerkraut, drained
1 small bay leaf
1 heaping tablespoon brown sugar
⅓ cup ketchup
½ cup water
Wieners
Freshly cooked peeled potatoes, halved or quartered

Fry bacon slowly.
Add garlic and onion and sauté slightly.
Add remaining ingredients, except for wieners and potatoes,
Cover and cook slowly for 30-45 minutes, stirring occasionally.
Add wieners, or a similar sausage, to heat through.
When done, if liquid is thin, thicken with small amount of cornstarch dissolved in cold water.
Just before serving, add potatoes and heat through.

Mother's Sloppy Joe's

Here is another ground beef recipe that we grew up enjoying. Assuming that everyone has at least one pound of hamburger in their freezer for unexpected company, but not a single can of Sloppy Joe sauce on hand, try this. We think it's great.

1 pound lean ground beef
½ cup chopped onion
¼ cup chopped celery
¼ cup chopped green pepper, optional
8-ounce can tomato sauce
¼ cup catsup
1 teaspoon vinegar
1 teaspoon sugar

continued

Mother's Sloppy Joe's *continued*

1 ½ teaspoon Worcestershire sauce
1 teaspoon salt
1/8 teaspoon pepper

Brown ground beef, onion, celery and green pepper.
Drain only if necessary.
Add remaining ingredients and simmer, covered, for about 20 minutes.

Hot Dog Sauce

Think Coney Island as in hot dogs with a spicy meat sauce slathered down the center of a wiener about to be embraced by bun. Paul Hansen's mother, Mary Torretti Shampo, has been making this for years so it's no surprise there's a soft spot for the flavor in the bottom of Paul's heart.

1 ½ pounds chopped meat
Chopped onions
Salt and pepper to taste
1 tablespoon dry mustard
2 tablespoons prepared mustard
1 cup vinegar
2 cups ketchup
½ cup sugar
1 cup water
½ package mixed spices tied in a sack

Fry meat with onions, salt and pepper. Drain.
Add remaining ingredients and simmer until blended and thickened.
Remove spice sack.
Serve sauce over hot dogs.

Beef and Pork Barbecue

The first year my column was introduced in the Wisconsin State Journal, a reader requested a good barbeque pork recipe similar to what she remembered being served years before at a State Street restaurant in Madison. Although the restaurant no longer was in business, I did some searching and came up with one found in an Italian community cookbook from Rockford, Illinois. I gave it an A+, included it in my column and it remains one of my favorites since August of 1993.

2 pounds beef roast
2 pounds pork roast
2 large onions, chopped
1 stalk celery
½ wine glass of vinegar
1 small bottle ketchup, or a little more
1 tablespoon brown sugar
Salt and pepper

Ask butcher for his suggestion as to the best cut of meat.
Remove any fat.
Combine all ingredients in a deep, heavy pan.
Cover and cook meat and sauce for 2 hours, or until tender.
Remove meat from pan and allow to rest in a dish until cool enough to shred with a fork.
Return meat to pan with sauce and mix well. Serve on buns.

Note: If a more intense flavor is desired, add some of your favorite barbecue sauce to pan and stir before adding shredded meat.

Italian Beef Roast Amato

Amato is a well-known and respected name in Madison as one of the city's most popular and successful restaurant owners from the past. As Sicilian immigrants whose family members are my friends, they treated their guests to authentic food to be remembered. This is just one of many recipes they still prepare for family gatherings… and one you will be proud to serve when you have company.

8 pound center slice round steak, 2 ½ to 3 inches thick
Garlic cloves
Kitchen Bouquet
2 envelopes Lipton dry onion soup mix
2 8-ounce cans tomato sauce
Green pepper, cut into thick slices
2 cups water
Cornstarch or flour for gravy

continued

Italian Beef Roast Amato *continued*

Poke holes in meat and insert whole or halved garlic cloves.
Place in heavy roasting pan and seal meat with Kitchen Bouquet.
Sprinkle with dry onion soup.
Pour tomato sauce on top of roast and place green pepper slices on top.
Pour water around sides of roast, not on top.
Cover and bake at 350 degrees for two hours.
Baste while cooking.
Uncover for 30-60 minutes and continue to baste.
When done, remove roast to large platter.
Make gravy with cornstarch or flour mixed with cold water.
Serve as entrée or in Kaiser buns.

Serves 10-12 generously.

Sicilian Breaded Steak

Along with caponatina, spaghetti and meatballs, frittata and spiedini, this was another recipe Daddy grew up with and rated ***numero uno.*** *I liked it, too, but never appreciated it as I should have, but then, who does as a youngster? When I think back to the evenings when he sat down and saw this on his plate, nothing else could have been finer.*

Cut ½ inch round steak into serving portions.
Pound slightly with tenderizing mallet.
Dip meat in olive oil, then coat with Italian seasoned bread crumbs.
Grill or broil meat until crumbs are a golden brown.
Turn over only once.
Just prior to removing from heat to serve,
coat top of meat with a thick tomato-based garlic sauce.

Note: Dipping the meat in olive oil before breading is for grilling.

If you want to make this indoors in a fry pan, dip meat in egg-milk wash instead of oil before coating with crumbs and fry in pan with olive oil.

Italian Sausage, Potatoes, Onions and Green Pepper

Here's another delicious and quick way to make an Italian dinner for family and friends the way we Italians have been doing for years. Start with a roaster to accommodate the amount of ingredients you will use, slip it in the oven and relax. It doesn't get any better than this and the flavor is out of this world.

Olive oil
Average-size potatoes, peeled and quartered
Green pepper
Onion
Salt and pepper, optional
Italian seasoning
Italian sausage links (See: Note)

Coat bottom of oven roaster with olive oil.
Layer, beginning with potatoes, then very large pieces of green pepper.
Over peppers place quartered onions.
Salt and pepper is optional.
Sprinkle with Italian seasoning.
Place Italian sausage links on top.
Prick a few sausages for juices to moisten and season the vegetables.
Roast partially covered for 45 to 60 minutes.

Note: I prefer using Johnsonville sweet Italian sausage links because fennel is added. Also, chicken parts can be added to the sausage links.

Teriyaki Steak Marinade

This marinade imparts a flavor I can't seem to get enough of and, as a result, whether at home or at the cottage, chances are that my steak has been marinated with this recipe.

2 garlic cloves, split
½ cup soy sauce
¼ cup packed light brown sugar
2 tablespoons olive oil
Sesame seed oil, optional See: Note
½ teaspoon ground ginger, or grated fresh ginger
2-4 steaks

Marinate steaks in refrigerator, covered, for 1 ½ hours, turning occasionally.
Grill to desired doneness

Note: Sesame seed oil is optional. However, if you have some on hand, add about ¼ teaspoon to the marinade.

Tenderloin of Venison

Anyone who knows me is aware that I am not a hunter. Nor is anyone else in my family. If you wonder, then, why I'm offering a venison recipe, it is because a young neighbor back home who hunts, but doesn't eat venison, once gave me a package of venison tenderloin. Searching for a recipe, I found this in ***With a Jug of Wine,*** *an old cookbook written by Morrison Woods. I'll remember this forever for its flavor, succulence and presentation. For those of you who take advantage of deer hunting season in Burnett County, add this to your favorite venison recipes.*

6 tenderloin of venison
6 strips of bacon
¼ pound butter (1 stick)
1 medium-size onion, sliced *julienne*
4 large mushrooms, sliced *julienne*
2 bay leaves
Pinch thyme
Pinch caraway seeds
½ cup dry white wine
1 ½ cups cream
½ pint sour cream
Salt and freshly ground pepper
Dash Worcestershire sauce
Juice of ½ lemon

Wrap tenderloins with strips of bacon and pan broil over a medium flame for about 6 minutes on each side.
Put in a warm oven while the sauce is being prepared.
Place ¼ pound of butter in a saucepan with onion, mushrooms, bay leaves and a pinch each of thyme and caraway seeds.
Let this simmer for about 3 to 4 minutes before adding wine.
Continue to simmer until the onions and mushrooms area tender.
Add cream and let it simmer for about 20 minutes more.
Remove from fire and add sour cream, salt and pepper to taste, Worcestershire and lemon juice.
Reheat.
Serve tenderloin of venison with this sauce poured on top.

Venison Tenderloin

This recipe appeared back home in The Capital Times on December 15, 2000. I clipped it because I thought it was too valuable not to, just in case I get lucky again and receive venison tenderloin from someone who loves to hunt deer, but doesn't like to eat it.

1 tablespoon olive oil
1 pound venison tenderloin
Freshly ground black pepper, to taste
2 tablespoons finely chopped shallots
¼ cup dry white wine
¾ cup chicken broth
2 teaspoons cornstarch
½ teaspoon Dijon mustard

Remove all visible fat from tenderloin.
Cut crosswise into 1 inch slices.
Place cut side down and flatten each slice with the broad side of a chef's knife or a glass bottom.
Sprinkle with pepper.
In large, heavy, nonstick skillet, sauté tenderloin for 3 minutes.
Turn, add shallots and continue cooking for 3 minutes.
Stir in white wine and cook over medium-high heat for 1-2 minutes, or until wine has reduced by half.
Meanwhile, whisk together chicken broth, cornstarch and Dijon mustard.
When venison is nearly done, add chicken broth mixture to pan.
Cook over medium-high heat until venison is done and sauce is thickened and bubbly, about two minutes.
Serve with noodles or rice.

Mom's Bread Pudding

My husband's mother made a bread pudding that Dick and his brothers, Bob and Roger, and their sister, Phyllis, remember with great fondness. I learned to make it shortly after we were married and have continued to enjoy it through the years. It's perfect for a quick, warm, soothing, dessert made with leftover bread and is almost as soothing when served cold from the refrigerator the next day.

4-5 slices dry bread
¼ cup sugar
½ cup raisins
2 eggs
¼ cup sugar
2 cups milk
1 teaspoon vanilla
Dash of nutmeg

Break bread into casserole.
Sprinkle with ¼ cup of sugar, raisins and salt.

Continued

Mom's Bread Pudding *continued*

Beat eggs with remaining ¼ cup sugar, milk and vanilla.
Pour over bread and mix together.
Sprinkle with nutmeg.
Bake at 350 degrees for 45 minutes until knife inserted comes out clean.

Sauce

½ cup sugar
1 tablespoon cornstarch
1 cup hot water
1-2 tablespoons butter
1 teaspoon vanilla
nutmeg

Mix together sugar and cornstarch in small saucepan.
While stirring, gradually add hot water.
Cook 1 minute.
Add butter and vanilla and a sprinkle of nutmeg.
If desired, add a splash of rum or brandy to sauce.
Serve warm over each serving of bread pudding.

Po' Boy Pudding

Berniece Thompson knows all about cooking and what people liked best when they stayed at Thompson's Resort. Acres of wooded southwest shoreline property was developed by Glen and Molly Thompson and passed on to their son and daughter-in-law, Stuart and Berniece, who continued to operate the American Plan resort until it closed many years later. Today the resort is a special reflection too good to forget.

14 slices white bakery bread
1 cup seedless raisins
14-ounce package/box of shredded coconut
½ cup butter
1 cup white sugar
6 eggs, beaten
14 ½-ounce can evaporated milk

Cube bread in 1-inch pieces. Place in buttered 9 x 13-inch pan.
Sprinkle raisins first, then coconut over bread.
Cream butter and sugar.
Add eggs and blend. Stir in milk.
Pour mixture over coconut layer.
Bake at 400 degrees for 20 minutes.
Serve warm with lemon sauce or Half & Half (cream).

Wild Cranberry Pudding

Soil conditions plus the abundance of water made Burnett County a perfect place for cranberries to grow. The Native American first discovered cranberries growing in bogs and sold them in what may have been one of the earliest county industries. Years ago, cranberries grew in abundance in the area of Thompson Bay on North Sand Lake.

4 cups cleaned and washed cranberries (See: Note)
3 cups water
3 heaping tablespoons cornstarch
1 cup sugar
Sweet cream

To cleaned and washed cranberries, add 3 cups water and boil until skins burst.
Rub through a sieve and discard seeds and skins.
To the strained liquid, add cornstarch, mixed well with sugar.
Stir well and let cook until thick.
It will thicken somewhat as it cools.
Serve with sweet cream.

Note: Wild pincherries may be used instead of cranberries.

Blackberry Delight

Bobbie and Tom Leopold are blessed with spectacular property laden with blackberry bushes. Their south shoreline location provides ideal conditions for blackberries to reward them each year with enough to fill baskets and tins to use immediately, or freeze for the months ahead. I don't know about you, but dessert is important to me and it tastes even better when you've gathered the main ingredient from the woods. Leopold's say this is delicious.

1 1/2 cups graham crackers crumbs
¼ cup sugar
⅓ cup melted butter
8-ounce package cream cheese
¼ cup sugar
2 tablespoons milk
1 1/2 cups Cool Whip
2 pints blackberries
2 small boxes instant vanilla pudding
3 1/2 cups milk
2 cups Cool Whip

Blend together cracker crumbs, sugar and melted butter for crust in 9 x 13-inch pan. Chill.

Continued

Blackberry Delight *Continued*

Mix together cream cheese, ¼ cup sugar, 2 tablespoons of milk and 1 ½ cups Cool Whip.
Spread over graham cracker crust, and cover with blackberries.
Prepare instant pudding with milk as directed on package and spread over blackberries.
Top with remaining 2 cups of Cool Whip.
Garnish with additional blackberries.
Chill overnight.

Note: May substitute blackberries with strawberries, blueberries or raspberries.

Apple Crisp Pie

This recipe was found in a 1989 Williams Sonoma catalog and has been a favorite since then. If you like apple crisp and like pie, you'll love this. You can make your own pie crust, or use a good quality refrigerated pie crust to simplify preparation.

Single Pie Crust:
1 cup flour
1 tablespoon sugar
¼ teaspoon salt
6 tablespoons chilled, cubed, unsalted butter
1 ½ to 2 tablespoons ice water

Combine flour, sugar and salt.
With a pastry blender, cut in chilled butter until granules form.
Add ice water and mix lightly until dough forms a ball.
Wrap in plastic and chill for 2 hours.
Roll out and fit into a 9-inch pie dish.

Note: Otherwise, use store-bought refrigerated pie crust.

3 to 4 Granny Smith apples, peeled, cored and thinly sliced
2 Tablespoons butter
¾ cup sugar
¾ cup flour
½ teaspoon cinnamon
¼ teaspoon salt
8 tablespoons unsalted butter, chilled and cubed

Toss apples with 2 tablespoons sugar and fill pie shell, rounding up in center.
For topping, combine ¾ cup sugar with flour, cinnamon and salt.
Mix in 8 tablespoons butter with fingertips until crumbly.
Sprinkle evenly over apples.
Bake for 15 minutes in 425 degree oven.
Reduce heat to 350 degrees and bake another 30 minutes until golden brown.

Wild Blackberry Pie

Blackberry picking in Helen and Gary Rohde's family's south shoreline backyard has become a late summer family tradition. Where the Francis farm once was, and Henrietta Bauer's cows roamed years later, and Bauer's cabin renters took August delight in picking and eating berries on the spot, today sits Rohde's stunning new duo-family home surrounded by bushes with berries to fill countless pies for the entire family throughout the cold winter months.

Use your favorite two-crust pie recipe for an 8- or 9-inch pie pan
4-5 cups blackberries
1 ½ cups sugar
1/8 to ¼ cup brown sugar
⅓ cup flour
Sprinkling of nutmeg and cinnamon
1 tablespoon lemon juice
Butter, optional (See: Note)

Place berries in large in a large bowl.
Add sugars, flour, spices and lemon juice and carefully mix together.
Place in unbaked crust, top with second crust and perforate crust with fork tine or knife to allow steam to escape.
Bake 15 minutes at 400 degrees, then cover crust edge with foil to keep from getting too brown.
Turn oven to 375 degrees and bake for 45 minutes.

Note: If desired, add some butter to berry filling before covering with top crust.

Pear Crisp for Two

One thing nice about this recipe is that you won't have any leftover to pick at the next day. Another nice thing is that you can experiment with other fruits and have a different flavored dessert every night of the week. The third nice thing is that it is absolutely delicious!

3 ripe pears, peeled and cut into chunks, about 2 cups
3 tablespoons butter, softened
¼ cup light brown sugar
¼ cup quick oats
¼ cup flour
Cinnamon, 1/8 teaspoon or less

Grease a 6x6x2-inch baking dish.
Place pear chunks in dish.
With fork, mix together butter, sugar, oats, flour and cinnamon until crumbly.
Place over fruit.

Continued

Pear Crisp for Two *continued*

If topping seems dry, melt additional tablespoon of butter and drizzle over topping.
Bake at 350 degrees for 35-40 minutes or until golden brown.

Fresh Red Raspberry Pie for Two or Four

This is another good recipe I received from a reader. After cutting it in half, I added toasted chopped pecans to the crust ingredients and came up with a delicious pie that would last only two days instead of four. If you want to serve 6-8, just double all the ingredients and use a regular size pie pan.

Crust:

1 ½ cups flour
½ teaspoon salt
2 tablespoons sugar
½ cup vegetable oil
2 tablespoons milk

Mix until oily ball forms.
Press into a 6-inch pie plate.
Bake at 400 degrees for 10-12 minutes, or until a very light golden in color.
Cool before adding fruit and glaze.

Note: If you don't have a 6-inch pie pan, use the deep top of a 6-inch Pyrex casserole dish. Also, chopped toasted pecans can be added to crust ingredients.

Glaze:

3 tablespoons cornstarch
¾-1 cup sugar
Pinch of salt
1 cup water
3 tablespoons Jell-O powder (flavor to match fruit)
4 cups fresh berries (See: Note)

Mix cornstarch, sugar and salt.
Stir in water, corn syrup and Jell-O powder.
Microwave until thick and bubbly
(can be made in a small saucepan on stove top if necessary)
Cool to room temperature.

Note: Strawberries, blackberries or peaches can be substituted.

Key Lime Pie

Three little boys, each so different, carried those personalities to the table with borderline likes and dislikes. Although healthy well-rounded meals were served every night, eating patterns didn't always jive the way I expected, or hoped they would. Mike liked chicken so much that the drumstick bones left on his plate looked like varnished knickknacks He also labeled black mushrooms I used in Chinese food as "leeches"—not exactly a winning description to warrant second helpings for his little brothers. Bill wanted the juice from everyone's steak to be poured onto his plate so he could drink it when his steak was finished. Give Bob cream of peanut soup and fried oysters and he felt like a king. One recipe that made them all feel like royalty was key lime pie. When Mother made one at the cottage, it was, without question, the highlight of the day. Authentic, delicious and too simple for words, this is how it was made many years ago in Key West at Brantley's Busy Bee Bakery on Francis Street.

4 egg yolks
1 15-ounce can sweetened condensed milk
Juice of 4 key limes, about ¼ to ½ cup
Grated rind
4 egg whites for meringue

In bowl, combine egg yolks and condensed milk.
By hand, mix in juice and grated rind.
Pour into baked pie shell.
Make your favorite meringue recipe with egg whites
Spread over pie, sealing edges to crust.
Place in 350 degree oven for 12-15 minutes or until meringue has golden brown tips. Refrigerate leftovers.

Note: **Authentic key lime pie crust was made with flour:**

1 cup flour
½ cup Crisco
½ teaspoon salt
2-3 tablespoons ice water

Mix first three ingredients until like cornmeal.
Add ice water to form a soft ball.
Roll out on floured board, place in pie tin, prick with fork and bake 8-10 minutes at 375 degrees. Pour in filling.

For meringue:

Beat room temperature egg whites with ¼ teaspoon salt and ¼ teaspoon cream of tartar. Continue until soft peaks form when beaters are raised.
Gradually add 6 tablespoons of sugar until stiff peaks are formed.
Spread over filling as directed and proceed as above.

S'More Pie

Okay, so we know there are people who don't mind spending time in the kitchen when everyone else is outside having a good time. If you happen to be one of them, here is an adult version of those little after dark treats toasted over a bonfire. Passed on to me years ago, it takes longer than a wink of the eye to prepare, but still is simple as well as making a delicious conversation piece.

1 ¼ cups graham cracker crumbs
¼ cup sugar
6 tablespoons melted butter
2 cups milk
2 egg yolks
small package of vanilla pudding mix (not instant)
1 cup tiny marshmallows
3 (3/4 ounce each) milk chocolate candy bars, broken in pieces
2 egg whites
½ teaspoon vanilla
¼ teaspoon cream of tartar
¼ cup sugar

Combine crumbs, the first ¼ cup of sugar, and butter; mix well.
Press firmly on bottom and sides of 9-inch pie plate.
Bake in 375 degree oven for 6 to 8 minutes until edges area brown; cool.
Combine milk and egg yolks; gradually add to pudding mix in saucepan.
Cook according to package direction.
Cover surface of pudding with waxed paper; cool.
Place marshmallows over crust; top with chocolate pieces.
Spoon cooled pudding evenly over chocolate.
Beat egg whites with vanilla and cream of tartar to soft peaks.
Gradually add the remaining ¼ cup sugar, beating to stiff peaks.
Spread meringue over pie, sealing to edges of crust.
Bake in 375 degree oven for 10 to 12 minutes, till golden.
Chill thoroughly before serving.

Rhubarb Crisp

Although there are countless crisp recipes floating around, for years I've searched for the simplest fruit crisp of all and this is it. I found it in a second-hand book purchased on the corner on Main St. at the lovely Webster Antique Shop that I remember once being a small town department store. I was so thrilled when I tasted the results that a week later I used fresh blueberries. At this writing, I'm preparing to make it with peaches for a supper dessert.

3 cups rhubarb, chopped
1 egg, beaten
¾ cup white sugar
2 tablespoons flour

Mix rhubarb with beaten egg.
Add mixture of flour and sugar.
Place in shallow greased glass baking dish.
Sprinkle with crumb topping.
Bake at 350 degrees for 30 minutes.
Serve warm or room temperature

Topping

¼ cup butter
½ cup brown sugar
½ cup flour

Serves 6 - 8

Mrs. Wood's Chocolate Cakes

Circa 1926

Another favorite found in "Nana's" collection was this recipe which Mrs. Woods claimed will ripen and be better after a few days. Bill Caruso admits that the cakes were so delicious they never had a chance to experience the validity of Nana's ripening claim.

1 bottle (1/2 pint) sour cream
¼ teaspoon baking soda
1 level cup sugar
1 rounded cup flour
1 teaspoon baking powder
3 squares bitter chocolate, melted
1 egg, beaten
Vanilla

continued

Mrs. Wood's Chocolate Cakes *continued*

Mix together sour cream and baking soda. Add sugar.
Sift flour and baking powder.
Stir in melted chocolate.
Add beaten eggs and vanilla.
Grease cupcake tins.
Bake in moderate oven (350 to 400 degrees) for 25-30 minutes.
Frost sparsely by stirring together cream, vanilla and confectioners' sugar.

Chocolate Chip Squares

Anything that can be made and enjoyed out of the hand is perfect cottage food. The nice thing about this bar recipe is that it can be consumed as is, on the run, getting in the boat, walking in the woods, or dressing it up for company with a small scoop of vanilla ice cream. Drizzled with chocolate or hot fudge sauce, it becomes a special treat on a plate.

From the **Sacred Heart of Jesus and Mary** *cookbook as submitted by Lucy Basler.*

½ cup shortening
½ cup butter
½ cup white sugar
½ cup brown sugar
2 egg yolks
1 tablespoon water
1 teaspoon vanilla
2 cups flour
1 teaspoon salt
1 teaspoon baking soda
½ cup chocolate chips
2 egg whites
1 cup brown sugar
Chopped nuts, optional

Mix together shortening, butter, and sugars.
Stir in egg yolks, water and vanilla and mix well.
Mix together dry ingredients and add to butter mixture.
Mix well and spread into a greased 9 x 13-inch pan.
Sprinkle with chocolate chips.
Mix together 2 beaten egg whites and 1 cup brown sugar.
Spread over chocolate chips and, if desired, sprinkle with chopped nuts.
Bake at 350 degrees for 35 minutes.

Sand Lake Swiss Bars

Although Burnett County is more Scandinavian than Swiss, this should become a favorite of everyone. A few more calories, but, oh! So delicious!

First Layer:
1 cup butter
½ cup white sugar
½ cup brown sugar
2 egg yolks
1 tablespoon water
2 cups flour
1 teaspoon baking powder
½ teaspoon baking soda
Pinch of salt

Cream butter and sugars. Add egg yolks and water; mix well.
Sift dry ingredients and add to butter mixture; mix well.
Press into 9 x 13-inch pan.

Second Layer:
1 cup brown sugar
1 cup chopped nuts
12 ounces chocolate chips
2 egg whites

Sprinkle chips and nuts over first layer.
Beat egg whites and brown sugar until fluffy.
Spread on top of first layer.

Bake at 350 degrees for 25-30 minutes

Beacon Hill Brownies

I know that a box of brownie mix is much easier, but these are too good not to include. If you can't bear to be inside on a beautiful day, save this recipe for when the wind blows or the sky rains. Then enjoy them with a glass of cold milk.

8 ounces unsweetened chocolate
1 cup butter, room temperature
5 eggs
3 cups sugar
1 tablespoon vanilla
1 ½ cups all-purpose flour
1 ½ - 2 cups coarsely chopped walnuts (See: Note)

continued

Beacon Hill Brownies *continued*

Melt chocolate and butter together over very low heat, stirring to combine.
Beat eggs, sugar and vanilla for 10 minutes with electric mixer, then blend in chocolate mixture.
Add 1 ½ cups flour and stir in by hand just until blended.
Fold in nuts.
Place in greased 9 x 13-inch pan.
Bake at 375 degrees for 35 to 40 minutes.
Be careful not to overbake as brownies will be dry.
Top should be dull and might have cracked edges.
Cool on wire rack.
Frost with your favorite dark chocolate butter/powdered sugar frosting.

Note: Toasting walnuts before adding to batter adds a better nut flavor.

Oatmeal Crispies

You most likely have your own favorite oatmeal cookie, but this one is too good to leave out. It was given to me a few years ago by Celoris Hinz who was a good friend of Mother and Daddy. Because it is so important to keep the cottage cookie jar full at all times, add this to your list of favorites.

1 stick butter
1 cup sugar
1 egg
¼ teaspoon vanilla
1 cup flour
½ teaspoon baking soda
⅛ teaspoon salt
2 cups dry quick oatmeal

Cream butter and sugar.
Add egg, vanilla and dry ingredients.
Add oatmeal and refrigerate for several hours.
Roll into small walnut-size balls.
Place 1 ½ inches apart on ungreased cookie sheet.
Flatten slightly with fork coated with granulated sugar.
Bake at 375 degrees for 10 minutes.
Allow to rest a few minutes before placing them on a rack to cool.

Another Best Oatmeal Cookie

Is there anything wrong with having two favorite oatmeal cookies? I doubt it. This way you can have one in each hand to nibble on. Because I store all my cookies in glass jars, they are good keepers as most oatmeal cookies are.

1 ¼ cups Butter Flavor Crisco
¾ cup firmly packed brown sugar
½ cups granulated sugar
1 egg
1 teaspoon vanilla, or more
1 ½ cups all-purpose flour
1 teaspoon baking soda
1 teaspoon salt, optional
1 teaspoon cinnamon, optional
1/4 teaspoon nutmeg
3 cups dry oatmeal
½ - ¾ cup coarsely chopped walnuts
Raisins and/or chopped dates, optional

Beat shortening and sugar until light and fluffy.
Beat in egg and vanilla.
Combine dry ingredients.
Add to shortening mixture and mix well.
Stir in oats, then add remaining ingredients.
Don't worry about any looseness of dough.
Scoop with a tablespoon and bake on ungreased cookie sheets at 375 degrees for 8-11 minutes depending on how crisp you want them.
These cookies will not spread while baking.
Leave on cookie sheet for one minute before removing to racks to cool.

Spellbinder Cookies

This was a last minute addition to Up North Food, a recipe sent to me by Jenny Pyle. It was passed on by her mother, Lee Cerk, who found it years before a Wisconsin State Journal reader responded to my request for a cookie made in church cookbook. Although I'm not required to prepare reader's recipes included in my column, I decided to try it and since then it has been added to my list of all-time favorite cookies.

1 ½ cup flour
1 ½ teaspoon baking powder
1 teaspoon baking soda
1 cup butter
1 cup firmly packed light brown sugar
1 egg
1 cup quick oatmeal
1 cup flake coconut
1 cup salted peanuts, chopped
½ cup finely crushed Cornflakes

Sift flour, baking powder and soda.
In another bowl, cream butter and sugar until light and fluffy.
Add egg and beat.
Add flour mixture and blend well.
Stir in oatmeal, coconut, peanuts and Cornflakes.
Drop by rounded teaspoons onto ungreased cookie sheet.
Flatten lightly with fork or bottom of small glass dipped in sugar.
If icing is not desired, sprinkle with finely Cornflake crumbs.
Bake at 350 degrees for 12-15 minutes.

Note: I used chopped salted dry-roasted peanuts.

If desired, drizzle with icing:

2 tablespoons butter
1 tablespoon hot water
1 cup powdered sugar
1 teaspoon vanilla

Melt butter, add sugar, water and vanilla. Beat until smooth.
Drizzle or spread thinly on cookies.

Part VI

Mother and Daddy's new cottage on the south shore, 1965.

It probably never occurred to Daddy that someday he might own his own cottage. Satisfied to rent a place on the lake for the family each summer, he was content to stay in #5 for the rest of his life. If owning ever entered his thoughts, he never discussed it at the supper table. When he heard about the resort closing, he worried that the good times on the lake were about to end.

Cottage Life on the South Shore

...And the Best of Times Got Even Better

It probably never occurred to Daddy that someday he would own his own cottage. Satisfied to rent a place on the lake each summer for the family, he was content to stay in #5 for the rest of his life. If owning ever entered his thoughts, it was never discussed at the supper table. So, when he heard about the resort closing, it left him with an empty feeling. Good times on the lake were about to end. Staying there each year had become one of those great pleasures in life that wouldn't allow the reality of an eventual end to it all. Florence Hansen offered to sell to Daddy #5--the cottage we had stayed in for 19 of the 20 years since the resort opened. Asking price was $4,000, but after Mother and Daddy discussed it privately, he politely declined.

Meanwhile, development on the south shoreline was sparse. We would learn that North Sand, Green and Mallard lakes had been temporarily connected years before when water levels were unusually high. In fact, old plat maps show Mallard Lake labeled as Sand Beach Lake.

Bobbie Dietrich Preiner had grown up on the south shore of Mallard Lake and was concerned about the proposed landfill between the two lakes. When the first attempt failed and caved in, no one was surprised. A second attempt was successful and the North Sand Lake southwest lots with 100 feet of shoreline on the newly created isthmus between North Sand and Mallard lakes and its carpet of sand began to draw interest.

Desperate to continue summer treks from Madison to the lake we all loved, we were alarmed when hearing of the proposed closing of the resort and sale of its cottages. Other possibilities were immediately investigated and, after much searching, we reluctantly reserved cottages on Oak Lake for the following summer. The next day Gordy, who built homes in Madison, drove to Webster and learned that four connecting North Sand Lake lots along the newly created south shoreline isthmus were selling for $1800 each. When he returned to the resort to describe some particulars, it was quickly agreed that he would buy all four lots, sell one to Mother and Daddy, one to Dick and I, and keep two for himself, thus assuring us of many more years of family togetherness at the lake.

As lake property owners, each day was embellished with tidbits about the history of the immediate area. We would learned that the land encircling the lake was granted to the state of Wisconsin in the mid-1880's for the construction of a Chicago, St. Paul and Minneapolis and Omaha railroad that would run from the St. Croix River or Lake to the west end of Lake Superior. By 1902 the United States sold the land to Loren Moody who eventually sold it to Nora Lavell and her husband, Anthony Lavell, which appears on many North Sand Lake abstracts.

At the time Gordy purchased the lots, the wetland in the immediate back of the pie-shaped property was shooting forth earthly treasures through the fill. Cattails, pin cherry trees and sumac complete with a variety of undetermined weeds added seasonal glamour to the area we would fondly refer to as The Swamp. In its natural innocence, the narrow strip of wetland offered a place to hide if those of us without basements were threatened by a tornado. I often wondered what it would be like to lower myself into a swamp of frogs, snakes and who knows what else, aware that if it meant survival, there wouldn't be time to give much thought to the unknown.

Jim and Margaret Moore's cottage three lots away, which would be sold later to Len and Rosalie Heuer, was the lone dwelling along our new shoreline from the base of Rubin's Hill to the slough and back bay. I remembered a day many years before as a young teen rowing across the lake from Hansen's Resort in pursuit of big fish and dropping anchor out front when there was nothing but a sandy bottom with bull rushes in shallow water and trees, weeds and bushes as a backdrop. Not pulling up on shore to see what was beyond my view from the boat, I had no idea of its make-up. Unbeknown to me at the time, it was exactly where our family cottages would be built, side by side, years later.

When the shallowness separating North Sand Lake from Mallard Lake was being dismantled to create a buildable isthmus, vegetation was removed by heavy equipment to give a long strip of Mallard Lake the look of a beautifully nurtured sandy beach. At the top of the hill on our service road was another area opened, leaving nothing behind but pure sand in an area we labeled The Desert that extended down to our North Sand Lake shoreline near Moore's. Although roots have sprouted in The Desert through the past forty years and a garage today occupies a large portion of the area now with new growth, it was where our little boys played with their toy trucks and G. I. Joe's and Mother used as her own private golf driving range. When the boys were older, the desert was also used for BB gun and rifle practice and even became their own baseball diamond with new growth here and there that served as bases, home plate and a pitching mound. After many homerun baseballs were lost in the swamp, we switched to my old tennis balls. Although the sea of sand has since disappeared, taking on a new look, memories remain vivid.

The triangular-shaped lowland directly behind our four lots that we referred to as The Swamp remains wet, especially when water levels rise. During drier years, one could walk through much of the area without dampening their shoes. As for the entire triangle bounded by two South Shore Roads and Mallard Lake Road, Mother and Daddy, for some reason, called it The Horn. When someone wanted to go for a short walk around the horn, we knew exactly what it meant. It was yet another addition to Tripalin family *up north* jargon.

The four connecting lots on 400 feet of shoreline that Gordy purchased lifted us to a new level on the lake as property owners. Having never before driven Mallard Lake Road, this was new territory for all of us. Any previous conception of what kind of property was required for summers at the lake was quickly dismissed as building plans materialized. The openness of what we were used to at the resort on the north shore with A in our back yard shifted to the south with a quiet bay in front and the small beautiful Mallard Lake behind us. On each side was the privacy of woods and vacant lots.

Daddy was still working at Oscar Mayer in 1964 when he and Mother decided to start building the following summer. Gordy drew up a simple blueprint for a small two-bedroom, three-season cottage, similar to the floor plan they had grown to enjoy at Hansen's Resort. Every Friday afternoon at 4:30, Mother would pick up Daddy at the meat packing plant and drive 300 miles north to help Gordy clear the lot. Friday and Saturday evenings were spent at the motel in Webster and Sunday, after Mass at Sacred Hearts Catholic Church on H, they'd return to the lot for a few extra hours of work before leaving for Madison for another five days home before the routine was repeated on Friday. When the foundation was finally poured and the framework began, they knew that before long the walls, two doors and a roof overhead would welcome them with their own simple overnight accommodations. More than once Gordy and his friend, Bud Steele, drove a truck

Daddy in his garden of sand, flowers and vegetables.

from Madison weighing heavy with $1500 in lumber and trusses that kept shifting along the way. Another time, upon their arrival at the lake, one of their wheels sunk deep in loose soil over the septic tank. Except for the unpredictable, what a relief it was to see their truck appear at the top of the hill on the service road to know the long trip north had ended.

The completion of the cottage seemed like one of those miracles in life that would never have a parallel. Like childbirth, it was a new chapter in their lives to be celebrated. Each moment was a blessing. And finally, taking deep breaths, they were speechless as they walked through the open door to see their combined living room and kitchen, two bedrooms, and a half-bath with shower waiting to welcome them. Everything they saw and touched triggered comments, so innocent, so humble, so appreciative. At the moment, Daddy, literally, was being crowned king of his own summer castle with Mother at his side as his queen. From then on, everything would be remembered and savored like the finest of wine.

With Daddy exercising his rights as a lake property owner, tending to everything with loving care, Mother began her search back home for nice second hand furniture and antiques at the St. Vincent De Paul Shop on Williamson St. to recover, strip and stain or paint. Both in their 60s, yet fine-tuned to the area and the lake, and assuming that staying at a resort for 20 years was just the beginning to what would guide them through many more summers of lake living to the twilight of their lives, they now yearned for retirement when they could stay in the cottage from early April until late October.

Retirement was still a few years away. Once the cottage was opened each spring, it meant a repeat of the late Friday afternoon departures from Madison for the long drive north for an all-too-short, yet fully enjoyed weekend until 3 p.m. on Sunday when they'd leave for home. When Daddy retired in 1969, they anxiously packed for six months instead of 2 ½ days.

In 1967, Gordy and Elaine built a small cottage next door to Mother and Daddy. Like Mother, Elaine opted not to have kitchen cabinets and, instead, narrow floor to ceiling open shelves where dishes, silverware, and pots and pans were kept. Matching curtains hung over the kitchen window and in front of the sink and counter to hide the waste basket and storage shelves underneath. It was small and charming as seasonal cottages were back then with an arrangement that was inexpensive, yet sufficient. The combined kitchen and living room, two bedrooms and a full bath provided ample space for them and their son, Tom.

During this time, Dick was assigned to Boston's Logan Airport for a nine-month probationary period as a new TWA pilot. When not in the cockpit of a 707, he would head north to Bangor, Maine to fly jet fighters with the Maine Air National Guard. Leaving behind a newly built home in Madison and a slot as a military fighter pilot with the Wisconsin Air National Guard in Madison, he found a large two-story, century-old summer home to rent on the ocean in Nahant, a two-part peninsula north of Boston. When we returned to Madison the following June, there was much excitement knowing that we'd be driving *up north* to the lake as soon as things settled down at home. A few months later, we were caught up with dreams of building our own cottage—the only problem was deciding which one of the two remaining lots to choose.

When the four lots were originally purchased by Gordy, there were eleven lots in a row beginning with lot # 1, 2, and 3 belonging to Ray Rubin. The rest had 100 feet of shoreline each, many in pie-shaped parcels. At the narrowest point, to the east, was lot #4, the shortest lot in depth with the closest proximity to Mallard Lake. Elaine and Gordy built on #5 next door to Mother and Daddy on #6, with #7 next door. Dick and I continued to weigh the possibilities of #4 and #7, both end lots, #4 butting property owned by Ray Rubin and the cottage he built for his parents, Eric and Lucille, on 150 feet of shoreline. If we built on #4, we'd have the privacy and solitude of a narrow strip of woods separating us from the Rubin's--a strip that could never be developed. However, on the other side of Mother and Daddy was #7, the deepest of the four lots and, although there was more room to build, there was a shack close to the property line that must have bothered us at the time. A factor in making a decision was recognizing that someday Mother and Daddy would be gone and, if we chose the lot #7, Elaine and I would be separated by another family. Considering this, we decided to build on #4, the smallest, most private lot, a move we never regretted: #7 would remain vacant and saved for Tom.

Although the years we all were together were the best of times, Elaine and Gordy sold their cottage long before Mother and Daddy, leaving us with hindsight that we should have bought it to prepare for the future when our own family expanded with marriages and grandchildren who could stay next door to us. Years later, the empty lot #7, which had been saved for Tom, was sold to Curt and Ginny Mommsen, who didn't develop the parcel and eventually bought Ray Rubin's parent's cottage on the other side of us. Today lot #7 is the summer home of Dick and Carol Langdok. Elaine and Gordy sold their cottage to Dick Carpenter who sold to Bob and Gayle Magee who sold to Bob and Barbara Zeimer who sold to Dave and Linda Regel, today's owners.

Back in 1970, after learning that new shoreline setback restrictions the following year would deem our property almost worthless, a foundation was quickly poured. Without doing that, we would have been forced to build on the service road in the backyard. As soon as the cottage was roughed in, the level of excitement escalated allowing few dull moments thanks to Mike 11, Bill 7, Bob 5, and Tom 11. Each day was highlighted with surprises and learning experiences for everyone. Discoveries included Indian mounds and Indian arrowheads. Fish of all sizes were caught and raccoons frequently raïded our garbage. Intermittent BB gun practice with empty cans propped on sticks probed deep in the sand would eventually take place at The Desert and, weather permitting, bike rides and walks would take us through the woods and around Mallard Lake. Toads, frogs, beautiful birds, and chipmunks were everywhere. We saw our first black squirrels and flying squirrels and witnessed storms that turned the sky a scary black when waves dismantled piers, flipped boats and once sent an aluminum canoe end over end like a wheel running along the shoreline. We hid in the storeroom during such storms, carrying blankets, pillows, a flashlight, candles and matches and, the dog. Of course, this usually occurred when Dick was on a trip. The calm after the storm found us much relieved with the return call of the loon, the soaring of an eagle, and the Great Blue Heron that stood motionless at the end of the pier or in ankle-deep water, if only for a silent moment.

Without forgetting the past and what we had gathered and treasured on the north shore, we quickly found there were more jewels to add to the lake crown as our south shoreline strip began to fill to capacity. With the Moore's already settled a short distance away, Mother and Daddy were next, followed by Chuck Cashman who built at the mouth of the back bay where Roger and Pat Larson reside today. Next door to the east of Cashmans was the Christianson family and next to them was Clyde Leedberg who owned many properties on the lake. The Korans, with five children, built next door to Clyde and, on the other side of the Korans were the Moores. Around 1975, Joe and Lenore Kuelbs bought the empty sandy lot that had been scooped out to fill the narrow strip between both lakes. Joe built a large garage with living quarters before starting work on their adjacent lake home. Next door was another lot owned by Clyde and on it sat a small weathered shack once used as Clyde's office on his St. Paul car lot. When the property was sold to young Jerry Paulos of Danbury, the shack became a combination fishing shack and weekend retreat for Jerry and his friends. Next door were our lots # 7, 6, 5, and 4 bought from Ray Ellis in 1964.

It would be nice to have family weigh heavily on the scale of good things in life, but balance doesn't seem to take precedence as time goes on. It is the inevitable that's not always easy to handle. Did we ever think the good times wouldn't last forever? No one ever talked about that. We bathed in optimism and relished each day spent at the lake, absorbing its flavor to the fullest, forever anxious for the next minute, or day, and the return trip back the following summer so we could all be together again in the place we loved most. Before each of our returns, Daddy would spend hours that day mowing our lawns and pulling the tiniest of green weed flecks from the shoreline to make everything look perfect. While he was manicuring our yards, Mother was in the kitchen preparing a welcome-back-to-the-lake meal of Sloppy Joes, potato salad, Jell-O, pickles and dessert to enjoy at whatever hour we arrived.

Looking back to this time in our lives reminds me of seasonal cottages and wooden row boats with oars, and piers, and an occasional water skier…when early morning fishing welcomed us in the peace of daybreak…when Daddy would struggle alone at the end of the pier to reel in and net big northern pike well before breakfast and have a picture taken with each one, insisted by Mother, to fill scrapbook after scrapbook…when dates were never written on the back of any developed picture because we all thought we'd never forget the year, but did, because Daddy never aged, nor did his fishing attire of gray or tan wash pants, faded red plaid flannel shirt and the equally faded red Oscar Mayer hat that he wore almost everyday, rain or shine. Unless one or all of the boys stood next to him in the picture, we will never be certain exactly what year the picture was snapped…because the northern pike were all huge and never changed either.

They truly were the best of times and were about to become even better.

A Three Season Year

After years of celebrating our presence at the lake during July and August, we finally tasted the flavors of three seasons. As years passed, we often frivolously toyed with the possibility of returning in November to celebrate Thanksgiving at the cottage. The thought, however, never reached fruition. Once the piers were pulled in, the pipes were drained of water, and the cottage was boarded up for the winter, the 300 mile trip seemed like a long road to travel for turkey and mashed potatoes. And, although the distance was whittled down to 285 miles by the new I-90 system, it was easier to stay home.

When Daddy retired in 1969, the cottage, opened in April, is where they stayed until the end of October. Only once, on a whim, did they drive to the cottage during the winter, out of sheer curiosity, on a cold, clear, sunny winter day to see what it looked like blanketed with snow. After spending an hour walking around the cottage through snow and onto the frozen lake, they got back in the car and returned home for a one day round trip of 600 miles (See: Diaries)

Everything settled down in retirement. Unexplored adventures were at their fingertips with an endless array of surprises and treasures. Mother's early spring letters described scattered melting snow piles and a still frozen lake. Within days they'd find themselves sitting at the coffee table, looking out at the lake and listening to the deafening snaps of the ice breaking up. If the direction of the wind changed, they'd witness the ice shifting, hoping it wouldn't head toward the cottage where its strength could easily erode both shoreline and lawn.

Once the ice was gone, new chapters began with hints of spring emerging from winter dormancy. Buds on tree branches and bushes seemed to appear overnight. Weeds and wild flowers nudged through the sandy soil and any winter-browned growth left from the year before was raked away allowing new shoots to breathe. Aside from welcoming in New Year's Day, these were nature's magic moments signaling the birth of another year.

The phenomenon of spring brought other seasonal surprises—ticks for example. We never encountered the nasty little blood-sucking insects at Hansen's Resort because by the time we arrived for our late July to mid-August vacations, ticks had all but disappeared. Come spring, however, we were introduced to them and learned it was nearly impossible to avoid them. Any form of yard work necessary to prepare the place for the waiting summer months meant thoroughly checking ourselves throughout the day and again at night to make certain they weren't crawling on our clothes, resting in the creases of pleats or, worse yet, already attached to our skin. By July 4th their fun and games had ended for another year. By that time, we had also witnessed the miracle of black flies and fish flies, and were about to battle swarms of mosquitoes that came out every night about 9:25 p.m. like squadrons of dive bombers.

We learned during those early years that painting a picture of the north woods was impossible to complete as nature continually kept us on our toes with slivers of the unexpected. The property, lake and weather were just portions of the overall picture. There were new sounds, new smells and new sights. Wildflowers appeared everywhere in the woods, roadside and wetlands. Fish, reptiles, birds, ducks, black squirrels and insects became our new neighbors. City cats and dogs that wandered through yards back home were replaced with white-tail deer, raccoons, skunks, beavers, badgers, muskrats, gophers and chipmunks. Although we heard stories of bear, none were seen by us for years. Regional trees offered beauty, shade and, oftentimes, fruit. The stars were so incredibly bright on cloudless nights that we became intrigued with astronomy like never before. When weather permitted, Daddy acquired new fishing holes to haunt on a daily basis while Mother searched for and found unusual rocks to paint. She also learned that wildflowers didn't like to be disturbed and transferred to man-made gardens.

By mid-summer, the water was warm enough to swim without first having to count to ten. Crystal clear, cold or not, submerging yourself in the lake was a teasing milestone. Although Daddy entered the water about 4 p.m. each day, Mother swam only when the temperatures were unbearably hot. Another awakening for all of us were horse flies attracted to splashing that attacked us while swimming, just as the deer flies were bothersome when we walked the road. We also found that by leaving the windows open 24-hours a day when the temperatures rose brought southerly breezes from Mallard Lake behind us to cool the cottage and make hot summer days much easier to bear with nature's own air conditioning. At the same time, the heat and sunshine made the garden grow.

Summer

Chilly evenings snuck in around the last few weeks in August making us aware that it was nearing a time to rely on the furnace for comfort. The chill also chased away the deer flies which made long walks a pleasure. It was time for Mother and Daddy to walk around Mallard Lake. The four mile stroll was a sign summer was about to disappear and the third season meant that before long the cottage would be put to sleep for another year.

With a chill in the air, autumn colors suddenly became breathless backdrops for everything in view. Once again, good fishing kicked in and Daddy continued his quest each day for a stringer heavy with bluegills or great catches off the end of the pier, until the weather required a heavy winter coat and warm gloves. Chipmunks scurried everywhere. Fuzzy caterpillars crawled across sun-warmed concrete, gardens withered, and acorns from the oak tree branches hanging over the cottage bounced from the roof with the slightest breeze. Plants were pulled, the garden was raked clean, pier sections were dismantled and pulled up to rest on the lawn,

Fall

chairs were carried to the garage, and the Johnson 6-hp white motor was taken to someone in the area to leave for a winter tune-up. After that was done, the boat was dragged up on shore and turned upside down near the cottage. Later, after the garage was built, the boat slept inside until spring arrived. The day before Mother and Daddy left, homemade wood shutters were hooked and secured over each window to discourage break-ins and prevent windows from being broken by tree limbs or animals. In darkness brightened only by end table lamps and overhead lights, the cottage was thoroughly cleaned one last time.

The next morning, local plumber "Iggy" Hersant stopped by at 9:30 for a cup of coffee and a little chit-chat while he drained the pipes. As soon as he left, coolers packed with dry ice, bluegills, northerns and bass, and suitcases and other boxes were packed in the back seat of the car and the trunk. Only when the lights were turned off for the last time was the door locked and secured before the last wooden shutter was nailed over the side door. Once in the car, Mother and Daddy said goodbye to their cozy three season cottage, drove off the service road and headed for County Road A and a highway connection for the long ride home.

The Diary

Saturday, February 12, 1967

Mother wrote...

Left Madison at 2:30 a.m. heading toward North Sand Lake to our cottage, near Webster, Wisconsin. Surprised to see so many cars on the road at that time of the morning for February. It was nice driving. We stopped at Black River Falls for gas and coffee and take out. Sure was dull in there, not the action you see in the summertime with travelers hurrying in and out to continue on their trip.

Somewhere around Jim Falls, on a lonely country road, we had a flat tire about 5:45 a.m. Still dark out. We were glad it wasn't raining or 24 below zero. Found out later it had been 40 below two weeks earlier.

Got to Spooner at 7:10. Had breakfast in the same restaurant we always stop in. After all these 19 years, I still don't know the name of it. Will have to check next time we make the trip. Gordy had tire fixed while we were having breakfast. Ran over to the gift shop to look in the window before I got back into the car. Even the gift shop window didn't have the summertime sparkle. Nothing I wanted that I could see.

We took Highway 70 to Webster to the lumber company. Nothing doing in Webster. No one around. Didn't even get out of the car while Gordy went into the office. After that we drove to the cottage. Took County Trunk C--Country Trunk A was under construction. Side roads aren't too good to drive on--all ice. We turned onto Leef Road, then Mallard Road, stopped at mail box to pick up a letter mailed to me in November. This was my first time back since then. Continued on toward the cottage.

Finally see it, standing all boarded up so lonely looking with the frozen lake in front and back. Can't say it has that coziness about it in February. Even the evergreen trees we planted didn't look too good. In fact, one is drying up and the others don't look any better. Have to wait until spring to make sure which ones are still good. It's dreary out, so quiet except for the wind rustling through tree tops. No birds, no chipmunks scampering back and forth. Some animal was digging at the insulation around the water pump. Some of it was gone, probably to make his nest with. We take a quick look up and down the shoreline and then turn to open the cottage door. We are anxious to see if anything has happened during our absence. We open the door and Gordy yells "anyone home?" No answer. I hurry from one room to the next to see if everything is in place, and to see if any mice had gotten in somehow.

Very surprised to see how clean it looks and no dust, bugs or cobwebs. But, is it ever cold in here. We hurry to get the heat started. Every step I take I feel the cold air through my wool slacks. After about two hours, it is starting to warm up. My feet are freezing, the floor is like ice. Mike wanted me to put on another pair of socks--his socks--but was afraid my shoes would be too tight then.

I went over to Gordy's cottage. It wasn't as cold in there as it was in ours. Gordy claims it is because the air was getting into his cottage and wasn't as damp. Saw a man ice fishing. Gordy and Mike walked out to talk to him. Someone from around here.

The fellows killed two field mice in the garage. Mike fell down chasing one of them, but finally got it.

North West Patrol officer stopped in. He was driving by checking the cottages. Saw our car and wanted to say "hello." He tells us about the break-ins.

Cottage is finally getting nice and warm. Gordy says "it's too hot, it must be 90 degrees in here." Well, it doesn't seem that hot to me and I'm not about to turn the heat down yet. Although I did take my coat off then. All the moisture is coming out of the furniture and woodwork. Sat down on the desk chair and my seat felt damp. Walked over to stand near the stove to dry out.

I'm passing sandwiches around, we are having our lunch. We have just decided to leave for home. Don't want to stay over and get caught in a snowstorm--from all reports. The side roads around here are all ice, and as we left Mallard to turn onto Leef road, the car swerved over to the edge of the road.

Trip back home was pleasant. We left about 10 o'clock. Stopped to get gas in Augusta, and Mike walked across the street to get our usual treat on the way back to Madison--ice cream cones.

Through Jim Falls on the county road, we stopped to pick bittersweet. They didn't look too bad yet, and thought they would be alright, but found out later they were too dry and dropped off easily. So after all that picking and cutting and bringing them back to Madison, we threw them away.

Getting into Madison, the sun was down, but the sky was so beautiful with colors, it made us think of a sunset in the desert. Back home in Madison (300 miles one way), the 600 mile trip in one day in February is out. No more. The best thing to do in February is to go to Florida and forget about the north.

We are going back to the cottage in April.

The End.

And so it was. A diary began, capturing each day in their lives as North Sand Lake property owners and the excitement of owning their very own humble little summer cottage that brought them from Madison to Spooner and back in one day with nary a complaint or concern about the distance. Mother did not think about starting a diary at the very beginning of this new episode in their lives when the land was untouched and stakes were pounded into the sandy soil to give them an idea of where the cottage would be built. However, once the land had been cleared and the cottage was completed, coupled with the indescribable joy of each day's experiences, she would never turn off the lights at night without recording her thoughts in a hard-cover, daily planner-turned-diary. When she and Daddy decided to sell the cottage in 1988, there were volumes of memories wrapped and packed carefully for the final return trip home.

The next entry in the 1967 diary follows:

Saturday, April 8

Started out for North Sand Lake at 5 o'clock a.m. Saw hundreds of Canadian geese fly out of the swamps on I90. Got to Spooner at 9:45. Stopped for breakfast at the Top Hat on the main street of Spooner's business district. We discovered when we arrived at the lake that the shoreline was free of ice and open.

Weather was mild, nice day for traveling. Saw patches of snow after we left Spooner on the side of the road. Arrived at the cottage about noon. Everything was in fine shape. Parts of our fence had been broken, either from heavy snow or the deer. Went for a long hike after getting things organized. No one around at any of the cottages. Came back to cottage and prepared a chicken dinner. After dark, went for a walk. Pitch dark out. No moon or stars. Next morning ate a big breakfast and then decided to leave for home about 11 o'clock. It was foggy. Got back to Madison at 4:30 p.m. Went to church, came home and had hamburgers for supper.

Friday, April 21

Left today at 6 p.m. It was raining, but cleared up later. Got to the cottage at 11:30 p.m. Very cold. Temperature about 27 degrees.

Saturday, April 22

Gordy and Mike put the new pier up this morning. Mike fell into the water, had to hang all of his clothes on the line. They all froze stiff as a board. Was trying to snow all day long.

Sunday, April 23

Left for Madison at 1:15 and arrived home at 6:15.

These were the ingredients of each seasonal weekend before Daddy retired from Oscar Mayer. Mother packed a lunch of sandwiches and cookies, picked him up at the plant at 4 o'clock, and away they went on their 300 miles journey north. Sundays brought them back home, with thoughts already brewing about the next Friday evening when they'd begin the trek again. Friends and acquaintances couldn't believe they'd drive the long distance for such a short weekend. Little did they understand the power of North Sand Lake and horizon of Daddy's retirement plan. The very thought of having their own little cottage fueled their enthusiasm. Many of their meals consisted of hamburgers and fried fish when they weren't patronizing small restaurants in the woods.

Friday, June 23, *Left at 4 o'clock from Oscar Mayer for the cottage. Arrived there at 9 o'clock. Cathi and the children drove up with Gordy, Elaine and Tommy. Glad to see them. Michael is staying for the week.*

Saturday, June 24, *Misty weather this morning. Billy (age four) fell off the end of the pier while fishing. Gordy and Mike pulled him out of the water. Good thing he had his life jacket on.*

Monday, June 26, *Another beautiful day. Cathi and the children left for home at noon. Enjoyed having them for the weekend. It was fun having the family together.*

Saturday, July 8

Cloudy this morning, but cleared up later in the day. Churchills, Fell and Flagstads came over at 6 o'clock. Had cocktails on the patio. It was a beautiful evening. We all went to Perry's for dinner. Stopped at Schultzie's on the way home, and then over to Churchills cottage just to see it. Very rustic, very nice.

(Perry's today is known as The Channel House and "Schultzies," as they referred to it, is Mulroy's Hunter's Inn located on A between the cottage and Webster.)

The first week in July, Mother and Daddy drove to the cottage and spent a week of rest and relaxation. Well, kind of...

Thursday, July 27

A most beautiful day. Lake so clear and smooth, we could see everything on the bottom. Walked over to Mallard Lake and collected lupine seeds. Added them to my new rock garden and transplanted two fir trees plus some more wild flowers. Looks real nice. Went swimming for a while--just then Gordy drove in from Madison about 4:30. Having meat loaf for supper tonight at their cottage.

Saturday, July 29

Very chilly morning. Sun was shining and the lake was smooth, but by noon it had warmed up. Cathi and Elaine took the sail boat up to the service road to the slough to investigate the area by boat. Came back on the lake. Said it was so interesting. Had cocktails that night in the screen house and a delicious steak roast cooked outside. Billy turned the stove burners on in the cottage. The bread board caught on fire. Nothing happened otherwise.

On August 18 they headed north again. Without stops along the way, the trip seemed to take a total of about five hours. Being gone for just five days they found everything dry from lack of rain. The thirst of sandy soil and rocks that filled the low swampy area to make the property buildable never seemed quenched. Although evidence of a drought appeared everywhere, blackberries continued to ripen and waited to be picked. Some were used for pie, while others were drenched with milk and sugar.

Monday, August 21

Went berry picking this morning. Very cold out. Found a new patch of berries near Oak Lake. Got quite a few of them. Hope to take some home. Tried to ride a bike--fell off and hurt my ankle. It is a beautiful day--bright sun, went walking--it was nice and quiet. No one around. Having a fish fry tonight.

Picking blackberries continued day after day and ingredients in the freezer became a jigsaw puzzle of berry and bluegill packages. Rain fell August 26 and continued all day. The sun came out the next day to warm the temperature and everything seemed to be a fresh new shade of green. Elaine decided to stay for another week which made Tommy and Michael very happy about not having to go home. By August 30, the berry bushes had been emptied of fruit and evenings were becoming very chilly.

Wednesday, August 30

Beautiful day, but windy and cool, sun bright. Drove to Rice Lake this morning to lunch and shop. When we returned I walked up Mallard road to check on berries. Just got a half of cupful. As I was walking back over the hill on the road saw this huge bonfire. Thought our cottage was on fire, but then realized people who own lot #8 were burning all the brush on their lot. Sure hope every spark is out when they leave.

Just when she thought berry season had ended, Mother would discover another patch and returned home from a walk the next day with four more cupfuls. Elaine, Tommy and Michael were enjoying their time at the cottage and ventured out for a bike ride around Mallard Lake. With Gordy and Daddy at work back in Madison, Mother and Elaine were responsible for driving to Scalzo's (A & H) when they needed groceries. Friday night Gordy and Daddy returned to the cottage and everyone dined on bluegills and blackberry shortcake at the beautiful round oak Queen Anne-style table that Mother purchased at St. Vincent de Paul and stripped of its age. Fall had set in and school was starting so Elaine, Gordy and the boys left for home on Sunday, September 3.

Monday, September 4

Another gorgeous day. Walked toward the mailbox to check on berries. There are plenty, but didn't take a container along., so just picked flowers on the way. Came back and sat on the pier and had coffee and a doughnut. Fixed my nails and read a story. Watched the water shine--it was so beautiful--water so clear--sun so bright. Just hate to think of leaving this place to go home. Mike went fishing. Caught several pan fish and a large sunfish. Caught two nice bass earlier this morning. Having fish for supper. Leaving early in the morning about 5 o'clock for home. This is the end of our vacation. Had a glorious two weeks but will be coming back for weekends. Just can't describe the beauty of the north. It is unbelievable.

Mother and Daddy left the cottage the next day at 4:20 a.m. in the fog. When they reached Rice Lake and Chetek, the fog seemed just as bad. As the sun rose, she described it as a big red ball. She also confessed that she wished she could stay at the cottage for the rest of the summer. While getting acquainted with other lakeshore property owners, as well as the locals, they were creating a niche for themselves and anxiously awaited another Friday when they were greeted by wind and cold and white caps on the lake.

Saturday, September 9

Went to Webster and stopped at Hopkins to pick up some blocks to make a sidewalk. On the way back stopped to see "Dubie." Their new home is very nice. They gave us squash, potatoes, parsnip. It all looks so good. After getting back to the cottage I went berry picking, came back with coffee can full of beautiful ripe berries. Mike caught a beautiful bass. Had cocktails and hamburgers for supper. Sat by the window and really enjoyed sitting there and looking out. It was so comfortable. Also went blueberry picking. Got about a cupful. Decided not to pick anymore. I almost stepped on a bee's nest. They were chasing me.

After Sunday Mass, Mother went berry picking again. Anyone who loves the woods and the pleasures of picking berries knows only too well that it isn't easy to pass a bush with branches dangling with ripe berries and nary give a thought to picking just one or two more. Later that day, she returned to the berry spot with an empty coffee can and quickly filled it to the brim before heading back to the cottage. The berries in Rubin's swamp were all gone so she didn't have to return there and worry about bears, a thought that never left her mind when she was deep in patches away from the road. Daddy dug up a red berry tree and transplanted it in the yard, caught another bass and cleaned it before they locked up and headed for home... once again.

Saturday, September 16

A beautiful day. Mike caught a 28-inch northern this morning. Went to Webster to pick up cement blocks. Stopped at a roadside grocery store. Very interesting. Beautiful flowers on the grounds and around the store. After getting back to the cottage, I went for a long walk up toward Thompson road and down toward Mallard resort. Just absolutely beautiful out. Took my time coming back. Picked gentian buds today. Went blackberry picking toward the mailbox and filled a #1 can. Had to wrap my scarf around the can to keep them from falling out. Went to Schultz's later. On the way back stopped at the old gray building (tavern) to pick wild plums. They were so ripe when you grabbed one to pull it off, several others would drop to the ground. Stopped at Stranigan's home. Saw his children. He gave us some frozen corn, frozen tomatoes and frozen fresh cranberries.

Each day became an event to remember. Weekends at the cottage that September blessed them with clear skies and plenty of sunshine. Berry picking continued well into September. On Sunday morning, September 24, they discovered frost on the car windshield. Daddy had to scrape it off before they left for 8 o'clock Mass. After lunch they headed back to Madison.

The following weekend, they saw the northern lights driving past Jim Falls. Leaves were beginning to turn at the cottage and temperatures that warmed the day to allow Mother to have her coffee on the pier, plummeted in the evening. The weekend of October 7 and 8, rained the entire weekend, yet there were no complaints. Mother drove to Spooner to shop and have pie and coffee at the Top Hat before returning to the cottage to put a chicken in the oven for supper.

Other than a few wet weekends, the sun seemed to greet them every Saturday morning. They heard about a break-in at Mallard Lake which caused fear and concern that sometime in their absence the same thing might happen at their place. Fortunately, it didn't then, but would in the years ahead. A little time each October weekend was set aside to prepare for closing. The November 10 weekend trip was interrupted when they followed a new road out of Black River Falls, made a wrong turn at Baldwin and ended up in Prescott on the Mississippi River.

Saturday, November 11

A beautiful morning. Mike caught a northern before breakfast. Went to Spooner to shop, really enjoyed that. Got back to the cottage about 1:30. Sun went down and a terrible wind and rain storm came up. It only lasted about 15 minutes. Decided to go for a walk. The sun came out again and it was beautiful and warm. By the time I got back to the cottage the sun had gone down and it was getting colder. Mike chased a huge cow out of the yard. He also boarded up all the windows today except the three front ones, until tomorrow. Also took the pier down. I took all the drapes and curtains down to bring back home to clean. Went to 6:45 Mass in Webster and then drove to Perry's for dinner.

Sunday, November 12

After breakfast we started packing the car. Plumber came about 10:30 and drained all the pipes. Left for home at 11:30. Drove back on the new road. Drove through a beautiful little town called Amery. The countryside is beautiful on this new highway. It was a dreary day, but we enjoyed the trip. Got home at 4:30.

The end for summer 1967. Enjoyed every mile of driving and our stay at the cottage, rain or shine.

La Dolce Vita

The honisuckle that groweth wilde in every hedge, although it be very sweete, yet doe I not bring it into my garden, but let it reste in his owne place, to serve their senses that travel by it, or have no garden.

John Parkinson (1567-1650)

"The sweet life." To a writer, the very thought of being able to capture what was so overwhelmingly wonderful in life eventually becomes a therapeutic treasure. Offering a plethora of thoughts so personal at times, and so vital to our existence, each page enables the pen to highlight the moments we long to preserve for others to enjoy in the years ahead. And only then can we hope each entry and description will be genuinely appreciated. If a hug is needed from the past, we turn the page, read, smile and say, *yeah, that's the way it was*... The finished product, with a page for each day of the season, a chapter for each week, month, year, becomes a priceless document to serve as a conversation piece at a moment's notice.

Mother didn't begin to record her daily thoughts until 1966. All that preceded us at the lake from 1945 to 1966 had been left behind and we relied on our memories to remind us of the past. We thought of the slightest breezes that took away our electricity and plunged us into darkness time and time again. Forced to light candles and kerosene lamps, we sat around and waited to be reconnected with life in general. Despite the storm and its aftermath, those of us who had gas stoves could be nourished. Of course, that, too, depended on whether we could open the refrigerator for a quick five second grab of a food item to make sure all the coldness inside didn't escape.

While at the cottage, Mother described in detail her jaunts while exploring nature's nooks and crannies where she borrowed from the earth wild flowers to plant in her newly turned over garden. She learned that despite soil being the same in both places, wildflowers didn't appreciate being uprooted to plant elsewhere. And so, her plan to establish the color and charm of wild flowers in the cottage yard was put to rest. Daddy hadn't yet established favorite fishing spots at his new south shore location, but typical of his personality, he patiently explored the lake until he knew exactly what spot to return each morning at 9 o'clock.

The evening of July 24th, before Mother went to bed, she entered in the diary what happened to Daddy the day when he ventured out for a 4:30 afternoon gathering with Wally "Red" Flagstad, his good friend from Madison who had built a cottage on A across from Lily Lake. They were to meet new local friends, "Dubie," Bert and Don for a couple of beers at Schultzies before supper. When Daddy turned the key in the ignition, he noticed that the car was low on gas. Instead of staying home, he pumped air in the bike tires and pedaled all the way to the tavern at the corner of A and T to meet his friends. Getting there was described later over supper as a miserable ride of being attacked by bugs the entire trip. After their usual two tap beers, one of the guys lifted Daddy's bike into a truck and drove him back to the cottage to prevent him from making a return bike ride home with bugs that turned out to be deer flies. Even though he was in great physical condition for a 63 year-old man, we had no idea what he had endured, yet felt relieved when he walked through the kitchen door in time for supper. Typically Daddy, despite the deer flies, life was…sweet.

When fall arrived that year, Mother continued to describe in letters and her diary that the weather was beautiful. Daddy was driving back and forth to Webster to purchase cement patio blocks at Hopkins Sand and Gravel Pit to place in front of their cottage and the abundance of berries kept her returning to the woods each day for new pickings. The warmth of September allowed her to sun on the pier with coffee while the colors of the trees around the lake slowly changed. October brought rain during their weekends until October 20 when they arrived to begin the closing process necessary for the winter months ahead.

The home base of the cow Daddy chased from the backyard would remain a mystery until someone told him it most likely belonged to the Bauers who owned Deer Haven Bay Resort (property today owned by Gary and Helen Rohde). It was an unexpected experience that remained vivid in their minds, and ours, and one shared often through the years in *up north* conversations.

When it was time to leave for the winter, the feeling was bittersweet. As much as they loved their new place on the lake, life on Talmadge Street awaited their return. The year had been sweet and rewarding with promises of many more wonderful years ahead.

Up North 101

We thought we knew a little bit of everything about the area and the lake during the first 20 years as summer guests at Hansen's Resort, but once our July/August resort vacations expanded to three seasons as property owners, lessons exploded with intensity and intrigue.

At the resort, there were the simple take-for-granted things-- sand, water, woods, frogs and fish. If we were lucky, we'd spot a deer in the woods at dusk, or early in the morning on the way to the outhouse we'd tiptoe through the nasty telltale signs that snoopy raccoons had taken more than a peek inside our garbage can. Poison ivy we already knew by the shape and number of leaves on each stem that caused tiny watery-like pimples days after innocent romps in the woods. Requiring Calamine lotion dabbed with white cotton balls, the dreaded aftermath of such walks was not one easily forgotten. One in particular sent Mother, Daddy and Elaine to bed in pain one late summer, not with pimples but huge blisters, while I strutted around for days with nary a single pimple after picking countless juicy berries apart with my little fingers.

At Hansen's Resort we had learned about fishing with worms, minnows and the ever-reliable Daredevil near drop-offs and weed beds, methods to remove bones from fish, and how cold the lake was well into the late summer months when the heat of August finally warmed an inch of its surface, only to change again with the onset of chilly evening air. A new beauty of *up north* sunrises and sunsets fascinated us as did the eerie calls of loons late at night. We also learned that if we stood too close to the wood burning stove to warm our pillows before jumping in bed, our quilted nylon tricot bathrobes could scorch like toasted marshmallows.

Because we didn't vacation at the resort during spring and early summer, we knew nothing about wood ticks, *schistomsome dermatitis*, aka "swimmer's itch," or Canada geese which seemed non-existent on a lake whose shoreline fluctuated from one year to the next depending on water levels. Once our south shore summers embraced tail-ends of Aprils and full Octobers, it was as if we had completed UP NORTH 101 with a new semester ahead.

There were black flies, fish flies, dragonflies, deer and horse flies to deal with at intervals and, suddenly, after a walk in the woods or a few rakes of last year's oak leaves, we'd find little brown ticks crawling on our clothes in pursuit of a warm cozy place on our skin for a meal of blood. Every night before slipping into bed we felt like monkeys looking through each other's hair and body parts. If we missed one, it became evident the next day or days later when it had grown to look like a small gray jelly bean. By July 4th, the tick regime had gone into hiding and we could relax once again.

Years later, to make things even worse, we learned about Lyme disease, became somewhat paranoid, and crossed walking in the woods off our list of early spring *up north* activities. Unlike wood ticks, deer ticks were the size of pin pricks and often required immediate medical attention, especially if found on children. If a red bulls-eye rash appeared, chances were that the inflammation was caused by an infected deer tick that probed its mouth parts into you about 4 to 20 days before. Considering the fact that your life had been virtually threatened, it remains as something not to treat lightly. In fact, if you have any questions whether it is a wood or deer tick, after removing it place a piece of scotch tape across its body or seal it tightly in a jar for the doctor to inspect.

Swimmer's itch was something else we new nothing about, but when we did it became as dreaded as a fat tick. And maybe even more so as a tick could be removed, but swimmer's itch made life miserable for a week or two. While staying at Hansen's, we never saw snails in the water. In the past 10 or 15 years, maybe more, the lake bottom around our pier became thick and crusty with snails. In the beginning I questioned it, yet remember thinking how nice it was to have snails feeding off the bottom of the lake to clean it of impurities. I didn't learn of the connection between snails and swimmer's itch until an article appeared in a 1999 Lake Tides newsletter describing what had been causing me discomfort a few times each summer.

Schistosome, or flatworm parasite, lives in suitable mammals and birds, one being the duck. The worm sheds its eggs into the water where they hatch into a free-swimming stage called a *miracidium.* The miracidium swim in search of a proper second host animal, in this case, a particular type of snail. After penetrating snail tissue to develop even more during a three to four week development period, another free-swimming stage called *cercaria* emerges from the snail in search of the proper primary bird or mammal host. According to the newsletter, this usually occurs when the water temperatures reach their near-maximum summer temperature in late June or early July.

There are medicinal sticks and lotions to rub over the itchy red welts caused by swimmer's itch, but one method suggested to avoid the itch is to immediately dry off after swimming by briskly rubbing your skin with a towel to crush the cercariae before they penetrate the skin. Water quality has nothing to do with swimmer's itch which often occurs in the cleanest of lakes. Another method to prevent swimmer's itch is to shower immediately after a swim, which isn't always convenient.

As for the Canada geese, I remember one day about twenty years ago when my nephew, Tom, an avid runner, was completing his early morning trek around North Sand Lake. While still on Thompson Road he noticed something standing in the middle of the road and realized as he got closer that it was a huge goose. Having never seen one of these magnificent beauties on the ground, Tom returned to the cottage to fill us in on the details all of which seemed exciting at the time. Today Canada geese are in abundance and considered to be pests for the mess they leave behind.

Oh, for the old days when frogs were in abundance. Push a boat from the shore's sand and water early in the morning and a dozen frogs would leap in different directions or escape from view by diving into the shallow water. The year 2002 marked the first summer without seeing a single frog on our shoreline. It was also the year of absentee toads. I grieved, realizing something was wrong. Then at night I momentarily forgot as I watched a few tiny tree frogs at the window in the glow of the floor lamp that enticed them for a meal of insects on glass.

Mosquitoes must be of a different variety than those encountered back home in the city. Mosquitoes at the lake are like dive bombers, coming out about 9:30 in the evening like a military squadron scrambled on alert. Battling these blood thirsty machines required understanding them more than ever before. Being on the planet for 200 million years, it's a sure bet they are here to stay. Having learned that mosquitoes are responsible for more deaths than all of the wars in human history, there's good reason to avoid them at all times wherever you are.

Actually, mosquitoes don't bite. They penetrate their victims with a hollow, flexible snout composed of six parts. Four parts cut your skin, while the other two allow the mosquito to gorge on her meal—her because only females attack while their male counterparts, being vegetarian, feed off the nectar of flowers. The itch in her bite is caused by her saliva which she spits into the wound to thin the host's blood to keep it easy to draw. On a lighter side, in flight, they beat their wings 1,000 times a second, reaching speeds of eight miles per hour, to produce the familiar humming sound.

We already knew that skunks stunk and to stay as far away from one as possible is an understatement. Badgers are mean and if you see one, just stop, observe, and don't approach. The same is true for porcupines and their quill defense that we sure didn't want in any way, shape or form in our own bodies. But what about the great blue heron, the prehistoric-looking bird that perches like a statue on the end of the pier during early morning hours in search of breakfast? Splendiferous in every way, and ever watchful of the slightest movement around it, the heron eventually turns and moves toward the shoreline before entering the water. Stepping high, making not a single ripple as each foot penetrates the surface, patient beyond words, and suddenly, like the snap of a fired pistol, its long beak pierces the water to remove a succulent morsel of fish. With far more grace than one could imagine from a bird with such design, almost appearing in slow motion, the blue heron lifts off and takes flight to disappear over tree tops toward the slough...a sight and an experience never before seen back home.

Most magnificent of all has been the first sighting of an adult American bald eagle. Was it because I hadn't been privileged before to see one in the wild? That the wing span often measures seven feet? Or that in flight the eagle is a glorious sight? It had to be a combination of all three, plus everything else that fits in between. To sit in a boat and catch a glimpse of an eagle approaching, circling, and diving to pick up a fish injured or dead, perhaps one you've thrown back, is a sight never to be forgotten. Watching as it heads back toward the huge white pine trees where its nest rests to dine alone or with its young is a sight to behold. One day, while sitting on the shoreline in front, I watched as the eagle returned home. Reaching for my binoculars I witnessed its destination and arrival, then saw it settle down on a branch with its white head and brilliant yellow beak exposed over the dark greenery of the pine needles. The next best thing would have been to have a camera with a telephoto lens to capture the moment.

In July of 2004, I watched as an adult bald eagle landed on our short pier six feet away from a shoreline decoration of a tin white egret poked firmly into the soil and weeds. The eagle kept looking at the fake bird while trying to put some weight on its right foot. Obviously painful, the foot was lifted to expose dark metal prongs or long heavy nails stuck in its claws. We watched for less than five minutes, trying to identify the foreign object that had caused the injury, but our binoculars were being repaired and we had to rely on our eyes alone. When the eagle took off, his right leg appeared to be crooked and stuck out at an angle. I contacted the DNR who returned my call to tell me that other calls had been received at the station regarding the eagle. Someone came out to the shoreline in search of the eagle, to no avail. The DNR felt that as long as the eagle could gather food and feed itself, it might be okay. If it couldn't and was found injured, there was an assurance a phone call would send someone out immediately to take the bird back for treatment.

Enter the black bear. It took 50 years before seeing one in the wild and then it was at a distance, thinking I had seen a large black dog crossing a road near Oak Lake. The same year, as we were turning from Mallard Lake Road onto Thompson Road early one evening, a mother and two cubs ran in front of our car. The third time that summer a young bear plunked itself down late in the afternoon to check out finch feeders hanging from the tree in front of our cottage. Watching ever so carefully without moving inside at the window, we saw the bear pull down one of the feeders and stuff himself with niger seed. When the feeder was emptied, the bear tried reaching for the second feeder. Having failed time and time again, the bear decided to climb one of the trees. That also failed when the bear's reach was not long enough to grab the plastic cylinder. Unable to solve the problem, the bear returned to the ground, looking over the mound surrounding the tree to make sure nothing was missed, turned and ambled through the yard to the openness of Mallard Lake Road before disappearing.

It was back on July 4, 1985, that I decided to walk around the horn, so named by Mother and Daddy for the triangular shaped land bordered by Mallard Lake Road and both South Shore Roads. In the sand off the pavement along Mallard Lake Rd. were huge hoof prints from two animals. So big, in fact, that I returned to the cottage for paper and pencil to draw them to scale. One print measured 6 inches in length with two 3-inch long toes in front, and two 2 ½-inch ones in the back. Later, when I showed them to Mother, she solved the mystery by telling me that Margaret and Jack Hansen, whose cottage was down the shoreline from us, encountered a pair of moose walking, days before, along the side of Mallard Lake at Corbin Road. Within a week, signs had been posted in the dirt road ("Cut Across Road") area alerting the public to Watch for Moose.

Returning home in the late summer sunshine after having dinner at Oak Lake Inn about ten years ago, we noticed what looked like a white goat emerging from a wooded hill along the side of County Road A near Thompson Road. Walking slowly, "it" reached the road, began to cross over, then stopped and stood still watching us as we carefully came closer. It wasn't until we stopped altogether to observe the animal that we realized it was a young albino deer. We remained at a complete standstill for the deer to decide what it wanted to do until it reached the other side and disappeared through the field and woods beyond. When I returned to the cottage, I began to read everything available on albino deer and learned they not only are a protected species, but because they usually are shunned by other deer, their life span generally is short. Being a sensitive person, the information saddened me. Although I read later about similar sightings in the immediate area, I wondered if the deer would survive the dismissal from other deer, much less the brutality of winter. Not only did it survive, but *she* was seen the following spring with fawns which told me a buck found her worthy of an affair.

And then there was the summer day when I sat on the screened porch and heard somewhat of a tropical sound cawing in the distance. Heading toward the cottage, the sound got nearer, stopped, then continued on its trip, stopped again, and after a few more starts and stops of getting closer and closer, a huge bird suddenly landed on the tree near the porch door. Stunned at having never before seen such a bird, I hoped it would stay long enough for me to study before it continued its flight. When it flew on, I went inside, opened my North American Wildlife book and found a picture matching what I had seen moments before. A pileated woodpecker. A gallant monster woodpecker with an incredible head design topped with red feathers ending in a flip at the back with a beak as strong as an electric drill to send wood chips flying in all directions. This north woods resident with a jungle-like call was truly a grand sight. The principal food of the pileated woodpecker is the carpenter ant, so this is a good guy to have around, not only to get rid of destructive carpenter ants, but also to add excitement and beauty to the occasion.

When we arrived at the cottage in the spring of 2004, two Jack Pines in our side yard that supported a basketball back board and its hoop for more years that I can remember, and were cut off just above the backboard last year because of their condition, were peppered with holes, some measuring 4- by 5-inches across and 6-inches deep as visual proof that one or more pileated woodpeckers had feasted on both trees. Carpeting the sand surrounding each trunk were pieces of bark removed by their powerful beaks. If there were bugs or ants occupying both trunks, no evidence of a single crawler was left behind. It might be of interest to those of you who remember Woody Woodpecker cartoons that he was fashioned after the pileated woodpecker.

I must be one of few women who truly appreciates the beauty of snakes and was mesmerized one day by an unfamiliar gray snake slowly moving through the vegetation surrounding one of the trees next to Mother and Daddy's cottage. Obviously concerned for my life, everyone was shouting at me to stay back as I carefully moved closer to lock in my mind what I was seeing for the first time. The snake hissed at me, then hissed again before rising up like a cobra and inflating its neck to a flat circle. Stunned at what I was seeing, I continued to watch from a distance of no more than five feet when, suddenly, the snake collapsed before my eyes and dropped to the ground in a motionless pile. At that point, I backed away having no idea what the snake's next move might be and returned to the cottage and my handy wildlife book where I found a description to identify it as a hognose snake. If actions of the hognose don't scare away predators, its final defensive move is pretending to die. Unfortunately, I never saw another hognose, but learned that a neighbor found a nest in the area directly behind us off the service road of unusual looking young snakes that she eventually killed.

It was late at night and I could barely see the huge moth on the screen, but I was in awe. Another treasure of the woods that I wished was more prevalent for fear I'd never see another one appeared to be a velvet butterfly with intense autumn colors. Clinging to the screen like a nighttime mystery making a brief stop for a free showing was a beautiful palm-size cecropia moth that emerges in late spring and early summer with a wing span of 6 inches.

Another incredibly beautiful insect is the gold bug, a beetle Edgar Allen Poe wrote about and one that I found at the lake in the 1950s and gave to Paul Knipping, my homeroom biology teacher at East High in Madison (though years later wished I had kept for myself). In 2001, while turning the soil in my garden in the back of the cottage, I was lucky to unearth another gold bug. It was placed in a tiny jar until it died, then moved to a minute plastic container where it could be viewed and studied in its dried state. The gold bug is about the size of an average-size woman's thumb nail and seems to preserve itself remarkably well in death, retaining the iridescence in its gold shell which constantly reminds me that designing a gold bug in gold would make a beautiful pendant.

And the stars. Oh, the beautiful stars! They seem so much more brilliant over our lake than anywhere else I've been. Many mosquito-less nights, when the skies were clear, we gathered outside to settle in our chaise lounge chairs, or propped our bodies against the deck steps to lean back and stare, wishing we had studied astronomy in high school to know much more about what mysteriously hung overhead twinkling and whizzing by in miniature rocket-like fashion.

We also learned never to talk about anything personal while on the lake in a boat if you don't want people on shore to hear what you are saying because conversations drift in mysterious ways, especially well with the wind. One day a couple in a small boat motored slowly past our cottages while discussing the possibility of building a cottage of their own. Apparently, the woman had ideas of her own as we heard him say in defense while pointing at our places, "See, you don't have to spend a fortune to build a cottage." Another time two people motored by and must have been aware that all three cottages belonged in one family as one said to the other, "The old man and his two sons live there." Well, Daddy wasn't old and Elaine and I weren't boys so we chuckled at the comment and probably should have shouted out to correct him, but allowed the misnomer to slide.

I can't help but wonder about the volumes of things I've never seen and wish I had, like the 30 ½ pound northern pike A. Glueheisen caught on North Sand Lake on August 24, 1933. Measuring 46 inches in length, the very thought of it stirs my imagination as to the sizes of other northerns that might be too smart in their old age to be snagged and landed. Or a repeat of the first walleye I ever caught one cold windy October night off the pier in front of Mother and Daddy's place where we had gathered for dinner. Weighing 7 ½ pounds and measuring 28 inches, the walleye was wrapped in newspaper, frozen and carried to a Minneapolis taxidermist by our neighbor Ray Rubin who returned weeks later with the fish mounted on a plaque to remind me of what I caught while celebrating my October 4th birthday.

And then there were the arrowheads-- beautifully crafted Indian artifacts found by the boys while playing on our property when the ground was disturbed and the cottages were being built. Somewhere along the way, each one would disappear.

Man of Habit

Whether in the garden, on the lake, or the shoreline, Daddy was a man of habit. Someone down the shoreline once asked if Daddy had served in the military. He hadn't. Wondering why he asked, we were told by the man that he could set his watch every day by what Daddy was doing at the time.

Daddy woke up every morning at 5:30. Not by alarm, but by biological nature. Before washing up, he'd go to the garage to remove his rod and reel and landing net and carry them out to the end of the pier where he'd reach deep into the bait box for a bluegill to use as bait. Once the hook was carefully slipped through its back, and a bobber was set at the correct depth, the bluegill was cast out as far as possible. After setting the clicker, he'd place the rod into a holder secured at the end of the pier and return to the garage where he'd pull on his galoshes, his garden gloves, and lift from nails pounded firmly in garage studs any garden tools needed while inspecting his flower and vegetable garden planted on Gordy's empty lot next door. Only then was the hose turned on for a good watering. Before going back inside, he'd also water the creeping phlox that carpeted mounds around the trees in front. This was done not only during spring when the phlox bloomed, but every morning to keep their roots moist. Without water, the phlox would eventually wither and die in the sandy soil

The next phase of each morning ritual was removing from the refrigerator a large glass jar of bluegills caught the day before that had already been scaled and gutted in the small screened fish house at the side of the cottage. Soaking the cleaned fish in water in the refrigerator overnight made the flesh firm and much easier to filet in the calm of the kitchen, leaving little or no mess.

After removing the bones, each filet was thoroughly rinsed, divided, and placed in baggies to wrap with white butcher paper before sealing with tape. Before being placed in the freezer, the date and number of bluegill pieces was written on each package. One year the number caught and cleaned totaled 2600, many of which were enjoyed at the cottage and throughout the year by family members and close friends. When packages filled the refrigerator freezer to capacity, they were transferred to someone's commercial freezer in Webster until it was time to close up for the winter, pick them up and return home.

By 6:30, it was likely the bobber on the line off the end of the pier was no longer in view. Still being somewhat of a quiet bay, big fish moved into the area early in the morning to feed and we have countless pictures to prove it. How I wish we had kept a monthly chart to keep track of each fish he caught and landed before breakfast.

For as long as I can remember, Daddy's breakfast consisted of half a grapefruit, corn flakes with bananas, toast browned well, and coffee with cream and three teaspoons of sugar, a practice he claimed was the result of drinking chicory coffee when he was attending college back in the 1920s near New Orleans. It didn't matter where he was, at home or at the cottage, the breakfast menu never changed and was enjoyed like a man giving thanks to God. When breakfast was finished, he shaved and cleaned up before putting on an old faded red-plaid flannel shirt over a clean white crew neck undershirt with sleeves, lifted his faded red Oscar Mayer hat from the hall hook, and headed outside to the garage where he kept his night crawlers.

Before the garage was built, night crawlers were stored under a shaded side of the cottage. Later, packed in large worm boxes with plenty of feed, they were kept in the coolest corner of the garage and checked daily. From those boxes, a certain number of crawlers were lifted and placed in empty half-gallon milk cartons that he cut the tops from and removed. By slitting each corner to about 3-4 inches down on all four sides, the cartons could be folded flat on top and kept in place with a heavy rubber band. Each carton was filled with dirt, crawlers and shreds of newspaper dampened with water. Although Mother wasn't pleased to have worms stored in her refrigerator, Daddy insisted on keeping some of the cartons there when the weather was unusually hot. She gave in only after he promised to place each milk carton in a large Baggie secured tightly with a wire twist.

A wooden bench in front of the cottage served as a narrow table by loosening screws, readjusting and tightening the screws once again. Daddy would spread the top of the bench-turned-table with newspapers, dump out all the worms from a milk carton and, lifting each crawler, count what was there and add to another container the number he thought he'd need that morning for fishing. Once that was accomplished, he grabbed the oars he stored in the garage each night, his tackle box, bluegill basket, a cane pole and, with arms and hands full, walked down to the pier to place everything inside the boat. By that time, he had probably caught a northern on his rod and reel, but, if not, he'd reel in the pole, remove the bait, and place the pole in the boat in case he wanted to still-fish for northerns while fishing for bluegills. After the tires were lifted from each of the two pier posts to release the rope, he'd begin slowly and methodically rowing out to what had become his favorite spot-- an angle to the east, straight out between us and our neighbor's place. The time was 9 o'clock, give or take a minute, but no more.

If there was little or no action there, he'd move a little bit at a time, rowing with the drop line draped over the index finger on one hand, while the cane pole was propped on the seat in front of him. When he felt a bite or saw the bobber go down, he'd stop rowing, set the hook and bring in the bluegill. If it was a decent size, he'd drop anchor and stay there for awhile. Whatever was accomplished during that time stopped at 11:30 when the fish basket was pulled in, the pole wrapped and set aside, the drop line wound up and placed back in the tackle box, and the anchor pulled up to row or motor back to the cottage. After washing up, he'd sit down at the kitchen table for lunch and by 12:30 p.m. was settled into his favorite chair to watch, with Mother, Monty Hall's *Let's Make a Deal* television game show.

A beautiful walleye.

During the early afternoon hours, Daddy tended to other chores. If the weather was hot, he'd sit for a short time in the shade of the old oak trees out front and enjoy breezes from either lake. At 3 o'clock, his morning catch was cleaned in the screened fish house. By 4 o'clock, he was bathing in the lake before leaving at 4:30 to meet Don Pateck, Bert Morrill and others for a few beers before supper. These daily one hour gatherings were held at Schultzie's on A. Later, when the place was sold and known as Lily Lake Inn, tap beers no longer were available. After one of the guys suggested going where tap beer was sold, The Pineapple (Crow Bar), Mallard Lake Inn, and the Sandbar rotated as being daily meeting spots. Although "Red" Flagstad, brothers Don and John Pateck, Bert Morrill, "Hannigan" and "Doobie" all gathered on occasion, Daddy, Don and Bert established themselves as regulars with others like Joe Klecker and a young man named "Rich"who lived in the immediate area. All were special men from different

Daddy and another big northern with Bob looking on.

Daddy cleaned fish at the same time each day in his screened outdoor fish house.

walks of life who thoroughly enjoyed each other's company, if only for an hour each day.

After supper, it was time to rest from a full day. Weather permitting, Mother and Daddy sat in chairs on the brick patio out front with coffee and talked about whatever had happened during the day. Before the mosquitoes attacked, they'd go back inside to watch television. If Daddy's favorite old cowboy serials or Charlie Chan movies were listed in the *TV Guide*, he'd stay up late into the evening. Otherwise, a perfectly synchronized day had ended and it was time to retire for a repeat performance the next day which would begin promptly at 5:30 a.m.

Mother

She eagerly awaited the day Daddy retired so they could extend their annual five week vacations at Hansen's Resort to six months at their own place on the lake. Although it meant the house they both loved on Talmadge Street would sit empty from spring to fall, they were anxious to shift gears and head for Webster.

As Daddy's well-cared backyard flower garden at home shrunk in size, Mother's beautifully arranged bouquets also began to disappear. Golfing with her lady friends ended all together, but a place on the bowling team was saved for her return in October. Mother had truly enjoyed the camaraderie gained from both, yet neither seemed particularly important considering what awaited them. If she wanted to golf at the cottage, there were courses in the vicinity she could reach by car. She was not active in civic organizations, so there were no concerns about missing meetings.

Springtime

One of the first things Mother bought for herself was a portable sewing machine. A private person who was artistic and incredibly talented with the needle and thread, she was like a child with a new toy. Just knowing that she could plug in the machine and make curtains, cover cushions for the couch and a variety of chairs, design and sew clothes for herself, as well as mending anything Daddy owned pleased her immensely. While she occupied herself at the sewing machine, Daddy tended his *up north* flower and vegetable garden, lawn and shoreline, or fished among newly found weed beds.

Because a portion of the hill up the service road had been scooped out by machinery when our property was being prepared to build on, left in its aftermath was The Desert. A North Sand Lake Sahara Desert wonder, not a single green leaf or stem was left to peek through the sand that mother adopted as her own driving range and sand trap. She carried her clubs a short distance up the hill to The Desert any time of any day where she practiced her wood and iron drives and sand trap shots.

Mother never feared being alone in or near the woods and felt comfortable walking alone in search of what *up north* offered. Recorded in her diary are experiences with blackberry bushes, raspberry bushes, wild grapes and poison ivy. Each was a gift, whether touched, tasted or viewed from a distance. Identifying wild flowers became a daily lesson learned and she carried back to the cottage in the depths of her pockets unusual rocks and stones.

With a small box of tiny model paint bottles and an assortment of paint brushes, Mother's talent surfaced in a variety of ways. She had an eye for finding rocks that resembled different things—a perfectly smooth egg-shaped stone, a slice of bread, or a wooden Dutch shoe. Other rocks seemed to beg for her clever touches. Painted, speckled with interpretations of tiny flowers, buds, branches and leaves, minute openings were entered with toothpick ends coated with colors while brush strokes covered larger areas. Once finished, some were signed and dated—others were not.

Each completed stone or rock would sit unattended overnight until the next day when the paint had dried to allow a clear coating brushed on as a protection from dust and other ravages of time before being placed on a small knick-knack shelf on the paneled wall.

On the opposite side of the patio at the side door and protected against the garage was her own garden. As you'd expect from any artist, perennials and wild flowers were planted according to height and color and whether they'd prefer the warmth of the afternoon sun or the protection and coolness of morning and evening shade. For an old-fashioned touch, an iron hand pump that once brought cold water up from the depths of local earth to fill someone's buckets was found at an antique shop in Siren and placed in the center of the foliage after she painted it red.

Although Mother fished with Daddy on occasion during the early years when both tried to absorb everything in and around their new location as quickly as possible, she preferred staying on shore. She loved having her morning coffee and a cigarette on the patio in front. Using a large shell I brought back from Boston as an ashtray, she filled it with dry sand from the shoreline and rested it on the outside coffee table made for Daddy by Bert Morrill. Surrounding the cottage and the patio were circles of striped and solid dark green hostas. When the weather didn't cooperate, she would sit inside at a long coffee table made from a door and placed against the large front room windows where the view made it almost as nice as being outdoors. It was where Mother and Daddy sat during the early April spring days and listened to the explosive cracking sounds of ice breaking up. And, when the wind shifted, huge chunks moved in careless fashion to destroy whatever was in their path until coming to rest along the shoreline.

Furnishing their own cozy cottage was also a result of Mother's talent and trained eye. Constantly combing antique shops back home and garage sales *up north* supplied her with conversation pieces of character that she paid little for and made charming with stains and paint colors and fabrics to complement each cottage room.

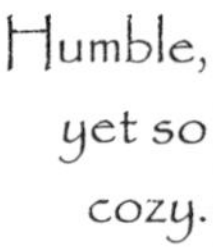
Humble, yet so cozy.

Because of limited counter space, Mother prepared most of the meals on the round kitchen table protected by plastic or newspaper as she worked. It was where she spread out the necessary utensils to make jam each fall and where she'd make Key Lime pies, a favorite of the entire family. Her fish fries will never be forgotten as she had her own system that worked perfectly. When, for a few weeks, she decided to try something different and used a beer batter for the blue gills, which we all thought was tasty, we asked her to return to the old way of using an egg-milk wash before coating with a dry lightly seasoned flour which didn't fill us up so quickly.

While the boys were growing up, she treated them to breakfasts of oatmeal made the old-fashioned way. Willingly devouring, they claimed no one made oatmeal better than Grandma, who served it with orange juice, toast, jelly and cocoa with marshmallows. At night, they gathered on the patio blocks out front around a heavy old metal pot hauled back to the cottage from a garage sale or antique shop, filled with fire to roast marshmallows. Love for her grandsons made each moment with them extra special.

The Boys

Above left: Mike and Tom during their first summer on the south shore, 1965.
Right: Dick and me, with Mike, Bill and Bob, 1968.

Born with innocence and gifted with inquisitiveness, the boys oozed sweetness laced with typical little boy mischief. Despite around the clock activity, occasional chaos and hair-raising moments, I would give anything to return to those days to begin their *up north* adventures all over again. Mike, born in 1958, Bill in 1963, Bob in 1965, and nephew Tom in 1959, all began infancy at the lake. Today, hanging on the wall behind my computer at the cottage is an enlarged 16x20-inch black and white picture snapped in 1968 of the four boys sitting on Daddy's wood pier. In the background is a beautiful sand beach complete with oak trees stretching down 900 feet of shoreline to the entry of the slough and back bay. Each precious face exudes innocence and unique personalities. As I study the picture and melt inside, I wonder if I ever disciplined or spanked them when it wasn't really necessary. Knowing that I was destined to be a great mother for boys, being a bit of a tom boy myself while growing up, it was easy for me to relate, absorb, understand and appreciate their ways and rarely questioned what

Tom, Bob, Bill and Mike, 1968.

made them tick at times. Yet, there had to be moments when my patience thinned to transparency.

Another wish would be that I had recorded everything they did because it would be an interesting and often hilarious account of the fun they managed to have together at the lake. As a TWA pilot, Dick was based at O'Hare in Chicago and commuted from Madison and because he was on a trip the boys and I rode *up north* on Friday, June 23rd with Gordy, Elaine and Tom. It was misty when we woke up the next morning and chilly enough to dress the boys in their winter jackets. While Elaine and I enjoyed coffee with Mother at her cottage, Bill, who had just turned four May 6th, was fishing off Daddy's pier and fell off the deep end. He managed to cling to the pier until Daddy and Gordy, who were working outside, heard him holler and ran down to pull him out of the water. Lesson learned for all involved.

Looking back, I wonder what Bill's horoscope was that day because falling off the pier was just the beginning. Once dry and warm in another outfit, Bill stayed with us in Mother's kitchen. While we continued to chat at the table, thankful a tragedy hadn't occurred, Bill took Tom's loaded BB gun and hit the butt of the gun on the floor so hard that it discharged and shot Tom in the elbow just inches from the barrel. Later that day, we were shopping at the corner grocery store in Webster when Bill grabbed the grocery basket filled with food items and accidentally tipped it over, sending everything scattered and rolling up and down the aisle. About six weeks later, he turned on the gas burners on Mother and Daddy's kitchen stove and the bread board caught on fire setting yet another example of what moments were like for a mother of an overly active little boy.

Daddy and Mother, Tom and Mike

Once our own cottage was built, summers blossomed into long vacations as Dick would drive us to the cottage, then commute to O'Hare from Minneapolis. Leaving Madison meant a five hour trip with Mike, Bill, Bob and the dog, each confined to their own small space in the back of the station wagon. As parents sitting alone in the front seat with plenty of room to move around, we were foolish to expect the same harmony in the back which usually lasted about the time it took to back out of the driveway and reach the corner of the street. We survived those travel experiences, except for the time we were on our way home on a Labor Day weekend and were hit from behind near Portage. Instead of going directly home we stopped first at the hospital for the emergency staff to remove embedded bits of glass from Mike's back.

Our cottage had three bedrooms—a small one for Mike, the next size for Bill and Bob, and a large one facing the lake for Dick and I. After the lights were turned off during the *Willie Wonka and the Chocolate Factory* days, the boys would begin their own Oompa Loompa song with silly verses about each other that pierced the paneling dividing their rooms. They'd giggle and, from my own bedroom, I'd quietly laugh with them until they wore themselves out and fell asleep.

Experiences. Each one is what life is all about. Together, the four boys learned to fish, identify birds, and karate-kick small rotted trees to topple in the woods. They shot at chipmunks (I never knew about that until later), put firecrackers in the mouths of frogs (didn't know about that, either) and shot rubber bands at people in pews in front of us one Sunday during Mass at the Catholic Church near A & H (became aware of it only when a rubber band flew past my face). I gave them "the look" and that was the end of that.

Elaine and the boys

When the water level was low and the beach was wide, they played football on the shore, golfed on the shore, and buried Bill up to his neck in the dry sand on the shore. Years later, after the water level rose, then receded again, Mike, Bill and Tom bet Bob that he couldn't walk across the swamp. He took advantage of their $20 bet, carefully ventured out and won only because of the dryness of that particular summer.

With age, they were allowed to go off on their own to play with the Koran kids and Scott Christianson who summered with their families down the shoreline. One day they spent hours autographing Mallard Lake Road with jack knives to carve their names in the blacktop near the split entry to one of the two South Shore Road entries.

Although they always had fun together, occasionally friends from home were invited for a week or weekend. We went through the beer can craze when Bob got hooked on collecting them and willingly accompanied him to many places hidden from the road, deep in the woods where people once tossed their trash. More than one can became a keepsake during those haunts, and one day Bob got a dose of the unexpected when he returned home with 26 wood ticks crawling inside the jeans he was wearing.

Last summer, when each of the boys, now grown men, was asked to share some things I hadn't heard before, Mike told me about the day Bill carried the BB gun over his shoulder while climbing a tree on Rubin's property so he could get a better look at the eagle's nest—the gun being carried merely as a form of protection. Like Tom, Bill was establishing himself as a diehard fisherman and relished the 5 pound bass he caught from the end of our pier, the 16-inch crappie from the edge of the boat, and the day a few years ago while fishing out front in the area in Daddy's old spot when he reeled in his line and a northern pike following the lure, leaped, unhooked, out of the water and into the boat.

Mike, Ray, Tim – Jeff in front, 1974.

When Mike became a junior in high school, he invited three of his good friends to vacation with us for a week. Tim Riddiough, Jeff Olson and Ray Mayne were also good friends of Tom, making it a total of seven boys for me to care for as a mother. I went on a cooking rampage, making everything they asked for, one night preparing three different specialties because of likes and dislikes. When Tim broke out with a heavy dose of poison ivy on his legs, I dabbed them with cotton pads soaked with Calamine lotion each night before he went to bed. During the day, I joined them like one of their buddies in certain activities around the cottage. Little did I know what was going on when they left the premises.

Somewhere, somehow, they acquired two six packs of beer which they cleverly hid late at night in the coolness of Mallard Lake behind us. By the next morning the dampness had caused the cardboard to loosen and cans were bobbing everywhere. Mike remembered the time he and Jeff asked for permission to drive Daddy's car and roared down Mallard Lake Road going about 80 mph. The recollection horrified me and I prefer to think of it as being overly-exaggerated.

And then there was the priceless and timely trick played on Ray after he hooked a bluegill on his line which he cast out from the end of the pier before asking if we'd watch the bobber in his absence. I don't know where all five went, but while they were gone, Bob filled a large Baggie with stones and tied it tightly before Bill rowed him out to Ray's bobber. They removed the bluegill, attached the Baggie to the line and dropped it into the water to keep the bobber down and out of sight.

When the boys returned, Ray glanced beyond the end of the pier and not seeing the bobber assumed there was a big fish at the other end. He ran out on the pier, slipped and fell on the way, got up and grabbed the pole to set the hook. He did the best he could while reeling in the fish, but struggled with it until Tom, Bill and Bob rowed out to where the fish seemed to be caught in the weeds to help Ray land it. Suddenly, the line went slack. While a few of us knew the Baggie must have torn loose, Ray was furious at the thought of losing what he thought was a giant northern. So mad, in fact, that he never noticed a small piece of plastic bag still attached to the hook when he reeled in his line.

Many years went by until one of the guys confessed to Ray what really happened that day. Ray claims that someday he will get even with everyone. They are still waiting.

Another time, Bob cut out a piece of plywood in the shape of a shark fin. He attached it to a flat piece of plywood, painted the fin black, then rowed out to the point and open lake and placed it in the water. We watched it float in a perfect upright position before turning the boat around and returning to shore. It was the last time we saw the North Sand Lake shark, and never overheard a single word from any conversation that something resembling a shark had been seen on the lake, but still hope it created some momentary confusion and a little bit of excitement for someone.

Through the years, other friends visited the boys-- Pete Merrill, Joe Pellegrino, Scott and Steven Rohde, Ted Butler, and girls, Kari, Mary and Sandra. All were a joy to have with us.

One night, three years ago, when Mike was 44, Tom 43, Bill 39 and Bob 37, and all four were visiting us at the same time, someone got the idea to go through the chest of drawers in one of the bedrooms and remove way-too-small outdated clothes they had worn years before that I had washed, pressed and saved just in case someone much younger visited and forgot to pack sufficient clothing. The little boy giggles I remember hearing from behind the door so many years before were now deep throaty laughs and when the door finally opened it was like an updated scene from the television program *Happy Days* as they strutted out, one-by-one, in ill-fitted clothes and style-show fashion to show us that their humorous side, mixed with a little leftover mischief, still existed.

It's hard to believe that my little boys...so precious...are now in their 40s. Yes, with all the things I did to keep them happy and healthy and all the unexpected things they did that I managed to survive, those were, without doubt, among the most wonderful cottage experiences. Each morning began with a bowl of cereal and each evening ended with a bowl of cereal, enjoyed at the kitchen table. Everything else packed in between was a roller coaster of experiences. How I wish we could do it all over again, right down to finger-shooting rubber bands during Mass.

Mike, Bill, Bob, Tom and Sugar, 1969.

Mike, Bill and Sugar, and Bob at the desert, 1974.

Gordy and Dick

Mother and Daddy couldn't have been happier with our selections of husbands. Both fit in perfectly and established a deep love and respect for them. In essence, Gordy and Dick were the sons Daddy never had and the interaction was that of a father and sons, not just father and husbands of his daughters. As for Mother, she glowed every time they walked through the door. It warmed our hearts to see how much they all meant to each other, which made life even nicer.

Dick, Daddy and Gordy, cleaning up after a storm.

Gordy was a bright, handsome, blond-haired, blue-eyed quiet Lutheran Norwegian who served in the Navy. He was confirmed Catholic at St. Peter's in Rome by Pope Pius the XII during his ship's tour of duty in the early 1950s and attended Mass faithfully from that moment on. Not that he needed to be anything other than a wonderful husband to Elaine, but being converted was an added plus. When Gordy was discharged from the military and returned home to Madison, he became a highly respected builder of homes. That talent came in handy more than once through the years when Daddy needed something done that he wasn't qualified to do himself, such as building new cabinets in the kitchen, installing windows in the dining room to capture a backyard view, enclosing the old-fashioned bathtub and adding narrow closets for storage on each side, jacking up a slightly sagging front porch, removing and turning each board on the exterior of the house, and a bunch of other things that updated their lovely, but aging home on Talmadge St. Most important of all, of course, after spending memorable vacations together at Hansen's Resort, was initiating buying the property on the south shore and building Mother and Daddy's cottage, as well as his own and ours. Establishing a humble family estate on the lake was well beyond anything Daddy had ever imagined happening.

Dick was a bright, handsome, light-brown haired, blue-eyed quiet Scottish Episcopalian who flew jet fighters in the Air Force and the Air National Guard, and flew passenger jets for TWA, retiring from both the military and airlines with 25-years of service. He was not confirmed Catholic, but pretended he was and still does today when he attends Mass with me. He attended General Motors Institute of Technology, Ohio State and graduated from the University of Wisconsin-Madison.

Building was not Dick's forte. What he did build was beautifully done, but it took him much longer to complete because of the amount of patience necessary to achieve perfection. Gordy, on the other hand, was known to knock down a wall in the morning and by suppertime have a totally new look with built-in bookcases on each side of a carved wooden antique fireplace frame that Elaine had bought at an estate sale. Dick's expertise was in the air and in more than one cockpit, having to know each plane he flew like the back of his hand. His job kept him on the move much of the time either flying military or domestic and international airline routes, all of which fascinated Daddy. Being gone from home so much allowed me the pleasure of spending long periods of time at our cottage when the boys were young, with Mother and Daddy one lot away.

Our favorite stories about the two begin with Gordy who, having grown up in a calm Norwegian household suddenly found himself a member of a family who gathered for crackers and cheese and cocktails every late afternoon at the cottage about 5:30. They were fun times and, granted, we were far noisier than his family had ever been, but then...Italians are like that. One afternoon we all gathered at Mother and Daddy's place at about the same time before the supper hour and chatted and laughed and became louder by the minute before we noticed a boat and a fisherman cruising by the cottage, most likely to fish. We thought it looked just like Gordy, noticed that Gordy wasn't in the room anymore, then decided that it was Gordy after all and, we asked each other the same question, "When did he leave?" When Gordy returned about 30 minutes later, he walked in and said, "Do you people have any idea how loud it gets in here at times?" Well, no, we didn't because we were used to it. Apparently, the noise decibels had reached a level he no longer could deal with and decided to leave without telling anyone.

Daddy and Dick, having a cold beer on a hot afternoon, 1978.

Everyone knows that a pilot is expected to check the fuel tank of any vehicle before leaving home. One day, however, Dick left to fish with a half-full gas tank and no extra tank pushed under the seat, and the oars still on shore. It was a windy day and when he ran out of gas, the waves started pushing him toward the end of the peninsula. As the boat reached closer to shore, he slipped over the side of the boat thinking he could pull it along the shoreline until reaching our pier about ten lots away. Reliving another Humphrey Bogart scene from *The African Queen*, fully clothed he trudged through the water wearing tennis shoes, pushing and pulling when he suddenly found himself dangling from the side of the boat as it moved over a steep drop-off. Working through the waves and back to another spot to gain footing, he was able to pull the boat on shore and tie it to a tree before walking across the entry to the back bay and over to the shore and through the yard of a new home, before continuing through the woods to Leef Road and on to Mallard Lake Road where he turned left toward our cottage. Totally disheveled, and looking like a bum, we can only imagine what anyone thought who had passed him on the road.

The interaction with Daddy and the respect Gordy and Dick had for him created an indescribable father-son bond that remains as one of the highlights in their lives.

The Styrofoam Boat

Although the size and depth of North Sand Lake make it perfect for sailing, we never dabbled in the sport until the summer of 1967 when Gordy purchased a sailboat at a sporting goods store in Madison and hauled it *up north* for the boys to learn the basics of sailing. It wasn't a heavy sailboat made with highly polished wood, a tall mast and beautiful white sails, or a small neatly painted impression called a Sunfish, but instead, a ninety-nine dollar white 10-foot, light-weight Styrofoam wonder that clipped along the surface of the lake on a windy day like a bat out of hell. The mechanics of sailing big or small boats might be fairly similar to a certain degree; but this boat was as much like the big boys as a light single engine airplane would be to a Boeing 747. But, hey, it was a start and we were all ecstatic to think that something new had been added to our summers at the lake besides our beloved flat-bottom fishing boats that we either rowed, or maneuvered with 6 to 15 horsepower motors.

Well aware of what can happen in the middle of North Sand Lake on windy days, we insisted that navigation of the new sailboat stay well within the circle of our south shoreline and in plain view from the cottage. Unfortunately, though every precaution was taken not to disillusion the boys during their lessons, they eventually lost interest and returned to doing other things readily available and within reach despite the weather.

That may have put a damper on our expectations until something else emerged, thanks to the intuitiveness of kids. The sturdy Styrofoam boat, minus the sail, became a raft the boys balanced themselves on, standing two at a time with legs spread for balance as they rocked the raft from one side to the other, back and forth until one of them lost his balanced and jettisoned through the air and into the water as…the loser. It was a new form of competitiveness the boys took part in for hours on end, and for years that followed until one day when the boat split in half and became two rafts of different sizes that meant double the fun.

A few years later one of the raft halves split again, this time leaving a smooth heavy arrow-like portion of the front of the original sailboat that now could be tied with a rope to the back of one of our motorboats. We weren't a family of sailors or water skiers, but this new toy covered a lot of lake territory in a short period

Tom and Mike on half of the styrofoam boat, 1969.

of time as each passenger held on for dear life with their skinny legs dangling in the split wave behind them. It served much the same as colorful disks made especially for pulling behind a boat, but our old leftover piece of Styrofoam was far more endearing, just as flattened cardboard boxes had been years before if someone didn't have a sled, following a heavy snowfall.

When it was time to close the cottage each autumn, the Styrofoam rafts in their different shapes and sizes were shoved under the front porch, behind lattice panels. Worried that someone might take them during the winter months, we were always happy to find them in the same place, blanketed with dry brown oak leaves that found their way through the lattice to become trapped until spring raking took place.

One warm summer day the styrofoam halves serviced another purpose. Instead of rocking back and forth as the boys did so masterfully, Elaine and I, well into adulthood as wives and mothers, played *African Queen* by using the largest piece as a raft to enter the slough. Despite how slough is described in a dictionary, it can be a magical place that should be appreciated, but didn't exactly turn out like that on that particular day. Expecting a wet wilderness ahead, we weren't paying attention to the water levels as our journey began and half way through the shallow canal became stuck among the weeds and lily pads. Because the small oar brought to push along the way wasn't doing the job, one of us had to get off the raft to make some headway and it wasn't Elaine.

Anyone who knows us well also knows that I became Humphrey Bogart that afternoon, only because my sister, "Katherine Hepburn," couldn't fathom dipping her twinkle toes into what might be a bottom of muck and crawly creatures. We giggled as our imaginations carried us away while conjuring all kinds of morbid situations. What if we didn't return to the cottage in time for cocktail hour? Who'd fix supper? Would someone have enough sense to take the boat, check the back bay, and look to the left to see that we were helplessly stuck in the pathway to the open slough? Would I be in the water, pulling Elaine on the raft by a rope? What would we do if a bear appeared at the edge of the woods? If that happened, one thing was certain. Elaine would have to get her feet wet.

By the time we finally reached the safety of the open water, I had become a hero to my older sister and we both had a good story to share later with everyone during cocktail hour.

Sugar, Honey and Snickers

Sugar was the first dog we brought to the cottage from home. A small white poodle, she was a sweetheart who traveled well and shared the back of the station wagon with the boys. After she died, we bought another white poodle, same size but with a subtle hint of beige mixed with white. Before Honey died, Snickers crept into the picture as a little kitten that enjoyed curling up with a poodle.

Snickers was the offspring of a Corry Street affair in Madison between Michael's cat, Dusty and a tom cat that had to be big. As a kitten, Snickers had strange looking fur. How would I have know that the little kitten with the funny fur would grow into a 17 pound beauty with long beige hair, beautiful golden eyes, and measure 36 inches from the tip of his nose to the end of his plume-like tail. He was a magnificent specimen, a gentle soul for his size that did not enjoy riding in the car. And once at the lake, he never left the confines of the cottage for obvious reasons set by the family.

One day, while standing in the kitchen surveying his new cottage surroundings, Snickers found something of interest overhead and the next thing I knew he had leaped from the floor to the counter to the top of the refrigerator to the top of the single-shelf bookcase securely nailed to the wall. In it were cookbooks and a few heavy pans hidden behind gathered muslin and, underneath the shelf hung 12 pots and pans within my reach as the cottage cook. There was no more than 8-inches between the top of the bookcase and the ceiling which created an open space that Snickers chose as his throne and hiding place. Like a lion in a tree in the jungle, there he lay, 7 ½ feet off the kitchen floor, overseeing the goings on inside and whatever was visible outside through the screens and windows.

Snickers in his favorite spot.

Everyone had retired one night except Snickers who, being nocturnal, enjoyed patrolling the screened porch in the dark. Suddenly, I heard him gallop through the cottage toward our bedroom with the sound of something bouncing on the floor as he ran. He jumped on our bed and in his mouth, hooked into the roof of his mouth was a dropline hook. Trailing behind it was the leader, sinker and line wrapped around a six-inch piece of wood. Calmer than I thought an animal could be in that situation, Snickers laid himself down on the blanket and allowed me to do everything possible to move the hook back and forth, hoping to free the barb, but it was to no avail. Finally, we called a veterinarian who assured us that the cat would probably work on it himself and not to be surprised in the morning if the hook, line and sinker were no longer hanging from his mouth. If the hook was still attached, we were to bring him in for medical attention. The next morning, Snickers jumped in our bed free of the dropline that had smelled good enough to eat the night before.

Another time, Snickers required medical attention for uremic poisoning and was cared for at the Spooner Veterinarian Hospital. His weight had dropped to eight pounds and we were extremely concerned, not realizing how thin he had become due to the thickness of his fur coat. Doctors there nursed him back to good health and we were a happy family once again.

Snickers' second favorite spot—the screened porch.

Later, in Snicker's long life, on a weekend before Christmas, we boarded an American Airline flight at Chicago's O'Hare Airport to fly to Los Angeles and Universal Studios where Snickers was invited to appear on *America's Funniest Home Videos* as their little drummer cat. Star struck, Snickers had his own dressing room with a star on the door. Competing with three Cuban immigrants who tried to scare someone on Halloween, Snickers took second place for $3000 and the prestige of being shown countless times in clips of reruns.

By the way, Bob Saget loved Snickers!

So did we!

Snickers was a ripe old 17 when he died, put to sleep because of a malignant tumor the size of a small tennis ball on his shoulder that couldn't be removed. Since then, we have come to the conclusion that the big gentle giant with the purr of a motor was part Maine Coon.

The Great Sucker Mystery

I had spent most of my life summering on the lake and fishing its depths, yet never before saw a single sucker much less a shoreline full of splashers. It happened one spring morning shortly after we all had settled into our own cottages. I was outside doing yard work and every now and then I'd hear something splash. Lasting only a few seconds, another one would follow, then another, and another. While some were single splashes, others were doubles and triples. Aware of no particular rhythm to the noise, my curiosity got the best of me and I turned my attention to the base of Rubin's Hill and began to walk along the shoreline as the splashing became louder and clearer with each step.

When I reached the base of the hill, my eyes were opened to hundreds of big fish swimming and splashing in shallow water covering the rocks. For a brief second or two, I wondered if they were carp because of their robust sizes. Already aware of there being no carp in North Sand Lake, I stood and watched in great amazement. While witnessing the activity, I carefully studied each movement to absorb as much as possible of this south shoreline phenomenon. Anxious to pass it on to my family, I quickly returned to the cottage to share my discovery with Mother and Daddy at their place.

They were not the least bit surprised when I described what I had seen. In fact, they even had answers to my questions. After Daddy retired, they drove up about the first of every April to open their cottage and were well aware of what took place each early spring at the base of Rubin's Hill. They assumed that I already knew about the annual spawning of the suckers on the lake, and reminded me that North Sand Lake was carp-free.

Suckers? In our lake? I asked myself where the suckers hid the rest of the fishing season as never, not once, in all my years of fishing the shallows or depths of the lake had I ever seen, much less caught a sucker. Bowfin, aka dogfish, yes, but never a sucker.

Daddy explained to me that early spring when the suckers spawned, his local buddy Bert brought a clean galvanized garbage can to the base of the hill, filled the container to the brim with suckers and returned home with them. After they had been smoked, Bert would give Daddy some of the delicious efforts as a token of their friendship. At the coffee table, made from a door and placed against the large front windows, we'd sit together, look out on the lake, and enjoy the smoked fish, fruits of Bert's labor, stacked on crackers as evening appetizers. And then we'd wait until the following spring when the ritual began all over again for Bert and the spawning suckers.

Learning about one more miracle of nature has kept the scene fresh in my mind, yet to this day, the great sucker mystery remains as to how, after each annual spring sojourn to spawn at the base of Rubin's Hill, the suckers seem to disappear for another year…

The Weather Report

During our late July and August vacations at Hansen's Resort, we weren't privy to an entire summer season of weather conditions. Once settled on the south shoreline we were exposed to a new set of weather patterns, ones that weren't familiar. Spending Aprils through Octobers in cottages with no basements, when the skies threatened with shades of frightening purple-navy blue-black combinations and white caps on the lake looked dangerous and vicious enough to kill made us wonder, at times, if we'd ever see daylight again.

Elaine, Daddy and Gordy, 1981.

Back then, a slight breeze triggered a loss of electricity causing us to quickly move from room to room to light candles and kerosene lamps. Some storms were so scary that Mother sprinkled Holy Water in each room. One night during a storm I lifted my head from my pillow and, without glasses, wondered what I was seeing moving rapidly past the cottage. It turned out to be our Sears aluminum canoe flipping end over end like a misshapen wheel zooming down the length of the shoreline at the water's edge. Seeing a storm of such strength during the daylight hours would convince anyone that being on the lake at the time would be nothing less than a foolish gamble. If questionable skies moved in, one should immediately return to shore.

Of course, those storms always seemed to take place at night when Dick was on a trip and I was alone with the boys. We'd hide in the small pantry/store room, sit on the floor, wrap ourselves in blankets and have pillows handy to prevent fry pans or heavy dishes from falling on our heads from the shelves above. With a radio and flashlight, and a pet that didn't know what was happening, together we'd weather the storm in a tight little circle without letting them know how busy I was praying to the Blessed Mother.

After the storm, 1984.

As the boys grew older, they became "Heat Wave Burly" weather forecasters. Despite ferocious wind, rain and hail beating at the house and roof, dismantling piers, flipping boats, and downing trees, we've all been lucky…knock on wood. On Tuesday, June 8, 1993, a tornado was sighted at 3:55 p.m. near Big Sand Lake. Closer yet, a funnel cloud touched Gaslyn Lake Road as it spread out along the way, passing over Alden and Mallard Lake roads. Destroying everything in its path, it missed Jackson Town hall, but left its mark at Jackson Cemetery on Alden Road and through Voyager Village Campground. Barely skimming the west side of Green Lake, it continued across A and wound down just past Culbertson Lake off C. It had sent everyone in the immediate area to the depths of their dwellings, except for us and anyone else without a basement or storm cellar. The big question during these storms is…do we stay dry and warm hiding in the cottage store room, or should we run out to the backyard to dive deep in the overgrown swamp? Needless to say, everyone opts for protection in the store room.

Weather in *up north* Wisconsin is seldom monotonous. Seven months later, on January 19, 1994, temperatures were so cold that schools closed. Daytime temperatures hit a high of minus 14, but by evening, winds of 25 to 30 mph with a reading of 30 below zero sent wind chill temperatures to 70 below. Life was literally cancelled during that three day period as the brutality of the elements continued to fluctuate temperatures between 35 and 40 below.

Three years later, during Labor Day weekend, six inches of rain fell with wind so strong there were no waves, only sheets of water piercing the air. The paddle boat filled and overflowed, hail peppered our windows, and we all waited for the wind to sound like a train that never arrived.

Storms puzzle those of us who are admitted novices. We read in the paper about straight-line winds snapping off tree trunks like pretzels, and fickle tornadoes that skip and bounce along the way until they grow weary. We try to understand how and why it is. Just a few years ago on July 31, something else strange happened as I watched an eeriness coming from the northwest. It was 5:30 in the afternoon when I looked toward the back bay to see a sheet of solid white close off the opening to the bay. The wind picked up speed as whatever it was ripped along the shoreline through 12 lots, as large hail peppered our cottage. I ran into the storeroom and sat on a child's wooden step stool a foot off the floor and covered my head with a pillow. During those brief few minutes a roar was heard and a rumbling was felt through the stool I sat on. Seconds later, everything was silent.

After leaving the store room I looked outside and saw downed trees everywhere, some resting on porches and roofs while others were uprooted. Piers had been readjusted and heavy water equipment and rafts secured with anchors down the line were re-anchored near our pier. The neighbor's flag pole had snapped in half and his TV antenna was down. A tree rested on our front porch and a Jack Pine in the backyard was pulled out by its roots. Apparently, no one else on the lake was aware of what happened except those of us in the storm's path. The powerful storm crossed Mallard Lake Road and downed four big trees on Doug Staub's log home and property. The weather department in Duluth was notified by Nancy Jappe, an InterLeader newspaper reporter I contacted to question about the storm, but neither she nor the weather department were aware of any problems in our area. Not being educated in the field of meteorology, an innocent guess was a water spout, but recently was informed that it could have been a wall cloud and straight-line winds. Whatever it was, it was scary and very damaging.

In April of 2004, violent storms ripped through Minnesota and into Wisconsin, one tearing its way through the woods and lakes near Webb Lake, causing major damage along Dhein Road off A near Oak Lake. Closer to Thompson Road young pines were seen uprooted on a hilly, open field. When we saw the damage a week later, again we asked ourselves how the storm had been categorized. When does a straight-line wind become a tiny short-lived twister?

"Low tide" during the drought of 1978.

After the F3 tornado roared over the hill and through Siren on June 18, 2001, destroying everything in its path with winds over 200 miles per hour, we feel more vulnerable than ever before on our narrow isthmus in a cottage without a basement or storm cellar. Although the neighbors with basements have generously offered their shelters, when does one decide to run and, by that time, would we get there in time?

It's a...Cougar!

A compilation edited and printed years ago by the Burnett County Historical Society sheds a welcomed light on Jackson Township. Documented recollections shared by Lucy Dean Gatten, whose family moved to Burnett County in 1896, and those of Agnes Mickelson O'Brien, who arrived with her family in 1913 from LaCrosse County, have nourished those of us who crave local and regional history.

Weary of farming hilly terrains in an area of rivers and creeks, Mr. Mickelson selected Burnett County as his destination because of family and friends who had arrived earlier to settle in the Township of Jackson in a community called Leef. Homesteading near North Sand Lake and Agnes's accounts recorded many years later with names, dates and locations, plus life in general, painted vivid pictures of the area and helped me piece together the history of the lake and its periphery. Something that took place back in 1919 merely reinforced what I saw during the 1980s that wasn't supposed to be and no one believed.

Agnes wrote...

It was at this same school (North Sand Lake School) in 1919 I had another frightening experience. The building was located in an acre clearing in the woods with a woodshed on one side and two outdoor privies out back. These buildings each had a high wooden wall that extended round the front affording more privacy with a side opening that led to the door. One winter day, I asked permission to leave the room and journeyed down the frozen path to the little white house for girls. Since no one was about, I left the door open and, looking out, I saw what I thought was the neighbor's big Collie jump just over the brush pile at the edge of the playground. Just then I heard the most blood-curdling scream I have ever heard coming from the region of the path, and the next thing I knew, a huge lion-like cat walked past the opening of the wooden wall and not over four feet away. I was paralyzed with fright. Hearing nothing more, I slammed the door with a bang in hopes I would frighten the creatures away. Growing more confident, I opened the door and peered beyond the building corner. There, across the white expanse of a swamp, were two rows of tracks, each footprint the size of a saucer. I was told those animals were lynx that Oscar Pratt was tracking, and so I believe until years later, when I was teaching school, I read from an encyclopedia and discovered I had seen a male and female cougar.

How I wish I could have shared with Agnes my own experience that happened in 1983 as Dick and I were on our way to Webster. While still on Mallard Lake Road heading in the direction of A I looked to the right as we passed Alden Road. Had I been reading a book as I often do in the car, or blinked as we passed the road, I wouldn't have seen the cougar cross in the split of a second from one side of the road to the other about 50 or 60 feet away from my eyes. For a moment, I was speechless. I knew that I saw a big caramel-colored cat, very long in body close to the road with a long thick tail that curved slightly at the tip. It crossed Alden Road with such lightning speed that it was there and seconds later already had disappeared in the woods. If it took 50 summers to sight a bear sitting in front of our cottage eating bird feed late in the afternoon, I consider seeing a cougar off Mallard Lake Road a gift that should be considered a once-in-a-lifetime experience.

There was no question as to what I had seen, but how would I convince family members that sighting such an animal wasn't a figment of my imagination? And why is it that friends and acquaintances are more likely to believe what immediate family members don't? The rest of the way to Webster I was interrogated by my husband to the point of exasperation. Upon our return to the lake, I quickly glanced down Alden Road as we passed by, just in case...and have been doing so ever since. I knew what I saw, didn't imagine it, and that was it. It took me back immediately to our vacations at Hansen's Resort and an evening in the early 1960s when we returned well past the midnight hours from a dance at Webb Lake. We no sooner closed the door to the cottage that the shrillness of a screeching cat pierced the air with subsequent vibration around the cottage as though something running was being chased. When I read Agnes O'Brien's description of the piercing screech she heard from two cougars racing past the outhouse where she sat, the pieces began to fit snugly together.

During the 1980s, there were other random cougar sightings in the immediate area and, although the descriptions seemed credible enough for newspapers to mention in their outdoor columns, those of us who have experienced the excitement of seeing a magnificently beautiful caramel-colored cougar in the wild, for some strange reason, are still doubted.

Disappointments

Like everything else in life, there are carpet rides of happiness and roller coasters of grief. If given time, we survive the bad times even though some create enough heartbreak and disappointment to linger through the years as reminders of a time and a place.

Going fishing with Daddy, 1978.

There always was a fear that what we left in good condition wouldn't measure up when we returned in spring to open up. Would there be enough anti-freeze in the pipes to prevent them from freezing and breaking? What if a tree fell on the roof during a storm? If someone broke in, would they take a few things and leave or would they vandalize, leaving a heart-breaking mess because of their own personal problems? What if the door was left open and an animal sought shelter to create even more damage? Or worse yet, to nest until springtime? Even the thought of mice invading each room drew a picture that no one wants to be greeted with at the onset of a new year.

For starters, walleye have found a niche in front of our cottage during the winter months. We weren't prepared, however, for those who ice fished out front and cared little for our property. Cars parked in our backyard crushed many of our young pines. The Champlins in the A-frame on the Point once described our yard as resembling a winter parking lot. We learned that to blame the damage on snowmobilers was a mistake when it was due to more than a few insensitive ice fishermen.

Lack of respect veered in many directions. Some fishermen set fires close to our cottage to keep warm during cold spells. Others drank and smashed their bottles into slivers on our lawn and the mounds around our trees in front. And some used the protection provided by our side steps as their winter outhouse. When we found evidence of fires burned a few feet from the cottage, we decided we had had enough and contacted every law enforcement office in the area. When a heavy wood fence was installed at the entry from Mallard Lake Road to keep vehicles from parking in our yard, the abuse stopped. Perhaps it was also due to a concerned Constable who visited the immediate area twice each day to record license plates of cars parked nearby. We felt bad for those who weren't responsible for these despicable acts, but it was the only way to weed out problems and prevent a catastrophe from happening.

Unfortunately, two major problems occurred during that time frame. It was during the first two weeks of March 1983 that our tan 14-foot Lund 314 Sportsman 1975 fishing boat disappeared. Dick had secured it along the side of the cottage on a trailer without tires and chained it to a tree. Heavy tire tracks showed that a large vehicle backed up to the trailer and boat and hauled both away after the snow melted.

When the Constable called either New Year's Day or the day after in 1984, we knew something else had happened and learned that our cottage had been entered. The next day we drove *up north* to see what was taken. Items had been piled in the middle of each bedspread and hauled out like huge over-the-shoulder duffle bags, some dropped and left in the snowy service road behind us while others found their way elsewhere. Mother and Daddy's cottage was also broken into as was my sister's place next door. Left on the service road in the snow was Mother's sewing machine. A few feet away was one of my bedspreads filled with a new set of pots and pans along with other items. Missing, unfortunately, was a beautiful light blue quilt with tiny white flowers, trimmed with white crocheted lace that I had made the summer before.

Also missing was a rifle and power tools, kerosene lamps and, worst of all, my tackle box. The metal *My Buddy* box from Montgomery Wards that Daddy gave to me on my 13th birthday was filled with old lures, the dropline he made for me and other items reflecting 30-plus years of fishing together. Also missing was the rod and red West Bend reel he gave to me for the same birthday. All had been my prized possessions. I cried and wondered if they had been dropped along the way and were buried in the snow, not to be found until spring by someone else. I wondered who would be using them when fishing season opened that spring, or who they might be sold to. For years we thought we were safe from break-ins because of the proximity of our property to the road. We had been wrong.

I had trouble coming to terms with the break-in, what I lost and the insensitivity of those responsible. For years, while driving through the area, whether on my way to town or elsewhere, I'd peer through yards at everyone's laundry hanging on outside lines, hoping to see my quilt and wondered at the same time what I'd do if I did. I was never confronted with having to make that decision. Life went on. We survived each episode, but pain and disappointment in what had happened and what I lost still remains today.

A few years ago, during a conversation with a shoreline friend about the break-in, I noticed his expression change immediately as he told me about something he remembered happening that same evening. He described the weather that night as being well below zero and brutally cold. He and his wife had enjoyed a New Year's Eve gathering with friends and decided to return home shortly after midnight. About 12:30 a.m., while passing our place just off Mallard Lake Road, the couple noticed two very inebriated men wearing shirts, but no jackets, standing alongside the road directly behind our cottages. Not wanting them to get into the car with his wife present, but fearful they could not survive the sub zero temperatures in their condition, he quickly drove his wife home and returned within minutes to find them gone, leaving only footprints in the snow leading onto Mallard Lake. He drove around for a short time in search of the men, then gave up and returned home.

Another mystery, somewhat solved, but probably never, totally.

Virginia Miller

During the early days of the Labor Day Voyager Villager Craft Fair held in the field next to their stables on A, a decision was made one summer to apply for space to sell historical cookbooks I had written and published about the old Italian Greenbush neighborhood in Madison, WI. Being accepted by their panel of judges, I looked forward to exposing my work to others in an area removed from gift and book stores. It turned out to be a dry hot weekend without a breeze as I sat in the sun with thoughts about the coolness of the lake back at the cottage. While sitting there, a woman stopped by to page through my books. Before long, Virginia Miller and I were engaged in conversation about Italians, their gardens, cucuzza (squash) and favorite recipes before moving on to express our appreciation for our immediate area and the passion we shared for our summer cottages. The following March, Virginia wrote from her winter home in Cincinnati, Ohio to thank me for the cucuzza seeds I had forwarded for her spring garden planting. Although, at that time, I had no inkling of someday compiling a book about North Sand Lake and my experiences that began there in 1945, her letter was so interesting that I saved it.

March 4, 1991

Dear Catherine,

Coincidences seem not to end. The summer of 1945 was my first in the Jackson Township area of Burnett County. That spring I had finished my freshman year at Ohio State University. I worked for a time at a small furniture factory in St. Marys, Ohio, near my father's farm. One day my fingers were caught up in a drill press in the process of making army cots. I was off work for a time during the healing process. When I could have gone back to work the factory was cutting back production since WW II was winding down.

The girl I roomed with at OSU called me one day to ask if I would like to go along with her and her parents to spend two weeks with her aunt and uncle at a lake in northern Wisconsin. Having nothing else to do, I said I would go. What a trip! Her father, who owned a garage in the small town where they lived, had just put new rings in his car. In those day that meant a new break-in period for the engine. We traveled 700 miles at a maximum speed of 35 MPH. And, of course, after you left Spooner it was all sand roads.

Betty's Aunt and Uncle, Charles and Mae Wren, had an old house, a small cabin and a bigger cabin on a lake early known as Middle Loon Lake, later as Myre Lake, and again today on the Platt Map as Middle Loon Lake. They had gotten the property for back taxes during the 1930s. It is off County Highway C and down a trail about one-half mile long. If I had thought that growing up on a small farm was remote it was nothing compared to the isolation of Myre Lake! Somehow I lasted two weeks.

In January 1946 my husband-to-be (Charles) was back from the army. He went to school that next summer to catch up with me. In the spring of 1947 we were married. We both worked that summer to augment the fabulous $105.00 per month married veteran student allotment we would be receiving.

We went to school in the summer of 1948 and graduated at the end of the term. In the fall I got a job teaching Home Economics in a small town east of Columbus, Ohio. Charles enrolled in graduate school with a teaching assistantship and finished his M.A. degree in psychology that year. We had thought of living in Columbus and having me commute to my job. It turned out the man who was executive head of the school where I was to teach took a job in an army school in Germany. He offered to let us rent the house where he was living in Summit Station, OH, using his furniture to save him the cost of storage, for $35.00 per month. What a deal! So Charles commuted to OSU in the 1935 Dodge we had bought from his grandmother's estate and I walked to work, probably about four blocks.

At the end of the school year Charles had his M.A. Degree and a certificate as a school Psychologist, but no job. We decided we wanted to vacation for a week, job or no job, broke or not. I would have liked to travel through the southern states, but it was so hot that summer that we decided against that trip. Instead I contacted Mrs. Wren and she told me that we could rent the small cabin at Myre Lake for a week. We have gone to Burnett County every year since then.

After our second summer vacation at Myre Lake we began talking about how nice it would be to have a place of our own. During our vacation in 1951 we began looking around and in 1953 we decided on a lot on Des Moines Lake in Webb Lake Township. The next few summers our vacation time, one, two, and one summer three weeks, was spent building our place. With my brother's help, Charles and I built it ourselves. None of us knew anything about building. We did it by the book. At some critical points we had help from fabulous friends. Col. W. A. Lewis, U.S. Army, Ret., whom we had known at Myre Lake and who built a home for himself on North Sand Lake off Leef Road gave us help with establishing the pitch of the roof. Also, later in the building process, he installed the electrical wiring without charge. Two brothers we had met who were originally from northwestern Indiana helped us shingle at the roof. For the first few years we had roll roofing. That cost us one roast beef dinner that I fixed and a few cans of beer. They also installed the plumbing for an almost unbelievable charge. Another man, Roy Radke, a farmer who lived on A towards the Lone Pine Tavern (now the Crow Bar) laid the blocks for the basement in about 12 hours at $1.50 per hour! Charles, my brother and I helped. I screened the sand and mixed the mortar. He later put up our chimney for the same rate! So many wonderful people!

Do you remember the little cabin that was east of Hansen's Resort and just east of Kilkare Road on A? A few years ago it was moved from there and onto the property of Voyager Enterprises where it sits so forlornly. A new home was built on the property after considerable grading and filling. Mr. And Mrs. Wren had owned that little cabin. We stayed in that cabin a number of times over the years. One year we stayed in Mrs. Wren's Sand Lake cabin for one week and then, because she had promised some other people that cabin for the following week, we found that Barney Hansen had a vacancy so we moved over there. The following week we went to Myre Lake. There are several stories to be told about those three weeks!

We know, and have known, a number of people around Sand Lake. Robert Grindell, an attorney from Frederic, has a place near where Col. Lewis lived. We have used his services a couple of times relative to property. Dick Pierce has had a place for many years on the east side of the lake. Last year he bought Lakeview Inn (formerly the Brown Jug). Before retirement he worked for and with Mr. And Mrs. Wren's son, Cameron, in Elgin, IL! There are other people around the lake who we know but enough of that for now.

In January, when we stayed at Tommy Bachman's cabin at the Sand Bar, Vi Moser, who owns the Voyager Superette across the road, told me that that cabin had been Hansen's Number 10. It is a nice cabin but does have some peculiarities not uncommon in hastily constructed resort cabins.

Thank you for forwarding the cucuzza seed and Mr. Capacio's letter. Between your two letters in February, we saw an ad from a local discount department store advertising a pre-season sale on garden seeds. Charles says that with me that is analogous to ringing a fire bell in front of a veteran fire horse! Imagine my surprise when among the seeds I found a squash called cucuzzi. The picture on the packet looks very similar to the picture in your cookbook, Volume II, page 207. I suspect that the difference in spelling of the final letter "a" in one and "i" in the other many be another difference in dialect, but will await your hypothesis or explanation. Thanks for your help.

We undoubtedly drove past your place on Sand Lake when we were there in January. Rather late one afternoon we drove back to Mallard Lake Resort. Charles had to collect his winnings from Carl Hanson's football board. We talked to Carl for a time and then a man we know from Des Moines Lake came in and so we talked some more. Even though it was just past five o'clock it was, as I'm sure you know, already dark. We intended going down (up Thompson Road to Lakeview Inn for dinner, but at a juncture turned left instead of right. In a little while we found ourselves on Leef Road rather than Thompson Road. The map tells us we were on the road past your place.

We should indeed try to talk next summer. Another coincidence: We, too, are on an isthmus, between Des Moines Lake and Long Lake on Arbutus Drive.

Sincerely,

Virginia

Mallard Lake Connection

I first met Mrs. Frank Preiner about 25 years ago when she was visiting Mother and Daddy at their cottage. Mrs. Preiner admired Daddy's flowers in both front and backyards of the cottage, but was especially fond of the brilliant pink creeping phlox that blanketed mounds surrounding each tree during springtime and spread across our family's four lakefront lots. In his typical generous manner, Daddy offered to dig up many of the perennial phlox and that day packed them in cardboard boxes for her to duplicate the same colorful profusion along her Mallard Lake shoreline property.

Mrs. Preiner was a member of the Dietrich family who homesteaded the south end of Mallard Lake back in the early 1920s. That day she shared with me stories of the Chippewa and Sioux tribes and how the Sioux were forced to move away from the immediate area that we enjoy during the summer months. Left behind with the battleground were mounds and arrowheads, Indian relics, bones and skulls. Surrounding one mound were 200 stones, each one representing the number of Indians supposedly buried below. Her childhood friends were children of the Indians who lived along the periphery of Mallard Lake and, as a result, she grew up fluently speaking their language.

The Dietrich homestead on Mallard Lake.

And, when their seasonal shoreline evening gatherings roared with bonfires, and culture was being preserved with their native music and dance of ceremonials, she was welcomed as one of the tribe. Although the intriguing beat of drums from other camps were often carried with breezes to Mallard Lake, she remembers, as a youngster, taking it for granted as a way of life for her and her family. To others who understood the rhythm of words, the breezes carried messages in the silence of the night.

John A. and Elsie Dietrich had moved often. When they farmed in Minnesota and owned a furniture store in Superior, the store closed each summer so the family could drive directly south to Mallard Lake in Burnett County. Property during that time cost very little. Many wealthy landowners sold their farms and came to Burnett County to make another fortune. Unfortunately, when the Dietrich's arrived, they would also discover how different the soil was from that on their farm and, before long, what fertility remained under the surface of the soil was quickly exhausted and everything was lost. Elsie surprised everyone by purchasing 144 acres of land on Mallard Lake. She and her husband homesteaded the area with the farm house completed in 1924 on a hill overlooking the entire lake from the south. In 1927, a porch was added. Instead of growing corn or other regional crops, John became a strawberry farmer and added a few cattle for good measure.

The Dietrich's were blessed with seven children. In 1902, Frances became their first born. Richard was next, followed by John, Jr., Violet, Jack, Bill and Elsie who was known by everyone as "Bobbie." Frank Preiner married Bobbie and they had two daughters, Valli and Fran. Valli Preiner Sauer and her husband, Ted, today own the original Dietrich farm house.

Property on Mallard Lake sold for $500 per lot, probably much the same as lots on many other quality area lakes. A deep spot in the lake was referred to as "musky hole" because of the musky caught from its depths. It is believed that the Indians who lived nearby fished out the musky. Although musky never again inhabited the lake, proof of this bygone era are pictures found in Dietrich photo albums of family members who were fortunate to hook the monster fish and even more fortunate to land them.

John and Elsie Dietrich were concerned about the long distance between their house and the small one-room school the children attended on Gaslyn Road. To shorten the trip, John cleared a path through the woods from his farm to the school and the narrow two-rut road continued to serve his children during the 1920s and into the 1930s. Although private, with room for only one vehicle at a time, the handy short cut was discovered years later and locals, as well as vacationers, began using it to trim miles from their own trips. In the spring of 1973, the Preiner family arrived to open one of their seasonal dwellings and discovered that Grandpa's private short-cut, two-rut road was widened to accommodate more vehicles and connect with Gaslyn Road. When a county employee was asked why this was done without notifying the family, John was told that the private Dietrich-Preiner family road had been used by others for a length of 40 years, thus making it...public property. The unpaved road that still connects Gaslyn Road today is referred to by our family as the "dirt road," while others call it "short cut road" or "cut across road."

The lush wooded land that surrounds us today looked much different after the turn of the century. Logging camps finished their work and moved on leaving behind virtually treeless land. Mallard Lake was no exception, except when lake levels rose for any length of time, Mallard and North Sand lakes became one. When the water drastically receded, it took on the appearance of a giant sand beach, which, most likely, is the reason why Mallard Lake is referred to on the 1915 county plat map as Sand Beach Lake.

Other roads in the immediate vicinity of North Sand and Mallard lakes bear names of farmers who came and settled there when land was offered by the government for small amounts of money. After the Depression, some were forced to sell their land back to the county to pay back taxes. Today's paved strip of Mallard Lake Road that connects Thompson and Leef roads disappeared many times in the past from high water levels. Valli Preiner Sauer remembers driving the route with her family when water came up to the bottom of the car door. If the car wasn't carefully steered, the driver would find himself and his passengers in the lake.

Low land near a portion of the property owned by Richard and Madaleine Lambert that extended from North Sand Lake to Mallard Lake also was submerged when lake levels rose. When the isthmus, or narrow strip of land between the lakes was filled in, making it suitable to build summer cottages, Bobbie Preiner was concerned. She remembered her childhood when lake levels rose and how she and her brothers and sisters used to walk in shallow water connecting the two lakes. When the water rose even higher, they would pile in their boat and row back and forth. Yet, for those who yearned to have property on North Sand Lake, complete with a nice sandy beach, the property was very appealing and what it used to be in years past was overlooked. Actually, it was doubtful that any prospective buyer, including us, was made aware of this. A near half-century later, the man-made foundation of filled land remains solid and safe.

Other stories passed on by family members or heard during conversations include tales shared by Valli's aunt who worked as a waitress at the Five Oaks Resort on Oak Lake. Mobsters from Chicago frequented the resort and restaurant and celebrated their illegal financial status by lighting cigars with $100 dollar bills. Al Capone was a familiar name and face in the vastness of Burnett and adjoining counties and in the woods near Couderay at his hideout. John Dillinger stayed in a cabin in the woods on Des Moines Lake near Roamer's Inn on Long Lake Road. And there were others. It was the Roaring Twenties and life here, at times, hinted of what was happening every night in the big cities that Prohibition molded into a never-to-be forgotten era.

John A. and Elsie Dietrich played an integral role in the development of the land that oftentimes connected with North Sand Lake. Instrumental in the development of Mallard Lake Resort, John would be in awe today of the resort and campground well in view from the hill they homesteaded back in the 1920s, and of the seasonal water activity it creates on any given day. The days when Indians camped along the lakeshore and sat before shoreline bonfires with their families to practice and preserve their culture and heritage are memories of times that will never return.

Note: *John and Elsie's son, Bill, 86, wrote many books about the Indians in the Mallard Lake area and those they were preceded by. At the time of this interview on October 21, 2000, the Dietrich's surviving children were John, Jr., Fran, 95, and Viola, 94.*

Celebrations

Without verbal commitment, spur of the minute or planned, simple or elaborate, life at the cottage was to be celebrated. Whether a birthday, love and marriage, children, a 25th or 50th wedding anniversary, holidays, the new generation, having company, a great catch of bluegills, a huge northern, a Great Blue Heron standing on the pier in the morning, a magnificent bald eagle soaring overhead, or sunrises, rainbows and sunsets, there was something special attached to each with a feeling of being blessed.

The beauty was in recognizing, appreciating and celebrating the moment. A kiss, a hug, cake with candles, key lime pie, toasted marshmallows, firecrackers, champagne with dinner, beer and hamburgers, wine and spaghetti, a simple hot dog, the first blossoms of spring, red tomatoes in August, purple grapes in September or pulling into the driveway after driving 300 miles from home. The bottom line was that we were lucky to be where we were and be together.

In 1979, Mother and Daddy would celebrate their 50th anniversary and plans were made for them to spend a few days in Duluth. Just the thought of leaving the cottage to spend a few nights elsewhere was a major accomplishment as they weren't fond of dismantling their daily schedules. Yet, on June 26, the date they exchanged vows in 1929, suitcases were packed with enthusiasm and at 7:30 in the morning they headed north on Hwy. 35 for a memorable out-of-town celebration that would begin at the Radisson Hotel in Room 1214 at $39.50 per night. They shopped that afternoon and stopped at a jewelry store where Daddy bought Mother a gold charm bracelet and a gold charm. That evening, they ate at the hotel's Top of the Harbor revolving restaurant offering fine dining and a spectacular view of Duluth and Lake Superior.

Our reservations were for 8:30 p.m. The view was breathtaking and it was almost like being up in a plane. We had champagne ($12.50) and lobster tail ($12.50) and a surprise cake beautifully decorated. After dinner we went downstairs to the Whale Back Lounge for an after dinner drink. The orchestra played our favorite song (Sweet Georgia Brown) and they announced our 50th year over the microphone. Offered to buy us a drink, but we gracefully turned them down. Too much for one evening.

After breakfast the following day, they shopped more, did some sightseeing, and boarded the Vista Cruise excursion boat in the afternoon to tour the Duluth Harbor. Mother writes in her diary of how shocked she was at the size of the ore, grain and cement ships and mentioned seeing in a distance trucks being loaded at Jeno's Pizza Factory. Before heading back to the hotel they stopped at the jewelry store to pick up the bracelet and charm that had been engraved with their 50th anniversary date. After returning to their room, they rested and cleaned up before stopping at the hotel's lounge bar for a drink and appetizers before walking a short distance to the Chinese Lantern Restaurant (which has since burned down).

Thrilled with everything they managed to do in two days, Mother kept track of what they spent which included gas, hotel, meals, gifts, boat trip ($8.00), even two ice cream cones and the bell hop tip, for a grand total of $114.70. You would have thought someone had given them the moon.

At 10:30 in the morning of June 28, they checked out of their room and headed back to Webster and the cottage where we waited to greet them with a 50th anniversary poster taped to the side door. The next day, everything was back to normal. Daddy fished, then spent time working in the strawberry patch and Elaine and I had coffee with Mother on their patio. According to Mother's diary, by June 29th Daddy had caught and cleaned 333 bluegills for the year.

Getting ready to leave for the party: Elaine, Mother, Daddy and me.

On June 30th plans for a 50th anniversary celebration with the family were finalized at Voyager Village Country Club. Shirley, the club hostess, took great care to make sure everything was handled according to Mother's wishes and we all had a wonderful time.

Mother and Daddy at Voyager Village, June 30, 1979.

It was so fabulous. Manager presented us with a beautifully decorated anniversary cake. Can't say enough about how delicious the food and everything was. Passed pieces of cake around to waitresses, the cook, manager and his wife, etc. Everybody so pleased. A wonderful time. Had champagne. Dick took pictures. Mike got cake frosting all over his sport jacket carrying the cake to the car. What a laugh we had. Wonderful, wonderful anniversary week. So happy about it all. Perfect weather.

June had been a busy month. Besides this milestone in Mother and Daddy's life together, Tom celebrated his 20th birthday June 10, Dick celebrated his 46th birthday June 12, and on June 30th Dick and I celebrated our 17th wedding anniversary. By October 12, Daddy had caught and cleaned 2227 pan fish. October 18, they closed up and headed for home.

Above: Elaine and Gordy celebrating their 25th anniversary, July 9, 1980.

Right: A special moment with Dick.

5:30 cocktails and celebrating life at the cottage, together.

l-r, Dick, Mother, Daddy, Elaine, Gordy and me.

Coffee on the patio with Mother, Sugar, and Daddy.

Our up north domain — worth celebrating.

Fish Galore

Michael, Daddy and Tom, 1967

Countless scrapbooks include pictures of exciting catches along our south shoreline area. If fish weren't biting in a handful of places out in front of the cottages, Daddy seldom rowed or motored beyond either east or west points in view from our piers because something would be biting within that radius. It was just a matter of being patient, of which Daddy was a diligent master.

Daddy and Bob with an early morning northern, 1978.

Fishing was just one of many things that made owning property on the lake as special as it was, yet fishing was the undeniable factor in what kept the adrenalin flowing every day in all kinds of weather. Because Daddy was a happy individual with a great outlook on life, he never expressed an interest in state-of-the-art fishing equipment. Instead, he was perfectly happy with a bamboo pole, a dropline, and an old-fashioned rod and reel. All three did a fine job, thank you, as did rowing or using his white Johnson 6 hp motor.

Seldom did he use chubs or minnows, opting instead for simple things like meaty night crawlers divided in segments, carefully pushing a hook through the length of its innards to entice panfish with a bamboo pole or dropline. I sat across from him so many times in my life that I can picture his hands and the methods he used as easily as having watched mere moments ago. His favorite northern pike bait was a bluegill hooked across the top and thrown out to still-fish with a bobber. Never did I see him stand at the end of the pier with a spinning rod and reel to cast incessantly with minnows. He had everything he was comfortable in doing down to a science, never wanted anything more, and that's the way it was.

Bill's 4½ pound bass, 1978.

Bob and Daddy, 1975.

All the fish he caught were either shared with others or consumed by Mother and Daddy or the rest of the family, or given to extended family or to good friends back home. Never did he keep anything beyond the daily limit and never did he use any parts of the fish as fertilizer for fear that animals would investigate gardens during the nighttime hours. In fact, leftovers were carefully wrapped in layers of newspaper and kept in the garage in a garbage can tightly secured with a top until it was time for his weekly trip to the dump off Alden Road. On hot days, the garage grew nauseatingly fragrant even though it was opened and aired from daybreak to about nine o'clock each night. If the wind blew in our direction, it had the power to take your breath away, but then that was just a part of being *up north*. Previous visits from raccoons that made massive messes prevented any straying from his convictions. He felt that it was best to be more safe than sorry and he was right.

Daddy's 10 pound northern, 1981.

Bill, 1976.

These pictures capture just a fragment of many exciting catches with the simplicity of hook, line and sinker, sometimes with a bobber and, oftentimes, the landing net resting at the end of the pier that he carefully maneuvered with the other hand.

Tom, 1970.

Visitors

Mother and Daddy didn't often entertain friends from home, but when they did, they were very proud to welcome work related, club and social friends for coffee, beer, dinner and occasional overnight accommodations. Most people never understood why anyone would want to travel so many miles from home to settle on a lake that took at least 4 ½ hours to reach. Once they arrived, they knew why.

Daddy, Mother, and Daddy's brother Joe, 1980.

One who always understood was Daddy's brother, Joe. If you recall, Joe was the person who first visited the lake with a bunch of fishing buddies from Madison at the onset of the 1945 fishing season. Although the group stayed at Thompson's Resort along the southeast shoreline, Joe noticed the newly opened Hansen's Resort with their four unpainted pine cottages on the north shoreline and thought it would be a perfect place for Daddy and the rest of us to investigate. We did and, as they say, the rest is history.

Life on the south shore opened many opportunities. Elaine and I had our own cottages, had visitors of our own, and Mother and Daddy's two bedroom cottage became ample enough to welcome another couple. Uncle Joe and his wife, Mary, visited Mother and Daddy a few times each summer merely reinforcing every reason why the long trip was well worth the miles.

Through the years that followed, my family grew and our own three-bedroom cottage that once seemed so spacious suddenly wasn't big enough to comfortably fit everyone. With marriages and grandchildren and great-grandchildren, we burst at the seams. The important thing is being together, just as it was years ago and hopefully will always be in the years ahead.

Uncle Joe and wife, Mary, 1980.

The Gang's All Here!

This is what we all look like today. When the family visits, the previously ample three-bedroom cottage shrinks in size. No longer able to find corners for everyone and their sleeping bags, we watch as the backyard quickly sprouts with cozy tents and then we all keep our fingers crossed that the weather will cooperate the entire time. Otherwise, knock on wood, some may have to sleep in the garage on a cement floor.

Our sons, now in their 40s, still play basketball with the same intensity, but in a different location. For years, the backboard was nailed to Jack Pine trees at the side of the cottage. With sand under foot, hard fought games were played barefoot and when the game ended, everyone raced for the lake to cool off. A few years ago, when pileated woodpeckers began to feast on the trees, they left little or nothing behind but cavernous holes and piles of wood chips. The trees were cut down and the backboard was moved to the other side of the cottage and nailed to the back of the fish house. With a few initial games, the little grass that grows underfoot will eventually turn into soft sand like before making it easier for older bare feet.

Through the years, most everyone has taken giant steps to polish their skills as temporary North Sand Lake anglers. While they all mastered the droplines that Daddy made for them years ago, someone each year seems to dazzle us with a new plug that brings out a little envy in those of us who are still using old-fashion artificial bait. Grandson Jordan was the winner this year with a white "rattler." With the sound of tiny BBs, the action was exciting and now, of course, we all want rattlers in our own tackle boxes. I have the new invisible line that appears to be yellow out of the water, yet becomes invisible while fishing. I haven't used it yet, but maybe when I do, I'll be envied, too.

Cleaning fish is an "iffy" job for everyone but Dick and Bill who enjoy the camaraderie in the fish house and competition of who ends up with the best looking fillets. Mike had some heavy duty cleaning to do during the family's late June visit this year because the fish were biting on everything. Bill caught 180 bluegills one day (threw all but 25 back) and said they all seemed to be at the surface of the water, something he had never seen before. Bob doesn't get to clean fish often, but if he did I know he'd be a perfectionist. Now and then I help out, but usually leave the cleaning to Dick and the boys. Besides, I haven't had time for things like that since 1994 when I started this book. Maybe now I can return to my own fishing holes by rowing and trolling and enjoying everything around me.

When the gang comes at the same time it seems that I spend a lot of time at the kitchen sink. A few years ago I decided to place a TV tray in the kitchen with paper plates, bowls and cups and an empty can filled with plastic eating utensils. Why didn't I think of that before?

At about 9 o'clock, we pull out the games. Hearts, Pit and Michigan Rummy are three of the favorites played, of course, with popcorn and pop on the side. Other nights, we gather around a bonfire to make S'mores or just toast marshmallows to a golden brown. When Dick and I are alone, I spend an evening hour playing Solitaire on the screened porch while he reads or watches television. Songs from the swamp and loons on the lake serenade us to sleep and, in the morning, we wake up early to the fascinating language of the crows.

Although things have changed through the years, they really haven't. We may get older and wiser, but cottage life remains the same. We think of the past when we established ourselves on the north shore as resort guests, then the south shore as property owners and reminisce about when the boys were little, and now laugh at their shenanigans. We share fishing stories about all the big ones Daddy caught off the pier before moving on to those that got away, and remember Mother's old-fashion oatmeal in the morning, key lime pies early afternoon, and fish fries for supper. We think about our long walks on Mallard Lake Road in the pitch blackness of night and how we wondered what might lurk beyond the edge of the road and of the crackling noises we'd hear from the woods. One dark evening something big and white ran from the woods and across the road in front of us to send everyone running in all directions. A ghost? Only the Shadow knows.

We talk about Mother and Daddy and the fun we had together through the years and how lucky we are for what we had then and still have today and agree the only difference from days gone during each moment at the cottage on North Sand Lake…is their absence and how much they are missed.

The Scrapbook

Front: l-r, Shawn, Mike, Baby Jordan and Bob.

Back: Tom, Dick and Bill, August 1986.

Below: Four generations: Mother, Michael, Baby Jordan, me and Daddy, 1986.

Devin, Jordan, and some nice crappies, 2000.

Tom, me and Bob, 2000.

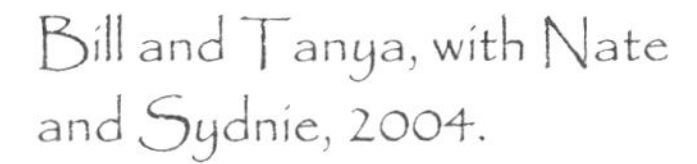

Bill and Tanya, with Nate and Sydnie, 2004.

Debbie, Devin, Jordan and Michael, 2000.

Shawn, Becky and Halle, 2000.

Kacie and Nate, 2004.

In a Nutshell

About to complete this book, I came across something from my own diary. Like Mother, my experiences at the cottage were recorded every evening. This entry sheds light on a spring day in 1984.

May 29, 1984

I woke up this morning to a spectacular north woods sunrise on the lake. Once again, it is time to open the cottage for the summer. The ice took huge bites from the shoreline which caused the concrete blocks to buckle leaving spaces and scalloped edges to our lawn. We've never seen the water this high and the swamp in back looks more like the slough. One could canoe through it. The mosquito population should be nothing less than a nightmare.

The high water levels mean that the pier sections have to be readjusted before a final placement. Because the concrete blocks that make up a narrow sidewalk from the cottage to the water are also buckled from the ice, carrying pier parts from their storage place will be little more difficult than usual. All of this must be done before we leave for home because the next time we come up there will be other jobs to do. There's always something waiting, unexpected or otherwise.

Daddy and Dick are trying to locate the cement blocks that for so many years protected the sod from waves. As I watch, they have spotted another corner of a block and are removing it from its burial place under the water and deep in the sand. When all of this is done, they'll re-position each one again, against the pitch to the grass to prevent what's underneath from being washed out by high waves.

Back in the swamp, with what must be a huge gathering of frogs, deep-throated sounds of a chorus, not necessarily in unison, vibrates with each note. Some of the tree roots back there have been loosened due to the water level causing their trunks to lean precariously toward the service road. A soon-to-be mother Mallard duck has been swimming back and forth with a drake through a film of fuzz blown down here from the cottonwood trees near the Desert. This spring there is a wide path through the poplars that was carved out of the woods by a telephone company in preparation for lines that will bring service to new lake residents. The changes make me uncomfortable as I loved it as it was. I can accept changes caused by nature, but resent changes due to progress. The long strip cut to provide access for the wires looks like a huge scar trying to heal following surgery. It is so obvious and painful to see.

I'm wondering if high water killed the Jack Pine in the back, or if it is an example of winter kill. Its needles are brown to match the old cones still hanging from last year. The pussy willow tree next to it looks sick, too, except for new young shoots at its base.

Out in front is a blaze of pink as the creeping phlox are in their glory. May is their month to show off and the high water levels must have nourished it like a magic potion.

This year the phlox are slightly interspersed with a chartreuse blossom that we are not familiar with. When the succulent looking stems are snapped, each is filled with a bitter, milky-white juice. Actually, each plant with its color and bright green lacey leaves appears like a runner, but we'll have to wait and see if it will affect the phlox that carpet the area around each tree. They did add some beauty to our arrival so we must give them a chance. When we aren't here, Mother and Daddy make sure the phlox are watered every morning.

After all the shutters are removed from the windows and the screens replaced on the porch, pier sections will be carried out and secured. Glad I don't have to help. With all the activity, the chickadees are busy chattering their greetings. This is all a part of the precious world at the cottage that I hope I can enjoy for another 38 years. Let's see...that will make me 88. Wonder if I'll last that long. Daddy will be 80 in December and he's still raking, pruning, mowing, and weeding to reap the rewards of each new year of our heaven on earth. Mother will be 76 in November. She is watching over him more each year to make sure he doesn't overdue the chores outdoors that he enjoys so much such as mowing our yards to make sure they are perfect when we arrive.

And, there it was...in a nutshell...an ever so slight repetition with each new season. While Daddy continued to rise early each morning to begin the day by turning on the hose and watering the phlox he methodically planted years before on the mounds around each tree, Mother's day began with maternal thoughts as an overseer. While the tiniest of weeds that violated his carefully tended garden overnight were being removed, Mother made breakfast. Deep pink phlox ablaze with color and precious purple velvet faces of violas peeking through patches of grass were just the beginnings of mere hints of spring's awakening.

Each new year came equipped with surprises and downfalls, the uppers and downers that erase monotony in any place considered to be perfect in every way. As the boys grew, so did cottage life expand. Spring presented its usual wonder of surprises before summer began with its laid back attitude and open arms to remind us it was time to relax before autumn, beautiful autumn, hinted that the good times were about to end for another year. What followed with winter was concern about the property in our absence until the following April, when a page was turned and a new chapter began.

As we rode each wave from one year to the next, we realized even more how lucky we were to be there together. Someday, my own volumes of diaries will remind the boys of the magnitude of having our own places, side by side, summer after summer, with Mother and Daddy, their Grandma and Grandpa, to care for things until we returned.

Innocently established, our place on the lake and everything that surrounded us had become a father's legacy.

Mother, the ever-dedicated photographer, captures a moment of fun for me, Dick, Daddy, Elaine and Gordy, 1986.

Mother and Daddy with Dick,who commuted during the summer months from the cottage to his TWA domicile in St. Louis.

Part VII

June 29, 1987 – Mother and Daddy celebrate their 59th wedding anniversary at the cottage.

During the summer of 1987, they decided it was time to sell. The following spring they packed with reservation and headed north to make final plans that Daddy would announce to us June 5th. Sixteen days later, he changed his mind. We had spaghetti and meatballs that night for supper and later settled on the patio for coffee. We listened to him sing "When Day is Done" to Mother, and watched them jitterbug to my Fats Waller music. It was just like old times with another summer together.

Summer Legacy

Twilight

Daddy always walked fast. Even in retirement. If his pace somewhat slowed at the cottage, or came to a standstill, he was either sitting in the boat fishing or, after yard or shoreline work, he'd relax in a lawn chair out front with a cold beer. To watch him gaze out at what surrounded him was motionless poetry of a man completely satisfied with what he possessed. There were no wishes or hopes for something bigger or better the next day or next year. He never thought in those terms. This was a man who never had a garage back home. For 42 years, during the coldest and snowiest of winter days, he'd go out to his car parked at the curb in front of the house, turn on the engine and go back inside while it warmed up for about five minutes after which he'd leave again, this time to settle behind the steering wheel, shift gears, and drive to work a few miles away. He never returned home with a single complaint as to how the morning began for him. What he possessed in retirement was the ultimate reward with no added wishes. It all centered around family and the cottage *up north*

His incredible attitude about life in general made everything reach a notch or two above the rest for us. He loved his "little girls," and his grandsons, Mike, Bill, Bob and Tom. Gordy and Dick were the sons he never had and the respect and love they had for each other was especially heart-warming. All three were always willing and anxious to help each other with any chore or need that surfaced. And, although we knew that someday in the all too near future things would begin to change for Mother and Daddy, we erased the thought from our minds because it seemed impossible to prepare ourselves for anything less than what we experienced when we were all together.

Mother was more realistic and concerned than the rest of us. They were devoted to each other and being with him 24 hours a day allowed her to observe things like momentary dizziness during hot weather spells when he continued to keep up the same pace fishing, gardening and doing other outdoor jobs he enjoyed. When we weren't at the lake with them, she'd wonder what she would do if something happened to him while fishing. Although he was an excellent swimmer, and had a boat cushion in the boat at all times, he never wore a life jacket. With Mother on shore, how would she be able to rescue him? What if some unexpected medical problems occurred when they were so far from home? What if she had to drive him to Spooner during the day or night? Would she be able to handle life-threatening situations? It was natural that these and other fears crept into her mind to simmer on a daily basis. During the summer of 1987, they came to terms that it might be their last summer on North Sand Lake.

Needless to say, we were devastated. Elaine and Gordy had sold their place years before, so it wouldn't affect them. The cottage meant everything to me and being there without Mother and Daddy made me wonder if I would be able to cope with their absence. I had no qualms about being there with just my own family, but already knew it would never be the same without them. Both were the lake in front, the fish in its depths, the choir of frogs from the swamp, each sunrise and sunset, the stars above, the Northern lights, the call of the loon, and everything else from the rain that fell, breezes from all directions, waves tipped with white froth and the unmistakable overall beauty of the north woods that surrounded us. Could I cope? What would it be like for them? Every single day of his life Daddy thought about the cottage. Thirsting to spend another year at the cottage, his mind locked in it every January 1st until they could pack and head north in April. Would they drive to the cottage that spring for the last time, accepting that they were entering the twilight of their lives? I couldn't come to terms with the concept and was unable to prepare myself for the inevitable.

While doing research for my first book written about Daddy's old Greenbush Italian/ Sicilian neighborhood in Madison, many questions surfaced. I wanted to talk to him in private about the 1915 shooting death of his father in their yard by two men with guns that shot four bullets into his chest and heart. As a 12-year-old boy who lost his father in such a traumatic way, and whose mother's life was threatened, and then his own if he talked to anyone about what he witnessed, Daddy buried the truth for eternity. I longed to ask a few questions and thought the best place would be in the boat with Daddy and, while we fished for bluegills, I'd ask about that night in December so many decades before. I tried to be tactful by approaching the subject before, but Mother would protect him and interrupt before he could answer by saying that he couldn't remember that far back and wouldn't want to talk about it anyway. In the boat, we'd be alone and maybe...he'd open up for me. I knew that I was running out of time. For whatever reason, I can't remember if Daddy and I fished together very much that summer. By not remembering, was I subconsciously avoiding what was slipping away when I should have been intent to preserve every moment for the rest of my own life?

I have no answer to that question. However, I can remember how many times Dick and I casually discussed the possibility of buying their cottage to keep it in the family. As probable as it seemed, we weren't able to justify the investment for the boys and their families, considering the distance of 300 miles from home, to visit only once or twice a year and we had no desire to get involved in renting it when they weren't there.

Little did we know that a young couple from Hammond, Wisconsin were looking for a place on the same lake along the same south shoreline. The man's brother and sister-in-law, Arlo and Darlene Johnson, already had a place down the line about five lots to the west toward the back bay. When he heard the cottage might be going up for sale, word was passed on to his brother Eldon, and his wife, Sharon.

On January 1, 1988, Daddy's new year thoughts for the first time would seriously revolve around not opening in April, and possibly selling, as well. The spring started differently than usual with them still at home on April 29 when Dick and I drove *up north* to open for them. We found that a pipe froze and broke in their cottage so Dick went up to Len Heuer's place to borrow tools to temporarily fix the problem. When all of the initial opening chores had been taken care of, we returned to Madison.

On May 19, Mother and Daddy drove to our house at 8 a.m. so we could drive *up north* at the same time, taking both cars. During our trip we encountered more trouble. Plans to veer off at Wyeville for breakfast failed when Daddy missed the exit. About 12 miles later we pulled off at the Black River Falls Crossing to eat at Denny's. Just as we were about to leave the parking lot, Daddy's car stalled. It was hot out, our big long-haired cat, Snickers, was miserable, and we sat for two hours on grass until a new fuel pump was installed. After finally reaching the cottage for a 3:30 appointment with Webster plumber Tom Stuszek, we cleaned up and left to drive together for dinner at the Lamplighter. As we approached their cottage we noticed that Daddy was sitting in his car, alone. He told us he felt sick...that he couldn't find $1100 in cash he brought with him from home. We tried to assure him that he might have left it back home and we would look for it when we returned, but words did not console him. Many subjects were discussed during dinner that evening, but Daddy remained distressed about the money he thought had been lost forever. Later that evening, he remembered that it had been deposited in the bank the day before they left for the lake. Then, the next day, Mother dropped her train case and the mirror inside shattered. Were these omens?

By the time Dick and I left to return to Madison, we had become aware that Daddy seemed to tire quicker than ever before. On June 5, Daddy announced to us that they were going to sell the cottage. Again we pondered if we should let them sell their place to someone other than family and then, out of the blue, Dick Carpenter, who once owned Elaine and Gordy's cottage, decided that he wanted to buy it. Sixteen days later, Mother and Daddy told us they changed their minds and were coming up for another year. By August 7, we still weren't exactly sure how firm those plans were, other than both of them were feeling good. We had spaghetti and meatballs that night for supper and afterward settled on the patio out front for coffee and watched them jitterbug to my Fats Waller music. They were darling and it was just like old times!

Daddy, Elaine and me, 1988.

The shoreline continued to recede that summer and the swamp was ablaze with butter 'n eggs wild flowers. But summer would be ending earlier than usual. On September 15, Elaine and I headed for home with Mother and Daddy driving behind us. Everything went fairly well until we were about 33 miles from Madison and pulled over to the side of the road to wait for them to catch up to us. The interstate eventually opens to three lanes after leaving the Wisconsin Dells area for Madison and when Daddy saw our car pulled along the side of the road, confused about three lanes, he stopped in the right lane. With traffic whizzing by and a semi-truck approaching directly behind Daddy, the driver was honking and honking with Daddy oblivious to the situation as Elaine and I stood there and thought we were witnessing the death of our parents. Yet, with this and everything else that happened throughout the summer, Daddy talked about buying a new pier the following year.

In the fall twilight of 1988, with 1989 approaching to make it nearly a half century spent on North Sand Lake, we all tried to come to terms with what was happening, rationalizing without going overboard by remembering their reasons for selling being extremely valid, considering their ages. Sharon Johnson had spoken many times to Mother on the phone, but she and Eldon had never once seen the inside of the cottage. While on a trip to Madison to attend a football game, the Johnsons called Mother and Daddy to ask if they could stop by to say hello and share their interest in buying the cottage. Mother was happy to hear from them and Daddy, who sat in his pajamas while mending a few broken ribs from a fall, seemed to emulate her feelings. Nothing, however, was verbally finalized.

A dark and rainy May 4, 1989 was opening day for all of us. Despite tornado warnings, Mother and Daddy showed their cottage somewhere between 5:30 and 6 p.m. to Eldon and Sharon Johnson who reconfirmed their desire to buy it.

A few days after an agreement was made, I sat in their kitchen at the old round Queen Anne's table Mother had found years before at St. Vincent De Paul's on Williamson St. in Madison. With the usual tender loving care of stripping, staining and varnishing, it had been turned into a beauty that we all sat around during family meals and fish fries in their cottage. We talked about their decision, and they suggested that it was time for me to look around for things I wanted for my own cottage. Because their cottage would be sold furnished, and my own cottage was already packed with character, I was careful and considerate in what I selected.

I tried to keep a stiff upper lip as I looked at the nook and crannies in the small two-bedroom cottage they loved. Framed family pictures were saved, scrapbooks were packed away, and the rocks she had painted so many years before were set aside. Their bedroom dresser, the last remaining piece to the bedroom set they purchased when they first married went back home with me, as did a wicker dressing table and chair. The rattan chair Mother sat in every day to have her coffee while reading, watching television or looking outside through the front windows found a new corner in my own cottage. Other items included a few dishes, a few pots and pans, and a deep fryer and the aluminum pan that kept the fish warm in the oven between batches. There were cookbooks, nature books, wildlife and fish knickknacks, a bamboo magazine rack, and some of the antique wood side chairs she had hauled back from area shops to strip, stain and varnish like the kitchen table.

Mother and Daddy in the cottage, reflecting on the past.

As for Daddy, anything inside the cottage Mother offered was fine with him. When we went out to *his* garage, my heart began to hurt in a different way. I wanted his tackle box, all of his homemade drop lines, his cane poles, his rods and reels, nets and minnow buckets, and the boat cushions we sat on when we fished together. From his workshop bench at the rear of the garage, a hammer and other tools were removed from their hooks. So were the garden tools he reached for each early morning for his vegetables, berry bushes and flowers, and many filet knives he used like a surgeon every day to remove bones from the fish he caught. The old, red, faded Oscar Mayer hat he wore everyday fishing became yet another treasure to remove from a hook screwed into one of the interior studs. Mother discouraged me from taking the old, tattered, red plaid flannel shirt equally faded from years in the garden and in the boat. Everything else I wanted was...mine. His cane pole was attached to the wall over my kitchen sink and the wood sign with his name that had been nailed to a post on the service road was hung over the door to my pantry/storeroom. Hanging next to it was one of his caps.

The small screened fish house Daddy and Gordy built years before to the front side of the garage and under the trees, where Daddy spent every mid-afternoon, was left as is. He liked cleaning his own fish and it was about the only part of our fishing adventures together that didn't involve me.

On June 21, the longest day of summer, we left for the cottage again, this time to help pack things for Mother and Daddy and so they could say goodbye to people who had become good local friends. First stop was the Lone Pine, but it was closed. Next stop was the Sandbar. After that we drove to Mallard Lake Resort to say goodbye to Carl Hansen, Don Pateck and Bert Morrill. We stopped at Oak Lake and continued on to the Northwoods Inn on H before settling in at Voyager Village for dinner and to say goodbye to their hostess, Shirley, and others who had been so nice to them through the years and had helped them celebrate their 50th anniversary years before with a grand dinner at the clubhouse.

The next day Daddy walked though his flower garden with me and dug up a few perennials, especially the Turk's Cap Lilies he knew I loved. I also loved the curved trellis and the beautiful grapevine that never bore grapes, yet delicately wove itself through narrow slats worthy of a picture, and foolishly left it behind. Having removed a few other perennials, one without name, and the other an old-fashioned rose bush Bert gave him, Mother and Daddy left their cottage on Friday, June 23,

Making the rounds to say goodbye.

Below: Meeting at Mallard Lake Resort, l-r, Bert Morrill, Dick, Don Pateck, Carl Hansen, Mother and Daddy .

turning the key in the lock one last time. They moved into our cottage for a few more days before returning home for good. I can only imagine how painful those moments were for both of them, especially for Daddy.

Leaving behind a little bit of heaven on earth .

It was a warm sunny Saturday, June 24, when we drove to Siren to meet Eldon and Sharon Johnson at Attorney George Benson's office for the closing. When all the necessary papers were signed, the cottage we all loved like a member of the family belonged to someone else…someone who would, in turn, love the cottage just as Mother and Daddy did. After returning to the lake, Eldon and Sharon, Arlo and Darlene, Dick and I and Mother and Daddy sat on our screened porch and poured champagne to celebrate the changing of the guards. Later, as Mother and Daddy rested, Eldon and Sharon put an umbrella up on their new patio and sat to enjoy the property as its proud new owners. Ironically, two days later, on June 26, Mother and

Saturday, June 24, after the closing in Siren. Mother and Daddy with new owners Eldon and Sharon Johnson.

Daddy celebrated their 60th wedding anniversary while Eldon and Sharon celebrated their 24th anniversary with a cottage of their own.

With a check for the sale of the cottage tucked safely in Mother's purse, the era had ended. Daddy and I would never fish together again. My chance to spend two more hours in the boat with him over his favorite fishing spot was gone forever. And, although I felt like a page had been ripped from my life, I also felt blessed to have experienced the special bonding between a father and daughter as fishing buddies in the *up north* wonderland Mother and Daddy had created for me on North Sand Lake.

Amen.

June, 1989 – Goodbye. As Daddy always said,
"We've enjoyed it immensely."

Final Entries

The red hard-cover daily reminder did exactly what it was meant to do. It was the end of an era and Mother recorded it as she had done with every other day of every year.

May 23, Wednesday

Left Madison at 8:00 o'clock for the north to open our cottage. Stopped at Perkins for breakfast at Black River Falls. Got to the cottage about 2 o'clock.
People came to look at our cottage about 6:30. Rained hard.
Cathi, Dick, Mike and I went to Voyager for our meal tonight. Good food.
Barbara Z. bought my wash machine.

May 24, Thursday

Sunny and bright. Left the cottage at 7:30 a.m. Drove to Siren to have breakfast and stopped to see the lawyer about our cottage.
Stopped at noon to have lunch at a German restaurant at Target Bluff. Nice place.
Got back to Madison about 3 o'clock.
Good to be back.
Meter Reading 55678

June 21, Wednesday

Sunny and bright.
Left for the cottage this morning with Cathi and Dick at 8 o'clock.
Stopped at Perkins for breakfast.
Found everything fine at the cottage.
Plumber fixed our pump.
Got to the cottage about 1 o'clock.
Later went to Mallard Lake Inn.
Met Bert and Don P. Said goodbye to them as we are selling our cottage.
Left there and drove to Voyager for our meal. Good food.
Home by 8 o'clock.

June 22, Thursday

Dreary. Temp 70.
Rained and thundered hard last night.
Packed dishes, etc. furniture from our cottage for Dick and Cathi.
Drove to Oak Grove for lunch.
Stopped at the bank and post office in Webster.
Came back and finished packing.
Had supper at Cathi's.
Nice evening.
Rain.

June 23, Friday

Sunny, Temp 80
Finished cleaning the cottage.
Had breakfast and lunch at Cathi's.
Went to North Woods Inn for fish tonight.
Good food.

June 24, Saturday

Drove to Siren.
Stopped at Tom Stusek's home to pay him.
Then to the lawyer to close the deal on our cottage.

Went back to the cottage to meet the Johnsons.
Had champagne at Cathi and Dick's with everyone.
Cathi had a beautiful meal tonight.

Sunday, June 25

Raining. Stayed in all day.
MaGees stopped for awhile in the afternoon.
Nice to see them again.
Went to Oak Lake for our meal tonight.

Monday, June 26

Raining.
It is our 60th wedding anniversary.
Said goodbye to Ziemers.
Stopped at Target Bluff at Camp Douglas for lunch.
Got home to Madison about 3 o'clock.
Stayed three nights with Cathi and Dick at their cottage so the new people could take over at our place.
This is the end for us to be going up north for the summer.
Good to be home.

Summer Legacy

Legacy is a gift. Forever precious and treasured, it is meant to be respected and embraced for as long as time allows. Supposedly, memories are who we are and, without them, we literally don't know ourselves. If that is so, then you will understand why memories of the cottage and North Sand Lake became a mental scrapbook since 1945.

Establishing a legacy doesn't require an exact mirror of previous experiences, but it does lay the groundwork from which to build. What evolves is much like being consoled by wrapping up in the comfort of memories just as one might wrap in a quilt to provide warmth on a chilly night.

No one expected Mother and Daddy to create a form of legacy through the years. Each day spent together at the lake was part of life. They were incredible parents who understood us and encouraged independence as they carefully and tactfully locked in their guidance for the future. The blueprint was simple and life was a joy. Yet, in looking back, it is obvious that with childhood innocence, we took everything for granted. Although there was nothing wrong with that, we weren't able to face the inevitable, never casting a thought to last longer than a few seconds that someday all of it would end. It was a fairyland with all good and no evil. We appreciated how much they enjoyed themselves and took for granted that when we became adults and parents, our lives would fit comfortably into the same summer niche they had created for us years before.

Today, we find ourselves smiling to think of how structured their lives were. Typical of that generation, their sunrises and sunsets seldom strayed off course. When dining out in the evening where a trio was on hand to entertain customers, they danced until the group played "Good Night Ladies" before heading back to the cottage through the pitch blackness of the woods until reaching the service road which meant moments to remember with a safe return.

They attended local events, annual potlucks at the Crow Bar, estate and garage sales, church bazaars, cookouts with shoreline neighbors and welcomed friends from Madison for them to see what they had found a long 300 miles from home.

Life was good. After Daddy retired, things changed somewhat because life was different on the lake compared to back home in the city. As a talented seamstress with excellent taste, Mother made most of her clothes on the portable machine in the guest bedroom. When Daddy's collars on his favorite shirts frayed beyond acceptance, she'd snip the threads to remove and reverse the collar for a brand new look. If the heels of his socks wore thin, she'd settle back in her favorite chair and darn them for another few weeks of wear. She also took pride in the meals she prepared as being healthy with a balance of flavor and color to make each plate aesthetically pleasing. She took care of everything inside of the house and cottage and was the disciplinarian while Daddy, a patient and easy going people-person so typical of a salesman, absolutely thrived on the social aspect of life. When Sunday or Holy Days arrived, religion became *numero uno* and he headed to church, despite how bad the weather may have been, to attend Mass with a devotion firmly engrained from childhood.

Smiles still surface as we remember occasional dinner table conversations when we were young. If the subject matter was not for our little ears to hear, Daddy would try to talk to Mother in his native Sicilian and she, in turn, responded in German. Although their bi-lingual conversations were not always perfect, their good health was incredible. Considering a lack of medical attention as immigrant children, they were extremely healthy with virtually no complaints. We never were aware if one or the other suffered from an occasional ache or pain because it was something they never talked about. If they had the sniffles or a cold, it didn't last long enough to mention. They complemented each other in so many ways and were successful in handling every phase in life. The formula was perfect.

Typical of others, they were proud of their children and proud of their grandsons and great grandchildren. With each arrival, both were anxious to introduce them to cottage life and the same fun and experiences we had as children. One day they woke to realize they had spent 44 years at the lake and, both in their 80s, sensed that it was time to leave for good.

And so it was, after every sunrise and sunset at the lake from the first morning they unpacked in 1945, each morning of oatmeal, corn flakes, grapefruit, toast and coffee, Key Lime pies, fish fries, the undeniable magic of nature, *up north* gardens, grape jam, fickle temperatures, moving from the north to the south shoreline, trophy fish caught off the pier, the call of the loons, noise from pileated woodpeckers, sound of the American bittern, scurrying of chipmunks, soaring of eagles, each spring return to the cottage and every new generation, their existence on North Sand Lake was ending.

When they packed to return home for the last time in the spring of 1989, Daddy was 85 and Mother was 81. The torch was passed on to me just as I will pass it on to our sons and grandchildren in the years to come. And only then will I understand what it was like for them to leave the service road, wave goodbye and head for home for the last time.

The Kitchen Window

For the duration of the summer, I found myself standing at the kitchen counter staring through the window as I prepared food and washed dishes. It seemed so strange to see someone else on Daddy's pier and shoreline and not see Mother sitting on the patio drinking coffee. My heart seemed to skip a few beats at times when I looked through the screen, hoping to see them again, but it was a wish that never came true. I tried to handle things in an adult manner, but in essence, I was a little girl looking for her parents.

Back in Madison, in the home they had lived in since 1941, their life went on, only at a slower pace. We continued to gather there to celebrate birthdays, holidays and other annual events with theme-related table settings. As in the past, Mother insisted on having everyone over for Christmas Eve, but Christmas Day, Easter and Thanksgiving would be held at our house. For as many years as I could remember, their backyard was a showstopper with extraordinary beauty and balance from annuals and perennials. Now, the elaborate display that once wrapped along the lot lines was merely a vivid memory which didn't reappear except for the old rosebushes that climbed through the back fence to sport their brilliant red petals. Nor did the small tomato patch that once produced plate size slices, until Elaine utilized the space by planting tomatoes that everyone could enjoy. We helped each spring and fall with major yard work and manicured the yard throughout the summer months. If they missed being at the lake, it was never mentioned in any conversations. Daddy spent most of his day in his favorite chair watching his favorite television programs. He always had a smile, was anxious to see us enter the front door, had a kiss for Elaine and I and hugged us when we left. Life was still good to Mother and Daddy, but with a much different design in mind.

When Dick retired from TWA in 1991, summers offered extended periods of time for us to spend at the cottage. We tried to encourage Mother and Daddy to accompany us, but they declined and never changed their minds. At the time, it made me feel bad, but today I understand why they chose to stay home.

It took a long time for me to come to terms with how everything so wonderful had to change. There were many fleeting moments when I looked out from the kitchen window, still hoping to see fragments of the past with glimpses of both of them—Daddy in his work clothes, getting ready to fish after breakfast, and Mother sitting on the patio or sprinkling the creeping phlox with the garden hose. Oatmeal breakfasts prepared for the boys who claimed that "grandma's oatmeal was the best," never returned and neither did her the fish fries that have been passed on to me as an *up north* cottage family tradition.

Everything that happened in bits and pieces easily fell into place during their years on North Sand Lake and developed into a poignant formula that made our existence there an unforgettable experience.

That's just the way it was.

July 28, 1997

Daddy's physical condition was very good for a 92-year-old man, with no dependency on glasses or a hearing aid. The only problem was diagnosed multi-farct dementia caused by occasional mini-strokes we had initially been unaware of, which made it difficult for him to complete sentences.

My family had arranged to spend their vacation together at the cottage and began to arrive July 26. The day before Dick and I left home, I stopped by to see Daddy just as I did every day, this time telling him where I would be for a week before saying goodbye with a hug and a kiss. I made sure he had a dish of ice cream, which he enjoyed immensely, but when it was time to leave and I saw him watching me with a frightened expression, I hugged and kissed him again. This scenario was repeated three times, each time hugging longer before removing my arms from his shoulders. Although my tears dried by the time I reached my car in the parking lot, my heart was crashing inside.

Dick and I left for the cottage that afternoon to get ready for a busy week hosting the entire family. By Saturday, everyone had arrived. On Sunday, we visited the Forts Folle Avoine and shortly after we returned to the cottage the phone rang with the message from the Health Care Center. I'll never forget how impressed I was that they would keep me informed about keeping my father comfortable. I thanked her for letting me know and hung up. How would I have known that this was a typical phone call made just prior to a patient expiring? Daddy seemed just fine when I left three days before and there was no reason to be alarmed. Because of that, the remainder of the day went on as usual with no fear of the unknown while the family enjoyed the great weather outside.

At 3:30 a.m. the next morning, the phone rang again, this time the caller told me that Daddy had passed away. I returned to my bedroom and was joined by my three sons who held me as I cried. Dick called Gordy to tell him about Daddy and to go over to tell Mother sometime before breakfast.

There was nothing else we could do, but go back to bed. At sunrise, Dick and I got up, instructed the boys as to what to do with the boats and other things before locking up and returning to Madison. The two of us left immediately and they followed hours later.

Fragments of life together flashed through my mind all the way home. It was bad enough knowing Daddy died, but realizing he died alone made me sad, angry and confused. He didn't deserve that. For everything he did to make life so special for everyone, he should have been surrounded by his family. Because none of us were made aware that he had become dehydrated again, Mother was not with him during his final hours. And neither was I.

When Daddy was laid to rest, Mike, his first grandson, placed a North Sand Lake postcard in the casket as a reminder of his love for the lake and the cottage and everything he did to share it with all of us.

I Love You

When it was over, and all the wonderful years we spent together ended, I realized that I had never looked into Daddy's eyes to tell him how much I loved him. It was something we both took for granted. We had been so close throughout my life and, yet, I knew if I thanked him for everything he did to make my life so special, I would cry with emotion. I don't know why that worried me, but it did. I remember how he hugged me one day when I was little and had tears in my eyes and as he wiped them away he told me that I had to be stronger as I grew older and not to cry over little things. I remember sitting on his lap in the front room on Sunday mornings while he read out loud Prince Valiant in the funny papers. The story didn't intrigue me, but I pretended it did because of the passion that remained from high school days when he studied King Arthur and Knights of the Round Table. I remember how he sat in the front of the toboggan on the coldest winter nights so the wind wouldn't sting my face on the way down, and how he pulled me and the toboggan back up the steep hill time after time because my little legs were tired. And I thought of how he carried me on his shoulders while ice skating on Tenney Park lagoons because I was too little to skate alone. And there were the countless wiener and marshmallow roasts in the woods and how he tried to show how easy it was to brown each perfectly instead of an over-anxious roast of crusty black. I remember how patient he was when I started fishing with him, how he taught me to put the hook through the length of the worm...how to lower the drop line until the sinker hit bottom before pulling up about a foot or so to fish deep...where the big ones gathered...and to let the drop line drape over my right index finger to feel a fish bite, and how to grab the bluegill and hold it tight so I wouldn't get poked by a fin when I removed the hook. In the meantime, although he was maneuvering a drop line in one hand and a cane pole in the other hand, he never minded putting either aside to help me feel comfortable and enjoy a new hobby. And I thought of his kindness, his generosity, and his love for Mother, Elaine and me and that we were the most important things in his life.

On July 28, 1997, when I answered the 3:30 a.m. phone call at the cottage to inform me he had passed away, I felt the pain of knowing he didn't deserve to die alone and that he should have been back home, in the house he loved. And I knew that I should have taken a few extra moments before leaving for the cottage to tell him how much I loved him, even though we hugged three times, believing he was doing... "just fine."

Pateck's pickle jars, jelly glasses and work gloves

After Daddy passed away, we'd ask Mother if she would like to spend a portion of the summer with us at the cottage. She'd shake her head, softly repeat no three times, and finish with a legitimate excuse.

The most often used excuse had to do with distance. Three hundred miles away made it too far away. The second excuse was that she couldn't stand to be in the car that long. There was also that intuition, a gut feeling, that she should stay home to make sure nothing happened to the house or yard in her absence. I remember wondering about these concerns, recalling few when they left to spend six months at the cottage.

After a while, I didn't ask anymore. Sad that we couldn't convince her to share with us the joy she and Daddy were responsible for, I finally came to terms with her excuses when I realized one day that total withdrawal from the lake was out of fear as well as respect—fear that memories of the wonderful years together on the lake would become haunting without Daddy, and respect for each moment they spent together as a closure to be recognized and accepted.

At home, however, were scrapbooks filled with reminders that she could enjoy at any given moment. Each book swelled with pictures taken of the resort years and the cottages we rented and all the good times we had with the people we met there. Each picture taken on the trusty collapsible Kodak captured a era that would thread its way through four generations when we moved from the north shore to the south shore. Far removed from everything else in the world from 1945 to 1989 had been a dream come true. When Daddy retired in 1969, we offered him a trip for two to Italy and Sicily, his homeland, but he refused by asking why we thought he'd want to return to the Old Country when he had Webster, Wisconsin where his family would be and his summer friends lived. Those scrapbooks said it all. Each picture reinforced their love and respect for the lake, their humble summer cottage and its rewards with family togetherness. There was no need for Mother to return without Daddy. Once I understood why, the invitations were laid to rest.

On a January day in 2001, while cleaning for Mother, now a 92-year-old recovering from an illness, I opened a single draw in a table to the right of the couch where she sat to watch television. Discovered was a sheet of paper, folded in half and pushed to the back of the drawer. Removing the paper, I opened it and began to read a handwritten check list she made in 1988 as they were preparing to pack for the last full season they'd spend at the lake.

Beginning at the top of the list, written with a ball point pen in her beautiful penmanship was *Pateck's pickle jars, jelly glasses, work gloves...* It was as if pickle jars and jelly glasses were the first reminders of what to pack. The name Pateck meant Don Pateck of Prescott, WI who had become one of Daddy's valued summertime friends. Pateck owned a grocery store in his hometown, but spent much of the summer at his cottage near Lily Lake where an enormous well-cared for garden supplied him with produce to sell at his store. He was a kind and generous man who, with his brother, John, also did a lot of canning, making the best dill pickles we ever tasted. Pateck's *pickle jars* seemed to have prominence over everything as a reminder to return the empty jars to Don so he could use them again at the end of the season. The *jelly jars* were for grape jelly Mother would make at the end of summer with wild grapes Bert Morrill picked and delivered to the cottage. Bert lived on farmland in a large two-story house set way back, yet visible, from County Road A. He was a very bright and talented man whose company and friendship Daddy also appreciated and enjoyed. During each planting season, Bert provided Daddy with jars and bottles of what he referred to as "prune juice" (liquid manure) to fertilize a garden planted in sand.

It was no surprise to see *work gloves* finishing the trio of necessities that headed the list as they were what Daddy slipped on each morning at 5:30 a.m. when he went outside to begin his morning garden ritual.

And, I read on…

Turn water off
Outside water turned off
Masking tape on window
Sugar
Flour
Front porch rug
Leave broom and dustpan on porch
Clothes basket and pins on back porch
Garbage pail
Mike's belts
Clothes line down
Moth balls in closets
Unplug lights
Turn water off (hot)
Curtain on back porch
Thermostat down, cookies
Defrost refrigerator
Unplug cord
Lock storm windows
Bedroom clock
Toilet paper
Cameras
Chairs on front porch
Electric cords

Empty waste basket
Cookbook
Check book
Eye glasses
Curling iron and hair dryer
Money
Shampoo and color rinse
Pills
Ice packs
Tooth boxes
Empty cig. Butts
Open drapes downstairs
Elec. Fryer
Pills
Bank book
Recipe box
Jewelry box
Ice cooler
Liqueur
Ham
Pork hocks

Next to each item was a red pencil check. There isn't an answer as to why the list remained in an uncluttered drawer but a consoling assumption is that it provided an inconspicuous link to a time and a place for Mother, thus becoming difficult to part with. For me, it provided a hint of what each spring required before leaving for the cottage since their absence extended over a six month period. The list provided a view of a mind in recoding first things first, then moving in different directions with intermittent reminders of *money* which was sandwiched between the *curling iron* and the *shampoo.*

I wondered later what Daddy's list would have included. The first item most likely would have been meat from the plant (Oscar Mayer). Next, night crawlers, a staple he'd buy by the dozens in Madison to care for at the cottage during the fishing season. The small portable television set and a small table radio. Following were probably the usual items the man of the house would be expected to take care of before leaving: Contact someone to mow the lawn. Find someone to water the lawn and the flower garden. Make sure the post office would forward the mail. Change the mailing address for the newspaper.

He didn't have to worry about his 6 hp Johnson motor because that remained at the lake during the winter, either stored at a place that would condition it for the following year, or locked in the garage with the 14-foot aluminum boat and its wooden oars. Sharing garage space were garden implements, fishing nets of varied sizes and, balanced on hooks were cane poles and rods and reels. Resting on the floor and on his work bench at the back of the garage were clumsy items like boat anchors, minnow buckets, and worm boxes for night crawlers that would be filled with dirt and dampened strips of newspaper to hide beneath the cottage partially removed from summer's heat. Also waiting for him was his tackle box, laden with plugs he seldom used, but filled with stringers, and a gaff hook, and other gadgets needed for fishing emergencies. Most important of all were the narrow packages of No. 6 and No. 8 claw hooks used for bluegills, and his simple handmade drop lines that we treasured like family heirlooms.

The Grapevine

I never knew if the grapevine Daddy planted near the backyard in Gordy's lot was reminiscent of his heritage and the Italian Greenbush neighborhood where he lived as a youngster. If it was, the connection was never mentioned. Gordy's empty lot afforded Daddy lots of room to plant whatever he wanted except through a heavy growth of trees and bushes that prevented anyone from walking down a slight incline to the lake shore. Otherwise, the lot from that point and all the way to the service road was wide open and flat and welcomed his growing talents. Alongside vegetables, and to the side of the flower garden seemed to be a good place for a grapevine so a trellis was placed and secured in the ground and a grapevine was planted at both sides.

Once roots were well established, the grapevine grew larger and more beautiful with each year, however it never produced a single grape. Daddy remained optimistic that the following year would be different. He watered it each morning with all of the vegetables and flowers that surrounded it and its bright green shoots continued to wind in and around trellis slats. By August, Bert would stop by with a container of wild grapes so Mother could make jam. That, too, became a yearly ritual and continued until the cottage was sold.

After Daddy died, I decided to plant a grapevine in his memory in my own cottage backyard garden. There was a prolific grapevine growing up the service road, but the owners of the property wouldn't allow me to snip a few branches to root. So I contacted my dear friend back home, Anne Stassi Bruno, who not only had known Daddy, but had an old grapevine growing in her own backyard that was given to her husband, Joe, and transplanted years before. The connection became somewhat emotional and was shared with readers of my Wisconsin State Journal newspaper food column to feature a grape jam recipe.

Cooks' Exchange

June 5, 2000

Memories travel through the grapevine

June 18 will mark the third Father's Day since Daddy passed away in 1997. I would give anything to have him with us, if only for the day, to count nightcrawlers with him, to fish together, walk behind him to admire his garden, prepare caponatina and cucidati and coconut cream pie, and to kiss and hug him one more time.

The first spring following his death, I visited my friend Anne Bruno, who knew him years before. When I mentioned my desire to plant a grape vine in his memory at the cottage, she snipped four branches from a vine in her yard that Sam Corona had removed years ago from the old Greenbush neighborhood and given to her husband, Joe. Both men had great respect for Daddy, which gave the branches a special meaning and extension of their friendship.

A portion of each branch was submerged in water. In few days later, hair-like roots appeared at the bottom of the branches. Because a trip to the cottage wasn't planned for another month, I made certain the water was changed each day and the stems did not rot.

A few weeks later, the roots stopped growing. I made fresh cuts to encourage a new growth, yet when we finally left for the cottage, the branches appeared gray and brittle. Concerned that it was no longer possible to expect a grape vine connection between Daddy, his old neighborhood and friends who once lived there, I purchased a healthy hybrid grape vine from the local Austin Lake greenhouse. While the young potted vine immediately took hold, the

dry Corona-Bruno branches looked worse with each day. Refusing to discard them, as a last resort they were stuck into sandy soil next to a rhubarb plant as a child might poke popsicle sticks in a sandbox.

Each day I examined the branches, hoping to witness the slightest hint of life. Although convinced I had waited too long from the time of the initial cutting to planting them, I watered them daily. The evening before Father's Day, I checked the garden one last time before retiring for the day but found no change.

The next morning while coffee was brewing, I went outside to make my daily inspection of the garden. Glancing toward the forlorn branches, I noticed a green shoot with tiny leaves on two branches. With tears in my eyes, I knew that Daddy had made contact with me in a most extraordinary way.

Mom's Recipes

The following column appeared in Cooks' Exchange on Sunday, April 6, 2003.

Mom's recipes are something to cherish

Paging through my mother's photo albums and scrapbooks, I smiled through tears at reminders of how she made growing up almost storybook-like for my sister and me. As I looked for photos to display during visitation at the funeral home, I also noticed how her innate shyness as a new bride disappeared as the mother of two little girls she adored.

My mother was born in 1908 in a village near Budapest, Hungary. When she was 9 months old, the family came to this country and lived for a short time in Chicago before settling on Madison's East Side in a new house on Moulton Court. On March 20, at the age of 94, she died.

Her mother, my Grandma Kovacs, had been the cook in a rectory in Germany. When the family arrived in this country, Grandma's style of food preparation did not change. As a child, I remember her Sunday family feasts and the quart Mason jar filled with white raisins in the back corner of her refrigerator, always handy for the strudels and kuchens she made on a regular basis.

Mother didn't spend much time in Grandma's kitchen, so when Mother and my Sicilian-born father were married, not only was the preparation of German-Hungarian food a slight mystery to her, but there were new ethnic flavors and recipes to learn.

It couldn't have been much of a surprise to Daddy when her first spaghetti dinner as a newlywed was nothing more than macaroni and ketchup, to which he tactfully commented that the recipe needed "a little work." Before long,

with some Old World advice from ladies dressed in black, her spaghetti sauce and meatballs drew hugs and kisses.

By the time we were little, Mother had achieved greatness in the kitchen. Not only was she a good cook, she also possessed magical powers as she always knew if I poured my milk down the kitchen sink. It took years for me to realize that I should have rinsed the sink with water.

Back then, supper was served 30 minutes after the church bells rang and, because we couldn't eat meat on Fridays, she learned to make frittata, an Italian omelet Daddy loved. All of our meals seemed to be casual daily celebrations with a variety of food served, from morning oatmeal to evening gourmet fare like veal kidneys in wine sauce. Although she always wished she had learned how to make goulash the way Grandma did, she mastered Grandma's way to prepare sauerkraut and wieners. One night during supper, Daddy sat on a piece of bubble gum that found its way to his kitchen chair and when he got up from the table the gum stretched from the chair and his trousers well into the dining room while we giggled so hard we weren't able to tell him what was so funny.

And then there was the time...,

March 20 was the end of the first generation of my immigrant roots in America. What became a blend of nationalities with an extra dose of American pride was a wonderful life spent together on Talmadge Street. Because good memories often become an endless chapter to capture when one lives 94 happy and healthy years, they also prompt sharing a few of Mothers' recipes, appropriately named as such, that I loved.

Note: Mother's recipes can be found in the **Up North Food** chapter.

Reflections...

After Mother died, preparations were made for an estate sale before the house was put up for sale. It was difficult for me to separate myself entirely from things that had meant so much to her, and did the best I could. Many boxes were filled and carried back to our house and placed in the basement to return to later. The box packed with her cottage diaries found a convenient spot on a basement counter for me to reach into while I sat at the computer, picking away at this book. Folded in her 1987 diary, I found this letter, written by me on May 22 of that year, knowing that things were about to change at the lake.

Dear Mother and Daddy,

The five days up north were not as enjoyable as we would have liked. The weather was terrible and we were forced to deal with the facts, to be realistic and understand that all good things have to end sometime. I am sure this probably is your last summer at the cottage. I thank you and God for being blessed with 42 memorable and valuable years of summers at the lake. I would not trade any of them for all the money in the world. I think back to each year like it was yesterday, hearing the sounds, feeling the wind and summer heat and remembering the tastes of every fish fry. I must continue my years there so to offer my children the very same.

It doesn't take much to reminisce. Please enjoy your last summer and savor what it has done to make my life so wonderful. We all have benefited from it. I remember the shrine that waited for us on the corner in Middleton to hear our prayers for a safe trip on a double lane highway loaded down with appliances, clothes and fruit from Mazurskey's Market. The smell of the Diesel engines made me want to sleep soundly from Middleton to Spooner. The smell of the north woods and a crystal clear lake made up for the nausea. What fun it was to hardly unpack before we checked for playmates in other cottages. That first year was a treasure-filled week as we made connections with our cottage, the shoreline, the lake and the woods behind us, and a cabin next door still as it was on a cold winter day when a man's life ended due to frigid temperatures - - so desperate and barren, yet filled with artwork and Haviland china.

And I remember finding Little Bass Lake hidden in the woods behind us. How were we to know at the time about a path that wound around trees and zigzagged bushes to lead Daddy and me to its shoreline for quiet fishing on a quiet lake with no one else in sight? With poles, tackle box, net and bait, we would finish the trek with dew-dampened shoes that would dry quickly in the warm morning sun. When returning, we had to shift equipment so we could carry stringers heavy with bass and northern.

Evenings were spent, adults and children alike, down at the "store," a little bar-restaurant-grocery store behind Barney and Florence's home, a place where all the people spending that week at the resort got to be old friends by the end of their stay. It was where I learned that "Kilroy was here," written on the back of a shiny black Buick, was a product of a war I could barely remember. It was also where I learned, when I reached a certain age, what "kissing the Blarney stone" was all about.

Kilkare and Leef Roads were sandy and dusty and each extra step provided another piece of the north woods to investigate. I remember the stone silo basement that we discovered on a hill during one of our excursions. The farmer it once belonged to had used it as a private dumping ground when the silo disappeared and it lost its value. There were pots and pans, a stove and refrigerator and other household appliances that had seen better days. The excitement came when someone tossed a stone down into the junk and frogs and snakes jumped and squirmed in and out of the debris.

One day we were told that the resort would be sold. We searched for days for another cottage on a similar lake, but none could be found. So we bought four lots on the opposite shoreline, so far removed that it almost seemed undesirable until it settled in that the lake and the lots really did belong to us. It presented a new plateau in our lives. It was like homesteading. More investigating of the surroundings and the people who already had cottages along the shoreline calmed us and our short weekends there were devoted to making it all livable as soon as possible.

Elaine and I were married by then and, although Tom, Mike and Bill had enjoyed the north shoreline as little ones, Bob would become familiar only with our new settlement. Gordy and Dick had already established a love for the lake and continued by building cottages next to you. The kids played on their own private shoreline, walked the service road, explored the Mallard Lake area and played in the warm desert sand with their GI Joes. Although times were hectic with four little boys being boys, they established their own appreciation and created memories special to them. And, after twenty years of breaking in the isthmus off the service road, a fourth generation appeared. This summer will be Jordan's second summer at the lake and I pray there will be at least twenty more for him.

It is difficult to describe the pain in knowing that someone so important as the two of you will be missing next summer. To know that when I look over toward your place I won't see Daddy fiddling with his yard or cleaning the shoreline or carrying the oars to the boat for a few hours of fishing. I'll miss not seeing him sitting in the shade to enjoy the breeze and the view, and will know, Mother, that the coffee pot isn't plugged in anymore, and the chairs aren't set up in front for a relaxing hour with coffee and donuts or to realize that there are no Sloppy Joes and Patecks pickles with your famous potato salad waiting for us when we arrive…and that cocktails prior to those wonderful fish fries around the Queen Anne table from St. Vincent's have ended. All of that brings tears to my eyes, yet I know that I am 42 years ahead of everyone I know in the wonder of what you have made possible, and I love you for that.

I am aware that this is not an easy letter for you to read. It is not any easier for me to type or proof. It is a situation similar to death…to know that something so good is about to end.

So, please, for me, enjoy every second, every minute and each week that remains for even though the raspberries no longer grow and the flowers cease to bloom, while friends are leaving because some are sick and bones are sore and enthusiasm has disappeared, this last summer will be vital to me. The good memories will forever far outweigh the few bad ones and the overall beauty of the past 42 years will glow forever. It is the way I want to remember your last summer at the cottage because it will make it easier for me to accept it, remembering that if it hadn't been for both of you, life and its wonders at the cottage up north never would have happened.

Love Always,

Catherine

Epilogue

August 21, 2004. The sun already is lower, casting shadows on the pier in places where I sat two weeks ago in the glory of the shine and its warmth. Another season is about to end and this one will leave everyone wondering...what happened to summer? It was a strange season that hardly made an appearance until mid-July, about one week after my first dip in the lake, not because I didn't want to, but because the water temperature was still too cold.

At the moment, the only good thing is that I am about to finish this book. Ten years after my idea was first set in motion, I continue to rewrite each page to be edited. Once that is done, I can visit printers for price quotes. There will be no more ideas, no more interviews and no more memories to add overnight. Otherwise, this project will go on forever. What I believe, and hope, took place yesterday with the last interview after catching up to a man I've been chasing for the past five years. Meeting him and recording a few of his thoughts put closure on what started so innocently in 1994 as a 35-page handbook to treat newcomers with a reflection of what North Sand Lake was like back in 1945 when I was eight-years-old. Chasing dreams and ideas is one of the reasons why it took so long for me to finish. When I was at the lake, someone I wanted to interview wasn't available and that had to be put on hold for another week, another month, or until the following year. And besides, other writing assignments and deadlines forced my good intentions to the back burner for brief periods of time.

Although I am happy with what I have accomplished, there remain six things I regret:

First, that Mother didn't record our daily experiences in diaries beginning that first summer vacation at Hansen's Resort in 1945. The only recording I did was writing in pencil my name and the dates each year on a pine board in my bedroom plus a board in the outhouse while sitting over the hole behind our #5 cottage.

Second, that I didn't start this book sooner.

Third, involves the locals who welcomed me into their homes for an hour or two of conversation and have since passed away. How I wish they could have read the memories they shared for the book.

Fourth, regretting that a number of people who could have shared, chose not to respond to a decade of pleas in local newspapers as well as our own Lake Owner's Association newsletter. Having written four previous books capturing the history of Italian neighborhoods, I respect decisions and desires for privacy, and also understand that many people have a tendency to think they have nothing to share when, in reality, one or two comments help to fit all the pieces together. Their failure to respond is the only reason their names do not appear on any page.

Fifth, that we didn't buy my sister's cottage next door when they sold it in the early 1980s before prices escalated and my family grew. I think now of how convenient it would have been when the whole family visits and three more bedrooms and another bathroom would have eased the pain of cramped quarters.

Sixth, of course, is that Mother and Daddy didn't live long enough to see how I compiled this book with inherited talent and with every word and thought of how much they meant to me, how much the lake means to me, and how much I appreciate Daddy's insistence that the rest of his summers were to be spent on North Sand Lake.

And, so it is, the twenty-first of August. After five days of early morning temperatures of 35 to 40 degrees to greet us upon rising, the deer flies have temporarily disappeared and water temperatures keep me at bay in my swimsuit. My basil is spotty, my grapes, plagued again with black rot, await warm days for the healthy bunches to ripen before a race begins between me, the raccoons and chipmunks. And, although the deer have eaten every tomato, leaf, and stem in my garden, I look forward to another chance next year while dreading the thought of closing up and leaving again all of which has to parallel how Daddy felt when autumn arrived.

I will celebrate my 60th year on the lake during the summer of 2005 and can only hope the season will return to its old-fashioned ways with soaring temperatures and non-stop swims. I want electric fans to whir all night when sheets are kicked off and bed clothes become skimpy and late evening southerly breezes seep through the screens bringing a fragrance of the *up north* woods to put a smile on my face before sleep arrives. I want to waken in the morning to the fascination of the language of crows, wishing I could understand their messages like those of a chipmunk looking for a playmate. I want to sit on the shore or at the end of the pier with my morning coffee, wishing that all of what surrounds me will last forever. And, most of all, while gazing to the west, wish I would see Mother and Daddy out in front of their cottage, enjoying the place they loved best.

As I put the finishing touches on this chapter, the date is January 10, 2006 and all I can say is…Amen.

Sixty years have passed. Oh, where have they gone?
Each spring I rake dry oak leaves from the previous autumn, plant tiny vegetable and flower seeds, witness violet plants poke through the sand before their delicate purple petals unfold, watch the eagle soar, listen to chattering of chipmunks and the haunting evening call of the loon.
Though each sight and sound nourishes my soul, what I truly miss is being eight years old again when this up north adventure began.
I wish my sons were little boys once more and that I could gaze through the kitchen window to see Daddy on the pier preparing to fish while Mother sits on the patio to sip morning coffee.
And, suddenly I am reminded that all good things in life don't last forever…

Catherine Tripalin Murray
October 4, 2005

No time on earth is long enough to share with those we love or to prepare our hearts for the last goodbye.

Michael Robert Tripalin

December 3, 1904 – July 28, 1997

Mary Anna Kovacs Tripalin

November 13, 1908 – March 20, 2003

In one sense, there is no death.
The life of a soul on earth lasts beyond his departure.
You will always feel that life touching yours,
That voice speaking to you,
That spirit looking out of other eyes,
Talking to you in the familiar things he touched,
Worked with, loved as familiar friends.
He lives on in your life
And in the lives of all others who knew him.

Angelo Patri

When day is done,

And shadow's fall,

I think of you ...

Order Form

Up North: A Father's Summer Legacy

Compiled and published by author Catherine Tripalin Murray for the benefit of North Sand Lake. Additional information is available by contacting Greenbush4@aol.com -- 1-608-244-3359 or 1-715-866-8545.

Cost of the book is $20.00 plus mailing costs of $4.00. If more than one book is mailed to the same address, add $2.50 per book.

Wisconsin residents add $1.10 sales tax per book.

Number of copies __________ Amount enclosed $ ________

Name ____

Address ____

City ________________________ **State** ____________ **Zip** ___________

Make check payable, and mail to:

Up North...remembered
c/o Catherine Tripalin Murray
1421 Wyldewood Drive
Madison, WI 53704

- -

Order Form

Up North: A Father's Summer Legacy

Compiled and published by author Catherine Tripalin Murray for the benefit of North Sand Lake. Additional information is available by contacting Greenbush4@aol.com -- 1-608-244-3359 or 1-715-866-8545.

Cost of the book is $20.00 plus mailing costs of $4.00. If more than one book is mailed to the same address, add $2.50 per book.

Wisconsin residents add $1.10 sales tax per book.

Number of copies __________ Amount enclosed $ ________

Name ____

Address ____

City ________________________ **State** ____________ **Zip** ___________

Make check payable, and mail to:

Up North...remembered
c/o Catherine Tripalin Murray
1421 Wyldewood Drive
Madison, WI 53704